Fighting Chance

Fighting Chance

The Struggle over Woman Suffrage and Black Suffrage in Reconstruction America

FAYE E. DUDDEN

OXFORD
UNIVERSITY PRESS

OXFORD
UNIVERSITY PRESS

Oxford University Press, Inc., publishes works that further
Oxford University's objective of excellence
in research, scholarship, and education.

Oxford   New York
Auckland   Cape Town   Dar es Salaam   Hong Kong   Karachi
Kuala Lumpur   Madrid   Melbourne   Mexico City   Nairobi
New Delhi   Shanghai   Taipei   Toronto

With offices in
Argentina   Austria   Brazil   Chile   Czech Republic   France   Greece
Guatemala   Hungary   Italy   Japan   Poland   Portugal   Singapore
South Korea   Switzerland   Thailand   Turkey   Ukraine   Vietnam

Copyright © 2011 by Oxford University Press, Inc.

Published by Oxford University Press, Inc.
198 Madison Avenue, New York, NY 10016

www.oup.com

Library of Congress Cataloging-in-Publication Data
Dudden, Faye E.
Fighting chance : the struggle over woman suffrage and Black suffrage
in Reconstruction America / Faye E. Dudden.
p.   cm.
Includes bibliographical references and index.
ISBN 978-0-19-977263-6
1. Women—Suffrage—United States—History—19th century.
2. African Americans—Suffrage—History—19th century.
3. Women's rights—United States—History—19th century.
4. Reconstruction (U.S. history, 1865–1877)   I. Title.
JK1896.D79 2011
324.6'208996073—dc22   2010053188

1 3 5 7 9 8 6 4 2

Printed in the United States of America
on acid-free paper

CONTENTS

ACKNOWLEDGMENTS

In writing this book I incurred many debts over a long period of time, and it is a pleasure to acknowledge those who helped me. At an early stage in the work I benefited from a Fellowship for College Teachers from the National Endowment for the Humanities (NEH). Although the final product is not what I projected, the NEH provided crucial time in which I could begin to explore the boundaries of a new area of research. Colgate University's Senior Faculty Leave also enabled me to carve out time for this book, and I benefited from Colgate grants to cover research expenses as well. I want to thank the American Antiquarian Society (AAS) for a Tracy Fellowship, with particular thanks to Caroline Sloat, John Hench, Georgia Barnhill, and Ellen Dunlap. The AAS provides an ideal research environment, and I enjoyed working there.

I owe many thanks to librarians and archivists at a number of institutions, but especially to the Schlesinger Library in the History of Women at the Radcliffe Institute, the Houghton Library at Harvard, the Rare Books and Manuscripts Collection at the Boston Public Library, the Massachusetts Historical Society, the Sophia Smith Collection at Smith College, the Manuscripts Reading Room and the Newspaper Reading Room at the Library of Congress, the Rare and Manuscript Collections in Olin Library at Cornell University, the Huntington Library, and the Archives at Miami University. Special thanks are due Mary Huth and Karl Kabelac at the Manuscripts Collection at Rush Rhees Library at the University of Rochester, who offered encouragement and helpful ideas at various stages of the project.

The staff at the Kansas State Historical Society in Topeka was extremely helpful. Virgil Dean provided invaluable research pointers and was also kind enough to read an early version of Chapter 5. I am also glad to thank Margaret Darby and her sister and brother-in-law, Kathy and Bill Rich, who helped me to spend the time I needed in Topeka. Rona Gregory, an old friend, enabled me to explore Boston-area archives and also helped me to understand how lawyers think.

Students also provided research help and I wish to thank Taylor Buonocore and Gavin Byrnes, and to acknowledge the fine work of Sarah Hillick.

Colleagues and friends contributed to this work at various stages, generously helping to guide me to the final result. Joan Jacobs Brumberg and Barbara Sicherman read early and very rough drafts and each of them let me know, in the kind way of dear friends, that I needed to go back to the drawing board. It was not what I wanted to hear, but this book would never have taken its proper shape without their patience, insight, and goodwill. I also imposed upon Jean Harvey Baker, who read early work and encouraged me to keep pushing. Ann D. Gordon's meticulous editions of the papers of Stanton and Anthony were literally indispensable; I am grateful, and glad to acknowledge her influence. Ellen DuBois critiqued parts of an early effort; I profited from her comments and even more from her scholarship; I am much indebted to her. I extend thanks to Judy Wellman, Carol Kammen, and my colleagues in the History Department reading group at Colgate University. Thanks also to the anonymous readers at Oxford University Press, and to Julie Roy Jeffrey, who generously agreed to read a late draft of the manuscript. My colleague Jack Dovidio helped me understand the way social psychologists discuss race prejudice, while Nick Salvatore encouraged me to look into social movement theory. Joan Brumberg was supportive, shrewd, and steady in her judgments: she will always have my appreciation and affection. My editor at Oxford, Susan Ferber, made this manuscript better in innumerable ways, improving both the argument and the language, and I feel fortunate to have worked with her. Finally, Marshall Blake helped me structure the entire book by enabling me to understand how movement activists think about politics and agitation, and how their work can take its toll. At many points along the way he read, argued, edited, and served as a sounding board. He knows how I feel.

Fighting Chance

Introduction

She dipped her pen into a tincture of white racism and sketched a reference to a nightmarish figure, the black rapist. If the nation gives the vote to black men but not to women, she wrote, it will encourage "fearful outrages on womanhood, especially in the southern states." If the Fifteenth Amendment is passed, she warned, woman's "degradation" will be complete and "persecutions, insults, horrors" will descend upon her.[1] It was February 1869 and the Ku Klux Klan was terrorizing the South, but the author of these words was no female Klan member. She was feminist pioneer Elizabeth Cady Stanton editorializing in the *Revolution*, the newspaper she and Susan B. Anthony had been publishing for over a year. Stanton and Anthony repeatedly predicted rape—"fearful outrages"—and insisted that black men were their enemies, "more hostile to woman than any class of men in the country."[2]

A long-standing alliance, marked by incompatibility but durable nonetheless, was breaking up. How did the advocates of woman suffrage come to this? How did black rights and women's rights, causes that had formerly collaborated, come to such a rupture? At the same time she laced her editorials with racist resentments, Elizabeth Cady Stanton also wrote openly of her regret at "this antagonism with [black] men whom we respect, whose wrongs we pity, and whose hopes we would fain help them realize."[3] This falling-out, this "antagonism," has been called "one of the saddest divorces in American history."[4] In the upshot, black men would get the vote in 1870 and women would have to wait for suffrage until fifty years later.

Looking at the question largely as a matter of personalities, or assuming that, as a practical matter, woman suffrage lay far in the future, historians have concluded that Stanton and Anthony's racist outburst reflected their individual biases and/or political naïveté. How could they have believed they had a chance to win the vote when they had no mass movement and it would take decades more to build one? And if they had no chance to win the vote themselves, why should they have so meanly opposed black men's voting rights, except out of bigotry? Yet the race-gender split of 1869 cannot simply be explained as a prod-uct of racism among white feminists, although racism there was, and plenty of it. A fuller explanation demands reexamining the assumption that woman suffrage was "ahead of its time" in the Reconstruction era.

In theory, the 1860s should have been a propitious time for the women's movement. By the late 1850s, activists had developed a set of arguments that appealed to American society "from every standpoint of justice, religion and logic" and as Stanton said, men had yet to make "a fair, logical argument on the other side."[5] The women's movement also had part of the resources they needed, because they were rich in human assets. A group of remarkably talented individ-uals had assembled around the annual woman's rights conventions, radical women and men who tried, by their limited lights, to "seize the time" in this rare and roiling moment of American history.

Their movement began in the 1830s, springing up within the ranks of activ-ists who demanded both the immediate emancipation of the slaves *and* equal rights for free people of color—proposals so radical most Americans regarded them as sheer fanaticism. Abolitionists coalesced in the American Anti-Slavery Society under the leadership of William Lloyd Garrison, whose bright-eyed intensity spurred others to question conventional wisdom and follow abstract principles—principles like "all men are created equal"—*wherever* they led. "Do right, though the heavens fall," abolitionists told each other, refusing all compro-mise or concern about practical policy. When Garrison brought two southern white women, Sarah and Angelina Grimké of South Carolina, into the public spotlight to testify against slavery, he set in motion a new dynamic. The Grimkés soon found themselves condemned as women for having spoken publicly, drew obvious parallels between the bondage of slaves and the subordination of women, and then began to speak and write on *women's* rights. Meanwhile slav-ery's defenders and apologists reacted to the American Anti-Slavery Society with unanticipated ferocity. Southern slaveholders put a price on Garrison's head, northern bigots stoned abolitionist speakers and burned their meeting halls, and a split developed in the American Anti-Slavery Society over how to respond. In 1840, practical-minded incrementalists peeled off to take the fight against slavery into the political realm, while Garrisonians disavowed politics, famously condemning the Constitution as a "covenant with death and a pact with hell" for condoning human bondage.

Many women stayed with Garrison because he insisted women's rights could not be separated from those of black people and of all humanity, while political abolitionists tended to see women's rights as a distraction. A women's movement was being born, and Lucretia Mott, a composed, determined, and eloquent Philadelphia Quaker, led the way by advocating women's full participation in biracial antislavery activism and embodying its principles in her daily life. Mott was a revelation to a new generation of abolitionist women including Lucy Stone, an Oberlin graduate with a gift for antislavery oratory. Like other Garrisonians, Stone moved outside the established churches and political organizations to pursue a vision of a radical equality of souls in which race and sex were both just "accidents of the body."[6] Wendell Phillips, perhaps the most prominent, eloquent Garrisonian, became the women's most important male ally. Phillips defended the women delegates' right to be seated at the World's Anti-Slavery Convention in London in 1840 and subsequently crusaded for both abolition and women's rights. In an age of great orators, Wendell Phillips stood preeminent: he made thousands as a paid lyceum speaker but delivered his spell-binding speeches for free on behalf of the slave or the woman.

The women's movement crystallized in 1848, in the small upstate New York town of Seneca Falls, where a young mother named Elizabeth Cady Stanton found the words for her discontent by reworking the most famous phrasing in the American political creed: "We hold these truths to be self evident. That all men *and women* are created equal." And she proposed the most radical of all the various resolutions at the Seneca Falls Woman's Rights Convention, one that claimed the right to vote. Lucretia Mott feared that Stanton would make the cause "ridiculous" by demanding suffrage, but Frederick Douglass, the famous fugitive slave who was publishing his own newspaper in Rochester, had come down to Seneca Falls for the occasion and he stepped forward. The ballot was the guarantor of all other rights, Douglass argued, and women must be bold. Together he and Stanton persuaded the members of the convention to approve the demand. It was the beginning of a long relationship between Frederick Douglass, Elizabeth Cady Stanton, and the cause of woman suffrage.

As the women's movement gathered momentum in the 1850s, meeting annually in woman's rights conventions, a schoolteacher named Susan B. Anthony joined the cause and by the eve of the Civil War three vigorous, veteran activists—Lucy Stone, Susan B. Anthony, and Elizabeth Cady Stanton—emerged in leadership roles.[7] They first met in 1851 or 1852, and in the intervening years they had convened meetings, written, petitioned, lectured—had even worn the bloomer costume until ridicule wore them down. Each labored for other causes, especially abolition, which left them hardened to social ostracism, accustomed to being "warned at the dinner table, avoided in the street."[8] But the "W.R. work," as Anthony called it, had increasingly emerged as their common compass point—their "true North."

Lucy Stone, who was employed as an agent of the Massachusetts Anti-Slavery Society before she became a woman's rights orator, blazed a trail ahead of both Stanton and Anthony. A "tiny creature" with a sweet, girlish manner and a "musical and delicious" voice, Stone argued that gaining rights would make women *more* useful and "womanly" not less, and she became so popular with general audiences that at one point the impresario P. T. Barnum tried to hire her for a series of lectures.[9] Although she vowed to remain single, Lucy Stone finally succumbed in 1855 to a determined campaign of wooing by Henry Blackwell, an entrepreneurial go-getter from a large reform-oriented family.[10]

Stone kept her own name and their marriage became a highly publicized experiment in the new, more equal marital relationship that the women's movement promoted. In private, the marriage was difficult. While Blackwell went on the road pursuing business opportunities, few of his investments turned a profit, and after their daughter was born, Blackwell pressed Stone to stay home and care for the child, even though her speaking engagements generated their only steady income. Stone's self-confidence wavered, and her letters revealed signs of anxiety or depression. Cut off from her work, worried about money, and suffering from migraine headaches, Lucy Stone became absorbed in family responsibilities and marital problems in the late 1850s just as the women's rights movement was picking up speed.

Stone's absence left a gap in women's rights leadership, and in stepped Susan B. Anthony, a relentless fighter with big ideas. One of her fellow activists had dubbed her "Napoleon," and the nickname stuck. Her family was immersed in the reform movements that flourished in the antebellum years in upstate New York: Susan's parents and her sister actually attended a women's rights convention *before* she did. Anthony was a working woman with a slender purse. She wanted to attend the Second National Woman's Rights Convention in Worcester, Massachusetts, in 1851 but could not afford to make the trip. Appalled that women teachers like herself were paid less than half of men's wages, she went to teacher's conventions to protest but found that the women were expected to remain silent while the "old fogies" droned on.[11]

As a "strong-minded" single woman, Anthony was mocked in the press as an unattractive reject, and she developed a thick skin. Colleagues in the movement knew her as reliable, good-hearted, and high-minded, but she was also inclined to be bull-headed and blunt. Anthony was often tongue-tied in front of audiences and suffered through scores of embarrassing failures, so she could neither support herself as an orator, as Stone had done, nor hope to replace Stone as the voice of the woman's rights movement. Ultimately she was hired as the New York State agent for William Lloyd Garrison's American Anti-Slavery Society and thus found paid work as an activist. Anthony finished out the 1850s juggling women's rights, abolition, and a need to support herself.

Elizabeth Cady Stanton was born to a prominent family in upstate New York's Mohawk Valley, where her father had a distinguished legal career for over fifty years. Daniel Cady was legendary in the art of cross-examination and famous for pithy, compelling summations. Elizabeth had her father's brains and talents but as a woman she could not follow him into the law, though she picked up an informal legal education from a succession of her father's law students who boarded in their home. Her cousin Gerrit Smith introduced Elizabeth Cady to an expanded family circle and a commitment to radical causes. Smith inherited wealth from his father, a partner of John Jacob Astor, and gave generously to support a host of reforms, from temperance and pacifism to women's rights, but he was most devoted to abolition and was a determined advocate of using political means to get it. His home in rural Madison County was a stopover on the Underground Railroad, and there in the fall of 1839 Elizabeth Cady spent bright autumn days riding the countryside and starlit evenings at antislavery meetings full of "thrilling oratory."[12] One of the thrilling orators was Henry B. Stanton, and she accepted his proposal of marriage despite her father's disapproval.

The Stantons apparently had a complicated marriage, though most of the details have been lost in the destruction of family papers carried out by them or their children. Henry Stanton was intelligent, witty, and loving, but also impractical and self-absorbed. In his absent-minded way he could tolerate his wife's activism when other men might have tried to stop her. Among other things, the couple shared a love of oratory and an interest in "all political questions."[13] She was smart and sunny-tempered, and their marriage never dented her self-regard. But when Henry's work in politics, law, and journalism took him away from their home in Seneca Falls nearly ten months a year, Elizabeth Cady Stanton's exasperation with the isolation and boredom of housewifery famously spurred her determination to call the very first women's rights convention in American history in 1848. In subsequent years, feeling "like a caged lioness," she relied on her friend Susan B. Anthony to help her work for reform at a distance.[14] She continued to read voraciously in law, history, and political economy even while tied down by her growing family, and by 1859 Elizabeth Cady Stanton had become through her writings a major theoretician of the women's rights cause. But as the mother of seven children, the eldest seventeen and the youngest a newborn, she was at that point the least active of the three women's rights leaders.

The end of the 1850s found these women and their male allies at the center of the action, possessed of strong arguments and serious talent but still in need of money for the practical work of their movement—money to support activists, pay speakers' expenses, publish newspapers, and print petitions. Almost all social movements are underfunded, but women's rights particularly so because the laws prevented married women from owning property. The early women's movement faced a "catch-22" of rights and resources: to campaign for their rights, women needed resources, yet in the absence of those rights, women could not acquire many resources from their most ardent supporters—other women. Then in 1858 and 1859, the women's movement became the beneficiary of handsome bequests from two Boston abolitionists, Francis Jackson and Charles Hovey.

Finally they had some money—what Anthony called "the vital power of all movements—the wood and water of the engine."[15] They had just begun to use it to campaign when the Civil War broke out. Though the war disrupted their plans, as they shifted gears to campaign for abolition, it also precipitated the end of slavery and thus brought about a moment of extraordinary political realignment—the chaotic, desperate years historians call Reconstruction. Now at last these activist women had arguments, resources, *and* political opportunity.[16] It seemed that history had dealt them all the cards they needed.

But in 1865 their longtime ally Wendell Phillips insisted that it was "the Negro's Hour." Phillips told woman suffrage advocates they should defer to black (male) suffrage, because simultaneous agitation for woman suffrage would harm black men's chances. Stanton and Anthony thought that simultaneous agitation for woman suffrage would not harm and might even help prospects for black (male) suffrage, and they had a right to try. At first Stanton and Anthony tried to pursue the traditional abolitionist goal of human rights for all—votes for both black men *and* all women—through a new organization called the American Equal Rights Association. But their AERA came to grief in 1867 in Kansas, where referenda on black suffrage and woman suffrage were both defeated. After Kansas, Stanton and Anthony embraced racist Democrats and narrowed their focus to woman suffrage only as they desperately sought some way to win the vote. By 1869 they had run out of options but could not bring themselves to accept the Fifteenth Amendment, which protected black men's right to vote but left women behind. With Stanton's ugly rhetoric about black-on-white rape, the AERA's coalition across race and gender lines was shattered. The women's movement split into two rival organizations, Stanton and Anthony's National Woman Suffrage Association, which opposed the Fifteenth Amendment, and Lucy Stone and Henry Blackwell's American Woman Suffrage Association, which supported it. Thus in four short years, woman suffrage had been defeated, the old alliance between black rights and women's rights advocates had fallen apart, and a schism had split the women's movement. Who or what was to blame?

Stanton and Anthony themselves offered the first explanation in the 1880s in their monumental *History of Woman Suffrage,* where they retold the story to justify themselves by omitting information and reorganizing events. They argued that woman suffrage might have been won in Kansas if only more abolitionists had been true to both causes, but they also commented bitterly on the retrograde attitudes of black men.[17] Mostly, however, Stanton and Anthony bracketed the entire episode by insisting that its real importance lay in its sequel: having been deserted by their old allies, women had been forced to form their own independent women's movement, which was the historic achievement essential to women's emancipation. "Standing alone we learned our power," they wrote.[18]

When Eleanor Flexner published her *Century of Struggle* in 1959, the events of the late 1860s were finally analyzed by a historian working at arm's length. Flexner built her analysis on the assumption that woman suffrage had been "ahead of its time" in the 1860s. She implicitly affirmed that black male suffrage *was* timely, and Anthony and Stanton's position therefore reflected political naïveté as well as racial bias. They "failed to see that such a step [woman suffrage] was still far ahead of practical political possibilities," she wrote.[19] Since failure was inevitable, Flexner did not sort out events or adjudicate blame, and she devoted fewer than ten pages to the densely packed, pivotal years between 1865 and 1869.

Beginning in the 1970s, "second wave" feminists rediscovered the early women's movement and found much to admire in its founding mothers, including Stanton and Anthony's fiery radicalism on issues that ranged from sex to suffrage.[20] The second wave also fostered a new generation of professionally trained historians who studied women's history, though they mostly ignored suffrage in favor of topics like women's work or education. They imposed chronological coherence on women's rights historiography with the metaphor of waves, the "first wave" of feminism ending when the vote was won, and though it proved useful in other ways, the wave metaphor downgraded the events of the 1860s into a mid-wave hiccup rather than a full-scale turning point. But one second wave scholar explored this vexing episode and insisted on its importance. In her *Feminism and Suffrage: The Emergence of an Independent Women's Movement in America, 1848–1869* (1978) Ellen DuBois concluded that the outcome—a truly independent women's movement—was indeed most important, just as Stanton and Anthony had said.[21] DuBois portrayed them as politically aware and engaged, battling the Republican Party and turning to labor and working women because they recognized that economic and political power were related. In her view, Reconstruction politics gave these women an opening, but eventually it defeated them: the failure to win woman suffrage was "far less a result of hostilities within the movement than it was an aspect of the defeat of Reconstruction radicalism in general."[22] DuBois did not hesitate to label Stanton and Anthony's alliances and arguments "racist," but ultimately she reached a conclusion that emphasized their achievement, not their shortcomings.

In the 1980s, scholars of African American history began to point out that there was little to celebrate in the emergence of a women's movement that was nearly all white and deeply tinged with racism.[23] They challenged the long tradition of viewing the history of the women's movement through white eyes, insisted that black experience and perspective were important, and offered a strong critique of Anthony and Stanton's racist words and deeds.[24] A new generation treated the founding mothers of feminism to critical, iconoclastic debunking. Some "Stanton skeptics" even asserted that racism had always been fundamental not only to Stanton's beliefs but to feminism itself.[25] This argument was, however, typically based on events of the late nineteenth century rather than the 1860s.[26] Just as Flexner assumed that the bitter and contentious breakup in 1869 was inevitable because woman suffrage was ahead of its time, the Stanton skeptics perhaps assumed it was inevitable because of white racism.

The key to a new and deeper understanding of this crucial episode in women's history lies in Stanton and Anthony's belief that they actually had a "fighting chance" to win woman suffrage. Within the political disorder unleashed by the Civil War and its aftermath, that belief was *not* naïve—instead, it was rooted in considerable political savvy and a strong sense of history. And it explains Stanton and Anthony's actions and attitudes: they aimed for a limited breakthrough in a bellwether state, they came close to it in Kansas, and after that their sense that a historic window of opportunity was closing led them to compromise and finally to abandon their egalitarian commitments. Stanton and Anthony came to a sorry pass by pursuing fleeting and finite political opportunities—opportunities they believed, quite rightly, would never recur in their lifetime. Political opportunism, not naïveté, drove them onward: had they not believed they had a fighting chance, they would not have reached so far or stooped so low.

The conviction that they had a fighting chance meant that they needed funding urgently, and historians have not realized how a hidden conflict about money exacerbated their slide into overt racism. Wendell Phillips used his power as trustee over the Hovey bequest to deny Stanton and Anthony money to which they were entitled, money they desperately needed to campaign, and eventually their resentments about money spilled over from Phillips himself to the African American men he championed.[27] The perception of their odds also led them to argue instrumentally, and Stanton's lawyerly habit of arguing "in the alternative" as she sought to persuade white male legislators and voters resulted in a combination of both egalitarian claims and appeals to racism—a combination that set up a slippery slope down which she eventually moved to racist arguments alone. As the Stanton skeptics insist, racism is terribly important, but it should be accounted for as well as identified, explained and not explained away.

Primary sources not available decades ago confirm that Reconstruction era politics were crucial, but they also deepen our understanding of those politics.[28] Stanton and Anthony did not agree with Phillips that fighting for woman suffrage would harm black men's chance to win voting rights, and at first their experience in the American Equal Rights Association bore this out. In the AERA's campaign in New York in 1866–67, they cooperated with Frederick Douglass and other black activists who opposed the Fourteenth Amendment. This cooperation has been downplayed because Stanton and Anthony gave a confusing and inaccurate account of their relationship to the Fourteenth Amendment in the *History of Woman Suffrage*. Although the AERA campaign was brief, while it lasted, joint work did not damage black men's chances, and conflicts between woman suffrage and black men's voting rights were manageable, not intractable. The AERA's coalition across race and gender lines, and Stanton and Anthony's good faith efforts on its behalf, were more substantial than historians have understood.[29]

All accounts agree that the defeat of the Kansas referenda in 1867 marked a pivotal episode, but what led up to this outcome has not been adequately explained. As Stanton and Anthony insisted in their *History of Woman Suffrage*, Kansas was their best chance to win woman suffrage, and to do so *along with* black suffrage. But they lost because a conservative faction of the Kansas Republican Party deliberately set the two causes at odds, and by defeating both, took over party power—and without money to bring in outside campaigners, the AERA was too weak to stop them. Stanton and Anthony could not forgive Phillips for having withheld the Hovey money, but he blamed *them* for having sabotaged black suffrage, just as he had long assumed they would, by agitating for woman suffrage simultaneously. The facts were obscured by a lightning-rod figure, racist George Francis Train, who arrived in Kansas too late to affect the outcome but just in time to confuse the picture.[30] Flat broke at what they still believed was a moment of historic political opportunity, Stanton and Anthony decided to make a "deal with the devil" and accept money from Train, and they were promptly criticized as traitors to black rights. Unsupported when they tried to campaign for rights for all but condemned when they compromised by working with Train, Stanton and Anthony grew increasingly resentful and desperate to win results that would justify their compromises.

Train's promised funding soon evaporated and Stanton and Anthony feared Reconstruction's window of opportunity was closing, so in 1868 they sought new allies among Democrats. The key development, heretofore unnoticed by any historian, was the endorsement by their newspaper, the *Revolution*, of Democratic vice-presidential candidate Frank Blair in the 1868 presidential election. The Blair endorsement was an act of extreme political opportunism because Blair hinted that he endorsed woman suffrage. But it was even more harmful than the better known *Revolution* editorial Stanton wrote three months later (warning of "fearful outrages" if the Fifteenth Amendment were passed), because Blair was a virulent racist and the endorsement was publicized in the South, where it could only have encouraged Klan violence. And this last political gambit yielded no results, so that by early 1869 Stanton and Anthony were suffering from an accumulation of political dead-ends and personal frustrations, especially after Lucy Stone decided to side with Wendell Phillips in opposing them. Exhausted, broke, defensive, and unwilling to acknowledge defeat, Stanton and Anthony used their newspaper to oppose the Fifteenth Amendment and to express their resentments in appalling comments about black men.

By late 1869 it was clear that what Stanton and Anthony feared had come true: their fighting chance to win a breakthrough for woman suffrage in

Reconstruction had come and gone. Never again in their lifetimes would a moment of political opportunity like Reconstruction recur, and lack of resources would plague the women's movement for decades to come. Bad feelings between Stanton and Anthony and antagonists like Phillips and Stone would become deeply entrenched, and decades of organizational rivalry and personal sniping ensued. Over time, their arguments would continue to shift in ways that deemphasized equal rights and picked up on the Social Darwinist assumptions of the Gilded Age. From a late nineteenth-century perspective, racism appeared to be part of the warp and woof of white feminism, and the fragile and gallant coalition effort that smashed up in Kansas in 1867 was misremembered or forgotten.

This book focuses on a small cast of characters. Lively grassroots interest inspired Stanton and Anthony to keep fighting when they were bone weary, but the leaders of the women's movement, not the rank and file, were at the center of the action in this period. They cannot be replaced by a broader cast of grassroots feminists, or swapped out for a truer heroine in Lucy Stone, because they *were* so widely influential.[31] Stanton and Anthony dominated news coverage, interacted with powerful men, chose the movement's strategies, and crafted the arguments with which women's cause became identified.

This book also focuses on a small but important slice of history when the nation underwent a remarkable transformation. The destruction wrought by the Civil War and the consequent dislocation of the nation's political arrangements left everyone, not just southerners, disoriented. In the years just after the war "there was to be a brave new world" of social justice, and "the prospects for success seemed real, almost palpably so."[32] Reconstruction was a time of dizzying change even for forward-looking northern reformers. When uncompromising William Lloyd Garrison compromised and honest Wendell Phillips equivocated, why should women not chart their own course? And in the midst of so much innovation, who could really say what was ahead of its time? The political upheavals of Reconstruction persuaded Stanton and Anthony that they had to reach out to snatch the brass ring of history. But as cascading events and irreversible changes kept transforming the political context month by month and even week by week, a series of contingent choices brought these woman suffrage activists to a place far from where they began. In 1866, Elizabeth Cady Stanton warned against measures that might have oppressed southern black men while they enfranchised southern white women. In 1869, she apparently would have welcomed the same prospect. The story that follows emphasizes timing and contingency, politics and money, bigotry and faith in equal rights for all.

1

The Age Is Ripe for the Woman Question

On a fresh spring morning in May 1858, Susan B. Anthony stood at the podium as 1,500 men and women streamed into Mozart Hall in New York City for the Eighth National Woman's Rights Convention.[1] Tall, slim "practical Susan" had reason for a sigh of relief as she surveyed the hall that morning: it was clear that the size of the crowd would allow them to cover expenses and put this convention's finances in the black.[2] A veteran women's rights activist like Susan B. Anthony was reduced to counting the house because her movement had neither treasury nor dues, nor any formal organization to raise or receive money. Annual "national" women's rights "conventions" like this were simply meetings of whoever chose to attend, arranged by a few self-appointed volunteers.[3] By holding such meetings they agitated their issues, hoping to educate and arouse interest, and by charging admission, they generated a trickle of income to cover their costs and, with luck, publish the proceedings.[4] Mostly they had to rely on the overlap between their cause and abolition for their audience and constituency: Mozart Hall was packed with speakers and attendees fresh from the American Anti-Slavery Society (AASS) convention, including William Lloyd Garrison, Frederick Douglass, and Wendell Phillips.[5] Conventions like this were the sum and substance of the women's rights movement.

As the 1850s drew to a close, the effort to win women's rights was maturing and spreading but still unorganized and unfunded, the convention still its only activity. The relationship between activists for women's rights and activists for black civil and political rights was haphazard, and both were impoverished junior partners to the organized abolitionist movement. The connection between the two informally organized movements depended heavily upon key individuals like Frederick Douglass. Black women activists, who would have been ideally situated to help bridge the gap, were few in number. As Lucy Stone stepped back from her early leadership role and Elizabeth Cady Stanton stepped forward to team with Susan B. Anthony, Stanton's political savvy became influential. Anthony and Stanton were taking the reins at the end of the decade when large bequests broke the bottleneck that constrained the women's rights movement. The combination of material resources and momentum already built up over the previous decade promised a more assertive movement in the months following the convention. Together, the pair charted a bellwether strategy to win women's rights in one leading state. Stanton's interests encompassed far more than politics, but at this juncture she joined with Anthony to identify the vote as the next target, though not without exploring the possibility of putting divorce reform and sexual autonomy on the women's rights agenda.

Although they were casually organized and operating on a shoestring, women's rights advocates were nevertheless able to celebrate notable success by the time Anthony gaveled the Eighth National Woman's Rights Convention to order.[6] The blossoming confidence of the women's rights movement sprang in part from the preeminent place women writers had come to occupy in the literary market-place. These writers and their readers used the cultural scene to explore and critique existing gender roles. Their popular fiction, while sentimental and melo-dramatic, often contained implicit messages about women's strength, wisdom, and capacity for self-support.[7] While Nathaniel Hawthorne groused privately about a "damned mob of scribbling women," the activists who met in women's rights conventions grew accustomed to reeling off the names of famous "women worthies" who proved women's capacities. In 1858 the list included writers Elizabeth Barrett Browning, Charlotte Brontë, and Harriet Martineau, but it also stretched to include painter Rosa Bonheur, sculptor Harriet Hosmer, and actress and theatre manager Laura Keene.[8]

Only ten years had passed since the first convention in Seneca Falls, but the women's rights activists could see that their arguments had gained increasing public support. The business committee of the 1858 convention adopted a "march-of-progress" tone, and its resolutions celebrated "new and influential allies" and "the gradual admission of women into colleges, scientific societies and new trades and professions."[9] The movement was tapping into broad, preexisting discontent among women, which had arisen without organized movement legwork. Women's rights ideas did not just spring from the brains of its famous pioneers; they also popped up at the grassroots level from varied influences in diverse locales.[10] The activists in convention were thus trying to lead or steer a social trend they had not really created and could not actually control, and the disorganized and unfunded state of their movement did not matter much because the tides of social change in American society, in the North at least, were moving in their direction anyway. Lucretia Mott summed up the outlook: "The intelligence of the Age is ripe for the Woman question, and it only needs the *asking* on the part of woman, to *receive*."[11]

This peculiar state of affairs, in which a small cadre of activists tried to direct a pronounced but ill-formed shift in public opinion, made their choice of direction particularly critical. As the Seneca Falls proceedings attest, the wom-en's rights movement began with a long list of grievances, but no agreed-upon priorities. Instead, the activists set to work in Garrisonian style, which meant educating and agitating broadly to change hearts and minds.[12] But some women's rights leaders soon realized that they could benefit by identifying winnable short-term goals. As early as 1851, Elizabeth Cady Stanton identified the pointlessness of general agitation: "It is often said to us tauntingly, 'Well, you have

Elizabeth Cady Stanton and Susan B. Anthony in an 1870 photo that suggests their intensity and determination, and their close partnership, during this period. Courtesy the Division of Rare and Manuscript Collections, Cornell University Library.

held conventions, you have written letters and theorized, you have speechified and resolved, protested and appealed, declared and petitioned, and now what? Why do you not do something?'"[13] In the early 1850s, dress reform seemed one way to "do something" without benefit of funding or formal organization. Individual activists donned the bloomer costume in hopes of challenging the dictates of fashion and legitimizing simpler and more practical styles of dress, but by 1854 it was clear that the bloomer caused more trouble than it was worth, and leading activists went back to long skirts.[14]

By the later 1850s, the women's movement was shifting to a focus on political action—on campaigning to change state laws that discriminated against women. The 1858 convention signaled this new emphasis by resolving that progress in both education and employment could be "safely left to individual energy." Instead, "The most effective mode of agitating the whole subject is now by obtaining hearings before the legislatures of the several states."[15] Most abolitionists also gravitated toward political and legislative solutions during the 1850s, having concluded that "moral suasion is moral balderdash."[16] Massachusetts abolitionist Thomas Wentworth Higginson, one of the movement's strongest male supporters, urged the 1858 Woman's Rights Convention to undertake political action by simultaneously petitioning a number of state legislatures, but follow-through on Higginson's plan after the convention was a shambles.[17] Coordinated activity was impossible to manage when activists lacked the money to pay for postage, printing, or travel expenses.

At Seneca Falls in 1848, the Declaration of Sentiments had promised, "We shall employ agents, circulate tracts, petition the state and national Legislatures, and endeavor to enlist the pulpit and the press in our behalf," but the women lacked the means to make good on those plans.[18] Bootstrap efforts to start a women's paper, including the *Lily* and the *Una*, were underfunded and short-lived. Woman's rights advocates could usually rely on the *Liberator* and the *National Anti-Slavery Standard* to print notices or letters, but with no newspaper of their own, they made do by devising strategies to attract attention from the editors of major metropolitan daily papers, especially New York's *Herald*, *Tribune*, and *Times*, which reached thousands of readers far beyond the city via the "exchange" and their weekly editions.[19] Only Horace Greeley's *Tribune* was sympathetic to women's rights, but even critical coverage in the other papers had the unintended effect of arousing public awareness, and it was better than being ignored. Nor could they afford to hire "agents" who went into the field as itinerant speakers and organizers.[20] The participants in a women's rights convention in New York State in 1854 admitted, "Gladly—could they command the services of Lecturing Agents—would they thoroughly canvass the entire State."[21]

Women's fund-raising was part of what made them the "great silent army" of abolition, and looking back, Frederick Douglass would acknowledge that women had "in large degree" supplied abolition's "sinews of war"—a Ciceronian euphemism for money.[22] Although the founding mothers of the women's rights movement were well aware of AASS fund-raising methods, they did not reproduce them for their own cause. Perhaps their failure to create a comparable formal organization was functional.[23] But their failure to engage in fund-raising also made a virtue of necessity because women were uniquely impoverished: the laws of coverture still denied most married women the right to own property or keep earnings so they could not contribute to causes they cared about.[24] True, female benevolent and voluntary associations, thick on the ground in the antebellum years, raised and spent significant amounts of money.[25] But the self-sacrificing ideology of female benevolence, which might stretch to cover efforts to end the sufferings of slavery, offered little support for women asserting their own rights. Elizabeth Cady Stanton fumed that when it came to fund-raising, women sewed pin cushions for every cause but their own.[26]

Resource constraints thus amounted to a bottleneck that held back the women's movement on the eve of the Civil War, affecting individual activists as well as the group. Married women activists were responsible for housework, which meant they needed efficient domestic servants and husbands who could afford to hire them.[27] Lack of servants took a toll on Angelina Grimké and her sister Sarah Grimké, who boldly pioneered the women's rights cause in the 1830s but disappeared almost entirely from activism after 1841, due to poverty as well as ill health.[28] In contrast, Lucretia Mott was able to travel, speak publicly, and preside at conventions because James Mott was both ideologically supportive and comfortably middle class, enabling her to employ servants.[29] Women who worked for wages were restricted to a handful of "women's" occupations with long hours and low pay and had little time for activism. Single women from middle-class families were not obliged to find compensated labor, but they were often expected to care for aging parents or assist married siblings.[30] Only Lucy Stone managed to escape these resource dilemmas: she could support herself and agitate the cause simultaneously because she was such a compelling orator that audiences would pay to hear her speak, even on the unpopular subject of women's rights.[31]

Susan B. Anthony opened the 1858 women's rights convention on a note of solidarity with black rights, declaring that neither sex nor skin color could "rob human beings of their inalienable rights."[32] Before the convention was over, however, Charles Lenox Remond sounded a discordant note. Remond, an African American abolitionist and an early supporter of women's rights from Salem, Massachusetts, spoke on "women's rights and complexion" and "deprecated the idea of separating the interest of the two movements by private jealousies."[33] Anthony and Remond were both right: the interests of the two movements were identical at the level of universal human rights and yet they operated separately, their relationship complicated by "private jealousies" and by other factors as well.

Like the movement for women's rights, efforts to secure black rights in the antebellum era were unorganized and played a subordinate role to organized abolition. Free African Americans had helped to establish the American Anti-Slavery Society, but they often found that their own claims for civil and political rights were relegated to the back burner by abolitionists who preferred to focus on southern slavery, not northern racism and discrimination.[34] Black activists tried to move away from those white-dominated priorities by calling conventions of their own. Beginning in the early 1830s these conventions of "free people of color," or "colored men," convened sporadically to discuss efforts to improve access to education, employment, civil rights, and voting rights.[35] But they sometimes faced the threat of violent disruption and they had to wrestle with the divisive question of emigration: would it *ever* be possible to gain equal rights within racist American society, or might it be better to leave for Canada, Africa, or the Caribbean? Emigration divided black activists and siphoned off support from rights-oriented black activism.[36]

The earliest black conventions laid ambitious plans for formal organization, but it soon became apparent that the participants lacked the necessary support and resources. Black conventions tried again to launch formal organizations in the 1850s: a permanent "national council" was established at the 1853 convention, but it collapsed two years later.[37] Remaining unorganized and meeting irregularly, black conventions did impose a measure of formal organization by insisting on examining and approving participants' credentials. Most were inclined to err in the direction of openness, but black conventions never entirely abandoned restrictions on participation, probably because they had to fear racist disruption.[38] Meanwhile, black activists built other organizations, including African American churches and voluntary associations devoted to benevolence, self-improvement, and mutual aid within the black community. In this vulnerable and needy community, any such ventures were understood as contributing to the advancement of the race: antislavery, black civil and political rights, and community uplift were all part of the broad ongoing struggle for African American freedom and justice.[39]

The black conventions were dominated by black men, but in the 1840s they began to discuss the "woman question" more and more favorably, and black women increasingly took part in the deliberations. At the milestone 1848 black convention in Cleveland, the delegates passed a resolution that read, "We believe fully in the equality of the sexes," and "Three cheers for women's rights" rang out on the convention floor.[40] The following year, when black women threatened to boycott the State Convention of the Colored Citizens of Ohio unless they were allowed to speak, they won their point.[41] But in the 1850s, African American activists in convention increasingly came to view women's rights as irrelevant to their concerns. Battered by the effects of the Fugitive Slave Law, which caused large numbers of free northern blacks to seek safety in Canada, and by the Dred Scott case, which declared that free blacks had "no rights the white man was bound to respect," black men began to see women's rights as an unaffordable luxury, a separate cause that had no place on their agenda.[42]

With the "colored" conventions dominated by men and the women's rights conventions nearly all white, black women occupied an anomalous but potentially pivotal position. Maria Stewart, a pioneering black activist, spoke out for both black rights and women's rights as early as the 1830s, and in the 1850s a small number of black women chose to attend the mostly white women's rights conventions.[43] One was the legendary Sojourner Truth, who used an Akron Ohio convention in 1851 to deliver remarks that later became known as her "Ain't I a Woman" speech. At many points in her long career, Truth confronted white women about their racism and criticized black men for their sexism, but she did so as a liminal figure whose significance was partly invented by white reformers. The symbolic Truth reflected their deep need for a heroic black woman who could resolve race and gender differences and speak truth to power in both directions.[44] But Maria Stewart was an isolated figure, and because she came and went by her own lights and chose to remain illiterate, Sojourner Truth also stood at a remove. Truth was never a regular attendee at women's rights gatherings and was cut off from the letter-writing and resolution-drafting strategies of the mostly white women's rights network.[45]

Other African American women attended women's rights conventions over the years, including women from the Purvis and Forten families at the 1854 women's rights convention held in Philadelphia.[46] Though a number of biracial female antislavery societies had been formed in the 1830s, almost all had long since disappeared, victims of racist violence or factionalism.[47] The 1858 National Woman's Rights Convention introduced a promising new African American recruit, Sarah Parker Remond, who had toured New York State with Susan B. Anthony in an antislavery canvass the previous winter.[48] Remond was a talented speaker who chose that convention to announce her willingness to "identify herself with this [women's rights] movement," but she disappeared from its ranks almost immediately, departing for England where she spoke for the antislavery cause.[49] No black women participated in the 1859 or 1860 national women's rights conventions.[50]

The patterns of activism that had evolved by the 1850s saw two rights movements, one of color and one of sex. Black women could fight for gender equity at black conventions or for race equity at women's rights conventions, but both projects faced practical hurdles. At the black conventions, women were less welcome after 1850, and they had to fight for credentials before they could begin to debate substantive questions. Given the conventions' small turnout and meager clout, it was not entirely clear that the effort would be worthwhile. Attending women's rights conventions, which required the price of admission and the likelihood of encountering white women with biased attitudes, was also a dubious proposition.[51] Those black women who could muster the resources and the time for activism tended to choose a third way, working in mutual aid, charitable, and church groups within the black community.[52] Those who showed up and spoke up in the black conventions or the women's rights conventions did vital work, helping to keep both movements honest about the universality of human rights, but they were few in number.

Like white women, black activists, male and female, found that funding was painfully scarce and wealthy benefactors rare.[53] Though Garrisonian antislavery societies were sometimes willing to hire black agents, they looked askance at separatist black conventions.[54] Individual black activists struggled to patch together a living. Sojourner Truth supported her itinerant career by selling her photos and memoir, but she still needed help from wealthy abolitionists because it cost more to be an activist than to stay home, as one of her friends remarked: "Travel needs money and this is why I have tried to help her. . . . Everybody will give her a home and bread, but she wants to be at work."[55] Frances Ellen Watkins Harper managed a rare feat when she was able to support herself by public speaking and by selling her self-published poetry and fiction wherever she spoke.[56] Both the movement for black rights and the movement for women's rights were positioned as supplicants for crumbs from the table of white abolition, living (or dying) on a starvation diet.

The two movements had somewhat different goals and quite different prospects. Voting rights for black men were a reality in several New England states and had enough backing to get on the political agenda in others, neither of which could be said for women. On the other hand, the sharp edge of "Black Laws," to say nothing of violent riots and venomous hostility, far exceeded anything white women had to contend with. White racism grew more virulent from the 1830s on, as new discriminatory laws were enacted and incoming waves of immigrant men were taught to regard blacks as a threat to their jobs and to see white supremacy as essential to their manhood.[57] Prospects for black rights looked increasingly grim during the 1850s, at the same time the women's movement was profiting from shifts in public opinion. By the eve of the Civil War, any sort of effort to win black rights in white America had to be undertaken on faith.[58]

Beset by discrimination, black men were capable of defining the rights to which they aspired in terms of the patriarchal privileges enjoyed by their white counterparts. Sometimes black male leaders endorsed traditional female roles, and fiction in the black press idealized feminine domesticity.[59] But some black men went out of their way to take a stand for women's rights. Charles Lenox

Remond had spoken for women at the World's Anti-Slavery Convention in London in 1840.[60] William C. Nell and Robert Purvis were also early supporters of women's rights.[61] From Seneca Falls on, Frederick Douglass consistently lent his enormous prestige to the women's cause, was friendly with its leaders, and often spoke on its platform.[62]

For their part, white women in pursuit of their own rights might be willing to throw black rights overboard, as became apparent soon after the First National Woman's Rights Convention was held in 1850. Jane Gray Swisshelm, editor of the antislavery *Saturday Visiter* [sic], wrote that the women's convention was all she could have wished for "except the introduction of the color question." Veteran Garrisonian Parker Pillsbury responded and defended the presence of black women and men, and the question of their rights, on the women's platform. Though at first Swisshelm spoke in what seemed to be even-handed tones, urging that each cause might hurt the other, her language eventually betrayed special vehemence against black men. Women's "little boat," she insisted, was not strong enough "to bear the additional weight of all the colored men in creation.... We do not want him in our boat. Let him row his own craft!"[63] Swisshelm was unrepresentative though not unique: most women's rights activists came out of an abolitionist background and gave at least rhetorical support to black rights.

Even if black men endorsed gender equality and white women resisted racism, opponents tried to link them as a means to denigrate both. Sexual innuendo featuring black men and white women was the stock in trade of gutter racism in the antebellum period, and outrageous rumors about sexual relations across the color line helped spark riots.[64] Any occasion that brought black men and white women together in public might provoke ugly comments or coarse jests. For example, the *Albany Argus* sneered at Susan B. Anthony's "usual delicate manner, refined by her contact with Fred Douglass and other third-class colored people."[65] And popular minstrel shows found it humorous to connect blacks and "bloomers."[66]

Because the woman's rights and black rights movements were not organized enough to elect officers who could coordinate activities, mutual support among these activists remained haphazard, a matter of individual initiative and sensitivity. What then was the "personal jealousy" Charles Lenox Remond alluded to in his remarks at the 1858 women's rights convention? Perhaps he referred to friction that had developed between Frederick Douglass and Lucy Stone. In 1854, Douglass had accused Stone of selling out her antislavery principles after she went on a lucrative speaking tour in the slave states, where she drew large crowds and complimentary newspaper notices.[67] Stone also spoke on women's rights in a whites-only hall in Philadelphia, and black people to whom she sent complimentary tickets suffered the humiliation of being turned away at the door. Douglass, who had criticized the black activist Samuel Ringgold Ward for speaking in a segregated hall, was not about to excuse the same behavior by a white woman, and he publicly questioned Stone's integrity.[68] Stone explained that the Philadelphia fiasco was based on a misunderstanding, but Douglass still regarded her with skepticism at decade's end.[69]

Anthony and Stanton probably had better informal relationships with black activists. Anthony and her family socialized with Frederick Douglass at home in Rochester, and as an AASS agent Anthony worked with other African Americans. In the first year of her agency, for example, she toured northern New York with Charles Lenox Remond and Sarah Parker Remond for several months.[70] Stanton's relationship to black activists was largely through her cousin Gerrit Smith, whose racial attitudes were remarkably progressive, enabling him to develop friendly, trusting relationships with both Frederick Douglass and James McCune Smith.[71] Stanton and Douglass had met before Seneca Falls, probably in the early 1840s when Stanton was living in Boston, and he credited her with having persuaded him "when she was yet a young lady" that women were entitled to equal rights.[72] In the *History of Woman Suffrage* she credited Douglass with playing a pivotal role at the Seneca Falls convention by endorsing her woman suffrage resolution.[73] Yet contemporary sources also show that as a young woman, Elizabeth Cady Stanton had a lot to learn about racial equality. In her 1854 "Appeal to the Women of New York State," for example, she credited Douglass's perception of his own humanity and rights to his "few drops of Saxon blood," and at least one black activist complained about her racist assumptions.[74] Nevertheless Douglass apparently tolerated or corrected Stanton while he feuded with Stone.

Disorganized and unfunded, the women's movement was in danger of becoming little more than a debating society when two fortuitous gifts dramatically changed the outlook in late 1858 and early 1859. The money came not a moment too soon for Susan B. Anthony, who was gloomily contemplating her own empty purse and doubting the efficacy of holding more conventions.[75] The women's first benefactor was Francis Jackson, a wealthy real estate broker who had given generously to support Garrison's *Liberator* and the AASS, and had attended the First National Woman's Rights Convention in Worcester. Jackson's will left $10,000 to battle slavery, $2,000 to aid fugitive slaves, and $5,000 "to secure the passage of laws granting women, whether married or unmarried, the right to vote; to hold office; to hold, manage, and devise property; and all other civil rights enjoyed by men."[76] Jackson named one group of trustees for the antislavery funds and another for the women's rights fund, but Wendell Phillips headed both groups. Lucy Stone and Susan B. Anthony were named to join Phillips as trustees of the women's fund.[77] In the fall of 1858, although Jackson was still alive, he directed that the expenditures begin, and Wendell Phillips informed Stone and Anthony of what was at that point still an anonymous gift, asking their opinions on how to begin. He added, "I think some agitation specially directed to the Legislature very important."[78]

The second gift came from Charles F. Hovey, a Boston dry goods merchant. Hovey, who supported abolition and signed the call to the First National Woman's Rights Convention at Worcester in 1850, left a huge gift of over $50,000 to be expended on antislavery and other reforms "such as women's rights, non-resistance, free trade and temperance." Like Jackson, Hovey appointed a committee of trustees headed by Wendell Phillips to decide how to allocate the money. He stipulated that the money must be spent at a rate of $8,000 per year to ensure immediate impact. Unlike Jackson, Hovey did not earmark any money specifically for women, and the trustees he named included none of the principal leaders of the women's movement, so Hovey monies might flow to antislavery at the expense of women's rights.[79] But Hovey also looked to the long term and stipulated that if slavery should be abolished, the woman's cause was to be a residual legatee.

At last the women's rights movement had material resources to work with. Resources could not recruit more black women or teach white women and black men how to harmonize their efforts. But they did permit and encourage activist women to take action in ways that had been hitherto impossible. It was a turning

Francis Jackson. Library of Congress.

Charles F. Hovey. *The History of the House of Hovey.*

point, and the leaders immediately understood it as such. Elizabeth Cady Stanton wrote, "I never felt so thankful in the days of my life as when I read Phillips letter.... Praise the Lord!!"[80] Now they could, if they wished, move beyond education and agitation to engage in practical campaigning, but they needed to decide what to do, and where, and how. They decided to mount a campaign to influence the legislature to change the laws that discriminated against women. They headed into politics.

Lucy Stone had never been much interested in electoral politics, although she did want the right to vote and argued for it at the First National Woman's Rights Convention in 1850.[81] The job of the activist, she believed, was "to make the public sentiment on the side of all that is just and true and noble," and then public sentiment would take care of changing politics and the law.[82] She considered antislavery politics "a great waste of power" and recommended the Garrisonian program of "abstaining from voting and holding office under the present Constitution."[83] The timing of Stone's withdrawal from activism meant she did not participate in abolitionists' increasing rapprochement with political methods in the late 1850s.

Like Stone, Susan B. Anthony approached politics from a Garrisonian background, but she moved much further to embrace them, increasingly drawn toward political action by the events of the 1850s. Her father was an abolitionist who voted for the first time in 1860, and her brother, D. R., was a founder of the New York State Republican Party.[84] She had an unlikely but important tutor from the ranks of conventional politicians: Thurlow Weed, the legendary boss of the New York Whigs and later the Republicans. It is not clear how they first met, but in 1852, when Anthony and other women were not allowed to speak at a temperance meeting, the women repaired to Thurlow Weed's office "to talk over the situation with him." In 1859, when Anthony was in Albany to lobby the legislature for the AASS, she "called often" on Weed.[85] Weed was a close friend and political ally of Senator William Henry Seward, and the two were a force to be reckoned with in New York and national politics.[86] The "spinster" ex-teacher from Rochester had a surprising degree of access to Thurlow Weed, arguably the premier professional politician in the country. By the end of the 1850s, Anthony's experience lobbying state legislators and interacting with Weed made her comfortably conversant with conventional politicians.

Elizabeth Cady Stanton was by far the most politically astute of the three women's rights leaders; she was not just reconciled to politics, she reveled in it. She learned to think like a reform-minded politician from her husband. Henry B. Stanton was an antislavery democrat in principle, and—something more difficult—an antislavery Democrat in practice.[87] He sympathized with the common man against the wealthy and the privileged, which made him a classic Jacksonian Democrat, but he went further and argued that the true Democratic Party ought to be the logical home of antislavery and common men of all races, which made him part of New York State's famous antislavery "Barnburner" faction of the party.[88] Stanton sympathized with her husband's belief that democracy was a political system still in the process of unfolding, and she pressed to extend that idea to women. Theirs was a deeply partisan family: at one point she had to reassure her five-year-old, who asked anxiously, and with a touch of real concern in his voice, if the new baby was a Democrat.[89]

For years, Stanton watched her husband wrestle with the dilemma of the political abolitionist. It was the same dilemma Gerrit Smith struggled with and Frederick Douglass agonized over: how to be a politically effective radical, how to avoid the fate of the ineffectual outsider or the co-opted insider? In the spectacular 1840 split in the ranks of abolition, Henry B. Stanton rejected the antipolitical stance of the Garrisonians as irresponsible.[90] He worked hard to build up the abolitionist Liberty Party, but it remained marginal, and after the outbreak of the Mexican War, Henry B. Stanton realized that stopping the expansion of slavery—demanding "free soil"—could appeal to far more northern voters than immediate abolition ever had. In the summer of 1848, when his wife was convening the first women's rights convention in Seneca Falls, Henry B. Stanton was busy forging a third party, a "Free Soil" coalition between Liberty men, "Barnburner" Democrats, and antislavery or "Conscience" Whigs.

She also watched his political career go through a less admirable stage, when the free soil cause waned and, despairing of the isolation of a third party, he returned to the regular Democratic Party. Henry predicted jauntily that the Barnburners would out-maneuver their pro-slavery opponents, the Hunkers, but the result was more the reverse.[91] Although the Democratic candidate for president in 1852, Franklin Pierce, ran on a pro-southern record and an anti-abolitionist platform, Henry B. Stanton campaigned for Pierce anyway because he badly needed a patronage job to support his growing family.[92] He sold out his principles for nothing, because the Pierce administration passed him over.

In 1854 the Kansas-Nebraska Act provoked a political realignment on which the Stantons could both agree. The new "anti-Nebraska" Republican Party appealed to antislavery Democrats like Henry Stanton who believed their party had been captured by pro-slavery southerners. By becoming a Republican, he could become a political insider without fatal compromise and with the approval of his wife, who attended the Republican meetings in Seneca Falls.[93] Henry B. Stanton's migration from Liberty Party to Free-Soiler, to Democrat and then to Republican mostly reflected his continuing effort to find a party framework that furthered the interests of common people, *including* black people. On that principle—that "created equal" was not intended for white men only—the Stantons, husband and wife, certainly found their political sympathies convergent if not identical. On the specific question of women's rights, Henry B. Stanton apparently offered Elizabeth scant support, but thanks to him she understood regular party politics intimately.[94] When the party system of Democrats and Whigs fell to pieces in 1854, for example, Elizabeth Cady Stanton analyzed events like a pro: in an article in the *New York Tribune* she discussed the fortunes of the *eight* distinct political factions in New York with ease.[95]

At the point when the Jackson Fund became available in late 1858, both Lucy Stone and Elizabeth Cady Stanton were sidelined. Stone was pregnant, and she and Blackwell had moved out to Evanston, Illinois. Stone's pregnancy ended in either a miscarriage or a premature birth, and the death of her child deepened her withdrawal from activism.[96] Meanwhile, Elizabeth Cady Stanton had to cancel an engagement to deliver a prestigious speech in Boston because she, too, was pregnant, and unlike her previous pregnancies, this one took a severe toll on her energy, a disability she felt embarrassed to admit.[97] That left matters in Susan B. Anthony's hands, but she was busy with antislavery work for the American Anti-Slavery Society, which was, after all, paying her salary. Anthony spent six weeks in Albany in the winter of 1858–59 lobbying the legislature for a personal liberty law, and therefore little had been accomplished with the Jackson Fund when, in the spring of 1859, the activists received word of the second bequest from Charles Hovey.[98]

Anthony soon set to work, and with a physical energy that always exceeded Stanton's and a political bent that Stone never shared, she changed the pattern of women's activism by tapping the new monies to hire activists as paid agents to campaign to change the laws of New York State.[99] In the fall and winter of 1859–1860, six speakers crisscrossed the state carrying petitions, distributing pamphlets, and speaking to public meetings on women's rights. Anthony brought in three experienced orators from out of state—Frances Dana Gage from Missouri, Hannah Tracy Cutler from Illinois, and J. Elizabeth Jones from Ohio—and tested the waters herself in a joint speaking tour with Antoinette Brown Blackwell. The women's Jackson-funded salaries of $12 per week were essential because collections or admission fees at the meetings "hardly paid expenses, to say nothing of compensation."[100] Elizabeth Cady Stanton penned a campaign "Appeal to the Women of the Empire State" in which she declared frankly, "Want of funds has hitherto crippled all our efforts, but as large bequests have been made to our cause during the past year, we are now able to send out agents and commence anew our work."[101]

Anthony's speakers held conventions in forty counties, delivered speeches in 150 towns and villages, and climaxed the campaign at a New York State Woman's Rights Convention in Albany timed to coincide with the legislative session.[102] Lucy Stone played a limited role but delivered one major address in New York City, sharing the stage with Henry Ward Beecher, a prominent minister who had a huge congregation in Brooklyn and was a prestigious convert to the women's rights cause.[103] Elizabeth Cady Stanton also gave a speech as the campaign was ending, finally able to do so because her last child was out of infancy and her liberation from household cares was bolstered by a handsome legacy from her father.[104] She delivered her speech in Albany on March 19, 1860, to a joint session of the judiciary committees, before galleries packed with women.

The women's rights activists had mounted an earlier, unfunded campaign for women's rights in New York State in the winter of 1854, and comparisons were instructive. Then, too, Elizabeth Cady Stanton had researched the laws of New York and prepared a meticulously documented and strongly argued speech.[105] The women had also petitioned the legislature for their rights and held a convention in Albany. In 1854 Anthony had wished for "forty of the right sort of women" to volunteer, but in 1860, she had actually been able to hire six full-time canvassers.[106] Earlier experience showed that entrusting blank petitions to local sympathizers could not roll up many signatures or convert many skeptics, nor could it build a wave of favorable publicity. It also showed that canvassing cost money: in 1855, when Anthony canvassed the state by herself, she was parsimonious but barely covered her expenses.[107] In 1860, the funded campaign was different, as were its results.

The New York State legislature crowned the women's efforts with success by passing the 1860 Married Women's Property Act, a landmark law allowing married women title to their own earnings and giving wives joint custody of their children. The earnings provision in the new 1860 law was significant; many states had passed laws allowing married women to hold property, but the New York law allowed them their own earnings. This was a significant step forward because it pointed to the possibility that wives might be productive partners rather than economic dependents. Similarly, the grant of joint custody involved a new perception of marriage as an equal partnership.[108]

At the Tenth National Woman's Rights Convention in New York City in May 1860, Anthony happily laid down a blanket of details about how the New York campaign was conducted and Elizabeth Cady Stanton repeated her Albany speech for the benefit of the crowd gathered at the Cooper Institute.[109] Speaker after speaker hailed the new property and custody law. Convention-goers even heard from a Brooklyn judge who told how the new law had benefited three women who came before his court that very morning. At last the women's rights leaders were not just talking about ideas; they were using their convention to report on political action and celebrate legislative results. The speakers praised what had been done but also anticipated more to come. A polite but demanding resolution declared, "We return thanks to the Legislature of New York for its acts of justice to women during the last session. But the work is not yet done. We still claim the ballot, the right of trial by a jury of our own peers, the control and custody of our persons in marriage, and an equal right to the joint earnings of the co-partnership."[110] This ambitious list suggested that the activists still needed to prioritize different elements of "the work" and develop a plan. Which goal should they pursue next and where and how? Who would be their allies, and what would be their strategy? Their New York experience began to answer some of these questions.

The New York campaign showed the importance of outsider campaigning in conjunction with lobbying and inside assistance. On the outside, speakers prodded legislators by mounting a petition campaign sufficient to arouse broad expressions of public interest and support. But on the inside, male allies were crucial, and the activists relied on Anson Bingham, a Republican member of the Assembly Judiciary Committee, and Andrew J. Colvin, a Democratic member of the Senate Judiciary Committee. Bingham and Colvin found votes in favor of the new law among legislators interested in legal code revision and debtor protection, as well as those who advocated women's rights.[111] The women's rights legislation had to thread its way past notoriously corrupt legislators exchanging New York City street railway franchises for hefty bribes.[112] Well aware of the character of many of the politicians who voted for the women's bill, Ernestine Rose joked, "We 'Woman's Rights women' have redeemed our last legislature, by inducing

them to give us one good act, among so many corrupt ones. (Laughter)." Both
outside and inside efforts were needed, Rose warned, disputing "some ladies
who think a great deal can be done in the Legislature without petitions, without
conventions, without lectures . . . without anything but a little lobbying."[113] What
about goals? Their petitions had asked the legislature for a full range of women's
rights, including the right to vote and hold office, the right of married women to
control their property and earnings, and the right of mothers to have equal custody rights over children and property in case of the death of a spouse.[114] But, as
Rose observed, the women were willing to take half a loaf. As it turned out, the
"half a loaf" of property and custody legislation seemed easily won because the
bill passed by two-to-one margins in both Assembly and Senate.[115] Was more of
the "whole loaf" of women's rights within reach? Anthony's ally Andrew Colvin
told her that a majority on the Senate judiciary committee had favored woman
suffrage, but he had not pushed the issue for fear of overreaching.[116] Considering
that the Senate Judiciary Committee had only three members, of which he was
one, Colvin may have exaggerated the possibilities, but Anthony understandably
seized on his message. An impatient strategist like Anthony had to wonder
whether this New York experience suggested that possibly, just possibly, women
could win the vote in the short run, as Colvin hinted. A similar hint had been
dropped a year earlier when a representative named George F. Longenhelt, a
farmer from Otsego County, unexpectedly presented a resolution in the New
York State Assembly to strike the word "male" from the state constitution's voting
requirements. Longenhelt acted on his own, unprompted by the activists, and
although the officers of the Assembly promptly tabled his motion, it drew
extended notice from the *New York Times*.[117] Colvin and Longenhelt in effect
suggested that the ballot might be within reach.

Elizabeth Cady Stanton moved quickly to announce the vote as women's next
target. Her Albany speech was actually delivered after the legislature had already
passed the property and custody bill and it awaited the governor's signature.[118]
Stanton thus felt free to turn to the next priority, and she singled out the vote.
Stanton based women's claim to voting rights on key principles of American gov-
ernance—consent of the governed and no taxation without representation—but
she also addressed commonly voiced objections. She gave special attention to
one argument: "The majority of women do not ask for any change in the laws,"
opponents reasoned, so that "it is time enough to give them the elective franchise
when they, as a class, demand it." Stanton had to concede that many women were
indeed indifferent to having the right to vote.[119] But she rejected the relevance of
popularity and argued that because suffrage was a matter of individual natural
right, it did not need the weight of numbers. "No, gentlemen," she said, "if there is
but one woman in this State who feels the injustice of her position, she should not
be denied her inalienable rights because the common household drudge and the

silly butterflies of fashion are ignorant."[120] The lack of mass support for woman suffrage, understandable enough when the women's movement had been in its infancy, was becoming a problem as the movement began to appeal to legislators who were accustomed to consulting their constituents' opinions. According to Stanton's reasoning, the vote was an ideal goal for the women's movement at this moment precisely because its success did *not* require persuading a majority of women to demand it. The activists could, she implied, fight and win an early victory without first building a mass movement, and indifferent women could thereafter grow into the use of the vote gradually.[121] Suffrage rightly understood was not "ahead of its time"; it was the ideal first plank in a bridge to the future.

Thus Stanton in effect tried to use the end of the New York State campaign as the occasion for setting an agenda for the women's movement that prioritized the vote. But in this unorganized movement, no individual or governing body was authorized to set priorities, so the Tenth Woman's Rights Convention's discussion was diffuse, responsibility was unclear, and even close coadjutors like Stanton and Anthony could send mixed messages. Attendees at the 1860 convention must have wondered when Anthony told the crowd that next year, "We propose to expend our funds and efforts mostly in the State of Ohio," who this "we" was of whom she spoke, and how the goals were being set.[122] Was the plan now to go after property and custody legislation in another state, as Anthony seemed to say, or to push further by demanding the vote in New York, as Stanton in her speech seemed to imply?

The whole project of campaigning for votes for women, which Stanton sought to launch in New York State, took shape in a political context where women were outsiders with a foot in the door. In the early republic, the wives and daughters of prominent men created a "parlor politics" in Washington using their social networks to forge coalitions of like-minded politicians and select individuals for leadership roles. For example, in the 1820s, when the women's rights leaders were girls, Louisa Catherine Adams mounted an effective "campaign" to nominate her husband, John Quincy Adams, for president.[123] During the 1830s, politics moved out of the parlor and women's roles diminished as the right to vote was extended to all adult white males. The newly organized Democratic and Whig parties made politics popular by floating it on a tide of pageantry, oratory, and alcohol, and they deployed symbolic issues and charismatic personalities, not to mention job opportunities or "spoils," to cement party loyalty. Voter turnout ranged upward from 70 percent or 80 percent, and frequent and staggered election dates made for near-continuous campaigning. Many historians have argued that this "second party system" created an antebellum society in which "politics seemed to enter into everything"—a situation that rendered women's formal exclusion all the more egregious and disempowering. Certainly that was how the women's rights activists felt. But appearances were somewhat deceiving: a sizable minority of the white *male* population remained estranged from or indifferent to the political circuses of the day.[124] Not surprisingly, even larger numbers of women evidently felt the same.

Antebellum women were encouraged to make a virtue of this political exclusion by reactionaries like Catharine Beecher, who championed the womanly virtues—loving care, purity, and spirituality—within the separate, private "sphere" of the home. Beecher conceptualized woman's sphere as a wholly separate world and a crucial counterweight to the male vices—competitive self-seeking and coarse materialism—that marred men's public sphere.[125] In reality the world was not so bifurcated. Female academies helped to create a middle ground, a "civil society" where women learned to participate in national discussions about ideology and policy.[126] Even though they lacked the vote, women who were educated in this way felt able to write, speak, petition, and lobby on behalf of benevolent voluntarism and causes ranging from temperance to Indian removal to abolition.[127] While it may be misleading to label these activities "political," to call them only "public" risks missing the women's specific legislative and policy goals.[128] Stanton and Anthony built upon the educational, social, and cultural foundations laid by the female academies and women's experiences in civil society in order to claim entrée into the ultimate male bastion, electoral politics. In the 1850s women's quasi-political activity increased, in part because of the increasingly political orientation of the temperance movement, but even more because the new Republican Party gave women special welcome.[129] John C. Fremont, the first Republican presidential candidate in 1856, found his wife Jessie Benton Fremont was an essential political ally. Jessie, the daughter of Democratic powerhouse Thomas Hart Benton, acted as her husband's chief adviser and secretary, and she was hailed, not ignored, during the campaign. Women donned "Jessie badges," tootled away in "Jessie bands," and turned out in record numbers for public meetings held under banners hailing, "Fremont and Our Jessie."[130] Despite some bumpy episodes involving Republican men who wanted to focus only on actual voters, most leaders of the new party learned to welcome women's support.

A small but significant group of "female politicos," most of whom were related to male politicians, went further by wire-pulling behind the scenes.[131] During the campaign of 1860, Mary Todd Lincoln revealed herself to be a highly political wife—knowledgeable about politics, ready to talk to reporters, an aggressive campaigner with pen and ink. Yet she was sensitive to conventional beliefs about women's sphere, and when the press noticed her influence she hastened to claim she was "wholly domestic."[132] Wielding political influence in a private way, behind closed doors, satisfied Jessie Benton Fremont, who praised "the beauty as well as the utility of silent activity" and refused to support woman suffrage.

She told Elizabeth Cady Stanton, "I do not believe in suffrage for women. I think women in their present position manage men better." Stanton in reply "expressed doubt as to whether it was our business in life to 'manage men.'"[133]

Stanton considered separate sphere ideology "twaddle" because it promised female influence but delivered little more than sappy lip service, and she scorned private wheedling in favor of equal political rights.[134] But as she and Anthony sought to chart a course to the political promised land, they had to cope with the apolitical worldview of most women and even other activists like Lucy Stone. Stanton and Anthony were raising the issue of the vote in a context in which most women, absorbed in domestic life, were still indifferent to electoral politics, while others who did care about politics had an alternative theory about how to proceed. And yet, because woman suffrage did not require mass support, Stanton and Anthony felt emboldened to press the issue.

It made sense for Stanton and Anthony to choose a bellwether state because the state and not the federal government was still the basic unit of American political activity, not to mention the sole determinant of voting qualifications.[135] New York was a logical choice. The state wielded national influence because its population made it an electoral heavyweight, with the largest congressional delegation and bloc of electoral votes, and the New York City press gave the state extra clout.[136] As early as 1853, the call to the National Woman's Rights Convention asked, "Where can we better hold these [conventions] than in *New York*, the commercial capital of the country, whose press is listened to by the Nation?"[137] It had also seen early agitation, beginning in 1836–37 when Ernestine Rose petitioned the state legislature.[138] By the late 1850s, New York had a quorum of savvy and well-placed women's rights leaders and sympathizers.[139] The *History of Woman Suffrage* exaggerated but not excessively when it claimed, "A full report of the woman's rights agitation in the State of New York, would in a measure be the history of the movement."[140] Small wonder, then, that the 1860 National Woman's Rights Convention resolved that the state should take the lead: "The geographical position and political power of New York make her example supreme; hence we feel assured that when she is right on this question, our work is done."[141]

Elizabeth Cady Stanton and Susan B. Anthony had studied the art of political action in a sophisticated school because their home state had virtually invented antebellum mass parties. In New York, Martin Van Buren created the Democratic machine known as the "Albany Regency," and later the team of Thurlow Weed and William Henry Seward orchestrated patronage and power for the Whigs and then the Republicans. Geared to win in a closely divided electorate, New York's major parties were "probably the most sophisticated and efficient" political organizations in the country.[142] Competitive elections made for vigorous third-party efforts: in upstate's evangelically minded Burned-Over District, Liberty Party men like Stanton's cousin Gerrit Smith tried to use balance of power tactics. Close races also helped to fuel fierce faction fights within the parties, pitting, for example, antislavery "Barnburners" against conservative "Hunkers" inside the Democratic Party.[143] New York politics thus taught keen competition and "labyrinthine complexity." It also reinforced the lesson that campaigning for anything, whether public office or reform measures, took money. Political parties needed money for the very same reasons activists did—to support newspapers and pay for speakers—though of course they found fund-raising much easier than did the activists.[144]

Stanton and Anthony's first funded campaign in New York State gave them a yardstick for costs. Anthony reported to the 1860 National Woman's Rights Convention that total expenditures in New York in the past year amounted to nearly $4,000. Even though this total lumped together Jackson Fund monies and local contributions, the number was sobering.[145] Like any good fund-raiser, Anthony chose to emphasize the magnitude of both the bequests and the expenditures in hopes of encouraging other donors, but it was obvious that the Jackson Fund could not stretch to cover campaigns in very many states. But the vote had the merit of leveraging their limited funding: with the ballot in hand, all other measures in women's favor would be more easily won. All the more reason, then, to hope that victory in one state would inspire activists and legislators in other states, and they could topple many suffrage dominos by pushing over one.

Of course, there were other priorities than the vote, and other leaders who were much less political. One such priority was women's sexual autonomy, and the Eighth National Woman's Rights Convention in 1858 had featured an embarrassing episode that hinted at its significance. Susan B. Anthony, the presiding officer, recognized a bearded and bespectacled stranger who wished to speak; he turned out to be Steven Pearl Andrews, leader of a small group of "free love" advocates centered in New York City. The notorious "free lovers" claimed conventional marriage was oppressive and should be abolished; sexual relations should be formed or broken based on love, whenever individuals were so inclined. Free lovers like Pearl Andrews believed that women's rights were halfway measures; women's true liberation demanded sexual autonomy.[146] Taking advantage of the women's rights conventions' traditionally "free platform," where everyone had a right to speak, Pearl Andrews claimed he had often attended women's rights conventions but had never spoken because he appreciated "the delicacy of the position [in] which the ladies in advance of this movement might be placed" by his presence.[147] Offering himself as an ally, this free lover assured the convention he relieved them "individually and collectively, from all responsibility for anything he might utter."[148] Of course his remarks got everyone's attention, and his declaration had much the opposite effect. Pearl

Andrews set everyone buzzing inside the hall and triggered a storm of bad publicity outside.[149] The free love incursion into the women's rights convention in 1858 demonstrated that their free platform could be hijacked by self-appointed "allies." But it also suggested that sexuality and marriage were controversial subjects closely related to women's ability to control their own lives.

As the women's rights supporters met in conventions, national concerns about sexuality were intense.[150] The birth rate in the United States was dropping sharply as couples turned to abstinence and coitus interruptus as well as condoms and an array of other devices. Abortion became more subject to public controversy and probably increased as well.[151] In the rapidly growing cities, prostitution flourished and the press provided a steady diet of news about sensational crime and sexual misconduct, while moralists complained about pornography and decried divorce.[152] Meanwhile, criticism of conventional marriage came from all directions, from spiritualists, to utopians, to Mormons.[153]

Competition for leadership was intense, too. Susan B. Anthony faced a leadership challenge from Caroline Healey Dall, a bright, assertive campaigner who had presided over the 1855 Woman's Rights Convention held in Boston and who wanted to squelch all talk of sexual issues. Dall believed Stephen Pearl Andrews's talk of free love at the 1858 National Woman's Rights Convention had been damaging to women's cause.[154] Assuming that proper Bostonians like herself belonged at the head of the movement, Dall set about planning her own separate women's rights convention for the following year.[155] Anthony came up with her own plan to control the content of the 1859 National Woman's Rights Convention in New York by scheduling only one public session with a full roster of speakers. That would leave no time for free-love interlopers or tedious digressions. If we "trust to the occasion," she thought, "we shall then have *Pearl Andrews* and *innumerable bores*."[156] Anthony also sought to co-opt Caroline Dall by inviting her to New York as one of only four women scheduled to speak.[157] But rowdies packed the convention in Mozart Hall and greeted Caroline Dall with a chorus of hisses, groans, and boisterous laughter. Anthony, in the chair, appealed for order in vain. When the crowd tried to "stamp her down," Dall felt sure they were "taking advantage of their memory of Mr. Pearl Andrews." She told her diary she could have "mastered even this turbulent crowd...if it had not been for Miss Anthony, who plucked at my sleeve continually, saying...'that is too tame, they won't hear that.'" She had to take a seat, furious at what she considered her public humiliation at Anthony's hands.[158] The women speakers who followed Dall fared no better, and Anthony finally turned the podium over to Wendell Phillips, "who understood from long experience how to play with and lash a mob, and thrust what he wished to say into their long ears."[159] Dall was still seething when she returned to Boston determined to redirect the women's movement.[160]

Dall's Boston convention opened with a speech that warned against confounding the women's movement with "theories which claim unlimited indulgence for appetite and passion," thus firmly disavowing free love without mentioning it.[161] Speakers who wished to "invade" the Boston platform to speak of temperance or spiritualism were screened out, and Dall was delighted to see in the crowd many "women of wealth and position, never in such a throng before."[162] Afterward, Dall criticized Anthony privately, cultivated the support of Garrison and his *Liberator,* and sent reports of her Boston convention to influential people.[163] Dall tried to cultivate Wendell Phillips, too, because she had her eye on the Hovey Fund for money to found a New England Woman's Rights Society headed by a board of prominent men—"councilors"—chosen from among Boston's elite. Its agenda would of course exclude sexual issues. She worked with a more tactful ally, Caroline Severance, to draw up list of potential council members, and they exchanged ideas about how to avoid "concerted action against us."[164] Dall's rivalry with "Napoleon" Anthony became so pronounced that Wendell Phillips began referring to her as "Wellington."[165]

Not only did Dall want to avoid sexual issues but she also had little interest in the vote: "Many advocates of woman's rights place the question of her equal political recognition in the front rank, as the most important. To us, it does not seem so." Dall believed that women cared "very little about politics as such" though they must seek the right to vote because "without it, they can never rest secure in any other right, whether educational or industrial.... So the farmers, mechanics and merchants who fought at Lexington cared very little about political rights, until their avocations [*sic*] were interfered with, their market cut off, their commerce checked."[166] For Dall, the vote was little more than a necessary tool: she believed education and employment were the keys to women's emancipation. But Dall's leadership challenge faltered because while she planned, Anthony acted, and while the Boston society did not materialize, Anthony's New York State women's rights campaign did. Perhaps Phillips favored action over talk, or judged Dall's personality unsuited to leadership, because, while he approved some funds to be spent elsewhere, mostly they went to support Anthony's New York initiative.[167]

Even with Dall out of the way, questions of sexual autonomy remained a concern for women's rights advocates, and Elizabeth Cady Stanton tried to seize the initiative at the Tenth National Woman's Rights Convention of 1860. The first day's proceedings focused on politics, but on the second day Stanton abruptly changed the subject by introducing resolutions in favor of a right to divorce.[168] As Stanton understood, divorce had become controversial once antebellum state legislatures had transferred it from the legislature to the judiciary and then codified grounds. Most states eased divorce, pragmatically attempting to adjust the law to the fact that in an expanding nation with no central record keeping, it was easy for men to walk away from marriage.[169] A few states went so far as to become divorce havens, and moralists soon sounded the alarm about what they perceived as increasing divorce rates.[170] Stanton picked up on a recent divorce debate in the pages of Horace Greeley's *New York Tribune* and countered him by arguing that marriage should be like any other contract, dissolvable at the will of the parties, and that looser grounds would benefit women.[171]

Stanton miscalculated. Her divorce proposals aroused opposition in the movement's own ranks and triggered an uproar in the press. Antoinette Brown Blackwell offered a set of counterresolutions declaring all divorce "naturally and morally impossible" because marriage was ordained by God.[172] Blackwell argued that activists ought to give their attention to women's education and women's work, because economic dependency was the root of the problems in marriage, and she warned that liberalizing divorce laws might in practice favor the husband, allowing him to cast off one wife and take another.[173] Ernestine Rose disputed Blackwell and declared marriage was a human arrangement, not a divine ordinance. But, true to her ultra-radical reputation, Rose also confronted the unspoken tension that had arisen in the convention hall. "I presume," she remarked, "that the very advocacy of divorce will be called 'Free Love.'"[174] Although Stephen Pearl Andrews was nowhere to be seen, the free love question had resurfaced.

Wendell Phillips then took the podium and condemned the whole discussion on procedural grounds, moving even to excise it from the minutes. He invoked procedure in order to avoid a subject—free love—with which "our question is only unnecessarily burdened," and he urged that the women's platform, traditionally open, be closed to such subjects. He declared pointedly, "We had an experience two years ago on this point, and it seems to me that we might have learned by that lesson."[175] Phillips spoke as if he had the authority to set convention rules and the women's rights agenda. Recently named as principal trustee of the Jackson and Hovey funds, Wendell Phillips was more powerful than ever, and he acted with the confidence of a man whose intelligence and social standing had accustomed him to play a leadership role.[176] In this debate, however, he overreacted, and his motion to censor the minutes was defeated.[177] So were Stanton's divorce resolutions. Ironically, her political savvy probably led her to this misstep: she knew that in the New York State legislature a divorce reform bill had the support of many sober New York jurists and had come close to passage in the last legislative session. It would be reintroduced in the next session, and decades later Stanton would still recall that it ultimately lost by only four votes.[178]

The New York papers had a field day with Stanton's 1860 divorce initiative. The *New York Evening Post* complained that many who sympathized with women's rights would be "disgusted with this new dogma," while the gimlet-eyed *New York Observer* predicted Stanton's resolutions would "turn the world into one vast brothel."[179] James Gordon Bennett's *New York Herald,* ever hostile to reform, was especially ready to pump up circulation by breathless coverage of anything that had sexual overtones. Bennett decried the convention's "disregard of decency," and, mixing gutter racism with misogyny, he lumped women's rights together with "Communism, Fourierism, Spiritualism, Free Loveism, and Niggerism."[180]

Elizabeth Cady Stanton was so heavily criticized that she "often wept with vexation," but she also commented that the uproar proved that marriage and divorce were central. "We have thrown our bombshell into the center of woman's degradation, and of course we have raised a rumpus."[181] She took heart from the "sad-faced women…speechless with emotion" who had struggled up to press her hand after she finished speaking.[182] Anthony, backing her friend, noted that many letters of support came from women "not connected in any way with our great movement but sympathizing fully with our position on the question of divorce."[183] Issues related to marriage and divorce *were* important, even crucial, though of course Caroline Dall quickly seized the opportunity to criticize the New Yorkers.[184]

Women's rights leaders understood that ordinary women were deeply concerned with marriage issues—far more than with the right to vote. As she traveled around the country in the early 1850s, Lucy Stone had heard stories from many women like the one who "fled from her husband to the Shakers," a celibate sect, because he "gave her no peace either during menstruation, pregnancy, or nursing."[185] The women's rights activists had already spent much of the decade discussing marriage and sexual issues among themselves, but the discussion was inconclusive. Privately Stone might admit that the right to vote and own property meant very little "if I may not keep my body, and its uses, in my absolute right," but she was not ready to discuss the issue in public.[186] Other women's rights activists began to say in private that women had the right to "own our own bodies," and the list of rights claimed by one resolution at the 1860 convention included "the control and custody of our persons in marriage."[187] But how could they agitate such issues? They lacked the vocabulary, conceptual tools, and basic science needed to analyze the situation and devise remedies for what was called "unwilling maternity."

Divorce reform, Stanton's idea, was not much of a solution. Although inability to obtain a divorce trapped some women in cruel and abusive relationships, as Stanton said, it was also true, as Antoinette Brown Blackwell pointed out in their debate, that easier divorce might benefit *men* more than women. Hindsight reveals that divorce legislation was a blunt instrument to wield on behalf of women's interests. To the extent that divorce laws in the nineteenth century were liberalized, they did "reallocate marital power" by allowing women to escape an institution that buttressed male domination. But most divorcees, who were the victims of desertion, won little more than "single status, and with it, the right to remarry."[188] The divorce "rumpus" of 1860 showed that Elizabeth Cady Stanton had a wide-ranging understanding of what would be needed for women's true liberation, even while she was moving to an agenda that prioritized the vote alone.

By demanding the vote, women asserted self-ownership, claimed public power, and assumed the dignity of full citizenship, and once achieved, the vote would be the "guarantor of all other rights."[189] But the vote had practical, agitational advantages for Stanton and Anthony as well. They were looking to campaign and win, and the vote could be easily defined and logically defended, and as a natural right, it did not (they thought) require a mass movement. When it came to sexuality or marriage, there was no comparable single measure to unite behind. Stanton and Anthony did not prioritize issues related to marriage and sexual autonomy at this historical moment, but they did not act out of prudence or caution. In fact, when reflecting on the rumpus at the 1860 convention, Stanton reassured Anthony, "I shall not grow conservative with age," and declared she was more than ready "to fire another bomb into the heart of the metropolis."[190] But she refrained from firing that particular "bomb" again because she saw that issues relating to women's sexual self-ownership were divisive and could not be addressed by organized campaigning. As Martha C. Wright at one point told Susan B. Anthony, it was a mistake to deal with subjects "that no convention or legislative action can reach."[191] By choosing the vote, Stanton did not foreswear marriage questions altogether; she only postponed them. Once it was won, the vote would empower women to change oppressive "man-made" laws, including those of marriage.

By 1860 the impact of the new funding was being felt. Anthony's penchant for prompt political action in New York State trumped Caroline Dall's cautious plans for organization building in Boston, and practical questions about where and how to place the entering wedge for woman's rights were being resolved. The women's rights movement had become operational, campaigning for and winning expanded rights. If Dall had been less abrasive, perhaps her apolitical attitudes might have held more appeal, but behind Anthony and Stanton's leadership the vote was emerging as *the* central demand of the women's movement. As they saw it, the vote had great potential to elevate and empower women. As a matter of individual right, it did not require mass support and thus seemed like the best way to leverage the activists' small numbers and limited resources. They projected a state-level strategy and hoped it would snowball into other states after an initial victory in an influential state like New York.

2

Black Rights, Women's Rights, and Civil War

In the summer of 1860, Stephen Foster, a long-time "ultra" in Garrison's American Anti-Slavery Society (AASS), decided it was time to abandon his skepticism about electoral politics. Foster proposed to start a new political party demanding outright abolition of slavery, not just the Republican plan of preventing its expansion, and he invited both Elizabeth Cady Stanton and Frederick Douglass to attend the party's founding convention in Worcester. Stanton's political bent was so well known that she received two similar invitations that same summer.[1] Trying to decide where to go, Stanton wrote to both Gerrit Smith and Frederick Douglass.[2] Douglass had long been bitterly estranged from AASS Garrisonians like Foster, but he told Stanton, "I have been in a half and half condition about attending that Worcester convention ever since I got the call.... Of course your letter has taken something from one half and added it to the other. I am now strongly inclined to go." "I may call to see you," Douglass concluded, "on my way to Syracuse next week, and talk matters over with you."[3] The historical record does not reveal whether Frederick Douglass did in fact stop to talk politics with Elizabeth Cady Stanton, but their exchange of letters shows they recognized each other as radicals intent on political means. As the gathering sectional crisis pressed the existing political system to the breaking point, they were both looking for new opportunities for effective activism.

Beginning in 1860, the pace of events quickened and in response Stanton and Anthony reshaped their movement. Their focus on the vote put them into closer alignment with advocates of political rights for free black men, but there were few immediate results. In fact, the defeat of a New York referendum on black (male) suffrage in 1860 revealed some of the difficulties in winning voting rights, but its lessons were overshadowed by the secession crisis. Similarly, Stanton's pattern of arguing for woman suffrage along lines that sometimes maligned black men was established before the war, but its implications would not become immediately apparent. The war put women's activism for their own rights on hold while they shifted their gaze to the national scene and focused on ending slavery. They created a formal organization, the Women's Loyal National League (WLNL), but its goal was ending slavery, not winning women's rights. Events provided them with a swift and advanced political education, under the impact of a Customs House scandal, a gubernatorial election, and the presidential contest of 1864. In their effort to substitute Fremont for Lincoln in 1864, Stanton and Anthony saw evidence that they had indeed achieved a measure of political influence when they were recognized by the president himself. Yet the same episode left them shut out of the abolitionist press, a reminder of their dependence on resources they did not control. As 1864 came to an end, faced with Abraham Lincoln's reelection and Thurlow Weed's ascendancy, the women could hardly consider themselves political winners, but they were political players, with the insights, connections, and bruises to prove it.

As Stanton and Anthony made the vote their top priority in 1860, they effectively placed their cause alongside that of black men, who were also agitating for equal suffrage in New York. Although the state granted the vote to all white men, black men needed $250 worth of property to qualify as voters. In 1846, a referendum on eliminating this discriminatory property requirement failed by a wide margin, and prospects for equal suffrage seemed to dim thereafter, as the famine immigration from Ireland magnified the influence of tub-thumping racism nurtured in the New York City Democratic machines.[4] In the late 1850s, however, the rise of the Republican Party and its dominance at the polls in several state elections created a new opening. Frederick Douglass joined with James McCune Smith and Thomas Hamilton of New York City to press the fight to put black suffrage on an equal basis with white suffrage. Timing brought black and woman suffrage into closer proximity because the same 1860 session of the New York State legislature passed both an amendment to the New York State Constitution eliminating the property qualification for black men and the new law expanding property and custody rights for married women. Susan B. Anthony lobbied the legislature for the women's property bill and, as an agent of the AASS, she also carried petitions for and lobbied for a personal liberty bill. The record does not show cooperation between Anthony and the principal lobbyist for black suffrage, Stephen A. Myers, however, and public statements of mutual support were scanty.[5] The *Anglo-African*, in reporting Albany proceedings, mentioned the women's bill approvingly, but the women, lacking a newspaper of their own, could not return the favor.[6]

Among legislators, support for the two measures overlapped: 48 of 128 assemblymen, all Republicans, supported both bills, while 13 of 32 senators, again all Republicans, voted for both. Anson Bingham, the Republican who championed the women's bill in the Assembly, also took a leading role in the debate on black suffrage.[7] However, unlike black men's voting rights, women's property rights enjoyed some degree of bipartisan support and could win votes and even leadership on the Democratic side of the aisle. In the Senate, one of the women's warmest and most active supporters, Andrew Colvin, brought two other Democrats with him when he backed the women's bill. But when the black suffrage measure came up, Colvin was no help at all: he absented himself and refrained from voting. In fact, the black suffrage bill garnered not a single Democratic vote in either house. Meanwhile, Republican support for it was only partial. One Republican legislator declared that extending the vote to "degraded" blacks would "drive white people from the polls in disgust."[8] When the session ended, the women's property bill became law, but black suffrage still faced one more hurdle. Equal suffrage for black men would be sent to the voters and would take effect only if approved by a majority in November. It still needed support from Republican orators and newspapers during the fall campaign, and Republican county committees needed to print party tickets marked "yes" on black suffrage.[9]

Radicals would seem to have been in a good position to mount a campaign in support of the referendum. Throughout the antebellum years, they had often worked across race and gender lines in upstate New York in common settings and overlapping networks devoted to abolition, the Underground Railroad, and women's rights.[10] The congregation of the Wesleyan Chapel in Seneca Falls, for example, where the first women's rights convention was held in 1848, included both blacks and whites. Black activist William C. Nell joined Frederick Douglass as a speaker at the Woman's Rights Convention held in Rochester that same year, while in 1853 both James McCune Smith and Jermain Loguen participated in the New York State Woman's Rights Convention.[11] Efforts to realize black suffrage and woman suffrage should have been able to draw upon this upstate experience of proximity and personal acquaintance, but in 1860 activists' shared background did not help much, and there was little mutual aid. At the 1860 National Woman's Rights Convention, none of the speakers mentioned the New York referendum on black suffrage that would be held six months later.

An activist campaign for black suffrage in New York in 1860 never got started because Republicans assured black-rights activists that there was no need to campaign—"they would do the work."[12] In fact, Republicans advised quiet in the black community, and black activists even canceled a planned convention because it might attract attention and hostility from the Democrats.[13] James McCune Smith had planned to sponsor speakers and distribute tracts but he could not raise the needed funds. The Executive Committee of the American Anti-Slavery Society, which initially pledged $500, reversed itself and made no appropriation.[14] A number of well-known black speakers did not participate in the 1860 black suffrage campaign in New York, possibly having been drawn off by opportunities for paid work on another project, Haitian emigration.[15] The activists were lulled into inaction by Republican advice, but failure to campaign proved a losing strategy.

Black suffrage lost in 1860, because Republican voters failed to support the referendum as strongly as their presidential candidate while Democrats voted heavily in opposition. Abraham Lincoln defeated the Democratic fusion ticket headed by Stephen Douglas, but the voters rejected removing the property qual-ification by a wide margin. Obviously there were massive abstentions among the Republican Party faithful.[16] Frederick Douglass, who stood at the polls all day in Rochester, saw the problem: many Republican voters "refused to touch a ticket in favor of the amendment," and the party leadership had done little or nothing to convince them they should. "The Negro was stowed away like some people put out of sight their deformed children when company comes."[17]

In the aftermath it was clear that conservative New York Republicans had resorted to a time-honored tactic of factionalism: by campaigning half-heartedly or not at all for a measure they mistrusted, they sandbagged it.[18] The *National Anti-Slavery Standard* explained, "Many of the Republicans leaders...proved false on this question, keeping it out of sight as much as possible during the canvass, and then neglecting to provide affirmative ballots for the use of voters when they came to the polls. The Democrats, on the other hand, provided all their voters with neg-ative ballots."[19] Susan B. Anthony publicly criticized New York State Republican leaders as hypocrites.[20] And Frederick Douglass was bitterly disappointed to have come so far only to be defeated "by the supineness of our friends, [rather] than by the strength and activity of our enemies." He was not above expressing his resent-ment of the "No" voters, whom he characterized as "drunken Irishmen and igno-rant Dutchmen,...the tools of the negro-hating Democracy of this city, many of whom would sell their votes for a glass of whiskey."[21] If New York was a proving ground for the project of coordinating efforts to win black (male) suffrage and woman suffrage, little progress had been made.

Opponents of black voting rights in New York already had a history of invoking woman suffrage as a rhetorical foil against the expansion of voting rights for black men. During the debate over suffrage extension at the 1821 New York Constitutional Convention, for example, conservatives who sought to defeat black suffrage by denying that suffrage was a natural right had only to point to women as proof that not all the adult populace were entitled to become electors. At the 1846 New York State Constitutional Convention, delegates who opposed removing the word "white" from suffrage qualifications cited women's case to argue that the vote was a privilege rather than a natural right.[22] And in 1855, when a new Republican majority first gave hope for passage of the black suffrage bill in the Assembly, opponents had attempted to delay a vote on black suffrage by introducing the question of woman suffrage.[23] It was therefore important for the advocates of black and women's voting rights to develop arguments that would undermine such opponents and enable one cause to reinforce the other. In 1854 and again in 1860, Elizabeth Cady Stanton addressed herself to the state legislature and made the case for women, but how well did her arguments reinforce support for black rights?

Back in 1854, Stanton had surveyed the whole array of women's grievances and argued for all of women's rights, not just the vote.[24] But she spoke especially sharply on the vote, declaring, "We are moral, virtuous, and intelligent, and in all respects quite equal to the proud white man, yet by your laws we are classed with idiots, lunatics and negroes." Complaining that women did not feel honored to be placed in such company, she went further and claimed that women were actually treated worst of all: "In fact, our legal position is lower than that of either; for the negro can raise himself to the dignity of a voter if he possess himself of $250; the lunatic can vote in his moments of sanity; and the idiot too, if he be a male one, and not more than nine-tenths a fool."[25] She repeated the claim that women were treated worse than black men when she charged that women were taxed without representation, remarking, "here again you place the negro, so unjustly degraded by you, in a superior position to your own wives and mothers."[26] In her speech, Stanton expressed sympathy for black men precisely once—in that brief phrase "so unjustly degraded by you"—but then only to emphasize the idea that women were treated even worse. Stanton said almost nothing in support of black men's rights and instead used them to leverage women's rights with white legislators inclined to believe their white "wives and mothers" should occupy a position superior to black men.

Although Frederick Douglass commended her speech when it was issued as a pamphlet, he also criticized her "seeming assumption...of superiority over negroes." Douglass declared, "We are willing to allow and contend that woman has as good a right as we have to the exercise of suffrage, but we cannot grant even as a matter of rhetoric or argument, that she has a better."[27] He thus seemed to say that Stanton might be using "rhetoric or argument" in an instrumental fashion, arguing for results rather than out of conviction, but even so, such an argument fed racism. Bigots might conclude that inconsistencies ought to be resolved by *withdrawing* rights from black men rather than *extending* them to women.[28]

In her 1860 speech, Stanton constructed her arguments with more care to support black rights. She dealt only with the right to vote, and she began with a strong emphasis on universal human rights, reassuring men that women's gain would not be their loss. "You might as well carp at the birth of every child," she remarked, "lest there should not be enough air left to inflate your lungs."[29] The vote was important, she insisted, because it was the key to equal rights for all citizens. "The grant of this right would secure all others, but the grant of every other, whilst this is denied, is a mockery!" Without the vote, she said, woman was "honored with all the duties and responsibilities of the citizen, and at the same time... denied all his rights and privileges."[30] Stanton chose language that contained no hint that the individual citizen should be presumed to be white any more than she should be presumed to be male. Instead, she explicitly equated women and black men as both unjustly denied their rights by white men: "The prejudice against color, of which we hear so much, is no stronger than that against sex. It is produced by the same cause and manifested very much in the same way. The negro's skin and the woman's sex are both prima facie evidence that they were intended to be in subjection to the white Saxon man."[31] However, Stanton acknowledged that the legislators she addressed were not prepared to grant women "more than a partial legislation" on the "broad platform of human rights." Therefore, she announced, she would *also* plead woman's case "on the low ground of expediency and precedent."[32]

On this "low" ground, Stanton explored questions of comparative treatment and comparative worthiness and drew invidious distinctions. She compared the free white woman and the slave "Cuffy," and she chided the Republicans—"that party now so interested in the slave of the Carolinas"—for failing to see "the similarity in his condition and that of the mothers, wives and daughters of the Empire State."[33] If, she went on, the vote was to be awarded on the basis not of natural rights but of just desserts, women were *more* deserving than many men, including "the ignorant alien, the gambler, the drunkard, the prize-fighter, the licentious profligate, the silly stripling of twenty-one, the fool, the villain," and the illiterate Irishman "who saws my wood."[34] Although she omitted black men from her list, Stanton complained, just as she had in 1854, that New York law placed black men in a superior position to women. She explained how: "The few social privileges which the man gives the woman, he makes up to the negro in civil rights. The woman may sit at the same table and eat with the white man; the free negro may hold property and vote. The woman may sit in the same pew with the white man in church; the free negro may enter the pulpit and preach." For citizens of a republic, Stanton reasoned, civil rights were more important than social privileges.[35] She also detailed the way the suffrage and tax law worked to the black man's advantages: "If he is possessed of a certain amount of property, then is he permitted to vote, and pay taxes too. If he has not that amount, then he is not permitted to vote, neither is he taxed." Meanwhile women, white and black alike, paid taxes on property from the first dollar but could never hope to attain the vote.[36] Stanton argued, "The prejudice against sex is more deeply rooted and more unreasonably maintained than that against color."[37] And she concluded, "Your Constitution regards the negro, so unjustly degraded, with far more consideration than your wives and mothers."[38]

In this important 1860 speech on woman suffrage, Stanton offered two kinds of arguments, one universal and egalitarian, the other legalistic, comparative, and based on "expediency and precedent." She claimed human rights for black and female citizens alike and abandoned her insulting 1854 comparison of blacks to lunatics and idiots, but she employed a stereotypical label like "Cuffy," and made a tendentious comparison between free white women and slaves. She again hit legislators with the punch line claiming their laws treated black men better than "your wives and mothers." Using two different premises to reach the same conclusion in the same speech, she argued that women deserved the right to vote. Scholars have noted Stanton's puzzling tendency to contradict herself when she argued about black suffrage and woman suffrage.[39]

Lawyerly habits of mind authorized Stanton to offer an array of diverse and even contradictory arguments.[40] This mode of thinking came easily to her: as a child she thought it "fun" to slip into the courtroom to listen to argument, and as a mother she watched her husband amuse their children by presenting legal arguments on which the youngsters had to decide as mock judge or jury.[41] When Stanton offered "low" arguments based on expediency and precedent, she knowingly abandoned the argument for equal rights on moral grounds alone and ignored the contradictions between equal rights principles and invidious claims of black male advantage. In effect, she assumed that any argument that swayed a jury was a good argument. Douglass charged her with using "rhetoric or argument" instrumentally, calling it irresponsible because it reinforced racist assumptions. In 1860, Stanton's speech to the New York legislature in March had no impact on the fate of legislation that had already passed, or on what turned out to be a noncampaign for the black suffrage referendum in November. But as the two causes of black and woman suffrage came into closer alignment in the future, Stanton's style of argument would have greater potential for harm.

In 1860, the movements for women's rights and black rights were being overtaken by dramatic national events that would prioritize political antislavery over both their causes. As Elizabeth Cady Stanton and Frederick Douglass were drawn together by Foster's invitation to the Worcester convention in the summer of 1860, Anthony was not enthusiastic about Foster's plan, but she told Stanton, "If you see your way clear to help both woman and the Negro, or only the Negro, go [to Worcester] by all means."[42] Anthony's choice of words was revealing because it suggested that in the gathering sectional crisis, activist women's priority might go to "the Negro" alone.

Douglass and Stanton had both had been deeply influenced by Gerrit Smith's brand of radical political action. Douglass originally came into the abolitionist movement under the influence of William Lloyd Garrison, who favored moral suasion over political participation, but in 1851 he declared his independence and sided with the political abolitionists, especially Smith, who was able to help

Douglass with his newspaper, the *North Star*. Since then the Republican Party had emerged, but Douglass wanted far more than the Republicans were willing to offer. He tried to chart an independent course that included the black convention movement but also regular politics and the fruits of the American political tradition, as in his famous, anguished, "Fifth of July" speech.[43]

Each for his or her own cause, Frederick Douglass and Elizabeth Cady Stanton hoped to extract radical results from the American political process, which was designedly conservative and biased against radical projects of all sorts, not to mention routinely cynical and corrupt. Theirs was a project against long odds, although each one brought vast intellectual powers, nearly unquenchable optimism, and iron determination to the task. Douglass chronically shifted back and forth between principles and expediency, and "agonized between a moral worldview and the realities of political power, between detachment and action, between militancy and accommodation."[44] In 1860 Stanton too found it difficult to explain her political stance, at one point describing herself as "a full-blooded Republican and about three-quarters over."[45] Stanton and Douglass would both prove willing to compromise with mainstream politicians in ways that baffled activists who took a purist line. Both pursued what sometimes seemed an erratic course as they sought to leverage radical measures out of a political system rigged against them.

In any event, Stanton did not go to Worcester in 1860 but Douglass did. Stanton chose instead to attend a similar gathering of political abolitionists in Syracuse, hoping to give Gerrit Smith emotional support as he recovered from a nervous breakdown triggered by the failure of John Brown's raid on Harpers Ferry.[46] In Worcester, Frederick Douglass met a chilly reception. Although the convention laid plans for a "Union Democratic Party," much of the meeting devolved into a clash between Douglass and Garrisonians rehashing old debates about American Anti-Slavery Society policies.[47] Lucy Stone sided with the old Garrisonians, who were not quite ready to embrace politics even though Foster was prodding them to do so.[48]

As the crisis atmosphere deepened, Stanton and Anthony tried to find the best way to react by continuing to push for women's rights at the state level but also attempting to "get an oar in" on antislavery issues at the national level.[49] They issued an "Appeal to the Women of New York," urging woman suffrage, and Stanton also authored "The Slaves' Appeal," an abolitionist pamphlet to be mailed to every legislator, editor, clergyman, and elected official in the country, North *and* South.[50] Anthony hoped the pamphlet would be "a firebrand at the South," and outraged Democratic editors, apologists for the South, feared she might be right.[51] But there is no record of any response to the "Appeal to the Women of New York," and the differing fate of the two "Appeals" showed that women's rights questions were drifting into a state-level backwater while antislavery efforts rode a riptide of national events.

Frederick Douglass. Photographs and Prints Division, Schomburg Center for Research in Black Culture, New York Public Library, Astor, Lenox, and Tilden Foundations.

Once Lincoln was elected, southern secessionists swung into action, and the activist women had new decisions to make. In December 1860, Thurlow Weed used his influential *Albany Evening Journal* to urge that the South be placated with a fresh round of concessions, including a tougher fugitive slave law and even a restoration of the Missouri Compromise line—which would have violated the fundamental Republican principle of no further territorial expansion for slavery. Although William Henry Seward spoke more vaguely, it was assumed that he might hew to Weed's line. This "amazing" change of views by this powerful team of politicos galvanized New York radicals and abolitionists, who were only too well aware of Weed's ability to control events through patronage and intrigue, and Anthony organized a "no compromise with slaveholders" speaking tour to counter Weed.[52] By the time the tour kicked off, South Carolina had already seceded.

In this "mob tour," Elizabeth Cady Stanton joined Susan B. Anthony for several stops along the route from Buffalo to Albany and they were howled down in city after city.[53] Opponents simply packed their meetings, sometimes electing their own officers and passing their own resolutions, sometimes just making it impossible for the abolitionist speakers to be heard. A hefty admission charge excluded the rioters from one Rochester meeting, but elsewhere rowdies simply pushed in. "Ten cents sir," Anthony said to one in Rome, but he brushed her aside "as if I had been a mosquito, and cried, 'Come on boys!'" to the crowd behind him.[54] Local Republican authorities, who were trying to distance themselves from abolitionists and avoid the opprobrium of having provoked secession, assailed the abolitionist speakers in the newspapers and virtually invited the mobs to assemble. Anthony understood their game: "Good stiff-backed Union Democrats," she fumed, would have broken up the mobs.[55] As it happened, Lincoln set his face against compromise and Weed's proposals fell flat, but the political situation was being redefined, and Stanton and Anthony had moved nimbly to respond.

Stanton filled the space left by Stone's absence, sharing danger and cementing her partnership with Anthony, although together they were acting on behalf of "the Negro only." Still, Anthony had a chance to demonstrate her mettle in the face of misogynistic venom. In Syracuse, a mob manipulated effigies of Anthony and the Reverend Samuel J. May in obscene positions before burning them. At the next meeting, in Auburn, according to a reporter on the scene, "While the riot was at its height...Miss Anthony leaned over the desk and said, 'Why boys, you're nothing but a *baby mob*, and you ought to go to Syracuse to learn how to do it, and also learn how to get before the Grand Jury.'"[56] As she taunted them coolly, Anthony was in her element, but marriage, divorce, and woman suffrage were forgotten in this new national emergency.

Like almost all abolitionists, Anthony and Stanton embraced the war. In April 1861, a week after Fort Sumter was obliged to surrender under a southern bombardment, Wendell Phillips strode onto a platform at the Boston Music Hall profusely decorated with the stars and stripes, and the packed hall heard Phillips deliver "the greatest speech of his life."[57] For twenty years he had urged separation from the slave South, confident that disunion would somehow destroy slavery. But now that slave owners themselves had appropriated disunion tactics and plunged the nation into civil war, what should an abolitionist do? Phillips declared for war, for one "last appeal to the God of battles." He recalled John Quincy Adams's statement that slavery was not protected by the Constitution in time of war, and now war had come by the South's own hand. "Seize the thunderbolt God has forged for you," Phillips urged, and make this a war for *freedom* as well as for union.[58] Neither Stanton nor Anthony was among the cheering crowd that night, but news of Phillips's speech shot through abolitionist ranks and as usual his leadership was decisive. Anthony was persuaded by his "masterly address,"[59] and Stanton was "delighted" with the speech. Even though the war meant canceling the 1861 woman's rights convention, Anthony was thrilled: "What a glorious revolution we are in—emancipation must come out of it."[60] The women's rights leaders joined Wendell Phillips, Frederick Douglass, and other abolitionists hoping to use the war as an opportunity to destroy slavery. They did so because they believed it was right, and because they anticipated that emancipating the slaves would impose the immediate necessity of defining the rights of a free person—a process from which women stood to benefit. Of course, Lincoln at first intended to restore the union without touching slavery, but abolitionists hoped that their own persuasive efforts, together with what Frederick Douglass called "the inexorable logic of events," would make that impossible.[61] When Lincoln was elected, Wendell Phillips predicted, "The Republican party have undertaken a problem, the solution of which will force them to our position."[62] Anthony and Stanton hoped that, in the same way, the abolitionists and the nation were undertaking a problem—black freedom—the solution of which would force them to women's rights.

The Civil War drew northern women by the tens of thousands into voluntary "patriotic toil" devoted to the needs of the soldiers, but Susan B. Anthony and Elizabeth Cady Stanton reserved their efforts for politics rather than benevolence.[63] Setting aside her plans to push women's rights in New York in anticipation of the next constitutional convention, Anthony sat out the first year of the war at her family home in Rochester. She came to regret the decision to cancel the woman's rights convention but when she tried to arouse interest in another one, it was impossible. Much to her disgust, the 1862 legislative session in Albany repealed some provisions of the 1860 property and custody legislation.[64] Elizabeth Cady Stanton also sat home in upstate New York during the first months of the war, but her husband's moves soon took her to the big city. Henry B. Stanton had campaigned for Lincoln and was rewarded with a plum patronage job at the New York City Customs House, so they sold their house in Seneca Falls and moved to West 45th Street.[65] Elizabeth Cady Stanton had always been well informed, but in Manhattan she was at the center of northern journalism and became privy to the very latest news because her brother-in-law Samuel Wilkeson was chief Washington correspondent for Horace Greeley's *New York Tribune* and a quintessential "inside operator."[66] Stanton knew a lot but she told Anthony, "I long for action."[67]

Like other abolitionists, the women's rights leaders watched and waited to see how they could push the Union into attacking slavery as well as secessionists. In the fall of 1861, General John C. Fremont electrified northern public opinion by issuing a proclamation that freed slaves in his jurisdiction, and because Lucretia Mott's son-in-law served on Fremont's staff, the women's rights leaders were especially interested. But Lincoln ordered Fremont to rescind the order because he was concerned about the loyalty of slaveholding border states.[68] Abolitionists were appalled, and in the winter and spring of 1862 they began to push their ideas assertively. Month by month public opinion began to shift in their direction, audiences became receptive, and lyceums were eager to engage abolitionist speakers. One veteran abolitionist marveled that lectures could now "supply our Treasury instead of emptying it."[69] Stanton and Anthony saw old friends and longtime allies move into positions of great national influence. Wendell Phillips reached (by one estimate), five million people who either heard or read his speeches in the winter and spring of 1861–62.[70] And Frederick Douglass entered the political mainstream for the first time in his life as he pressed the Republican administration to stop ignoring the slavery question, stop returning runaways, and stop respecting their courtly southern opponents, whom he called "traitors worthy of our hemp."[71]

In the spring and summer of 1862, when appalling casualties at Shiloh and the collapse of McClellan's Peninsular campaign destroyed Union hopes for an early victory, abolitionists like Douglass and Phillips redoubled their effort to "compel a timid and reluctant administration to proclaim emancipation."[72] Appealing less to morality and more to military necessity, they insisted that slavery was the cause of the war and therefore only emancipation could bring victory, and they revived the old abolitionist tool of the petition.[73] Radicals in Congress pushed through a succession of antislavery measures, including one that abolished slavery in the District of Columbia. Lincoln seemed as hesitant as ever to emancipate, but with Jackson and Lee triumphant on the battlefield that summer, he was at last forced to abandon schemes for gradualism and colonization. Finally in September 1862, when McClellan turned back Lee's invasion at Antietam, Lincoln issued his Preliminary Emancipation Proclamation. Abolitionists were quick to see that this legalistic document only threatened future action, and even then it promised to free only those slaves in Confederate territory, so their work was far from over. This was the sequence of events that finally set Anthony and Stanton in motion.

After Lincoln issued the actual Emancipation Proclamation on January 1, 1863, abolitionists moved into new phases of work related to this revolutionary but halfway measure. They helped to build northern support for emancipation through new voluntary organizations, the Union Leagues, sometimes also called Loyal Leagues.[74] The Leagues were private membership organizations, some of them complete with lodge-like initiation fees and passwords, but their aim was to influence popular opinion as the North changed war aims midstream. By year's end they had enrolled 600,000 to 800,000 members, and their pamphlets, broadsides, and mass meetings helped Republicans to rebound at the polls in 1863. While the Union Leagues were organized on a broad basis of loyalty to the

Union, their ruling assumption—that saving the Union required destroying slavery—was often muted. These Union Leagues gave Anthony and Stanton a model for renewed activism, and their male relatives and abolitionist colleagues encouraged them to start a women's version.[75] In New York State, the Weed/ Seward conservatives organized a Loyal League of Union Citizens, whose members pledged to support "the Government in all its *constitutional* efforts to suppress the rebellion"—an important adjective, since opponents of the Emancipation Proclamation denounced it on precisely that ground, that it was unconstitutional. The radicals, including both Henry B. Stanton and Gerrit Smith, hastened to create a rival, the Loyal National League, which embraced emancipation wholeheartedly.[76] Thus Anthony and Stanton signaled their radical tilt within New York State politics by adopting the name of the *Women's* Loyal National League.

The purposes of Anthony and Stanton's new League came into focus at its organizational meeting on May 14, 1863, in New York City, when antislavery and woman's rights veterans like Angelina Grimké Weld and Ernestine Rose mingled with "delegates" who had come from local women's "loyal" societies around the country.[77] Lucy Stone was able to attend, and new talent included Anna Dickinson, a teenaged orator who was making a sensation with her political speeches, and who had struck up an increasingly close relationship with Susan B. Anthony.[78] The organizers presented resolutions in support of the government "in so far as it makes the war for freedom." With slavery destroyed, Stanton declared, a "true Republic...will surely rise from this shattered Union."[79] The League meeting considered a series of resolutions, one of which touched off debate because of the way it linked black freedom and women's rights. Resolution #5 read, "The property, the liberty and the lives of all slaves, all citizens of African descent, and all women are placed at the mercy of a legislation in which they are not represented." It concluded, "There never can be a true peace in this Republic until the civil and political equality of every subject of the Government shall be practically established."[80] Freedom as the WLNL leaders defined it meant more than not being bought and sold: it meant having equal rights, including the vote, and those equal rights extended to all alike—to white and black men, *and* to white and black women. In the WLNL, Anthony and Stanton defined loyalty to encompass emancipation, defined emancipation to imply equal rights, and defined equal rights as extending across race *and* gender lines.

Loyalty thus "fronted" for an expansive interpretation of freedom and equality, and some of the patriotic lady delegates were upset by these bold ideological equations. A Mrs. Hoyt of Wisconsin objected to women's rights as an unpopular "ism" that would damage the cause, which she defined as assisting the government in its struggle to defeat treasonous rebels. Rebutting Mrs. Hoyt, Anthony made the case for resolution #5, saying, "It brings in no question, no ism, it seems to me. It merely makes the assertion that in a true democracy, in a genuine republic, every citizen who lives under the government must have the right of representation in that government."[81] Mrs. Hoyt was not persuaded, but she was outvoted.[82]

The WLNL's founding meeting was more ideological than practical, but a business meeting finally agreed that the actual work of the League would be petitioning for an end to slavery in American constitutional law—a necessary move because Lincoln's proclamation was limited in scope and potentially reversible. The WLNL thus stepped into the established tradition of women's abolitionist petitioning.[83] They adopted the goal of a million signatures, decided to print and distribute a pamphlet to every volunteer who carried a petition, and confirmed that the new organization was to have a formal membership by setting an initiation fee ($1 or 100 petition signatures).[84] Anthony coordinated the work with Senator Charles Sumner, who was able to present League petitions containing hundreds of thousands of signatures the following February, thus helping to build pressure for passage of the Thirteenth Amendment.[85] The WLNL's petitions asked only for freedom for the slaves, leaving unspoken the rights claims of women *or* free black people. Elizabeth Cady Stanton and Susan B. Anthony— president and secretary, respectively, of the WLNL—thus embraced formal organization for the first time, but not on behalf of their own rights.

The summer of 1863 saw them grappling with organization's practical necessities, including an office, letterhead, and operations that extended through all the free states and into some occupied territory. They had to print, send out, receive, and collate massive numbers of petitions, and they employed a clerk in their office at the Cooper Institute as well as two agents in the West, Hannah Tracy Cutler and Josephine S. Griffing.[86] They got advice from Robert Dale Owen, an indefatigable, adaptable radical who had been transformed in the new political environment thrown up by the war from a far-out visionary to a hard-headed man of business who audited war department contracts and advised the secretary of war.[87] Owen became a crucial link between the WLNL leaders and the Radical Republicans in Washington. Owen was a radical-cum-insider, a type they hoped to emulate, and unlike many other abolitionists, Owen agreed that black rights and women's rights were related in principle and should, if possible, be combined in practice.

The WLNL had national ambitions with costs to match but little Hovey support. Abolitionist funding dried up during the war because British donors stopped sending contributions, antislavery fairs were suspended or forced to compete with soldiers' aid and sanitary commission fairs, and wartime inflation took a toll on family budgets.[88] Yet the cost of the *Liberator* and the *National Anti-Slavery Standard* rose sharply, and in this context the Hovey Fund took on special importance because it enabled the American Anti-Slavery Society to stay in the black and even carry forward a small surplus.[89] Under Wendell Phillips's leadership, the Hovey Fund trustees supported the AASS but refused to under-write the women's organization, though Owen dropped Phillips a broad hint about what he would do "if I had control of any anti-slavery funds," and Anthony told Boston abolitionists, "We find *money* to be the *grand desideratum*."[90] Parker Pillsbury urged his fellow Hovey trustees to grant the WLNL a subsidy, but they only authorized $100, though they did agree to pay Anthony a salary of $12 per week.[91] The WLNL quickly ran up a debt of over $5,000, and while enduring much "financial anxiety," the women begged donations of paper and printing, and tried to save postage by asking congressmen to frank their mail.[92] Finally they devised a way to generate their own income stream, by asking every person who signed a petition to contribute at least one cent.[93] In this way they eventu-ally covered about $3,000 of their costs, although the clerical work of handling small remittances was extraordinary.[94]

That massive clerical task made 1863 a summer of "drudgery," but it was also a summer of battle.[95] Elizabeth Cady Stanton's nineteen-year-old nephew, Bayard Wilkeson, was killed at Gettysburg. When the Union forces were outnumbered on the first day of the battle, Confederates under Jubal Early came pouring in on the attack, overwhelming Wilkeson's position. An artillery shell blew his horse from beneath him and nearly severed his leg. The young lieutenant put a tourniquet on the leg and completed the amputation with a penknife, but his wound was mortal and he had to be left behind as the Union forces retreated.[96] Too terrible to talk about and impossible to forget, this tragedy became embedded in Stanton's outlook.

Even for those who stayed at home the war brought inescapable, irreversible choices. Hard on the heels of the news from Gettysburg, the draft riots exploded in New York City, and because the rioters were targeting known abolitionists, Anthony and Stanton and Stanton's family had to take refuge with her sister and brother-in-law, where Horace Greeley was also forced to shelter.[97] Stanton saw her son Neil almost fall victim to the rioters when they snatched him up on the street shouting, "Here's one of those three hundred dollar fellows!" Neil was indeed able to buy his way out of the draft by paying the commutation fee, but in this case he escaped from harm by offering to stand treat as the group passed a saloon. And when everyone had drunk up, he cheerfully agreed to lead a chorus of "three cheers" for Jefferson Davis. Neil saved his life by "a bit of deception," but Stanton must have found the contrast between her boy and his cousin, a vol-unteer killed in action in a great Union victory, painful to contemplate. She qui-etly reflected that it might have been "far nobler" if Neil had died defying the tyranny of the mob.[98] Stanton left no indication of how this pair of experiences affected her, but perhaps these events help explain why the Reconstruction years would discover in Stanton a will that was surprisingly steely, and sometimes unreasonably rigid.

After the Emancipation Proclamation took effect, Frederick Douglass and other black leaders including William Wells Brown, Charles Lenox Remond, and Jermain Loguen became heavily involved in efforts to raise black regiments, recruiting for the Massachusetts 54th and 55th.[99] Douglass kept up a drumbeat of editorials and speeches and eventually he met directly with President Lincoln, tirelessly making the case for black freedom *and* black rights. As early as June 1863, Douglass began arguing for "perfect civil and political equality" for the former slaves, and hammered away on the idea that black suffrage was a crucial component of freedom.[100] At the same time, black women hurried to do what they could to meet the needs of the "contrabands" or refugee freedpeople who gathered in camps in large numbers around Washington.[101]

Meanwhile, through the WLNL, Stanton and Anthony associated themselves with black rights and black activists, both rhetorically and practically, as never before.[102] The League's badge depicted a black man "striking the blow himself with his own right hand."[103] At its meetings, Anthony displayed photos of Sojourner Truth and the whip-scarred back of a Louisiana slave, protested the mistreatment of African Americans on the street cars in New York City, and appealed for supplies to help "Moses"—Harriet Tubman.[104] At the 1864 anniversary meeting of the WLNL, an unidentified "mulatto woman" spoke in favor of liberty, justice, and equality—"especially the equality."[105]

By associating themselves publicly with black people and particularly with black men, the League leaders braved racist reactions to emancipation that harped on interracial sex. In late 1863, an anonymous pamphlet entitled "Miscegenation" appeared on the newsstands of New York City, and complimentary copies were sent to prominent abolitionists like Lucretia Mott and the Grimké sisters with requests for their endorsements. The pamphlet argued that interracial marriage was the solution to America's race prejudice, and some abolitionists incautiously praised what appeared to be a scientific treatise. It was in fact a hoax, devised by the Democratic press and designed to elicit "proof" that the *real* goal of abolitionists was to enjoy interracial sex. The miscegenation hoax, which played out in the background during the winter and spring of 1863–64, signaled that the opponents of emancipation thought they might benefit by scaring up the specter of black men associating with white women. But it also revealed the extent to which abolitionists, including women, were becoming political "players" whose opinions mattered.[106]

In 1864 Frederick Douglass led African Americans to create a rights organization of their own at the National Convention of Colored Men held in Syracuse, New York. The new National Equal Rights League was formed to fight for the interests of "colored men generally," and its "Declaration of Wrongs and Rights" complained, "As a people we have been denied the ownership of our bodies, *our wives*, homes, children, and the products of our own labor." [emphasis added][107]

There were no women listed among the officers, but two black women, Edmonia Highgate and Frances E. W. Harper, did address the meeting, so the role of women remained unclear.[108] Despite the question about black women's participation, Douglass's new National Equal Rights League and the Women's Loyal National League seemed to have related purposes, at least in Stanton's eyes. As 1864 drew to a close, she told Anthony, "I cannot tell you how happy I am to find Douglass on the same platform with us."[109]

Responding to the emergencies of the war meant Stanton and Anthony were throwing themselves into politics as never before, and rapidly acquiring a political education. As soon as abolitionist lecturing became popular enough to cover expenses, in the summer and fall of 1862, Anthony hit the road and gave many addresses on the need for emancipation, "entirely off old anti-slavery grounds and on the new ones thrown up by the war."[110] Then as election day neared in 1862, Anthony moved into a new, more explicitly political phase. In the New York State gubernatorial election, the Democratic candidate Horatio Seymour opposed the Emancipation Proclamation and campaigned against it.[111] But Radical Republicans had managed to overcome the Weed faction and nominate James S. Wadsworth, a red-hot Barnburner who endorsed the Emancipation Proclamation.[112] Gerrit Smith, Henry B. Stanton, and the women's old ally, Andrew J. Colvin, all publicly supported Wadsworth, and Anthony apparently did so as well in five speeches she made in Schuyler County the week before the election.[113] When the votes were counted, however, Wadsworth lost to the Democrat because the conservative Weed faction of the Republicans chose to sit on their hands, preferring to forfeit the governorship rather than lose control over party patronage to a radical like Wadsworth.[114] Lacking the vote herself, Anthony had done her best to participate, but her foray into electoral politics taught her a lesson in the hardball practices of cynical pols like Thurlow Weed.

In 1863, as the WLNL pushed its petition campaign, Anthony saw the need to educate the northern public about emancipation and its consequences, and she proposed a joint national canvass by the women's League and the American Anti-Slavery Society. Anticipating "the hour of adjustment"— reconstruction— she wanted "to educate the people to demand justice."[115] She apparently realized that asking volunteers to pass emancipation petitions was too narrow an activity to educate the public to the expanded understanding of freedom and equality—to black rights *and* women's rights—that the WLNL stood for. She proposed to send out four corps of lecturers operating in groups of three, with each group to include "a *white* man, *black* man, and a woman."[116] They would circulate emancipation petitions, but they would also personify the message that equal rights crossed race and gender lines. The Boston abolitionists turned down Anthony's proposal. Instead, the American Anti-Slavery Society executive committee authorized a petition campaign of its own and sent five speakers into upstate New York and New Hampshire that winter.[117] But none were women, and the announcements of their lectures suggest that they kept the focus on emancipation with no mention of black rights, let alone women's rights.[118]

Anthony was full of ideas for political action, but her proposal failed because abolitionists could not agree on what to do in the altered situation created by the war. They could not even agree on whether to continue their own organization. As early as 1862, well before the Emancipation Proclamation, some veteran Garrisonians had begun to argue that the work of the American Anti-Slavery Society was done and it was time to disband. The regular political process could now be relied upon to end slavery, they argued.[119] In January 1863, William Lloyd Garrison hinted that he agreed.[120] Of course, an early dissolution of the Society implied accepting a narrow definition of emancipation as simply outlawing the ownership of human chattel. Wendell Phillips disagreed. He joined black abolitionists, who had always insisted that liberty must include political and civil rights and now opposed dissolution strongly. They argued that freedom was meaningless unless it was accompanied by the full rights of citizenship.[121] The result was a faction fight inside the American Anti-Slavery Society pitting Garrison against Phillips. The WLNL's expansive definition of freedom as implying equal rights put the women firmly in Phillips's camp, and Garrison sniffed at the WLNL as not "wisely got up."[122] Anthony's proposal probably fell victim to the developing Garrison-Phillips feud.

Meanwhile, Elizabeth Cady Stanton was distracted by a family crisis that provided another chapter in her political education. In October 1863, New York papers broke the story of a corruption scandal at the New York Customs House, leveling accusations against her husband. Henry B. Stanton had to resign his position and then withstand a lengthy congressional investigation when information emerged that his son, Neil, acting as his clerk, had indeed taken small bribes seven or eight times.[123] Congressional investigators were not satisfied when Neil Stanton admitted misconduct and they embarked upon a fishing expedition in Customs House waters, rendering Henry Stanton an embarrassment to his patron Salmon P. Chase at a moment when Chase's presidential aspirations were flowering.[124] When the House investigating committee issued its final report, it had turned up no evidence of indictable crimes, but blasted Henry Stanton anyway, for "no uncommon carelessness, if not culpable complicity."[125] The House committee trained its guns on picayune misdeeds in an era rife with major misconduct, and the whole episode was suspiciously advantageous for the Weed/Seward faction in its efforts to undermine the radicals and take over the Customs House.[126]

Like the Wadsworth campaign, the Customs House scandal showed just how rotten contemporary politics could be. Stanton's brother-in-law Sam Wilkeson looked into the discrepancy between the inconclusive testimony and the report's harsh conclusions and declared flatly that its author, Representative Calvin T. Hulburd, had been bribed.[127] And "a man in high position" proposed that Henry in turn should pay a counter-bribe to be cleared.[128] The episode revealed that in New York, the state Stanton and Anthony knew best and hoped might become a bellwether for equal rights, radicals faced unscrupulous conservatives and corrupt placemen within their own Republican Party.

As the women's rights leaders delivered their emancipation petitions to Congress, they also hoped to wield some influence in the 1864 presidential election even if not armed with ballots. Stanton urged women to use "the only political rights we have under the Constitution, the right of petition, [to] build the platform for the next presidential campaign in universal emancipation."[129] Like many radical abolitionists, Anthony and Stanton considered Lincoln faint-hearted and his reconstruction plan, announced in December 1863, was the last straw. Wendell Phillips took the lead in condemning Lincoln, pointing to the way his policy was playing out in Louisiana. The new Louisiana government under General Banks refused blacks the vote, despite the presence of a large and well-educated cohort of free blacks from New Orleans, and it bound the Louisiana freedpeople to labor contracts that, Phillips charged, effectively substituted serfdom for slavery. Surprisingly, William Lloyd Garrison emerged as Lincoln's chief apologist within abolitionist circles. Having thundered against compromise for decades, Garrison now lowered his voice, embraced moderation, and argued that Lincoln's gradualism was good enough. This half-a-loaf reasoning from such an unlikely source was unnerving to many veteran abolitionists, even Lucy Stone who was absorbed in family life and usually ignored political news during the war years.[130] American Anti-Slavery Society ranks split wide open over Lincoln and Louisiana, pitting Garrison against Phillips.[131]

Anthony and Stanton agreed with Wendell Phillips that John C. Fremont was preferable to Lincoln because he was an advanced radical on both emancipation and equal rights. To push Fremont's candidacy, they strategized with Jessie Benton Fremont and permitted the "Freedom and Fremont" Club to use the WLNL office. Stanton even signed the "call" for a special convention in Cleveland designed to nominate Fremont.[132] Fremont was the better candidate, Stanton explained in a public letter, because he backed "the right of suffrage for the black man—that safeguard of civil liberty, without which emancipation is a mockery."[133] Privately, she lobbied Gerrit Smith, again making black (male) suffrage her central argument for Fremont: "When we demand suffrage for the Negro," she wrote, "we make freedom a fact."[134] Ironically (in view of where the next five years would take their opinions), in 1864 Stanton and Anthony made a point of insisting on votes for black men—and withheld any mention of woman suffrage when they did so.

Anthony and Stanton wanted to use the WLNL anniversary meeting, scheduled for mid-May 1864, to boost Fremont's candidacy, and they issued a "call" for the meeting urging women to be "a power for freedom in the coming presidential campaign." In an accompanying letter, Stanton mentioned both Fremont and the radical Massachusetts politician Ben Butler by name. At that, Caroline Dall, who was busy in Boston contributing needlework to the cause of soldiers' aid, took up the cudgels on Lincoln's behalf.[135] Dall criticized Stanton in an open letter in the *Liberator* and the *National Anti-Slavery Standard* where she declared that while women might "interest" themselves in national questions, they must not expect to "dictate." Women should be above ordinary politics, Dall warned, and the WLNL meeting should not be used for "electioneering." She revealed her own preference for Lincoln by declaring that, four years earlier, "God safely led an honest and humble man" to the presidency.[136] Stanton responded in an open letter of her own, in which she scoffed at the premise of dictation, raised a skeptical eyebrow at the assumption that God interested Himself in American presidential elections, and reminded readers that the WLNL was *already* political. In fact, it was "the first and only organization of women for the declared purpose of influencing politics."[137] Of course, Stanton strained a point, because the WLNL had no mobilized mass membership, but she was certainly trying to use it to participate in electoral politics as far as possible.

Dall and Stanton's public exchange about which presidential candidate women should endorse may seem like a minor episode, but President Lincoln noticed. Lincoln sent messages of congratulations to Dall not once but twice.[138] Did he do more? Just prior to the May 1864 WLNL meeting, Elizabeth Cady Stanton traveled with her husband to Washington where they "had a long talk" with the president at the White House. Scholars have missed the possible significance of this meeting because the letters describing it were misdated as 1863, and if the meeting had occurred in 1863, she would have been just a wife accompanying her politician husband.[139] But in 1864 Henry B. Stanton was in political Siberia owing to the Customs House scandal. Of course, Henry may have wanted to plead his case personally with Lincoln, but that does not explain why Lincoln should have agreed to meet him while the congressional investigation was ongoing. It is not clear who took the initiative to arrange the meeting, but Lincoln used personal meetings to win over or neutralize other impatient abolitionists, including Sydney Howard Gay and Anna Dickinson.[140] In short, it seems possible that the interview stemmed from Lincoln's desire to win over Elizabeth Cady Stanton and swing her influence away from Fremont. She was either a participant or a front row observer in politics at the highest national level. The war years gave Stanton every reason to feel confident in her political savvy, insight, and connections.

As it happened, Stanton refused to shift her support to Lincoln, but the WLNL leaders found that whatever public influence they might have hoped to exercise was undermined by lack of press coverage. When they held their big first anniversary meeting in May 1864, Garrison's *Liberator* refused to mention it at all, while Johnson's *National Anti-Slavery Standard* merely printed the text of the executive committee report.[141] Wendell Phillips was infuriated by the way editors Garrison and Johnson tilted toward Lincoln, and Anthony described the "spirit of the Lincoln press on Fremont" as "diabolical."[142] Only the *New York Herald*, traditionally hostile to both women and abolition and delighted to detect dissension in the ranks of its enemies, ran coverage of the 1864 WLNL meeting. The *Herald* reported that when an unnamed participant on the floor tried to defend Lincoln by declaring, "The intention of the President is to emancipate," Anthony in the chair riposted that she "didn't care a fig for his intentions. It was an old saying that Hell is paved with good intentions."[143]

Though little is known about discussion at the WLNL meeting in 1864, it probably included rhetorical efforts to link black rights and women's rights and looked forward to postwar reconstruction. The Executive Committee's report floated a proposal for a constitutional amendment "to secure the elective franchise to all its citizens who are taxed or bear arms to support the Government"—a formula that implied voting rights for some black men (those who fought) and some women (those who paid taxes). Stanton looked forward to the postwar era, saying theirs was "the only organization of women that will have a legitimate cause for existence beyond the present hour," and she described the WLNL as "based specifically on universal emancipation and enfranchisement."[144] She spoke as if they had formed a permanent organization that would be converted into a universal suffrage organization once the war was over, but the WLNL executive committee report, less expansive, had to admit they had proceeded thus far "with neither press nor pulpit to magnify our work, without money or the enthusiasm of numbers."[145]

The WLNL's electioneering efforts fell flat because Fremont was not the candidate they thought he was. He failed to endorse black rights, his support among radicals cooled, and his gestures to reach out to Democrats pleased no one.[146] After Fremont stumbled, almost all abolitionists rallied behind Lincoln, especially because the Democrats proceeded to nominate General George McClellan on a peace platform. When Sherman captured Atlanta in September 1864, Lincoln's reelection was secured. Frederick Douglass, who had considered supporting Fremont's candidacy, eventually came to support Lincoln though he held out as long as there was "any shadow of a hope" for a nominee "of more decided anti-slavery conviction and policy."[147] But Elizabeth Cady Stanton and Susan B. Anthony stuck together with Wendell Phillips as anti-Lincoln holdouts to the end. Stanton was convinced of "the utter rottenness of the present administration."[148] She was bitter about what had been done to her husband, whose career never really recovered, and she was disgusted with Lincoln, whom she held responsible for permitting Weed's skullduggery.[149] Apparently she was right: Lincoln had allowed Weed to take control of the Customs House in exchange for election year support.[150] The women's rights leaders were left to take consolation in the thought that they had, through their opposition, influenced Lincoln to include a constitutional amendment to end slavery in the Republican platform.[151] The Thirteenth Amendment *was* a long-desired victory for abolitionists like Stanton and Anthony, and through their WLNL they had worked hard to make it happen, but they were not inclined to rest on those laurels.[152]

The war precipitated a shake-up in the American political system that created the kinds of opportunities politically minded radicals like Stanton and Douglass had been hoping for. As the hammer blows of battle set a new and faster cadence for the political life of the nation, these activists were intent on making vast changes in a short time. They had already worked hard and seen results: the death warrant of slavery had been signed, a revolutionary social change that had formerly appeared impossible. The war's results suggested that radical dreams *might* come true, and the bitter sacrifices of the war made it seem that they *must* be *made* to come true. Stanton and Anthony did not expect woman suffrage as a reward for their war work—that rationale would be constructed later, in retrospect. But looking ahead they saw a social and political landscape in which black rights and women's rights would be more and more intermingled, to the benefit of both.

3

The "Negro's Hour"

In January 1865, as the end of the war came in sight, the Thirteenth Amendment abolishing slavery finally cleared Congress. During the war, Elizabeth Cady Stanton and Susan B. Anthony had looked ahead to a reconstruction of the nation in which black people would be freed and black men enfranchised. They were confident that black suffrage would, in turn, help bring about woman suffrage, but they had never explained exactly how they expected that linkage to work. In any case, it was clear that the short-run implications of war and emancipation would be determined by one man, the president. Although Lincoln's wartime reconstruction measures in Louisiana had included no voting rights for black men, many abolitionists took heart from observing his remarkable capacity to mature and liberalize his opinions. In a speech on April 11, 1865, just after Lee's surrender at Appomattox, Lincoln suggested that he was now inclined to extend the ballot to some black men: "I would myself prefer that it were now conferred on the very intelligent, and on those who serve our cause as soldiers." Listening in the crowd outside the White House, John Wilkes Booth immediately grasped the import of Lincoln's words: "That means nigger citizenship," the assassin snarled.[1] Four days later, Lincoln was dead. As the nation moved into uncharted waters, radical activists faced questions about how to proceed. What was the best way for activists to fight for social justice, now that slavery was abolished but civil and political rights for black men and all women were still far from won? With the war over and the North victorious, it seemed that history had delivered what the women's rights activists needed. They now had all three necessities for a successful social movement—arguments, resources, *and* political opportunity. But then Wendell Phillips declared that it was the "Negro's hour."

Stanton and Anthony were about to enter into an extended dispute with Wendell Phillips, who believed that simultaneous campaigning for woman suffrage would harm black men's chances. On the contrary, they thought the two causes might be stronger together, and they wanted to demand the ballot for all citizens—to "claim the uttermost." Activism often features debates like this, disputes between ultras who favor making bold demands (even if they remain prepared to settle for half a loaf), and incrementalists who opt for step-by-step methods and try to preempt opposition by narrowing their demands at the outset. Stanton and Anthony took the first approach and Phillips the second. Given the way events unfolded, it is tempting to assume that Phillips was right. But the question was not whether woman suffrage could assuredly be won after the Civil War; it was whether agitating for woman suffrage at that point would harm the prospects for black men. After all, simultaneous efforts can be mutually reinforcing, and sometimes ultras make incrementalists' demands seem reasonable by comparison. At the time, the strategic choice was not clear-cut, and other abolitionists, including Robert Purvis, Stephen Foster, and Lucretia Mott, thought Stanton and Anthony's ideas had merit.

Wendell Phillips's patrician self-confidence was such that he felt justified in telling activist women what to do, and when Stanton and Anthony refused to defer, he used underhanded methods and denied them funds to which they were entitled. By the middle of 1866, Stanton and Anthony had been forced to create a new organization devoted to the simultaneous agitation of black and women's rights, the American Equal Rights Association. They had no funds to work with, but they did have support from Frederick Douglass, who argued unambiguously that black men's voting rights were most important, but felt that was no reason to discourage women suffragists from agitating for their cause as well. As before the war, Stanton's arguments varied widely, from offensive racist rhetoric at one point to a principled defense of black men's voting rights a few months later, but in 1866 tensions across race and gender lines generally remained manageable. And when the Fourteenth Amendment was passed by Congress, it became the basis of cooperation, not conflict, between the advocates of black (male) suffrage and woman suffrage.

When they convened only three weeks after Lincoln's assassination, in May 1865, the activists of the American Anti-Slavery Society decided to continue their organization despite slavery's demise. William Lloyd Garrison's motion to disband was defeated and he stalked out, leaving an "anti-slavery" organization devoted to the premise that slavery was not really abolished until black men had voting rights. Assuming the presidency, Wendell Phillips delivered a keynote speech setting the organization's new direction. Although the women's rights leaders had backed him against Garrison and worked alongside him to challenge Lincoln in 1864, Phillips used this speech to disavow any link between the cause of black (male) suffrage and woman suffrage: "As Abraham Lincoln said, 'One war at a time,' so I say one question at a time. This hour belongs to the negro."[2] With the metaphor of the "Negro's hour" Phillips went out of his way to prioritize black (male) suffrage.[3]

Phillips softened the blow in his speech by giving women's rights activists good reason to hope that the "Negro's hour" would last only a few minutes. He informed the meeting that the new president, Andrew Johnson, had endorsed placing the ballot "in the hands of the black man."[4] Charles Sumner had assured Phillips privately that this was indeed Johnson's intention.[5] The women's rights activists therefore accepted Phillips's pronouncement without public protest because they understood that such a presidential proclamation would make for a short "hour" and leverage women's claims at the same time. But Elizabeth Cady Stanton raised questions in private, and Phillips responded that he would not "mix" the movements, saying, "I think such mixture would lose for the negro far more than we should gain for the woman."[6] Phillips's qualms harked back to the abolitionist schism in 1840, when the American Anti-Slavery Society had debated whether including women and women's rights on the abolitionist platform might detract from the fight against slavery. Garrison and Phillips had then taken the ultra position and argued that there were no men's or women's rights, no black or white rights, only human rights, while their incrementalist opponents preached practicality and caution and maintained they could not fight slavery "with forty incongruous things tacked on."[7] Phillips swapped sides after decades, just as he was embracing practical political methods he had previously scorned. As recently as September 1860, Phillips had argued that Stephen Foster's idea of using electoral politics to attack slavery—an idea Foster shared with Elizabeth Cady Stanton and Frederick Douglass—was simply "a farce."[8]

Phillips did not explain exactly what sort of loss he feared if radicals campaigned broadly for universal voting rights, in part because he continued to insist that he was simply working for "abolition." "I am now engaged in abolishing slavery," he told Stanton, "in a land where abolition of slavery means conferring or recognizing citizenship and where citizenship supposes the ballot for all men."[9] Stanton was not prepared to accept his judgment. In fact, the sequence he described—from emancipation to citizenship to equal rights—so closely paralleled WLNL projections that Stanton could easily spot the logical flaw in that last word, "men." She shot back a telling question in rebuttal: "Do you believe the African race is entirely composed of males?"[10]

The postwar discussion about voting rights was confused by unspoken assumptions and ambiguous language. People who talked of "black suffrage" almost always meant black *male* suffrage, and "impartial suffrage" or "equal suffrage" almost always meant that black and white *men* would vote on equal terms. Even proponents of "universal suffrage" sometimes meant votes for black and white men only, implicitly excluding black and white women from the "universe" in question. Typically women were not included in talk of voting rights unless they were mentioned explicitly, and even deliberate and determined feminists occasionally used "man" as generic for humankind.[11] Meanwhile many

Wendell Phillips. Henry W. and Albert A. Berg Collection of English and American Literature, New York Public Library, Astor, Lenox, and Tilden Foundations.

advocates of "woman suffrage" pictured only white women going to the polls. Sometimes activists like Anthony and Stanton tried to clarify matters by focusing on black women, mindful that it would take both "black suffrage" *and* "woman suffrage" before a single black woman could vote. Confused as it was, the situation did serve the women's rights activists by solidifying the transformation of their women's *rights* movement into a women's *suffrage* movement.[12] The vote was confirmed as their top and effectively their only priority—they wanted *truly* universal suffrage.

Throughout the summer of 1865, Elizabeth Cady Stanton debated Phillips's "Negro's hour" privately although she deferred to it in public. Her article on "Universal Suffrage" in the *National Anti-Slavery Standard* referred repeatedly to "men," and gave no hint she might be implying, let alone advocating, a wider definition of "universal."[13] Meanwhile, Susan B. Anthony, who had gone to Leavenworth, Kansas, to live with her brother, gave unambiguous public support to Phillips's priority. Anthony worked with black Kansans, including Sattira A. Douglas and Charles Langston, and supported voting rights for black people with no cavil if they were male-only measures.[14] In a July 4 speech in Kansas, Anthony urged granting suffrage to "black men" and near the end of her speech, she acknowledged, "When I speak of the inalienable rights of the Negro, I do not forget that these belong equally to woman." But, she hastened to add, the "one great work for the people at this hour" was to insist on "No reorganization [i.e., reconstruction] without Negro suffrage."[15] Anthony had mentioned woman suffrage but she hewed to Phillips's line by stating that the work of "this hour" was black (male) suffrage.

Soon, however, events began to undermine a key assumption behind Phillips's position: it became apparent that Charles Sumner was sadly mistaken about Andrew Johnson's intentions. The new president issued proclamations recon-structing Confederate states with no provision whatsoever for black voting rights and dispensed pardons for high-ranking Confederate leaders with a liberal hand; the new "Johnson governments" he created in the South emerged lily white and heavily staffed with the old planter elite.[16] Andrew Johnson was revealing himself to be an intemperate and pigheaded man who disdained black people as lesser beings, but he had almost an entire four-year term ahead of him and the patronage power to keep many reluctant Republicans in line. Phillips, Sumner, and other radicals now saw that they faced a tough campaign—a very long "Negro's hour"—trying to convince a hostile president and a reluctant Congress to enfranchise black men.

By midsummer 1865, both Phillips and Stanton were pleading for Susan B. Anthony to come back east, but for different reasons: Phillips wanted her to campaign for black (male) suffrage while Elizabeth Cady Stanton wanted her to work for women's rights.[17] The Women's Loyal National League (WLNL) was moribund, and veteran women's rights leaders either had to revive their movement or allow it to lapse altogether, Stanton wrote: "With the League dis-banded, there is pressing need of our Woman's Rights Convention. Come back and help." "I seem to stand alone," she wrote. "I have argued constantly with Phillips and the whole fraternity, but I fear one and all will favor enfranchising the negro without us. Woman's cause is in deep water."[18] But Anthony had already left Leavenworth for Rochester before Stanton wrote.[19] Passing through Chicago in late August, she still seemed to agree with Phillips, judging from a speech in which she did not mention women's rights and argued that "nothing but the admission of the black man to the franchise can save the nation."[20]

In the fall of 1865, the outlook for black (male) suffrage under Johnson went from bad to worse. In Connecticut, the Republicans put black suffrage on the ballot but failed to campaign for it. They "literally did nothing.... there was no canvass whatsoever," while the Johnson administration and the Democrats both opposed it, so it was defeated by a substantial majority.[21] President Johnson delivered a speech to black troops in which he defined freedom as no more than the right to work for pay and warned that emancipation was only an experiment, and if it failed they might be deported.[22] In the South, the new Johnson govern-ments proceeded to enact Black Codes that reduced freedpeople to serfdom, without most civil rights, let alone political rights, and reports of violent attacks on black people filtered back to the North. It seemed likely that when Congress reconvened in December 1865, representatives of these Johnson governments would join with northern Democrats, retake control of national politics, and confirm Johnson's Reconstruction policy.[23] Seeing the fruits of victory squandered, Wendell Phillips tried to galvanize northern public opinion with a powerful new speech, "The South Victorious."[24] At some point in this sequence of events Susan B. Anthony became convinced that Elizabeth Cady Stanton was right—that they must not defer to Phillips and wait for black (male) suffrage before beginning to campaign openly for woman suffrage.

Anthony visited a long list of women's rights veterans to take counsel about what to do. Her list suggested that she was herself the one-woman center of a women's rights network, but it also, tellingly, included no black women.[25] Anthony visited Lucy Stone at her home in New Jersey and together they went into New York City to call on Antoinette Brown Blackwell, Elizabeth Cady Stanton, and the editors of the *National Anti-Slavery Standard*.[26] For several years Stone had been busy caring for a sickly daughter and elderly parents and had moved frequently while Henry Blackwell continued to be an erratic breadwinner. The couple often lived apart.[27] She still suffered from migraine headaches, but Stone's money worries had evaporated because in 1864 Henry Blackwell's real estate speculations finally paid off, so much so that he could retire from business altogether.[28] Stone, "astounded," spoke of investing in government bonds and buying a place on Nantucket or Martha's Vineyard.[29] She still had to negotiate a complex family situation, however, because Blackwell now had time on his hands and was eager to join in, or even take over, what had formerly been her own distinctive work for women's rights. Though Lucy Stone was elected a vice president of the AASS at the May 1865 meeting, she moved back into activism at less than full speed.[30]

Throughout 1865, while Anthony and Stanton deferred to Phillips's "Negro's hour," other voices spoke for woman suffrage. Garrison's *Liberator* stirred their restlessness by publishing news of abolitionist meetings in which speakers endorsed this right.[31] The editor Theodore Tilton broke ground for woman suffrage in his *Independent,* and Senator Benjamin Gratz Brown of Missouri advocated it in a well-publicized speech.[32] Famed novelist Harriet Beecher Stowe endorsed woman suffrage in the *Atlantic Monthly*, interpreting it not as a right but as a duty—a new and potentially strong argument.[33] Anthony and Stanton were also goaded into action by Frances Dana Gage, who was working with freedpeople in the South. Gage contributed a series of letters to the *National Anti-Slavery Standard,* most of which emphasized the capacity and potential of the freedpeople, but in November 1865 her letter sounded a different note. Gage reported, "The negro men of Paris Island insisted (the smartest and most knowing ones) that the money for the women's labor should be paid over to the husband instead of to the laborer herself. Because, 'you know, missus, de woman she have short sense, and don' know how to spend it.'" These men were, Gage remarked dryly, "very much like white folks you see."[34] Gage's report that some freedmen were claiming their wives' earnings raised obvious questions about their willingness to support women's right to vote.

Finally and most urgently, Stanton and Anthony reactivated their movement because of proposals circulating in Congress to deal with what Robert Dale Owen called "the 3/5 principle in aggravated form." Under the Constitution the white population of the antebellum South had enjoyed added political clout at the national level because every slave counted as three-fifths of a person for purposes of representation in the House (which in turn enhanced a state's electoral vote in presidential contests). The three-fifths clause had given the South between twenty and thirty extra "slave seats" in every Congress and it was part of the reason that slaveholding southerners had been able to dominate national politics for over seventy years. As the prospect loomed of southern states resuming their membership in Congress, Republicans realized that, with the three-fifths clause effectively annulled by the Thirteenth Amendment, the ironic result of the war would be to count the ex-slaves as whole people and thereby to *increase* the representation and the power of southern whites.[35] The end of the clause, Robert Dale Owen argued, was an eminently practical reason to enfranchise southern blacks, a reason "not of sentiment but of calculation."[36]

The end of the three-fifths clause made it necessary for the ruling Republican Party to do *something*, but forcing the southern states to enfranchise black men outright, as Owen urged, seemed politically impossible, and halfway measures had implications for women. Although radicals like Charles Sumner and Ben Butler pressed for black (male) voting rights by stressing the loyal service of black troops and the practical argument that black votes were essential to southern reconstruction, conservative Republicans opposed black suffrage as unwise, and moderate Republicans feared it would be politically suicidal. Democrats denounced all black rights with gutter rhetoric and vehemently race-baited their opponents, but they were few in the 39th Congress. With their party in control but divided, Republican leaders tried to devise language for a constitutional amendment that would not *en*franchise black men but only reduce southern representation if they remained *dis*enfranchised. Some Fourteenth Amendment proposals stipulated that states would lose representation if they denied the vote to all adult males, thus introducing the word "male" in the Constitution for the first time.[37] Other proposals solved the problem by basing representation on the number of a state's "qualified voters"—which could reward states for enfranchising women.[38] These two possible changes to the Constitution—one harmful and the other hopeful—led the women to act.

As 1865 drew to a close, Anthony completed her tour with a visit to Boston, where Wendell Phillips consented to her use of $500 from the "W.R. fund"— that is, the Jackson Fund—and she "commenced W.R. work in earnest."[39] Together Anthony and Stanton drew up a petition asking Congress for woman suffrage, prevailed upon Lucy Stone to join them in signing its cover letter, and spent most of Christmas day 1865 writing to women's rights veterans about it.[40] Although they aimed at a minimum to prevent negative action—to keep retrograde "male" language out of a new constitutional amendment—their petition asked for positive action in the form of a woman suffrage amendment to the U.S. Constitution.[41] As before the war, Stanton and Anthony were engaged in a petition campaign for women's rights, and again they were drawing on the Jackson Fund, but now they were looking to the national scene. And they were openly challenging Wendell Phillips's "Negro's hour" priority.

Of course, Stanton and Anthony needed money to start campaigning again for women's rights, and they expected they could turn to the Hovey as well as the Jackson Fund. In fact, they stood to claim a much larger part of the Hovey Fund, because Charles Hovey's will stipulated that that "in case chattel slavery should be abolished in the United States" before the money was exhausted, the remaining balance should then be applied to the promotion of "Non-Resistance, Woman's Rights, and Free Trade."[42] With the final ratification of the Thirteenth Amendment at hand in December 1865, chattel slavery was about to be abolished. Because pacifism had shrunken in the wake of a righteous war and free trade was championed by many mainstream politicians, the women's rights activists had the largest claim on the balance of the Hovey Fund. But in the battle with Garrison over AASS dissolution earlier in the year, Phillips and his supporters had taken the view that slavery was not really "abolished" until black men had the vote. At some point the Hovey trustees under Phillips's lead began to apply this definition of "abolition" not only to justify the continuance of the Society but also to govern the disposition of Hovey money. They decided not to redirect the funds even after the Thirteenth Amendment officially and formally outlawed chattel slavery, thus ignoring the terms of the will.[43]

The disposition of this money was a matter of considerable interest because emancipation had precipitated a funding crisis for radical abolitionists, especially men who had made a career out of agitation. William Lloyd Garrison understood that there would be no more donations to pay his salary as editor once the *Liberator* ceased publication in December 1865. He therefore took a salaried position with a freedmen's aid organization and tried lecturing; eventually, in 1867, his friends raised a "testimonial" purse of more than $30,000 from among well-to-do admirers.[44] African American activists who enjoyed no such financial backing critiqued both Garrison and *NASS* editor Oliver Johnson for wanting to disband the AASS organization when its labor was "only half done." Thomas Hamilton of the *Anglo-African* could not resist a barbed comment: "It is an unfortunate coincidence that they have made the discovery that their work is done at the very moment that they also find that it no longer pays."[45]

A new cause, freedmen's aid, siphoned off donations from radical activism but was sometimes a boondoggle for white men. Veteran abolitionist J. Miller McKim brought together local and regional freedmen's aid associations into a massive national American Freedmen's Union Commission, which raised large amounts of money to send teachers for the freedpeople into the South.[46] Lucretia Mott complained that "woman was ignored" in the Commission's hierarchy but McKim, though "taken aback" by her criticism, failed to act on her complaint, and women continued to serve in only the lowest posts.[47] In fact, women who applied to serve as teachers were turned away for want of funds even while the organization was top-heavy with salaried superintendents, agents, and national officers, all of whom were white men.[48] The American Freedmen's Union Commission used Garrison's name to establish its bona fides with radical donors (and voted him a salary of $3,000), but despite its name, it soon began to give aid to southern *whites* on an equal basis with the freedpeople.[49] Nor did the Commission endorse a radical political agenda: it refused, for example, to publicize Susan B. Anthony's Chicago speech in favor of black suffrage.[50] Anthony suspected that the freedpeople's interests were being undermined by white men who wanted to "give themselves fat, easy posts as superintendents, missionaries, teachers, etc."[51]

Losing donors to freedmen's aid and worried about money, the American Anti-Slavery Society brought in a business-oriented manager to increase circulation and sell advertisements in its *National Anti-Slavery Standard* newspaper.[52] A market niche seemed open for a popular journal of radical opinion because Greeley's *Tribune*, which showed that such a venture could pay, had lost its radical edge, and Garrison's *Liberator* was about to publish its last issue. But the new manager clashed with editor Parker Pillsbury and had to leave, and the *Standard* remained a money loser.[53] Wendell Phillips therefore found another answer to the funding problem. As he explained to Susan B. Anthony, he would steer Hovey money to the *NASS*: "We [Hovey Committee] shall aid in keeping our *Standard* floating till the enemy comes down."[54]

Phillips's *Standard* was unwilling to mention, let alone promote woman suffrage. In April 1866, Elizabeth Cady Stanton prodded Phillips about it. "At the next meeting of your executive committee, A.S., there is one point I wish you would take into consideration," she wrote him, "namely, will you *sell* a page or half a page of the *Standard* to 'oppressed women' for the coming year?....We should then have a right to draw from the Hovey fund for its support." She thought this approach would meet his strictures against mixing black and woman suffrage: "There need be no 'turning in as mincement' of that sacred platform, or its organ!! The black man can be kept in one column and the women in the other. I suppose you are afraid of miscegenation!"[55] Stanton was challenging Phillips not only on the contents of the *NASS* but on the continuing use of Hovey money to support it. Phillips responded blandly, pretending to perceive no problem about Hovey's will: "I see no reason why the Hovey Cee [*sic*] cannot still support an Antislavery Journal." He told Stanton he was "wholly unwilling as at present advised to mingle any other question" with black (male) suffrage, which he continued to equate with the organization's abolitionist goal: "My present view is to hold to the society as it is—and keep its organ afloat if possible exclusively as an *antislavery* organ."[56]

Insisting that he was still fighting slavery, Phillips refused to be drawn into the strategic question at hand: was it more advantageous to combine the causes of black (male) suffrage and woman suffrage? And he could not acknowledge he was ignoring the terms of Hovey's will. Phillips told Stanton that his "Negro's hour" priority would not harm woman suffrage, saying he would "never so ask for negro voting as to put one single obstacle in the way of her getting it."[57] But that reassurance was hollow as long as Phillips controlled the purse strings and blocked funding for woman suffrage agitation until after black male suffrage was safely won—by which time the fund might well be exhausted. By keeping up the pretense that "slavery" was still at issue, Phillips justified not only the continued existence of the American Anti-Slavery Society but also its dubious claim on the Hovey Fund.

Elizabeth Cady Stanton challenged Phillips's priorities and disputed his strategic assessment in three letters published in December 1865 and January 1866. Her first letter went to William Lloyd Garrison and was published in the last issue of the *Liberator.* In it she encouraged women to rouse themselves by exaggerating the situation, saying the black man had "the most influential political party of the day" arguing for his voting rights, while woman was threatened by legislation that might "exclude her forever" from the vote—this last a reference to language proposed by Representative Jencks of Rhode Island. Saying nothing more about the freedmen, Stanton urged women, "It is unsafe to sleep now."[58]

Her second and most prominent public letter was published in the *National Anti-Slavery Standard,* which ran an immediate editorial rebuttal, probably written by Phillips himself.[59] In this letter Stanton challenged Phillips's "Negro's hour" idea directly and by name. She argued that black (male) suffrage was virtually assured because the end of the three-fifths clause would compel the Republican Party to enfranchise black men for its own political advantage, though she admitted that politicians might "wrangle" over the question for as much as "five or ten years." With the black man thus "in a political point of view, far above the educated women of the country," she asked, should women "stand aside and see 'Sambo' walk into the kingdom first"?[60] With this term Stanton labeled the freedmen as "degraded" and "ignorant," and asked her readers to contemplate the implications of enfranchising them first. It was not just a matter of women's rights being delayed, she argued, because the enfranchised freedmen might subsequently oppose women: "Are we sure that he, once entrenched in all his inalienable rights, may not be an added power to hold us at bay?" But not all black men were "Sambos," apparently, because she shifted to a more positive image of the black soldier with his "strong arm and blue uniform," and suggested that women ought to avail themselves of an opportunity to "walk in by his side."[61] Stanton expressed some sympathy for black women, who needed "all the rights, privileges, and immunities of citizens," but she also suggested their biggest problem might be black men, who she predicted would become domineering husbands, perhaps even worse than white slave masters. She did not oppose black men's voting rights outright, but with its negative references this second letter undercut support for them.

Phillips's editorial in the *Standard* responded, "We cannot agree that the enfranchisement of women and the enfranchisement of the blacks stand on the same ground, or are entitled to equal effort at this moment." Based on a count of votes in Congress, Phillips predicted that woman suffrage had no chance: "Mrs. Stanton must see that while there is a strong party in Congress who can be brought to vote directly or indirectly for putting the ballot in the hands of the blacks, no considerable portion of those votes could now be carried for an amendment to the Constitution which should include women." Agitating woman suffrage would be not only fruitless but risky, since "thirty years of agitation and four years of war" had created a historic opportunity, and "We have no right, from an anxiety for something beside justice to the negro, to throw away a single chance of securing it for him."[62]

In her third letter, published in January 1866, Stanton shifted ground, eliminating both the exaggerations of her *Liberator* letter and the denigrating comments and racial slurs that marked her second letter. She took a more measured and respectful view of why the freedmen's suffrage claims had emerged first but women should act now. Women had deferred to the black man, she wrote, because "we saw that the settlement of his claims logically included those of woman also," but now, she claimed, the question of his rights "is settled by all honest minds."[63] Although she had to concede an uncertain political outlook, she still expressed confidence that the Republican Party would carry the ball for black (male) suffrage out of party necessity, so that radical activists should demand more. This time when she cited the interests of black women, she linked them to a more sympathetic account of black men, suggesting that it was doing the black man a wrong by "striking down the civil, political and social rights of every woman of his race." She insisted on truly universal suffrage and argued that the nation would never be a *true* republic until *all* its citizens were enfranchised.

By describing the freedmen as "degraded," and "ignorant," as she had in her second letter, Elizabeth Cady Stanton used adjectives that came back to haunt other abolitionists in the wake of emancipation because for decades they had insisted on the harmful, degrading effects of slavery, decried the ignorance in which the slaves were confined, and laid the responsibility for these things at the feet of the slaveholders. They had used strong adjectives the better to indict slavery as a wicked system. Now that the slaves were free, however, it was hard to deny that they were in general much as they had been months earlier, and yet in this new context, to say so seemed to blame the victims.[64] Abolitionists might explain over and over that nobody in his right mind would expect to find the freedmen without "the vices of the slave," as one put it, but the opponents of black rights were eager to seize upon the condition of the freed slaves as an excuse for discrimination.[65] For example, one member of Congress condemned black suffrage outright on the grounds that he had often heard the eloquent Senator Sumner proclaiming that slavery degrades men, and "therefore I must oppose enfranchising them now."[66]

The women backed universal suffrage after considering educated suffrage. One way to avoid debating the freedpeople's (or women's) readiness for suffrage was to devise an evenhanded principle on which the vote could be granted to individuals rather than groups, and an educational qualification—extending the vote to all who were literate, whether black or white, male or female—seemed at first glance like a sensible proposal. It might disarm opponents and encompass women along with black men. Stanton and Anthony considered it, but as they began to agitate openly in December 1865 and January 1866, they soon realized it was a political nonstarter: it would have disenfranchised many white men and would have enfranchised far too few of the freedpeople to enable them to protect themselves.[67] Instead, the women's rights activists embraced a strategy of demanding truly universal suffrage—enfranchising black men *and* all women, black and white.

Advocating universal suffrage did not require denying all differences in condition. As advocates for women's rights developed their arguments in the antebellum years, they tended to argue either from a belief that natural rights were a gift of God, given equally to souls equally precious in His eyes, or from a belief in political principles forged in the crucible of the American Revolution, which held that individuals were entitled to equality before the law and to a government to which they had given their consent.[68] Either way, their theoretical principles implied a sweeping and unconditional gift of rights not hemmed in by tests of merit or capacity. Worthiness, except in very minimal requirements for "mental and moral sanity," did not enter into the picture.[69] They were not obliged to pretend that they thought ignorance was as good as education, idleness as good as diligence, or drunkenness as good as sobriety in order to insist that, by an egalitarian line of argument, everyone—and yes, that included the uneducated, idle toper—was indeed entitled to vote. Like other abolitionists, feminists even turned illiteracy into an argument in favor of enfranchisement by arguing that possession of the vote was in itself educational—a "schoolmaster" or as Wendell Phillips called it, a "normal school for the masses."[70] Stanton never opposed universal suffrage, even though she would often notice (and deplore, in ugly language) the characteristics of some enfranchised men as an argument for adding women voters to the mix.[71] Thus, despite having made denigrating comments about black men, Stanton took the position that, illiterate and even "degraded" though he might be, "Sambo" was nevertheless entitled to cast a vote—and women were, too.

Stanton summed up her strategy as "Claim the uttermost," which she credited to the Irish nationalist Daniel O'Connell. She recalled meeting O'Connell and asking if he really expected to secure Irish independence, whereupon he had replied, "It is always good policy to claim the uttermost and you will be sure to get something."[72] Claiming the uttermost meant fighting for the voting rights of *both* black men and all women, but it also implied that its proponents would ultimately be willing to settle for "something" less. Fired with enthusiasm, Stanton and Anthony probably could not anticipate how they might feel if that "something" finally turned out to be black (male) suffrage only.

Wendell Phillips defended his "Negro's hour" priority with a maxim of his own, "One thing at a time." He argued, "It is certainly perilous and may be fatal to relax any energy hitherto devoted to [the Negro's] emancipation, or to allow any fraction of our strength to be diverted to another issue."[73] He thus indicated publicly that he feared energy or resources would be diverted from black rights to women's rights, but he also wrote privately to Stanton that he feared that women's petitions would "block wheels that are only too willing to be blocked" in Congress.[74] This comment apparently referred to weak-kneed congressional Republicans who might seize on any excuse to refuse black (male) suffrage. But Stanton was well-informed and had her own views on the outlook in Congress: "In regard to blocking the wheels of action for the black man, I have not heard one leading Republican express the slightest hope that suffrage could be secured for the Negro during this session. I do sincerely believe the shortest way to get justice for him is to educate the people now into the true idea."[75] The votes were not there for black male suffrage, Stanton argued, and therefore activists' energy and resources would be well spent on combined efforts. She saw no point in conceding to weakness rather than arguing boldly and playing for time.

Phillips's comment about wheels "only too willing to be blocked" reflected concern that woman suffrage could be used to embarrass and paralyze proponents of black (male) suffrage. Opponents could use a "let us be consistent" argument for woman suffrage cynically, to repel arguments for extending the franchise to black men. This old debaters' ploy, used in the New York state legislature and constitutional conventions before the war, was sure to reappear. Both Stanton and Phillips could anticipate that conservatives who sought to undermine black (male) suffrage might portray it as a step onto a slippery slope that would lead to a ridiculous, embarrassing, positively unthinkable result—*women* voting! Conservatives counted on discrediting both black men's and women's voting rights not by engaging with proponents' arguments but by evoking visceral emotion. Cautious reformers reacted with moderation, reassurances, and every effort to calm irrational fears. Phillips had scorned moderation in the antebellum years but, impressed with the rarity of this historic moment, he had turned cautious. Stanton reacted differently, partly because she analyzed political action opportunities differently and partly as a matter of personal disposition. Elizabeth Cady Stanton actually relished provoking "holy horror."[76] She liked to poke fun at her scandalized critics, disarming them by her absolute refusal to be cowed. Sometimes the fearless self-assurance of a radical individual like Stanton is precisely what it takes to make "unthinkable" ideas begin to become thinkable.[77] But to moderates, her "claim the uttermost" sounded too much like conservative opponents who said "let us be consistent" and cynically argued for woman suffrage the better to undermine black suffrage. Moderates thought she was playing into opponents' hands, but Stanton believed that charging straight ahead with all flags flying was sometimes the best or the only way to go.

Stanton's and Phillips's disagreement about strategy was already complicated because it was also a covert struggle over money, and it soon deepened because it became a struggle for organizational control. Stanton and Anthony had come to appreciate the value of formal organization through their WLNL experience, they wanted the ability to tap into the Hovey funds, and the shortest route to both goals was to reorient the American Anti-Slavery Society and make it a truly universal suffrage organization, opposed to both race and gender discrimination. As early as October 1865, Susan B. Anthony lobbied Lucretia Mott with some version of this idea, and by year's end Pennsylvania abolitionists gave it a hearing.[78] Of course Phillips was opposed, but perhaps they could convince a majority of AASS members. At a January 1866 meeting, Stephen Foster proposed converting the organization into an "equal rights" society, arguing that the two causes would be stronger together and could marshal a larger force against a common enemy. But Charles Lenox Remond countered that woman suffrage would burden down the cause of black (male) suffrage, and Wendell Phillips insisted the society must secure "absolute safety for the negro race"—still seeing the "negro race" as all male. Lucy Stone tried not to take sides, saying that "in season and out of season the claims of woman to political rights should be urged, but she was always glad also to maintain the rights of the negro."[79] Stone was apparently thinking in traditional Garrisonian terms about agitating issues over the long haul without aiming at immediate political results, but other participants in this AASS debate were trying to assess the best way for them to function as a political pressure group in the short term.

Garrisonian abolitionists were peculiarly ill-suited to assess political strategy. Practical-minded incrementalists had long since abandoned the American Anti-Slavery Society for political antislavery, in the split of 1840. For over a generation, AASS members had prided themselves on their willingness to ignore electoral politics, only softening that position in the last years before the war. The shift among abolitionists in the late 1850s from moral suasion to political means created a context in the 1860s in which many of them began to prioritize politics, but most lacked any real experience with it. The postwar AASS aimed to exercise political influence over Republicans and perhaps even act as the party's "left wing," but to do so was complicated.[80] The results of the war had infused abolitionists with false confidence: it seemed they had brought about emancipation and been master strategists all along, simply by sticking to their moralistic guns. So did they really need to change tactics? Few members of the AASS could pretend to anything approaching the political savvy possessed by Elizabeth Cady Stanton. Phillips had certainly become politically aware and active during the war, but his closest confidant among politicians, Charles Sumner, took an almost perverse pride in violating the normal rules of the political game.

At this moment in early 1866, Phillips sought to evade debate over political strategy by moving to postpone the organization question. He told Anthony and Stanton that the proposed organizational change meant amending the American Anti-Slavery Society's constitution, which required three months' notice. The women accordingly deputized Aaron Macy Powell "to give the formal notice, in order that it might be acted upon at the coming May anniversary," expecting the society would then "widen its object so as to include universal suffrage."[81] In the meantime they pressed forward by forming a New York State Equal Rights organization to promote both black (male) and woman suffrage. Phillips wished they would limit themselves to the state level, but they told him that, on the contrary, they hoped to use New York as a stepping stone to national organization.[82] Stanton told Phillips frankly she hoped to persuade him to embrace her strategy and to lead "a national organization or committee with you as President, the *National* Standard as our organ." She did not hesitate to mix flattery with logic. "I do not feel fully satisfied to take a step without your approbation," she wrote, "I have more confidence in your conscience and judgment than in any living man."[83]

But Phillips refused her cajolery. Instead he set up a face-to-face talk with Stanton and Anthony in mid-February 1866 in New York City, predicting, "Half an hour's talk will open your ideas more than any letters."[84] Phillips recruited the editor of the *Independent*, Theodore Tilton, to reinforce him, and together the two men tried to convince Stanton and Anthony to defer to "the Negro's hour."[85] They laid it down flatly: there was simply no chance for woman suffrage in this generation. It was only an intellectual theory, but black (male) suffrage could become a fact. Asking for woman suffrage would be fruitless, and its advocates ought to be realistic and willingly lend a hand with the work of "the hour." Afterward Stanton described the talk as "very demoralizing" because of "all that was said of the distant day for the realization of our hopes."[86]

But the two women had not been persuaded. When it came to assessing political opportunities, Stanton (and, to a lesser extent, Anthony) had been schooled in New York political infighting for years, while Phillips had disavowed politics until recently and Tilton had more experience in poetry and publishing than in politics. Why indeed should these two seasoned women defer to the political analysis of these two relatively inexperienced men? Stanton and Anthony's skepticism was reinforced by Robert Dale Owen, who told them he thought women might have the vote in Massachusetts and New York within five years.[87] These different prognostications indicated that Owen and Phillips were focusing on different levels of government: Owen referred to state-level changes, while Phillips was fixated on the national scene and the federal Constitution.

The women were trying to combine state and federal aims by setting a three-pronged strategy. Before the war, they had pursued a bellwether strategy at the state level, but now that Reconstruction was redefining citizenship and its rights at the federal level, the activist leaders wanted to work at that level as well, at least to the extent of preventing the retrograde action of inserting the word "male" in the federal Constitution. But they chose to urge positive action at the federal level, too, by petitioning *for* woman suffrage.[88] As they saw it, claiming "the uttermost" and agitating *for* woman suffrage at the federal level would help to forestall retrograde action at that level *and* simultaneously reinforce state-level agitation for positive measures—and it might even pay off on its own. Lucretia Mott, who was persuaded by Stanton and Anthony, explained their three-pronged strategy: first, there was an opportunity for action on woman suffrage at the state level in the imminent New York Constitutional Convention; second, there was need for action at the federal level to stop the congressional move to insert "male" into the federal Constitution; and third, there was a chance that at the federal level, "the negro's hour was decidedly the fitting time for woman to slip in."[89] Of course winning woman suffrage at the national level was an exceedingly long shot, as Stanton and Anthony surely appreciated, but after all the astounding events that had come to pass in recent years, who was to say that it was literally impossible?

They knew it would be difficult at every level, but they believed they had a fighting chance—and they insisted they had the right to try.

As they tried in early 1866 to stop "male" language, and possibly even to "slip in" at the national level, the women were scrambling to identify insider allies who could help them influence the Fourteenth Amendment as it was being drafted in Congress. They knew no one who was a well-positioned sympathizer able to draft and steer legislation. Robert Dale Owen was an excellent source of information but not a member of Congress himself. Benjamin Gratz Brown of Missouri, who presented the women's petitions respectfully in the Senate, appeared to be a strong ally but announced he would not seek reelection.[90] Ben Wade of Ohio would prove to be a supporter of woman suffrage, but he was a stranger to them personally and spent most of his political capital on other causes.[91] And Charles Sumner was at best a half-hearted ally because he agreed with Phillips about the "Negro's hour" and presented the women's petitions apologetically.[92] Years later Sumner would claim he had wanted to help, and used up "nineteen pages of foolscap" trying to devise language that would keep the word "male" out of the Constitution. But this waste of paper was less than impressive because Sumner was notoriously incompetent at drafting legislation, and his effectiveness was limited because so many of his Republican colleagues despised his self-important manner.[93]

Probably the women's best ally, both sympathetic and influential, was Thaddeus Stevens, though he was also in failing health and already carrying heavy burdens as the co-chair of the Joint Committee on Reconstruction.[94] The women sent woman suffrage petitions to Stevens because his committee was charged with drafting the new constitutional amendment, asking that if the Joint Committee could not report favorably on woman suffrage, it would "at least not interpose any new barrier" to that right.[95] But the proceedings of Stevens's committee were secret, and the women realized that whatever was happening behind closed doors, they might also take advantage of public debates in the House. To get their woman suffrage petitions presented and thus publicized in the *Congressional Globe,* they sent copies to Representative James Brooks, a "copperhead" or peace Democrat who represented Elizabeth Cady Stanton's district in Manhattan. Brooks was a former newspaper editor with an irresponsible record of opposing the Union war effort and a "clownish" manner.[96] But Republican members in the House who had been sent woman suffrage petitions were refusing to present them and, as Anthony said, "the public hears not a word."[97] Anthony told Brooks they were using him to goad the Republicans, and Stanton told Sumner openly that she was advising women to send petitions to Democrats, "as they for their own purposes would give us more attention."[98]

The women thus inadvertently handed Brooks a weapon with which to attack black (male) suffrage and he tried to use it. During a discussion of proposed language for the Fourteenth Amendment, Brooks taunted Stevens by asking "if the Indian was not a man and a brother," and why women were not permitted to be represented. Stevens pointed out, "This bill does not exclude them. It does not say who shall vote."[99] Perhaps Brooks had been expecting a version that featured the word "male," but he rattled on, saying, "Indians are only Indians, but negroes are men and brothers; and why not, in a resolution like this, include the fair sex too?" and with that he read and inserted into the record a petition signed by Anthony, Stanton, Stone, and others, asking for woman suffrage. Brooks promised he would move to add sex to color as a proscribed basis of disenfranchisement, whereupon Stevens acerbically asked, "Is the gentleman in favor of his own amendment?" Brooks refused to answer the question and brought the exchange to an end by playing to the galleries: "I prefer the white women of my country to the negro." Brooks's antics showed that the request for woman suffrage at the federal level had, as moderates feared, the disadvantage of providing Democrats tools to make mischief. But no real harm had been done, and when Brooks's time expired, the debate proceeded without a ripple.

When the Joint Committee on Reconstruction reported out its draft of a Fourteenth Amendment in January 1866, Stanton and Anthony must have been pleased because Stevens had shepherded a version that used the word "persons" and made no mention of "male."[100] It seemed that Stevens had delivered for them and Anthony took some credit: "We have at least saved the nation from disgracing the Constitution by inserting the word *male* we can hardly estimate the value of that."[101] But her triumph was short-lived because Stevens's measure, though it passed the House, went down to defeat in the Senate, stymied not only by bigoted Democrats and hidebound Johnson loyalists but also by the ever-righteous Charles Sumner. Sumner would brook no compromise on the right of black (male) suffrage, and in his eyes the proposed amendment did just that by implicitly recognizing the right of southern states to disenfranchise blacks so long as they were willing to accept reduced representation.[102] When the Stevens measure failed, proposals revived the old "male" formulation.

As she watched the progress of events during that winter and spring when the Fourteenth Amendment was being debated, Stanton at one point spotted a chance that woman suffrage might do real harm to black (male) suffrage, in a proposal to base representation on "legal voters."[103] Even though doing so would have created an incentive for states to enfranchise women, Stanton warned against it in the *National Anti-Slavery Standard* because "the spirit of caste would impel Southern aristocrats to enfranchise their women sooner than their negroes," and if so, "the black man may be worse off." "Beware American Senators," she urged, "lest in this backward legislation you are foiled in what you attempt."[104] The proposal failed for other reasons, but Stanton had maintained a principled position.[105] In December she made derogatory comments but in March she was unwilling to see the freedmen's voting rights endangered.

The last act of the Fourteenth Amendment drama saw the activist women again come close to a favorable outcome. In April 1866 the Joint Committee was exhausted but Robert Dale Owen gave it a fresh start by presenting his own proposal for a Fourteenth Amendment. The most striking provision of Owen's plan was its measure granting the vote to black men after a delay of ten years, in 1876.[106] In the interim, states that disenfranchised on the basis of race would lose representation, but black civil rights would be protected throughout. Owen's proposal dealt with "persons" and from the women's point of view, it was even better than the previous Stevens plan because it not only avoided the word "male," but also, by granting black male suffrage outright, promised to make it easier to leverage woman suffrage. Thaddeus Stevens and William Pitt Fessenden, co-chairs of the Joint Committee, both liked Owen's version and it seemed ready to pass when Fessenden fell ill. The measure was laid over for two days—after which it was completely abandoned. Apparently New York, Illinois, and Indiana Republicans feared facing their voters with any grant of black suffrage, even a delayed one, and taking advantage of Fessenden's illness, they exerted powerful pressure to defeat the Owen plan.[107] But it was also scuttled by opposition from Charles Sumner, who insisted he could brook no deviation from principle in the form of a ten years' delay before black men got voting rights.[108]

Thus at the last minute the Joint Committee reported out a very different proposal, one that would go on to become the Fourteenth Amendment as we know it. The House passed it on May 10, 1866, and the Senate, after making some changes, followed suit about a month later. Like most legislators and journalists, the woman suffrage leaders focused on section two, which dealt with representation and contained the offending word "male." It contained no grant of the franchise to black men, only a representational penalty for not doing so. Section one guaranteed citizens "equal protection" and "due process," and defined citizens as "all persons born or naturalized," thus including women and black people. Despite its enormous future importance, section one did not excite much comment and certainly no great radical enthusiasm at the time.[109] Radicals therefore found little reason to welcome the amendment. On the contrary, when the Senate passed the amendment in its final form, Thaddeus Stevens lamented that his "bright dream" of political justice was dead, Theodore Tilton was tormented "to think of what might have been," and Wendell Phillips called it "a fatal and total surrender."[110] Although Garrison, playing his new moderate role, supported the amendment, Frederick Douglass blasted it as an insult: "To tell me that I am an equal American citizen, and, in the same breath, tell me that my right to vote may be constitutionally taken from me by some other equal citizen or citizens, is to tell me that my citizenship is but an empty name."[111] Stanton and Anthony had failed to influence the amendment and to keep the word "male" out of the Constitution, but they had come close to seeing a more positive outcome in both the Stevens version and the Owen proposal, and by deploring the disappointing results, they were not quarreling with other radicals. And if anyone had retarded the cause of black male suffrage by taking an impractical "ultra" stance, it was Charles Sumner more than these woman suffrage advocates.

Black activists' attitudes toward women's suffrage were unclear. The Equal Rights League that Douglass had helped to found in Syracuse in 1864 expanded rapidly at the war's end, but did activist black men intend to repeat the pattern of the 1850s, when women's rights seemed like excess baggage, or might they hark back to an earlier time when women had been welcomed as co-partners? Signals were mixed. Some Equal Rights League chapters clearly included black women. In Toledo, most of the members of the executive board of the new Equal Rights League were women. But in Trenton, New Jersey, while both sexes attended a "State Convention of Colored Men" in July 1865, only the men took part in the business proceedings.[112] The League's president, John Mercer Langston, claimed the ballot as an explicitly masculine prerogative, and complained, "It is said, women are citizens, and so are minors, but they are neither allowed to vote nor hold office.... Why put us in the category and condition of women and minors?"[113] The first annual meeting of the National Equal Rights League, held in Cleveland in October 1865, exemplified these mixed signals: though it had no female delegates or participants, the meeting approved provisions that outlawed discrimination by sex in state auxiliary leagues.[114]

In the South, freedwomen flocked to political meetings, apparently assuming that the ballot was the property of the black community and they had an interest in it.[115] Acting on their assumptions about the nature of freedom and rights rather than announcing their position on gender and the ballot, southern freedwomen did not usually take care to claim their rights explicitly as women's rights. Thus in Richmond, "men and women in crowds" made their way to the "First Colored Men's Convention of Virginia" and created the "Colored *Men's* Equal Rights League" of Richmond, but its bylaws made any "*person*" over twenty-one eligible for membership.[116] Southern black women had good reason to take politics seriously, and in the coming years, as white backlash developed, they would suffer violent reprisals for their political loyalties.[117] On the other hand, some southern black men opposed woman suffrage. The black-run *New Orleans Tribune* claimed the vote for black men "on the broad ground that they are men and they are American citizens," while its editors claimed for black women only "the same regard as for the white ones."[118]

No prominent black woman chose to become a spokeswoman for woman suffrage. In October 1865, Harriet Tubman spoke to Lucretia Mott "about the Freedmen & their right to vote," and Tubman "enlarged" on the subject in a "sensible" way that led Mott to exclaim, "She is a wonderful woman."[119] But there is no record of the substance of Tubman's remarks, and she took no public position on woman suffrage until much later in her life, when she would count herself a member of "Susan B. Anthony's association."[120] Sojourner Truth was specially cultivated by Anthony, who asked her to sign a woman suffrage petition and get her friends to sign.[121] Truth had sympathy for Anthony and Stanton's arguments emphasizing the rights of black women, but she had other, more urgent concerns. In 1865 and 1866 she and other northern black women focused on relieving the dire needs of refugee freedpeople who flocked to Union lines and gathered in urban areas like Washington, D.C.[122] Frances E. W. Harper would later have much to say about the freedpeople of the South, but she was only beginning to be acquainted with their situation.[123] Meanwhile, she delivered lyceum lectures making the oft-repeated connection between the bullet and the ballot, arguing that black men who fought to save the Union deserved the right to vote. But Harper also tried to avoid becoming involved in squabbles inside the AASS.[124] Thus none of these black women leaders challenged Phillips's "Negro's hour" priority, but none of them endorsed it either.

Frederick Douglass had been battling for the vote for black men for years, and he came out strongly in favor of woman suffrage, too, as early as 1848 at Seneca Falls and as recently as the 1865 meeting of the Massachusetts Anti-Slavery Society. "My heart and my voice go with the movement to extend suffrage to woman," Douglass then declared, but he immediately went on to say that the vote for black men rested "upon another basis."[125] Douglass could see that there were different and stronger arguments for black male suffrage than for woman suffrage, especially in black men's military service. By 1865 he already felt he had been urging "but one idea for the last three years"—the "immediate, unconditional, and universal" enfranchisement of black men.[126] In February 1866, Douglass argued the case at the highest level, leading a delegation of black men to the White House to meet with President Johnson (who dismissed the idea as sure to lead to a race war).[127] Although Douglass was no longer editing a paper, he was a popular public speaker and in these months after the war, suffrage was his prime topic: it would have been easy for him to echo Phillips's mantra about the "the Negro's hour," but Douglass did not endorse Phillips's rigid prioritization.[128]

Douglass clearly believed that at this historical moment, votes for black men were more important than votes for women, and said so repeatedly and unequivocally, but he was not willing to go a step further and tell the women activists they should not agitate for their own cause. Perhaps he was simply unwilling to tell the women what they ought to do. Perhaps he was wary of the standard for radical action that Phillips articulated in his December 1865 editorial response to Stanton. If having enough votes to pass Congress was the criterion for deciding what issues radicals ought to pursue, Douglass knew that black rights could be thrown over as impracticable almost as quickly as women's rights. At a June 1866 meeting of the Friends of Human Progress, Frederick Douglass took his characteristic position, strongly supporting black (male) suffrage but also endorsing (rather than disavowing) woman suffrage. In a powerful speech on impartial suffrage Douglass declared, "Because he is a man, the negro needs the ballot," but he also submitted two resolutions, the second of which claimed that "woman, equally with man" was entitled to suffrage.[129]

Frederick Douglass made it clear that he sided with Stanton and Anthony and not Phillips by becoming a vice president in their New York State equal rights organization. Douglass welcomed "the launching of the good ship 'Equal Rights Association'" and told Stanton there had not been another such since Noah's Ark. But though he shared her assumptions about the usefulness of joint race-and-gender organizing, Douglass also let Stanton know, deftly but firmly, that he did not appreciate her comments about "Sambo" and ignorant black men. "I have about made up my mind that if you can forgive me for being a Negro," he wrote, "I cannot do less than to forgive you for being a woman."[130] They had known each other for over twenty years, and each admired the other as an exceptional individual, but when it came to generalizing about races and sexes, Douglass was reminding her that they were both members of despised groups. Stanton ignored the implied rebuke and focused instead on the fact that Douglass did not agree with Phillips's strategy. She made sure to tell Phillips, "We had a long talk with Douglass, and he with the rest of us feel the time has come to bury the woman and the negro in the citizen."[131] Despite Stanton's willingness to employ harmful rhetoric, Douglass probably concluded that, in practice, the cause of black rights had many worse enemies and few better allies than Elizabeth Cady Stanton and Susan B. Anthony.

Anthony and Stanton confidently expected that May 1866 could bring a happy resolution of their dispute with Phillips. They thought they had the votes to convert the venerable American Anti-Slavery Society into an equal rights organization at its anniversary meeting, but when they moved to amend the Society's constitution, they were stunned because Phillips objected that "the necessary three months' notice had not been given." Aaron Macy Powell, whom they had trusted to give the notice, had not done so.[132] Having failed at their face-to-face meeting in February to persuade the women to desist voluntarily, Phillips apparently decided to enlist his ally Powell in procedural double-dealing to foil their efforts. Perhaps Stanton and Anthony could not have won a straight-up vote on reorienting the Society to their "claim the uttermost" strategy, but Phillips was unwilling to risk it. Dismayed, the women took the dispute to the floor of the meeting. The subsequent debate is mostly lost because the *NASS* suppressed all but the most cursory coverage, though the *New York World* and the *New York Tribune* sent reporters to the meeting.[133] Although Stanton and Anthony had at least one black supporter, the longtime abolitionist leader Robert Purvis, they could not muster enough support to overturn procedure, and Phillips retained control.

The Eleventh National Women's Rights Convention was scheduled for the following day, and the activist women had hoped to use the occasion to celebrate the conversion of the AASS into an Equal Rights Society. Instead they hastily moved to use the women's rights convention to create a brand new organization of their own. The American Equal Rights Association (AERA) was to be devoted to securing "equal rights to all American citizens, especially the right of suffrage, irrespective of race, color or sex."[134] Lucretia Mott became president, with Elizabeth Cady Stanton, Robert Purvis, and Frederick Douglass among the American Equal Rights Association vice presidents, and Susan B. Anthony sat on the executive committee. Lucy Stone and her husband also took on AERA leadership roles, he as recording secretary, and she on the executive committee.

Stanton opened the convention by emphasizing the urgency of the moment, saying Reconstruction was "*the* opportunity, perhaps for the century." She also expressed the hope that those who were "trained in the school of anti-slavery" would "still stand side by side in this crisis."[135] But there was little discussion of just how the organization would take advantage of Reconstruction opportunities, or how it would harmonize the twin causes of black (male) suffrage and woman suffrage. How would it relate to Wendell Phillips and his AASS, who might well be uncooperative, and where would it get the resources it needed to campaign? Because of the unexpected outcome of the AASS meeting of the previous day, many of the speeches at this first AERA meeting in May 1866 had clearly been prepared for a different occasion. Rather than addressing the direction of the new organization, many speakers responded to the theme that Stanton and Anthony had announced in the "call" to the convention—the problem of indifference and opposition among elite women who declared that they had "all the rights they wanted."[136]

Elizabeth Cady Stanton used her opening speech to respond just as she had in 1860, by pointing out that the rights of individuals were not a matter of popular demand. But she also used and emphasized the new Harriet Beecher Stowe argument that voting was a duty, and even women who did not want it would be educated by it. Stanton criticized women who "lounge on velvet couches" and remain lost in "frivolous externals."[137] These women, with their false views of women's rights and duties, made "society exclusive, religion

bigoted, and government aristocratic." Stanton proposed to speak for responsible middle-class women who repudiated the velvet couch ladies and needed
the vote to help those less fortunate: "The question I propose to you is not what
advantage you and I, who have friends, education and position, shall secure for
ourselves; but what shall we do for those who are perishing for work and
wages."[138] She said not a word about the freedmen, focusing strictly on women
and remarking only that many of the frivolous lounging ladies hailed from
"below Mason and Dixon's line."

The next speaker, the Reverend Henry Ward Beecher, provided oratorical
flourishes and star power, as he had done on the women's platform in 1860. He
too emphasized the good things women would do for the nation when enfranchised, and sounded the note not of equal rights but of special duties. "I argue
not a woman's right to vote: I argue woman's duty to discharge citizenship." In
sentimental tribute to women's sweet beneficence, he likened female influence
to the perfume of cherry blossoms or the glow of a candle in the window. Because
of women's special, spiritual powers, Beecher argued, it was "more important
that women should vote than that the black man should vote."[139] Beecher was a
prestigious voice in women's cause but he had inadvertently revealed the difficulty of holding firm to the AERA's position in favor of universal and simultaneous enfranchisement of all citizens, when he rhetorically prioritized, in the
manner of Wendell Phillips, but reversed the order and put women first.

Phillips himself then spoke, having had been invited to do so when the women
anticipated a happy merger between the AASS and the women's convention. He
used his formidable oratorical powers to "throw a pail of cold water" on the audience.[140] Phillips announced that because "Woman" was in thrall to fashion, the
ballot would be worthless to her: "Albany is nothing compared with Fashion."
Besides, he claimed, "Woman" already had power in her behind-the-scenes
influence. The southern rebellion depended upon "the enthusiasm and frenzy"
of southern women, he declared, and women were "corrupting the channels of
politics today." Having blamed "Woman" for secession and for Washington lob-
byists, Phillips even taunted the assembled women for their poverty: "A vote is a
great thing. Legislation is a large power. But money is a large power. Why do not
women make money?" It was only because they feared to be unfashionable, since
"there is nothing on the statute books to forbid" profitable employment. "No
ballot box will help you," Phillips concluded. "Go home and reform yourself."[141]
Phillips addressed the women in the hall as if they represented the shallow fri-
volity of fashionable "Woman." Of course, some of his audience was offended by
this "cold water" speech, but the order of proceedings called not for response or
debate, but for a speech by Frances E. W. Harper.

Harper refused to side with Phillips and his "Negro's hour" priority *or*
with the white woman suffrage leaders in their new organization and "claim the

uttermost" strategy.[142] She had not attended the previous AASS meeting, thus sidestepping the debate over organization, but she reacted strongly and spontaneously to the occasion by speaking about her own experiences in a way that was unusual for her.[143] Refusing to confine her concerns to the vote and positioning herself as an outsider, she reminded the group about the needs of black women, to whom the aristocratic snobs, ethereal angels, and fashionable fools discussed by the previous speakers were especially irrelevant. Harper took issue with Beecher's silly flatteries, saying, "I do not believe that white women are dewdrops just exhaled from the skies."[144] Harper spoke of her experiences of discrimination as a free woman of color in the North, observing, "You white women speak here of rights. I speak of wrongs."[145] She described her own recent treatment as a widow in Ohio, when the law seized her assets to pay her husband's debts. In conclusion she emphasized a point raised earlier by Stanton, that the ballot box would be educational for women, but sharpened it by saying explicitly that "the white women of this country" particularly needed such education. "I tell you that if there is any class of people who need to be lifted out of their airy nothings and selfishness, it is the white women of America," she said.[146]

Historians have tended to read Harper's remarks as critical, even hostile, comments on privileged white feminists.[147] Certainly she was picking up on the

Frances E. W. Harper. Manuscripts, Archives and Rare Books Division, Schomburg Center for Research in Black Culture, New York Public Library, Astor, Lenox, and Tilden Foundations.

critique of privileged women contained in both Stanton's and Phillips's remarks. But was she criticizing the activist white women in the room, like Phillips, or the frivolous women outside it, like Stanton? Perhaps it was both. Yet any hostility she felt toward AERA feminists was not enough to prevent her from attending and speaking at the second AERA meeting held in Boston shortly thereafter. The atmosphere there was reportedly harmonious and Harper's Boston speech was "happy" and "conversational."[148]

Sharp and unambiguous hostility still lay in the future. Phillips had withheld Hovey money unfairly and used devious means to retain control of the AASS, and then insulted the women and their new organization by telling them, "go home and reform yourself." Josephine Griffing probably spoke for many when she skewered Phillips for his inconsistency: "Yesterday he said the ballot, in the hands of the negro, was a talisman to bring to him every weal, and ward off every woe, while today he said that it was nothing in the hand of woman, that Albany can do nothing for us, that we must go home and go to work for ourselves."[149] Susan B. Anthony's biographer would describe a private meeting after this May 1866 AERA convention where Anthony fiercely refused Phillips's request that woman suffrage be deferred for another generation. At a meeting held in the *Standard* office with Phillips and Tilton, Anthony reportedly said she "would rather cut off her right hand than ask for the ballot for the black man and not for woman."[150] It seems likely that this story was a misdated version of the meeting held in February, since at both, Wendell Phillips took it upon himself to slap these women down. But in the AERA convention itself, Stanton still tried to defend Phillips, saying "he had spoken noble words for women the last twenty years," and his objective now "was to show women the need of doing for themselves."[151] Only in hindsight did the spring of 1866 seem rife with irreconcilable hostility between the advocates of the two causes.

In fact, within weeks, by the AERA's second meeting, Wendell Phillips had already begun to reconcile with the women's cause. In the interim, the Fourteenth Amendment had taken its final form and emerged from Congress. Although a few abolitionists like William Lloyd Garrison defended it, Wendell Phillips and Frederick Douglass denounced it fiercely for permitting the disenfranchisement of black men.[152] As Phillips did so, he took up common ground with the activists of the AERA. Phillips told the Boston AERA meeting the "hour" was "preeminently the property of the negro," but immediately added, "I stand here to plead the woman's cause," and warned that introducing the word "male" would "disgrace" the Constitution. "I wish to excite interest, everywhere, in the maintenance of woman's right to suffrage," Phillips declared. His *National Anti-Slavery Standard* editorialized in favor of amending the New York State constitution to eliminate not only "the odious property qualification for colored voters" but also "the restrictive word 'male.'"[153] Phillips was still rhetorically announcing the

"Negro's hour," but he no longer sought to stifle the advocates of woman suffrage or objected to "mingling" the two causes. He even held out an olive branch by suggesting that women were not barred from holding public office, though disenfranchised, and activists ought to consider running. On the other side, Elizabeth Cady Stanton had not repeated her obnoxious rhetoric, and in May 1866 she had seemed wary of claiming class privilege as she tried to position woman suffragists as advocates for working women.

Stanton and Anthony's opposition to the Fourteenth Amendment did not set them fatally at odds with black activists or white abolitionists who followed the lead of Wendell Phillips.[154] Stanton and Anthony misled the readers of the *History of Woman Suffrage* when they alleged, "Even in the Equal Rights Conventions the slightest opposition to the XIV Amendment called out hisses and denunciations, and all resolutions on that point were promptly voted down."[155] Not so. In fact, opposing the Fourteenth Amendment united these feminists with black activists in 1866, and their universal suffrage "claim-the-uttermost" strategy remained viable. (A few years later, Stanton and Anthony's opposition to the Fifteenth Amendment would have quite different results.) Racist rhetoric on Stanton's part and financial and organizational chicanery on Phillips's part had driven a wedge between them, and by mid-1866 they stood at the head of two rival organizations advocating two different strategies for radical action. But on the question of the hour, the Fourteenth Amendment, they agreed.

4

The Struggle for Equal Rights

"I cannot accept the honor you offer me," Wendell Phillips told the Convention of Massachusetts Workingmen who nominated him for Congress in the fall of 1866, explaining that he believed he could "serve our cause better out of Congress than in it." Elizabeth Cady Stanton deplored his decision, arguing that activists who were willing to take the plunge could clear the proverbially "muddy pools" of politics. Taking her own advice, she nominated herself as a candidate in 1866 for the New York congressional seat formerly held by James Brooks.[1] Stanton's one and only campaign document, an "Address to the Electors of the Eighth Congressional District," tried to appeal to the heavily Democratic electorate in her Manhattan district with a mixture of egalitarian idealism and free trade orthodoxy—arguing that the Republicans recognized free *men* while the Democrats recognized free *trade*, but a combination of the two was needed. She declared unambiguously for universal suffrage. But then her argument spiraled down. "In view of the fact that the Freedmen of the South and the millions of foreigners now crowding our Western shores, most of whom represent neither property, education, or civilization," were to be enfranchised, she reasoned, it was in the best interests of the nation that "we outweigh this incoming pauperism, ignorance and degradation with the wealth, education, and refinement of the women of the republic."[2] There it was again: Stanton's willingness to employ racist and elitist arguments that associated the freedmen with ignorance and degradation, with a proviso that female voters would be well-to-do, educated, and refined. Stanton lost the election, garnering just twenty-four votes.

Their different reactions to the 1866 congressional race revealed that Wendell Phillips was uneasy with politics and preferred an outsider role, but Stanton was eager, all too eager, to participate, even to the point of crafting a campaign document that catered to the prejudices of her electorate. She had carefully referred to the immigrants of the *West Coast,* who were Chinese, not the Irish who were numerous in her district. But even after Stanton's campaign-inspired lapse from equal rights principles in October 1866, the AERA's coalition across race and gender lines was not dead. For a brief interval in late 1866 and early 1867, when Wendell Phillips reversed course and funded the AERA, the organization carried on a lively campaign for universal suffrage in what they still hoped would be their bellwether state, New York. Teamwork across race and gender lines in that campaign was real, albeit sometimes flawed, but events overtook it. When southern intransigence indicated that the Fourteenth Amendment could not be the last word on suffrage, the national Republican Party finally determined to award southern freedmen the vote, and Phillips reacted to this new turn of political events by reinstating his "Negro's hour" priority. In March 1867 he cut off AERA funding and set his sights on a new goal: a Fifteenth Amendment to secure black (male) suffrage nationally. The AERA's New York hopes evaporated not only because there was no money to campaign with, but also because the leadership of the New York Republican Party fell into hostile hands. Then suddenly Kansas emerged as a new possible bellwether for woman and black suffrage—their best ever fighting chance.

Wendell Phillips's sympathy with the AERA position matured into an active alliance as a result of the congressional elections of 1866. At the polls the Republicans dueled with Andrew Johnson, nominally their president but now mostly identified with the Democrats. In vindictive and perhaps drunken speeches, Johnson bathed in self-pity and suggested that "traitors" like Wendell Phillips ought to be hanged. Repelled by Johnson's personality and his southern policy, the electorate gave congressional Republicans a smashing victory. Johnson's intransigence made radicalism look good by comparison. Sensing the shift in political tide, some northern Democrats began to argue that the Fourteenth Amendment actually offered the southern states a relatively good bargain, if by ratifying it they could prevent any further reconstruction measures and reenter the Union maintaining whites-only voting. A representational penalty might be a small price to pay to secure white supremacy and home rule.[3]

Wendell Phillips saw the danger, and he set about making New York State a firewall to stop it. He wanted New York to reject the Fourteenth Amendment and then amend its own state constitution to enact universal suffrage, thus throwing its weight into the balance of national reconstruction. Phillips needed ground troops in New York to campaign *against* the Fourteenth Amendment and *for* black suffrage: he needed Susan B. Anthony, a proven hand at running just such a campaign. He sealed the deal by endorsing her key demand as well: "We personally urge the importance of striking out the word male" from the New York Constitution, he editorialized.[4] Anthony had already named New York State as a priority, stating, "What we propose to do in New York the coming eighteen months, we trust to do in every other State, so soon as we can get the men, and the women, and the money."[5]

But would Phillips loosen the purse strings of the Hovey Fund and provide resources for "mixed" campaigning? Anthony asked him straight out, proposing a New York campaign including "a remonstrance against the proposed Con. Amendt on both grounds the Negro and woman and urging universal suffrage amendment." She requested $300 from the Jackson Fund, but also conveyed a much larger request from the AERA executive committee: they wanted $3,000 of Hovey money. "Of course our hands are tied," she wrote Phillips pointedly, "unless we can get the means to start."[6] The American Equal Rights Association's own fund-raising had yielded meager results. Small contributors pitched in, their names faithfully recorded years later in the History of Woman Suffrage, but the results were certainly no substitute for Hovey funding. "It is said ideas govern the world," Stanton had sighed wearily as she wrote fund-raising letters, "but there must be some money behind the ideas."[7]

The Hovey committee granted Anthony and her AERA the whole $3,000. Phillips thus reversed himself and the two causes of black men's and woman suffrage were allowed to "mix." The AERA kicked off this "mixed" New York campaign with a meeting in November 1866 at Tweddle Hall in Albany that attracted 3,000 people.[8] Lucy Stone, who was taking an increasingly active role, chaired the meeting and declared, "The law puts its foot alike on the colored man and the woman. Why should they not make common cause?"[9] Elizabeth Cady Stanton and Susan B. Anthony were on hand, as were Frederick Douglass, Charles Lenox Remond, and William Wells Brown, to inaugurate a cooperative effort across race and gender lines. When Anthony complimented Democrat James Brooks for his willingness to speak kindly of women's rights, Douglass remonstrated, saying Brooks's advocacy of women's rights was just "a trick of the enemy." When the discussion seemed to tilt too strongly toward women's rights, Douglass spoke up again to re-center their concerns, insisting, "The woman must take the negro by the hand."[10] But these exchanges were not hostile; indeed, applause seemed to indicate that the crowd sympathized with Frederick Douglass.[11] The only real debate arose when Henry Blackwell, revealing the brash, impulsive side of his personality, proposed an educational qualification for suffrage.[12] Douglass, Remond, and Brown opposed Blackwell's idea, as did Anthony and Stanton, on the grounds that it would leave the vast majority of the freedpeople disenfranchised. Stanton spoke sympathetically about the freedpeople's need for the vote: "The negro at the South has not the free school and cannot obtain it without first obtaining the ballot."[13]

Just as this New York campaign was getting under way, it got a boost from a publicity breakthrough at the national level. For three days in December 1866, the United State Senate debated woman suffrage.[14] A bill to enfranchise black men in the District of Columbia came to the Senate floor, and Senator Edgar Cowan of Pennsylvania (nominally a Republican but a reactionary backer of

Andrew Johnson) moved an amendment to enfranchise women as well. Cowan stated frankly that he opposed black suffrage, but if it were going to be enacted—and he conceded the Radicals had the votes to do it—he was in favor of enfranchising women as well. Cowan was cynically using a "let us be consistent" argument, and at one point he admitted that he really preferred that *neither* black men nor women would get the ballot. But he quoted at length from the woman suffragists and called them by name: "Mrs. Elizabeth Cady Stanton, Mrs. Frances Dana Gage, Miss Susan B. Anthony are on your heels," he warned the other senators. "They are after you and their cry is for justice, and you cannot deny it."[15] He was using woman suffrage to needle Radical Republicans about the inconsistency of their reasoning:

> I would ask gentlemen while they are bestowing this ballot which has such merit in it, which has such a healing efficacy for all ills, which educates people, and which elevates them above the common level of mankind, and which, above all, protects them, how they will go home and look in the face their sewing women, their laboring women, their single women, their taxed women, their overburdened women, their women who toil til midnight for the barest subsistence, and say to them, "We have it not for you; we could give it to the negro, but we could not give it to you."[16]

Cowan's ploy got traction because a few truly radical senators refused to be cowed by the threat of ridicule and took up his proposal on its merits. Henry Anthony of Rhode Island characterized Cowan's amendment as the product of mischievous intentions but declared he intended to vote for woman suffrage anyway.[17] Ben Wade boldly affirmed that he favored equal rights for every citizen regardless of race or sex.[18] Benjamin Gratz Brown quoted Caroline Dall about European women voting and affirmed that although he recognized "the impolicy of coupling these two measures," he would vote yes.[19] But more orthodox Republicans like Lot Morrill of Maine hastily rejected woman suffrage in order not to be embarrassed by it: "While we intend to give every male citizen of the United States the rights common to all, we do not intend to be forced by our enemies into a position so ridiculous and absurd as to be broken down utterly on that question."[20] Even in this group, however, the women scored a few points: Richard Yates of Illinois and Henry Wilson of Massachusetts both objected to having woman suffrage combined with black (male) suffrage and so opposed Cowan's amendment, but both also vowed they would support woman suffrage at a later time in a separate measure.[21] Ultimately Cowan's amendment was defeated 37–9, and of the nine who voted in favor only three—Anthony, Wade, and Brown—were true radicals, while the rest were either opportunistic

Democrats or conservatives of Cowan's stripe.[22] Woman suffrage had been defeated, but action at the national level had generated good press and reinforced the New York State campaign while the Washington, D.C., black suffrage bill moved along toward final passage.[23] Salmon P. Chase, who listened to the Senate debate, thought the embarrassment weapon had revealed its limits: "Some people who are anxious to defeat black suffrage endeavor to put its friends in an inconsistent position by propositions for woman suffrage but with little success actual or probable."[24] Though the Senate vote was not close, neither was the bill to enact black (male) suffrage in Washington harmed.

Working in the afterglow of the Senate debate, Anthony's teams of speakers went on to hold AERA meetings in over thirty different New York locations during the winter of 1867. At conventions in New York City, Utica, Rochester, Syracuse, Peterboro, and Penn Yan, speakers included Sojourner Truth as well as the prominent spiritualists Cora Hatch and Emma Hardinge. The AERA tried to organize local Equal Rights Association chapters along the way.[25] Campaigning in teams of two to four, AERA speakers were a mix of black and white, male and female. Anthony and Stanton were joined by Parker Pillsbury, Charles Lenox Remond, Louisa Jacobs (daughter of Harriet Jacobs), and newcomers Olympia Brown, Bessie Bisbee, and Elizabeth A. Kingsbury.[26] Anthony described the meetings as "capital," "the very best kind." "Remond never did better work," she wrote, and about Louisa Jacobs and Bessie Bisbee she reported, "It is great to have two new helpers and young too."[27]

These meetings permitted the woman suffrage activists to test and fine-tune their message with live audiences. They began to emphasize the needs of working women through "bread and the ballot" speeches arguing that the vote would raise wages and improve working conditions.[28] This new pitch might solve the problem of women's indifference to the vote, which had been thrown up to them repeatedly: Anthony declared, "We felt for the first time . . . that we had actually the women with us."[29] And Elizabeth Cady Stanton, mindful of her black allies, refrained from any offensive references to "Sambo" or "degraded" black men in her two major public statements, an appeal to the legislature and another major AERA speech.[30] The contents of Stanton's "Reconstruction" speech remain in doubt, though the National Anti-Slavery Standard's coverage at the time suggests it was also an even-handed appeal for both women and black men.[31]

Inside the AERA, teamwork across race and gender lines was not always smooth. Henry Blackwell betrayed the AERA's alliance between black and white when he published a broadside in January 1867, over his signature and apparently at his own expense, addressed "to the legislatures of the southern states."[32] These were the lily-white Johnson governments with their white supremacist Black Codes, and Blackwell proposed that they could "safely" accept black suffrage by enacting woman suffrage at the same time and using it to maintain white control: "Your four millions of Southern white women will counterbalance your four millions of negro men and women, and thus the political supremacy of your white race will remain unchanged." With this scheme, he wrote, "The negro, thus protected against oppression by possessing the ballot, would cease to be the prominent object of philanthropic interest."[33] Blackwell's proposal indicated muddled thinking or bad faith or both, because it assured southern whites of their continued supremacy while describing southern blacks as "protected against oppression." By casually consigning the freedpeople to the tender mercies of their former masters, it destroyed any pretense that Blackwell, an officer of the AERA, was equally concerned about black men's rights and women's rights. His proposal received at least some publicity in the South.[34] There is no surviving record of reaction from Anthony or Stanton, but Blackwell's proposal cannot have been helpful to an organization that purported to support equal rights for all.[35] Perhaps because they were embarrassed by Blackwell's pamphlet, Lucy Stone and Henry Blackwell held back from the New York campaign team and chose instead to campaign by themselves in New Jersey.[36] Stone was becoming more active through the AERA, but she was not rebuilding her ties with Stanton and Anthony; instead, she stuck close by her husband even as he revealed a tendency to act like a loose cannon.

On the other hand, some black men were less than supportive of woman suffrage. As Charles Lenox Remond canvassed New York for universal suffrage with an interracial team of speakers, one of the white women thought he tilted his message: "We could seldom get through a meeting without some bitter words from Mr. Remond illustrating the injustice done to the Negro as so much greater than the wrongs of women. He seemed to have no patience with the presentation of our claims." The tilt seemed a minor matter, however, because she concluded, "On the whole, however, the trip was most agreeable and apparently successful."[37]

A more disturbing incident occurred at a January 1867 meeting to form a Pennsylvania chapter of the AERA, when almost all the black men present disavowed woman suffrage. As Lucy Stone told the story, "Eight colored men gathered around us during the recess, and said they thought women were well enough represented by their husbands etc." According to Stone, only one black man, Robert Purvis, supported woman suffrage, and he predicted that the great mass of other black men "would give their influence like a dead weight against the equality of women.'"[38] Lucretia Mott, Elizabeth Cady Stanton, and Susan B. Anthony were all in attendance, and even if they were not present when this episode occurred, they would soon have heard Stone's account of it.[39]

Lucy Stone seems to have taken Purvis at his word, but he was in no position to speak for the black community. The son of a British cotton broker, Purvis had inherited a substantial sum, married into the well-to-do Forten family, and been educated at Amherst. A charter member of the American Anti-Slavery Society, he devoted himself to a career as a reformer and took the lead in radical circles in Philadelphia, organizing Underground Railroad support and encouraging black enlistments during the war. He always supported women's rights, as did his wife and daughter. But Purvis lived in luxury as a gentleman farmer and had little contact with the freedpeople of the South. He was also estranged from Frederick Douglass, who at one point described Purvis's inheritance as "blood-stained riches."[40] The leadership among black activists did not speak with one voice, nor did the leaders of the women's movement, which made cooperation across race and gender lines more complex. And as northerners black or white tried to generalize about the southern freedmen, they often did so with limited information.

AERA cooperation across race and gender lines, which was flawed but real, came to a screeching halt when Phillips and the Hovey Committee cut off the AERA funding in early March 1867. Anthony got the word and then kept the speakers in the field just long enough to fulfill prior engagements.[41] "We thought we had sure promise of at least $3,000 from the Hovey fund," she explained to Gerrit Smith, and so they had incurred debts printing tracts, and they owed salaries to some of their speakers. She begged Smith for cash to pay Remond's salary, saying he was especially needy, and angled for a new lead on a major donor. "It must be that new purses will open to our cause," she wrote Smith. "Have you not power with George Peabody? Can you not move some generous soul to put ten yes twenty thousand dollars into our hands to push on our work of agitation?"[42] Peabody, a wealthy banker, had just given a million dollars to support African American education in the South.[43] Anthony had a vivid understanding of what the loss of funding meant, telling Smith, "As I sat in that Senate chamber today and yesterday I felt continually, if only we had the *money* we could carry the Convention up to *equal suffrage* without a shadow of a doubt."[44] Anthony lamented that "nearly the *whole[Hovey] Fund is gone* and gone to the breaking the chains of chattelism," even though the letter and the spirit of Hovey's will meant every dollar should help fight for rights for "*all men* and *all women*."[45]

Phillips and the Hovey Committee had acted in response to a new turn of events on the national political scene that made the Fourteenth Amendment far less important. Although Andrew Johnson had been repudiated at the polls in November 1866, he continued to defy Congress and encouraged the southern states to refuse to ratify the Fourteenth Amendment. It thus became evident that additional measures beyond the amendment would be needed to reconstruct the South, and in this extremity, moderate Republicans became reconciled to enfranchising southern black men. Congressional Republicans finally united behind a plan of Military or Radical Reconstruction Act, which they passed over Johnson's veto on March 2, 1867. They imposed black (male) suffrage in new state governments to be formed in the ex-Confederacy.[46] In this way, section two of the Fourteenth Amendment, which provided for reduced representation in case black men were not enfranchised (and also contained the offending word "male") was rendered virtually a dead letter, although the amendment itself went on to be ratified in its original form.[47] The marriage of convenience between Wendell Phillips's AASS and the women's AERA based on their shared opposition to the Fourteenth Amendment was over.

As the anniversary meetings in May 1867 approached, veteran activists of the AASS and the AERA faced an interesting question. With black male suffrage having now been imposed by the Republicans throughout the South, might it be time for radical activists to take their demands a step further to encompass woman suffrage? Wendell Phillips thought not: he restated his "Negro's hour" priority with new vehemence, demanding that black (male) suffrage be protected and extended nationwide by an additional, Fifteenth Amendment.[48] At three successive meetings, the activists again debated whether the cause of woman suffrage should be joined with, or defer to, black (male) suffrage.[49] Henry Ward Beecher coined a phrase that crystallized the ideas of those who challenged Phillips on strategy: it was not the "Negro's hour," Beecher said; instead it was "the favored hour" for all: "If you have great principles to make known, this is the time to advance those principles. . . . Whatever truth is to be known for the next fifty years in this nation, let it be spoken now, let it be enforced now."[50]

Phillips opened the AASS annual meeting that May by congratulating the abolitionists as they stood "on the very eve of the accomplishment" of all the society had ever asked—they needed only stand firm in the "war of opinion and politics." Phillips claimed the AASS had a special role to play precisely because it had "no President to elect, no candidate to carry, no party to watch," and positioning the AASS as political outsiders, he declared they would not descend to "the bargain and truckle, to the bicker and huckstering of a political level."[51] Urging the impeachment of Andrew Johnson and warning against Ulysses S. Grant as a man without principles, Phillips assured AASS members the Republican Party would "use public opinion just as fast as we will manufacture it," but he also characterized the effort to influence Republicans as if it involved sacrificing principles: "I only want that if we sell out," Phillips vowed, "we sell in the dearest market and get the best price."[52]

Although he positioned himself and his organization as ultra outsiders, Phillips still saw women's aspirations as distracting, and when Stephen Foster and Anna Dickinson moved resolutions to add women's rights to the organization's goals, Phillips ruled them out of order as "ill-timed and premature."[53] Phillips kept the AASS platform closed to the topic of women's rights, but he did not escape criticism. Thomas Wentworth Higginson, who had commanded black troops during the war and spoke with the authority of his experience in the

South, endorsed "the extension of the suffrage to the women of the South"—
referring to black women and acknowledging their importance in the community
of ex-slaves.[54] Phillips also took a jab from Lucretia Mott who said "she regarded
the exclusion of the question of Equal Rights as rather hypocritical, and hoped
that in another year it would be found to be in order."[55]

The AERA met the very next day, and given the unanticipated, disjointed nature
of its founding meeting the year before, this was the first chance for the advocates
of universal suffrage to discuss among themselves how best to combine the two
causes. Wendell Phillips did not attend, but Anthony and Stanton were joined by
old hands like Purvis and Remond, Mott and Gage, as well as new faces like the
Irish immigrant James Haggerty and the Iowa cavalry commander, Colonel Charles
Moss. The meeting's distinctive feature was the presence of a strong black woman
who endorsed suffrage for both blacks and women. Sojourner Truth had been specially urged to attend because Anthony and Stanton hoped that a black woman
demanding the ballot could cut through inconsistency and challenge false assumptions among Phillips's backers.[56] Truth attended but she was nobody's puppet.

Truth immediately addressed the new situation in the South: "Now colored
men have the right to vote, and what I want is to have colored women have the
right to vote." If she had to "answer for the deeds done in my body just as much
as a man," she reasoned, her rights should be the same. Truth conceded she was
"about the only colored woman that goes about to speak for the rights of the colored woman." But she challenged Phillips's "Negro's hour" priority because she
did not see "the Negro" as all male. Truth put her case for the vote in economic
terms and described black washerwomen victimized by husbands who "go about
idle, strutting up and down; and when the women come home, they ask for their
money and take it all, and then scold because there is no food."[57]

The previous winter Frances Dana Gage had made a similar point. Gage
described ex-slaves who favored legal marriage in order to control their wives
who earn "as much money as we do and then they goes and spends it," and freedwomen who resisted "because when we are married in the church, our husbands
treat us just as old massa used to, and whip us if they think we deserve it."[58]
Though the *Christian Register* had indignantly denounced the report as a slander
on black women, Gage repeated it in this AERA meeting, and Truth was thus
adding her own testimony to such reports.[59] Truth challenged the assumption
that black women had the same interests as black men and could rely upon them
for protection: "There is a great stir about colored men getting their rights, but
not a word about the colored women," she declared, "and if colored men get
their rights, and not colored women theirs, you see the colored men will be masters over the women, and it will be just as bad as it was before. So I am for keeping the thing going while things are stirring."[60] Truth made a powerful case that
it was the "favored hour" for all, but her portrait of black men was not flattering.

I SELL THE SHADOW TO SUPPORT THE
SUBSTANCE.

SOJOURNER TRUTH.

Sojourner Truth, in an image she sold to support her activist work. Photographs and
Prints Division, Schomburg Center for Research in Black Culture, New York Public
Library, Astor, Lenox, and Tilden Foundations.

When the AERA proceedings resumed the next morning, the participants had had opportunity to mull over Truth's challenging remarks. Charles Lenox Remond defended black men, expressing confidence that when armed with the ballot they would "heartily acquiesce in admitting women also to the right of suffrage." Lucretia Mott promptly disagreed, saying "the colored men would naturally throw all their strength upon the side of those opposed to woman's enfranchisement."[61] The meeting was coming close to a discussion of the intentions of black men and the interests of black women—a thorny subject because it went well beyond the ballot and depended upon limited information and anecdotal reports out of the South.[62] Truth's picture of idle black men sponging off hardworking black women was enough to give everyone pause: it could undermine black men's claims to rights and even inadvertently furnish ammunition to white racists. Before anyone could respond further, George Downing rose to change the subject.

Downing represented the free black men of the North, most of whom still did not have the right to vote and who suddenly found themselves at a disadvantage compared with the newly enfranchised ex-slaves of the South. As the owner of a lucrative catering and hotel business, Downing was one of the foremost African Americans in the country. His father had run a successful oyster house in downtown Manhattan, and Downing combined a business career with a leading role in antebellum agitation for black rights and desegregation.[63] He had accompanied Frederick Douglass in the small delegation of black men who had visited the White House to challenge Andrew Johnson face to face the previous winter. Unlike Remond, Downing was not much interested in harmonizing black and women's rights; in fact, he would make a practice of attending equal rights meetings and demanding that woman suffrage advocates should cede precedence to black men.[64]

Ignoring Truth's challenge, Downing turned to Stanton and Mott and asked if they were opposed to the enfranchisement of black men unless women gained the ballot at the same time. At first Stanton resisted prioritizing and argued for simultaneous enfranchisement: "As a matter of principle, I claim it [the vote] for all." Politicians might plead they could do only one thing at a time, she said, but that was no reason why "philosophers" or activists should not enunciate broad principles. Then, however, she shifted to "a narrow view of the question," much as she had shifted to arguments based on "expediency and precedent" in her 1860 speech to the New York legislature. "When Mr. Downing puts the question to me, are you willing to have the colored man enfranchised before the woman," she declared, "I say, no; I would not trust him with all my rights; degraded, oppressed himself, he would be more despotic with the governing power than even our Saxon rulers are."[65] Downing offered a resolution saying the AERA "rejoiced" at the increasing sentiment in favor of suffrage for the black man, and said he understood Mrs. Stanton "to refuse to rejoice at a part of the good results to be accomplished if she could not achieve the whole." Stanton again conceded that Downing understood her correctly:

> If we are to have further class legislation, she thought the wisest order of enfranchisement was to take the educated classes first. . . . If all men are to vote, black and white, lettered and unlettered, washed and unwashed, the safety of the nation as well as the interests of woman demand that we outweigh this incoming tide of ignorance, poverty and vice, with the virtue, wealth, and education of the women of the country.[66]

Stanton thus associated black male voters with ignorance, degradation, and vice, compared them to women of "wealth and education," and argued, just as she had in her campaign pitch the previous fall, that women must be enfranchised to "outweigh" black men in an expanded electorate. Although she did not actually oppose black men's right to vote, her comments certainly tended to undermine it. By assuming that all women were middle class, she also undermined Sojourner Truth and working women of both races. Arguing for the priority of black men, Downing had pointedly ignored Truth as if a black woman's perspective was insignificant—and Elizabeth Cady Stanton had done likewise. The debate stopped short as it became clear that Downing's motion could not find a second, but the focus of the meeting had shifted.

Instead of talking about how to combine the two causes, Downing and Stanton led the way to polarized positions: he by advocating male priority and black men first; she by speaking for middle-class white women's superior claims based on class status and white privilege. Susan B. Anthony tried to reframe the issue as a matter of individual rights, rejecting the premise of setting priorities for social groups and refusing to be drawn into weighing comparative cases, but she had limited success. As recently as three months earlier, the partisans of black male suffrage and woman suffrage had been able to work together, but this debate suggested that without an active campaign to cement practical cooperation, conflicts could easily come to the fore. The new situation in the South, where Radical Reconstruction imposed black (male) suffrage, could make white woman suffragists feel that when it came to voting rights, black men's glass was more than half full. But northern black men, aware of the white South's resistance and often lacking the vote themselves, saw the black man's glass as more than half empty.

When Sojourner Truth spoke a second and a third time at this AERA meeting, she directed her comments toward activists themselves, especially men. She said, "I know how hard it is for men to give up entirely. They must run in the old track.

I was amused how men speaks up for one another. They cannot bear that a woman should say anything about the man, but they will stand here and take up the time in man's cause."[67] She was clearly criticizing Downing, but she softened her criticism by suggesting that if radical men wanted to change their ways, "We will help you out."[68] As the convention drew to a close, Truth commented on the mood of the meeting. Unlike many of the antislavery meetings she had attended, at the AERA she found nobody grumbling and muttering, nobody wanting to "pop up" in order to "gainsay." "I never saw so many people together and nobody tryin' to hurt anybody's feelin's," she said.[69] By insisting on the harmony of this group, she was apparently suggesting that Downing's initiative and Stanton's response had not been as disruptive as it appeared.[70] Although Truth smoothed over the dispute, she did not moderate her demand for the ballot or back off her implicit critique of Phillips's "Negro's hour" position. But she also offered no support to Stanton's elitist vision of woman suffrage. Instead, she concluded her remarks by suggesting that activists needed to examine their own motives.

Perhaps not surprisingly, this debate spilled over into a third meeting, the New England Anti-Slavery Convention in Boston where Wendell Phillips presided.[71] Because it was a convention rather than an organization meeting, he could not so easily rule an unwelcome woman suffrage motion out of order. Phillips again urged the antislavery faithful to stick to their unfinished business, which included not only guaranteeing black (male) suffrage but also blocking Grant's presidential candidacy.[72] Without Anthony, Stanton, or Truth present to debate him, Wendell Phillips was able to persuade this Boston audience by arguing that the antislavery societies must stick to their original purpose. He tried to dispatch the question of black women's rights by insisting that abolitionists were obliged only to put black women on a par with white women, no more. In this meeting William Wells Brown took up George Downing's role, telling the audience that at the equal rights meeting in New York "one of the leading women"—Stanton—had "said that the country would be safer in the hands of the educated and enlightened women of the country than in those of the ignorant and degraded colored man."[73] While Stanton did speak "as if all the women in the land were educated and enlightened, and all the colored men ignorant and degraded," as Brown charged, the stronger argument for woman suffrage had come from Sojourner Truth.[74] By taking a shot at Stanton, Brown was, like George Downing, turning away from Truth's straightforward demand for the vote. In these meetings it had been ominously easy for activists to take up polarized and stereotypical positions that pitted black men against white women, and overlooked black women's claims.

Probably no one understood the limitations of his arguments better than Wendell Phillips. He had declared the "Negro's hour" strategy to ensure that congressional efforts to pass black men's voting rights would not be encumbered by woman suffrage, but already he was repositioning himself as a moralistic outsider. The more he did so, the less reason he had to exclude woman suffrage from his platform. He was leaning on the slender reed of precedent and organizational mission when all his life he had preferred to stand upright on broad grounds of right and justice. Challenged by Sojourner Truth, rebuked by Lucretia Mott, and badgered by Parker Pillsbury, Phillips finally reminded the Boston meeting of "the gratuitous service of the *Standard* in behalf of the woman's rights cause" and claimed credit for having "voted liberal contributions" to what he called "the Equal Rights movement."[75] Taking a defensive tone, he was apparently trying to take credit for the Hovey funding of the AERA campaign, without mentioning that he had cut it off.

In addition to losing its funding for New York campaigning, the AERA's efforts to influence the New York Constitutional Convention faced other problems. As the state legislature's 1867 session proceeded, it became increasingly clear that the radical wing of the state Republican Party was in disarray and they had few insider allies. James Wadsworth, Anthony's candidate in 1862, had been killed at the Battle of the Wilderness, and Horace Greeley was so erratic and opportunistic that his "leadership" was worse than useless.[76] Governor Reuben Fenton was a radical, but he was also an "affable" lightweight.[77] Seward and Weed had long dominated the state Republican Party but they made the mistake of backing President Andrew Johnson and were brought down with him.

The contest in the legislature for the open U.S. Senate seat in January 1867 signaled the shift in New York Republican leadership: Roscoe Conkling emerged victorious. Conkling hailed from the same Mohawk Valley region where Stanton had grown up, but the emergence of this utterly cynical operator helped doom the women's hopes.[78] Conkling used and abused family, friends, rivals, and reformers. His attitudes toward women were unenlightened. He left his wife at home in Utica and carried on a not-very-secret affair with Kate Chase Sprague in Washington, but when it threatened to make him an object of ridicule, he hastily dropped her. While serving in the House in 1866, Conkling had been a persistent advocate of inserting "male" in the Fourteenth Amendment, and he was at best reluctant on black (male) suffrage, let alone woman suffrage.[79] Conkling was the quintessential "spoilsman," a self-seeking politico who stood in the path of all radical reform in New York State.

Under the circumstances, the AERA's best hope in the upcoming Constitutional Convention was to empower political outsiders via special rules for the election of delegates. The New York legislatures of 1801 and 1821 had extended the right to vote for convention delegates to disenfranchised classes, and if that precedent were followed, women and all black men could demonstrate the viability of their own participation and help to elect outsider delegates such as Frederick Douglass, Henry Ward Beecher, or Gerrit Smith.[80] Elizabeth Cady Stanton presented an address to the New York Senate and Assembly judiciary committees on January 23, 1867, making the argument to expand the electorate for convention delegates. As she urged the legislators to live up to "No taxation without representation," she made her familiar point about the effect of the combination of suffrage and tax law by citing the case of a black woman in Seneca Falls who owned $1,000 worth of property and paid taxes on it from the first dollar.[81] But her cause needed help from legislators, and her only real ally was state senator Charles J. Folger, an upstate lawyer.[82] The legislature left New York voter qualifications unchanged. In fact, "the leading men of the dominant party" were reportedly averse to holding any constitutional convention at all.[83] They went ahead but adopted a plan of electing at-large delegates that weighed against the women's cause, and ultimately that of black men as well, because it assured that a corps of party hacks would be scrutinizing every convention proposal for partisan risk and advantage.[84] The election for delegates left the women with only two solid allies inside the New York Constitutional Convention: Folger and George William Curtis of *Harper's Weekly*.

With diminishing hopes of any practical gains for women, the AERA leaders had to regard the 1867 New York Constitutional Convention as principally an occasion for propagandizing their cause, but scanty press coverage threatened to deny them even that. In January, Stanton's speech to the judiciary committees was "published in full by the metropolitan press and many of the leading journals of the State," but the *NASS* ran it with several passages omitted, the very passages in which she was at her most radical, making sharp comments about Republican policy.[85] Helpful press coverage in the *Tribune* was also endangered. Horace Greeley adopted Wendell Phillips's position, telling Anthony and Stanton, "This is the 'Negro's hour,'" so "Your first duty now is to go through the state and plead his claims."[86] They indignantly refused, just as they had rebuffed Phillips a year earlier. What would people think of Greeley, they asked—or Henry J. Raymond of the *Times*, or James Gordon Bennett of the *Herald*—if, while disfranchised, they pressed the claims of others to the ballot first? Greeley thought the two women flattered themselves, and threatened that if they refused to defer to black suffrage, they would forfeit all further help from him and his *Tribune*.

Greeley used his position as chair of the convention's Committee on Suffrage to push through black male suffrage but reject woman suffrage, ignoring petitions with over 20,000 signatures in its favor.[87] Greeley's report stated, "However defensible in theory, we are satisfied that public sentiment does not demand [woman suffrage] and would not sustain an innovation so revolutionary and sweeping."[88] Anticipating this, Anthony and Stanton arranged to have George William Curtis present a woman suffrage petition just at that moment, a petition headed by the name of "Mrs. Horace Greeley," and Greeley was thus embarrassed in front of the galleries.[89] Greeley was so offended by their maneuver that he angrily confronted Anthony and Stanton and refused to shake their out-stretched hands.[90]

During this period of convention maneuvers in the spring and early summer of 1867, Stanton once again elaborated arguments that included invidious remarks, both in her clash with Downing and in a public letter to the *New York Tribune*. In each case she began with an egalitarian argument: if suffrage is a natural right of all citizens, then, "women and negroes will no longer be known in law or constitution." But in each case she also proceeded to a second line of argument: if suffrage is judged "a gift of Society," then "it would be wiser and safer to enfranchise the higher orders of womanhood than the lower orders of black and white, washed and unwashed."[91] She resumed using these alternative arguments after the AERA's active alliance with black men had lapsed.

The New York Constitutional Convention was a disappointing affair for woman suffrage *and* black suffrage. On the opening day, one delegate shot and killed another delegate who had seduced his wife, and the ensuing scandal dis-tracted much of the press corps from substantive issues.[92] As the convention dragged on week after week with little accomplished, the press became impa-tient and dismissive, and discussions of woman suffrage were ignored along with everything else.[93] The culmination of this neglect came in July, when George William Curtis delivered a wonderful speech in favor of woman suffrage, a speech "regarded by many as the convention's finest."[94] But it was not published in any of the New York newspapers and the women had to print it as a tract in order to get it circulated. In antebellum days, a speech like Curtis's would have been printed in the *Liberator* or the *Standard*, and prob-ably in the *Tribune* as well. Now the *Liberator* was dead and the *Standard* and the *Tribune* passed it over. The *New York Times*, which also did not run the speech, informed its readers only that "Mr. Curtis' eloquent plea for female suffrage is looked upon as a huge joke."[95] With conservatives like Roscoe Conkling and opportunists like Horace Greeley atop New York's dominant Republican Party, not only was woman suffrage going nowhere, but black (male) suffrage was endangered.[96] The convention simply adjourned, fearing even to submit black (male) suffrage to the voters.

Just as their hopes for New York were waning, the activist women saw an alternative emerge. The Kansas legislature voted in February 1867 to strike out both "white" and "male" from its constitutional clause defining eligible voters, and Kansas would hold simultaneous referenda on both black men's and women's suffrage in the fall of 1867.[97] Kansas was not as influential as New York State, but in many respects it was a more manageable bellwether target. It had a small electorate—only about 25,000 votes were cast in the 1866 congressional election—and therefore the face-to-face "retail politics" of speech and debate had a better chance to carry the day.[98] Kansas Republicans included a cohort of seasoned abolitionists who had backed John Brown and were favorable to radical measures, and local feminists had begun agitating for woman suffrage as early as 1859.[99] Kansas Republicans also outnumbered Democrats two or three to one, so the measure could carry even if there were considerable "roll-off" among the party faithful.[100] Although the state did need outside speakers to help persuade Republican voters on a subject that was new to many, imported speakers would face few charges of "carpetbagging" given that every adult (except the Native Americans) was a recent immigrant.[101] And because woman suffrage and black (male) suffrage were separate ballot measures, a voter's position on one measure need not affect his vote on the other, and cooperative campaigning might get a "yes" vote on both. By the time of the May 1867 AERA meeting, Kansas was talked of as the best chance for its universal suffrage goals.

The activists needed money to campaign, however. Anthony at first assumed that the Kansas Republican Party, having voted for the women's measure in the legislature, intended to support it as a party measure at the polls, which meant

Leavenworth, Kansas, in 1867, when referenda on both black suffrage and woman suffrage were on the ballot. Kansas State Historical Society.

they would literally print it on the party ticket along with black (male) suffrage. "If the men of Kansas will only vote the *"strait," "clean"* ticket—to strike out both *"white male"* then we shall have the first brick knocked down and all the rest must go likewise," she wrote.[102] But soon she realized that Kansas Republicans were not united in support of these referenda. Kansas woman suffragists asked her to send "efficient speakers" to canvass the state, and Anthony published a notice telling *NASS* readers that "what we need is MONEY," mentioning the sum of $10,000.[103] The AERA had opportunities to campaign in other states as well, and "every mail" brought requests for articles, lecturers, and tracts. But the organization was flat broke—in fact $617 in debt—and she had to send word to Kansas, "The fact here at the east is, that *we cannot meet expenses.*"[104] At the AERA meeting Anthony called for funds to send "a dozen able men and women" and 100,000 tracts to Kansas.[105]

But Wendell Phillips and the rest of the Hovey Committee refused funding for Kansas, where black (male) suffrage agitation would have to "mix" with women's cause. Lucy Stone, who was devoting much hard work to Kansas, was so furious she urged Anthony to challenge the Hovey trustees publicly over their tendentious interpretation of the will. "I think you should insist that all of the Hovey fund used for the *Standard* and Anti-Slavery purposes, since slavery is abolished, must be returned with interest to the three causes which by the express terms of the will were to receive *all* the fund when slavery was abolished."[106] By demanding all the money "with interest," Stone sounded as though she had learned from her husband's entrepreneurship, but Anthony did not follow through on Stone's recommendation. Phillips seemed determined to ignore Kansas: he made a speaking tour of the West himself in the spring of 1867, delivering over sixty lectures and traveling over 12,000 miles but never setting foot in the battleground state of Kansas.[107]

The women's rights funding situation took a disastrous turn in August 1867, when the Jackson will case was finally settled.[108] Shortly after Francis Jackson's death in 1861, an heir had sued to challenge the bequests to abolition, fugitive slaves, and women's rights. Although Jackson's intentions were clear, and he had begun giving to those causes while he was still alive, a question arose about whether the will contravened the laws of Massachusetts. Six years later the Massachusetts Supreme Court finally ruled. The judge found that Jackson's two bequests to antislavery and fugitive slaves were valid charitable bequests and had not been terminated or destroyed by the fact that chattel slavery had in the meantime been abolished. But the judge ruled that women's rights was *not* a legal charity and that clause of the will was void, so the women's rights legacy must revert to the heirs of the deceased.[109] Anthony seems to have ignored the news of the initial court decision when it came out in February 1867, perhaps regarding the case as still unresolved. With hefty Hovey funding flowing into the AERA campaign at that point, there seemed no need to panic. But then Hovey Funds were shut off and now they had lost the remaining Jackson Fund as well.

The Jackson verdict reflected both Massachusetts law and lawyerly incompetence. Compared with other states, Massachusetts had a particularly narrow reading of what constituted a charitable trust.[110] In the will, the women's and the antislavery bequests were worded differently. The article on antislavery left money in trust to prepare and circulate books, newspapers, and other material "to create a public sentiment that will put an end to negro slavery," while the article on women's rights simply left money "to secure the passage of laws granting women, whether married or unmarried, the right to vote, etc." Relying on English common law precedents that defined a charity as "according to the laws, not against the law," the court ruled that the women's rights bequest "cannot be sustained as a charity" because it "differs from the others in aiming directly and exclusively to change the laws."[111] This difference in wording, on which the case turned, pointed to sloppiness in drawing up the will—and the lawyer at fault was Wendell Phillips.[112]

Nor had the women's cause been adequately represented in the Jackson will case. Anthony had "never known a thing about it" until after the case was decided.[113] Unless Phillips consulted with Lucy Stone—of which there is no record or hint—the majority of the named trustees of the Jackson women's rights fund had not been apprised of the legal situation or represented in the proceedings. Acting alone, Wendell Phillips almost certainly put more energy into defending the antislavery bequests.[114] Anthony was outraged, and she suspected Phillips was at fault: "Isn't it passing strange that any court should decide that heirs could take money *given by the owner during his lifetime into our hands* for the special purpose of securing the ballot for women?. . . . It does seem to me that if the money had been *in my hands*, and I a *Lawyer*, I could and would have saved it from so unrighteous a fate."[115]

But it was impossible to quarrel with Wendell Phillips about the Jackson Fund because he had invested the original bequest so well that it had doubled in size.[116] With the lawsuit having effectively frozen the fund since 1861, he apparently had in the meantime advanced some money out of his own pocket. In fact, Phillips would continue to disburse Jackson funds until the fall of 1867, perhaps by using the investment returns after having repaid the original bequest to the heirs.[117] There was nothing to do but inform people that the Jackson Fund had been lost. Anthony wrote to Kansas suffragist Sam Wood, "The Jackson Fund—$1800 is taken out of our hands by the Massachusetts Court," and to Martha C. Wright, "You see our little trust fund—$1800 of Jackson money is wrenched from us."[118] Garrison and Phillips went on to feud over how to spend the balance of the fund, and only one trustee, Henry Bowditch, seems to have recalled Jackson's original intentions. Bowditch told Garrison at one point that if Francis Jackson were still alive, he would want the *whole* balance of his money given over to women's rights.[119] But the women got not a penny. Stanton and Anthony and Stone's AERA limped into Kansas, their very best fighting chance, without the resources they needed.

‖ 5 ‖

Kansas

As spring turned to summer in 1867, Susan B. Anthony grew increasingly worried. Lucy Stone and Henry Blackwell had gone out to Kansas in the spring to campaign for universal suffrage on behalf of the American Equal Rights Association, and it was good to see Stone return to full-throated activism. But who could follow them? Anthony had hoped to raise enough money to send "10 good speakers, 5 women and 5 men," to persuade Kansas voters to support two referenda giving the vote to black men and to all women.[1] She wanted charismatic speakers like Frederick Douglass, Henry Ward Beecher, or Anna Dickinson, who ordinarily expected compensation and who certainly needed their travel expenses paid.[2] She and Elizabeth Cady Stanton were ready to go themselves and "do the work for nothing," but they too needed money to cover travel, not to mention printing tracts.[3] Anthony's letters reveal an almost pathetic scramble: "We need money as never before. I have to take from my lean hundreds, that never dreamed of reaching thousands, to pay our traveling expenses. . . . What an awful undertaking it looks to me. . . . I never was so nearly driven to desperation."[4]

Far out of sight of the eastern abolitionists, the women of the AERA were about to enter into an actual campaign to win woman suffrage, and an allied chance to win black suffrage. Each referendum item seemed to have a good, fighting chance, although Kansas was the first-ever referendum on woman suffrage, and referenda on black suffrage had been defeated elsewhere in recent memory. But they knew they had to mount a campaign, and Phillips held tight to the Hovey money, refusing even to fund black suffrage campaigners. In the absence of eastern resources, a faction fight inside the leaderless Kansas Republican Party determined the outcome.

This state-level test for black and woman suffrage took place in an unusual and promising political environment. As a territory in the 1850s, "bleeding Kansas" had been a lawless cockpit where armed partisans of free soil and slavery tore into each other, but it was also a frontier where millions of acres of Native American lands were opening for white settlement, setting off a massive wave of speculation in land and railroads.[5] Republicans outnumbered Democrats more than two to one in Kansas, though the party was badly factionalized, and the charismatic chieftain of the dominant faction, Senator Jim Lane, had committed suicide less than a year earlier.[6] The state Republican Party had a strong radical heritage dating from the antebellum free soilers and John Brown, but there were plenty of apolitical opportunists, too. Some antislavery Kansans had combined high ideals and low motives with distinctive flair: the so-called Jayhawkers used antislavery sentiments as an excuse for common thievery.[7] In the senatorial contest in the state legislature in the winter of 1867, dollars and promises had changed hands freely but no successor to Lane emerged, and leadership of the Kansas Republican Party was still up for grabs, along with the fate of the referenda.[8]

When Lucy Stone and Henry Blackwell traveled to Kansas in early 1867, they turned to the most prominent Kansas politician supporting women's rights, state senator Samuel Newitt Wood, and to Stone's relative, former governor Charles Robinson. Sam Wood was a "rough and ready" competitor who flayed his opponents with quick-witted sarcasm, but was also a sincere advocate of women's rights.[9] Having begun his career as a supporter of the Liberty and Free Soil parties, Wood had been an antislavery Democrat before he joined Republican ranks. A champion of the people against big money and professional politicians, he would later in life gravitate to the Greenback-Labor party and the Farmer's Alliance. Wood had alienated supporters of black suffrage by persistently amending black suffrage measures to include women, and voting against them when they did not.[10] But Wood had enemies mostly because he fought the Lane faction with an irritating combination of high ideals and expedient short-cuts. In his latest exploit, Wood helped to pass a measure creating new judgeships and then promptly secured an appointment for himself at a nice salary.[11] Supporters of woman suffrage worried, with some justification, that "Judge" Wood's advocacy did the cause more harm than good.[12]

Stone's other ally in Kansas was Charles Robinson, the brother-in-law of her brother Bowman Stone. Robinson went to antebellum Kansas as an agent of the New England Emigrant Aid Company, an organization that subsidized free soil settlers with everything from transportation to Sharp's rifles, but also a corporation that sold stock and promised profits to its investors.[13] Many regarded Robinson as self-sacrificing and patriotic, others saw him as self-seeking, and there was apparently evidence to support both views.[14] Although Charles Robinson led the fight for a free state in Kansas and was elected its first governor, he lost out to Jim Lane in a no-holds-barred struggle for Republican Party power and withdrew to private life, having concluded, as he told his wife, that

Sam Wood. Kansas State Historical Society.

"sheisters" constituted a working majority in Kansas politics.[15] When Lane committed suicide, however, Robinson considered returning to politics and he
angled for the open Senate seat, looking for support from both Sam Wood and
from "the Johnson or Democratic members of the legislature." Anti-Lane
Republicans like Robinson and Wood had cooperated or "fused" with Democrats
in 1864, and that history put their party loyalty in doubt and lent a suspicious
appearance to their advocacy of woman suffrage.[16] Lucy Stone wrote that she
found "no such love of principle here as I expected to find. Each man goes for
himself, and 'the devil take the hindmost.'"[17] But she seems to have been unaware
that Wood and Robinson carried such heavy political baggage.

Under the leadership of Robinson and Wood, Stone and Blackwell helped to
organize a State Impartial Suffrage Association at Topeka on April 2, 1867, aiming to ensure that the word "impartial" implied votes for women as well as black
men. At the state Republican convention the previous fall, the party had
endorsed "impartial suffrage" but left that fine-sounding term undefined.[18]
Stone proudly described Robinson as having "pulled every wire and set every
honest trap" to set up the Impartial Suffrage Association. Blackwell also

thought Wood was "a political genius" and Robinson "a masterly tactician," but their clever moves threatened the State Republican Central Committee by setting up a competing organization.[19] The *Leavenworth Daily Conservative*, which had been the organ of the Lane faction and boasted a circulation double that of any of its rivals in the Missouri River Valley, questioned the legitimacy of the Impartial Suffrage Association, asking if the intent was to "usurp the prerogatives" of the Republican Party.[20]

The Topeka meeting also went forward without the state's foremost black leader. The brother of John Mercer Langston and an important national figure in his own right, Charles Langston had long fought for black suffrage in Kansas.[21] He had taken a stand in favor of women's rights during his student days at Oberlin, and he had worked with Susan B. Anthony in 1865.[22] Charles Langston and Sam Wood had clashed before, when the question of suffrage was before the state legislature in February, and at that time Langston had upbraided Wood for "all the *dodging*, all the frivolous amendments" impeding the black suffrage measure.[23] Langston opposed having "male" amended to the proposition to remove the "white" qualification for voting. However, once a compromise enabled the two measures to be passed separately, Langston changed his position and wrote to assure Wood he was willing to cooperate: "There shall be no antagonism between me and the friends of woman suffrage."[24] Langston understood that adding women to a black suffrage bill in the legislature could cost it votes, but once the two issues had been passed separately and submitted separately to the voters, opposing one did not rule out supporting the other.

Charles Langston proposed two separate but parallel pro-suffrage campaigns. "I am ready to take hold and work for my race," he wrote, suggesting that his own speeches could be scheduled in coordination with Wood's Impartial Suffrage Association speakers. "I hope the cause of Negro suffrage will receive much help from your organization in canvassing the state," he urged. "I hope you will send out two sets of speakers and hold two sets of meetings. One to urge carrying the proposition for woman suffrage and the other that of Negro suffrage." He proposed to spend two months campaigning himself. Langston assumed (wrongly) that Wood's organization had "plenty of money," but he knew that resources in the black community were virtually nonexistent: "We are trying to raise money enough to send one or two good colored speakers into every community in the state. You must help us. Our people will do what they can."[25] Langston sent this detailed proposal to Wood while Stone and Blackwell were in Kansas, but there is no record of any response to it. Ironically, Wood had previously laid out a similar plan in a letter asking for help from the AERA back east, in which he too welcomed parallel positive campaigning.[26]

Instead of cementing an alliance with Langston, Robinson and Wood were busy flirting with their sometime allies in the Democratic Party. Robinson told

Charles Langston (center) in a detail of a group portrait of the "Oberlin Martyrs" at the Cuyahoga County Jail, 1859. Courtesy of the Oberlin College Archives, Oberlin, Ohio.

Wood, "I have talked it [woman suffrage] up with the Democrats and they are disposed to talk favorably of the *male* proposition. This will prevent the Republicans from openly fighting it."[27] Robinson's rationale was absurd: if the Democrats "talked favorably" about woman suffrage, it could only arouse suspicion of the measure among Republicans. If Robinson was negotiating with the Democrats, it was not because they could help woman suffrage (much less black suffrage, which the Democrats loathed). Probably, instead, he was still angling for their support for higher office, as he had the previous winter. But Lucy Stone and Henry Blackwell apparently bought in to Robinson's scheme without understanding its sources or its implications. Stone told Stanton, "The Democrats all over the State are preparing to take us up," and Blackwell reiterated, "The Democratic leaders are quite disposed to take us up. If the Republicans come out against us the Democrats will take us up."[28] Events would later show that Democratic support was practically the kiss of death for woman suffrage in a state where Republicans outnumbered Democrats so heavily.

The formation of the Impartial Suffrage Association at Topeka on April 3 still left the posture of the regular Republican Party organization toward the black and woman suffrage referenda unresolved. Stone, Blackwell, and Robinson heard rumors that a meeting of the Kansas Republican State Central Committee involved a "plot" to get the party to drop any support for woman suffrage, and they hurried to foil it.[29] The result seems to have been a meeting where everyone showed up and all parties politely agreed to support "impartial suffrage" but still failed to define the phrase. On the surface the meeting was harmonious and speakers predicted that both propositions would carry by large majorities.[30] The upshot was apparently a de facto division of labor whereby elements of the Impartial Suffrage Association focused mostly on the woman suffrage measure, while other Republicans who placed a higher priority on black suffrage would move forward on that front. The "Impartial Suffrage Association" of Lawrence, for example, was composed entirely of women and therefore probably gave its efforts to the woman suffrage referendum.[31] Meanwhile, Charles Langston toured the eastern part of the state speaking for black suffrage.[32]

Not everyone was satisfied to support both propositions. The *Leavenworth Daily Conservative* had originally dismissed woman suffrage as a farce when it was first proposed by its arch-enemy Sam Wood.[33] It now complained that woman suffrage was merely a ploy to defeat black suffrage.[34] By the spring of 1867, formerly indifferent Lane Republicans, like Republicans elsewhere, were concluding that giving the vote to black men was a party necessity, at least in the South. But many members of the Lane faction were Johnny-come-lately to the cause of black rights: Jim Lane's career was marked by startling shifts of position and his followers were united by patronage rather than policy.[35] The *Daily Conservative* had come to support black suffrage but its endorsements could be left-handed: one editorial, for example, tried to encourage support for black suffrage by warning that disenfranchised classes were dangerous, conjuring up the specter of armed revolution by black men.[36] The tenor of some of the *Conservative*'s editorials suggests that its opposition to woman suffrage was animated more by hostility to Sam Wood than by principled concern about black men's voting rights.

Lucy Stone and Henry Blackwell's campaign in the spring of 1867 elicited much positive response. The novelty of a woman speaking in public together with the entertainment value of any public event in isolated prairie settlements brought out good crowds, and Stone was persuasive as ever. Stone's tour also flushed out some vociferous opponents of women's rights, including John A. Martin, the editor of the *Atchison Daily Champion*, and J. W. Roberts of the *Oskaloosa Independent*.[37] Accused of being "free lovers," Stone and Blackwell published the testimony of the minister who married them.[38] They did not, however, use their time in Kansas to insist that Sam Wood mend fences with Charles Langston. In fact, if Henry Blackwell was distributing his pamphlet, "What the South Can Do," a black suffragist like Langston might have found Blackwell more objectionable than Wood.[39] Nor could Lucy Stone draw upon a prior acquaintance with Charles Langston, as Susan B. Anthony might have done. Stone wrote to Anthony about "an ignorant black preacher named Twine who is very confident the women ought not to vote," and remarked, "These [black] men *ought not* to be allowed to vote before we do, because they will be just so much more dead weight to lift."[40] Reverend Twine was one of the community leaders Charles Langston recruited to speak for black suffrage. As Wood and Langston continued to work at arm's length, Stone and her husband were less than helpful in forming a coalition of black men and white women. On the contrary, Stone concluded, as she informed Anthony, "The Negroes are all against us."[41]

In any other year, the events unfolding in Kansas might have attracted more national attention, but in 1867 the South was rocked by the enfranchisement of the freedmen under Radical Reconstruction.[42] In the summer and fall of 1867, southern black men began to vote, first for delegates to state constitutional conventions, and then in the new state government elections. Hidebound Republican politicians executed political somersaults and discovered newfound respect for black citizens.[43] The northern Republican Party hastened to form a Union Congressional Republican Committee to raise money and recruit talented speakers, especially "able and active colored men," to send as party agents into the South.[44] The Union Leagues, functioning as Republican auxiliaries, set up chapters and enrolled members throughout the South; they quickly became the most important political organizations among the freedpeople, overshadowing or displacing black rights organizations like the National Equal Rights League that Frederick Douglass had helped to found in 1864.[45] Spurred by the fear that the ex-slaves might be credulous enough to vote for their former masters, northern Republicans were determined to inculcate Republicanism among southern blacks in order to control the Congress and the Electoral College. Republican speakers who went south often sought to curb economic radicalism, trying to persuade their new southern recruits that political power should not be used to obtain "40 acres and a mule."[46] Some of the northerners who visited and spoke in 1867 also carried another, equally conservative, message about gender: they advised freedmen to put freedwomen in their proper (i.e., domestic) place.[47] Republican efforts in the South drew off speakers who had been invited to Kansas, including Anna Dickinson and

Senator Henry Wilson, and Charles Langston's brother, John Mercer Langston.[48] Frederick Douglass, who spent much of the year on a national speaking tour but found no time to visit Kansas, was working with the Republicans when he went south.[49] Frances Harper also lectured extensively in the South during the summer of 1867, probably with the help of Republican subsidies.[50]

But orators were badly needed in Kansas. Based on their speaking tour in the spring, Lucy Stone and Henry Blackwell warned that canvassing the state would be critical in the coming referenda. Blackwell predicted, "I think we shall probably succeed in Kansas next fall *if the State is thoroughly canvassed, not else.*"[51] Stone explained that the local Republicans could not be relied upon to do the canvassing and outside help was needed: "It will be necessary to have a good force here in the fall."[52] Elizabeth Cady Stanton remarked on the local talent shortage, noting "not a man in the state" could make a really good speech.[53] Yet Wendell Phillips and the Hovey committee continued to refuse to subsidize any campaigning that might have to be "mixed." Instead the Hovey trustees voted $1,000 to support Parker Pillsbury's lecturing on "impartial suffrage" but carefully confined his labors to New England.[54] They also supported Henry C. Wright, who spent a month or two in Ohio lecturing in favor of black (male) suffrage, the only suffrage on the ballot there.[55]

The AERA could afford to send only one speaker to Kansas. Olympia Brown was a single woman of thirty-two and an experienced extemporaneous speaker with a rugged constitution, a level head, and an unflappable demeanor. A graduate of Antioch and an ordained Universalist minister, Brown had attended her first woman's rights convention in 1866, when the AERA was formed.[56] She had promptly been hired by Susan B. Anthony to join the team of AERA speakers who toured New York State during the previous winter, and she agreed to take a leave from her pastorate in Massachusetts in order to spend the summer and fall campaigning for woman suffrage in Kansas.[57] A second AERA speaker, young Bessie Bisbee, was later sent to join Brown but proved too inexperienced to be a great help.[58] Olympia Brown arrived in Kansas on July 1, and she carried the burden alone until Anthony and Stanton arrived in the fall.

The Kansas campaign entered a new phase in early June when Charles V. Eskridge of Emporia opened fire on woman suffrage, publishing a remarkably scurrilous and abusive letter. He revived the free love charge against Stone and Blackwell, who were no longer present to defend themselves, and he predicted that if woman suffrage passed, a man's "children would be taken from his control," and "his wife would become the common property of the whole prostituted race." Eskridge led with the charge that woman suffrage was the work of "scheming, tricky politicians" who proposed it with the intention of defeating black suffrage.[59] A Baptist minister, the Reverend Isaac Kalloch, publicized Eskridge's screed in

Olympia Brown. Schlesinger Library, Radcliffe Institute, Harvard University.

the newspaper he edited, the *(Ottawa) Western Home Journal*.[60] Like Eskridge, Kalloch had begun by complaining, some months earlier, that the real purpose of woman suffrage was to weaken the cause of black suffrage.[61] Eskridge and Kalloch gave the appearance of concern about the fate of the black suffrage measure, but in fact, neither man was much of a supporter. For example, in an editorial nominally endorsing black (male) suffrage and predicting it would carry, editor Kalloch described blacks as inferior in "intellectual ability, and moral worth, and possible elevation."[62] Soon other Republican editors began expressing surprising anxiety—shedding crocodile tears—for black suffrage.[63]

Eskridge and Kalloch did not have to gin up their animosity toward women's rights but their main purpose was to bid for personal advancement and party leadership. Both were ambitious men currently out of office, although Eskridge was a member of the Republican State Central Committee and Kalloch had a platform as the editor of a Republican paper. Kalloch had made a play for the Senate seat in January 1867, but his bid ended in humiliating failure, while Sam Wood emerged from that same legislative session with a judgeship and a cause—woman suffrage—that was bringing him statewide attention.[64] It was beginning to dawn on some Republicans that woman suffrage, by enfranchising a large number of new Republicans, might empower the likes of Sam Wood or Charles Robinson and change "the complexion of political affairs," as one editor nervously remarked.[65] The *Leavenworth Daily Conservative* warned that woman suffrage threatened to bring about a "*political* and social revolution."[66] Eskridge and Kalloch realized that playing on that threat could present a political opportunity: by driving a wedge between the two causes they could open for themselves a path to power in the leaderless Republican Party. Eskridge was a ruthless adversary—"of the samurai caste in Kansas Republicanism"—and Kalloch was hiding a sex scandal, having been caught in adultery with a parishioner in Boston.[67] The woman suffrage cause had tangled with a pair of versatile, energetic scoundrels.

Woman suffrage supporters tried to respond to Eskridge's gambit. A genuine supporter of suffrage for both blacks and women such as Kansan James Rogers could dismiss Eskridge's letter as "billingsgate" and provide information to show that Eskridge only "pretends to be in love with negro suffrage."[68] Sol Miller, a principled radical with a long memory, recalled that Eskridge had played along

Isaac Kalloch. Print Collection, Miriam and Ira D. Wallach Division of Art, Prints and Photographs, New York Public Library, Astor, Lenox, and Tilden Foundations.

with the *pro-slavery* territorial officers as long as they had control of the patronage, only to swap allegiance when the state became heavily Republican.[69] But Sam Wood was not so effective because his own credentials on black rights and party loyalty were shaky—he had been willing to block black suffrage at earlier points, and he had been a party rebel. Wood had to concede, "Suppose I was wrong a year ago, is that an argument against being right now?" and his old enemies like the *Leavenworth Daily Conservative* editor made hay.[70] Wood might have helped himself by cooperating with Charles Langston, who again wrote to say he was willing to be part of a differentiated but coordinated effort to pass both measures, but once again Wood apparently ignored the letter.[71] Other leaders shrank back: Governor Crawford, nominal head of the Impartial Suffrage Association, found that Indian trouble in the western part of the state absorbed his time, and Charles Robinson made himself scarce.[72]

In July, Eskridge opened a new chapter of violent personal abuse in a second letter. He taunted Kansas women who wanted the vote as "male women," accused them of having used the word "slut" in their published communications, and prophesized that if they voted, the legislative session in Topeka would degenerate into an orgy. Eskridge attacked male supporters of woman suffrage, calling one a "poodle pup," and implying that another had had an affair with a "girl" who worked in his office. Woman suffrage, he declared, "would break down any party, demoralize society, overthrow the Christian religion," and ultimately bring about "a conflict of races and sexes."[73] Eskridge's second letter made it clear that Kansans who supported the woman suffrage cause would be subject to public vilification. Sam Wood's wife, Margaret, although a supporter of woman suffrage, had at first questioned his decision to push it because she had anticipated just such a "deluge of abuse."[74]

The sheer ferocity of Eskridge and his ilk probably intimidated women who wanted their rights but lacked the courage for a public donnybrook. For example, Mrs. J. H. Slocum carried a pro-woman suffrage petition around Eskridge's hometown of Emporia in early August and gathered seventy-four ladies' names. But after she presented this petition to a local newspaper editor, Jacob Stotler, who had cast his lot with Eskridge, Stotler chose to publicize the petition with the comment that seven influential women had since asked their names to be *removed*. By transferring those seven names Stotler came up with a list of sixty-nine local women who had NOT signed—thus, he concluded triumphantly, showing that a majority of Emporia ladies opposed woman suffrage.[75] Mrs. Slocum protested that if seven names had been withdrawn, it looked "very much as though somebody had taken them to task for what they had done, and that the pressure was so strong that they could not resist it." "It is just this intimidating policy that we protest against," she wrote, "Women *dare not* assert their views on this subject." Editor Stotler proceeded to prove her point by publishing a lengthy editorial abusing Mrs. Slocum as "prevaricating," and threatening, "The quieter she keeps—the less 'personals' she has in the newspapers, the better she will get along."[76]

Eskridge demonstrated how to use sexual innuendo to slime woman suffrage proponents. Opponents spread ugly gossip about Bessie Bisbee and took any chance to make coarse jests at the expense of woman suffrage advocates.[77] One accused Olympia Brown of being a free lover who had come to Kansas only for the privilege "of wearing short dresses and riding about the country with fast young men."[78] Jacob Stotler slyly added *Venus's Miscellany,* a pornographic weekly published in New York City, to a list of Kansas newspapers that favored woman suffrage.[79] The *Oskaloosa Independent* equated female voters with the scantily clad dancers in a touring "leg show": "It is proposed to admit women who thus expose themselves for the gratification of depraved tastes to the ballot-box...to purify politics!"[80] On election eve the *Leavenworth Daily Conservative* asserted that woman suffrage would foster "infanticide and criminal abortion."[81]

Woman suffrage supporters who were tempted to fire back might score points, but at the expense of seeing the whole discussion degenerate into personal vituperation. Sol Miller could not resist responding to an anti-woman suffrage article by one Colonel Utley: "The burden of Utley's song is, that if women were allowed to vote, politicians would come around to log roll his wife; and that probably whenever he came home, he should find some political rake holding a private interview with her in the parlor, log rolling her. It is to be presumed that Utley is better acquainted with his wife than any one else, and knows what weak points to guard against, etc."[82] Such responses did nothing to reverse the dynamic Eskridge had set up, whereby the public discussion of woman suffrage had become heavily sexualized and thus difficult or impossible for women themselves to participate in. One woman who attended an Eskridge-Kalloch meeting claimed she never in her life had heard "such low jests and blackguardism." She described how in the speeches a local woman was attacked by name as a free lover, and when that woman's mother tried to defend her daughter's reputation, she was hissed and jeered, and the meeting "almost broke out in a row."[83] Both Lucy Stone and Susan B. Anthony believed that the opposition of men like Eskridge and Kalloch would boomerang, saying, "The opposition is low and scurrilous, and will really help more than it will hinder," but it probably did discourage many women.[84]

Meanwhile the Democratic press was mounting its own nasty campaign against black suffrage. Democratic papers fed racism by printing a steady diet of "news" reports from the South alleging that freedmen were refusing to work, stealing everything that was not nailed down, and demanding to marry white women.[85] One Democratic paper ran a story about the marriage of a black man and a white woman in New Jersey, and warned that when black men had political rights, "They will force themselves into your families and feeling 'free and easy' will take unwonted liberties."[86] It also described a minor scuffle at an emancipation celebration as if it had been a black riot in which "almost every man had a revolver and almost every other woman a razor."[87] Democrats charged that black men, when they got the vote, would oppose extending it to white women—thus reinforcing the Eskridge-Kalloch line that woman suffrage and black suffrage were at odds.[88] Democrats' opposition to black suffrage probably gained traction due to the fact that the black population of Kansas had mushroomed between 1860 and 1865 from less than 1,000 to over 12,000, encouraging white backlash.[89] With Republicans slamming woman suffrage and Democrats howling down black suffrage, negative campaigns were the order of the day. This was a dangerous development for black male suffrage because, as the New York and Connecticut experiences had shown, a referendum was unlikely to pass without strong positive campaigning. The Republican State Central Committee met at Topeka on July 24 and conceded that some more vigorous positive efforts on behalf of black suffrage were needed, but it did little.[90]

The AERA lacked the resources to support a strong positive campaign. They could not bring in charismatic radical speakers from back east who might have altered the local dynamics or rallied and reconciled supporters of black (male) suffrage and woman suffrage. There was simply no money. Susan B. Anthony wrote to Sam Wood on August 9 explaining that the eastern help he had counted on would not be coming, informing Wood that the Jackson Fund had been taken away "and *we are left without a dollar.*" As she explained, far from being paid, "*every speaker who goes to Kansas* must *now pay her own* expenses *out of her own private purse.*" She warned Wood not to contract "*debts* under the impression that *our Association* can pay them—for *it cannot.*"[91]

As the summer progressed, Eskridge and Kalloch were reinforced by the *Leavenworth Daily Conservative*, and more Republican newspapers lined up behind them.[92] The *Daily Conservative* continued to show more spirit in slamming Sam Wood than in boosting black suffrage.[93] At one point while urging passage of the black suffrage amendment, it observed that Congress held the power to grant the vote to black men and was sure to do so in the future. Given the extent to which concerns about the fate of the party nationally had previously undergirded support for black suffrage in the state, this passing remark was quite a concession. Although the *Conservative* argued that Kansans should still enfranchise black men on their own, it was also implying that a "No" vote would not much matter.[94]

Searching for ammunition to fire back, Sam Wood began publishing his own newspaper, the *Chase County Banner*, beginning August 3. Apparently he realized, when eastern help was not coming, that he needed to fight this out with other Kansas politicians. In the first issue Wood did not oppose black suffrage, though he could not resist a passing fling at his opponents' concern for "the lovely darkey."[95] Instead, Wood tried to attack his critics by arguing that *they* were not truly or strongly in favor of black suffrage, recalling recent votes against it by several members of the Republican State Central Committee. But Wood lacked credibility on this point. The *Daily Conservative* dismissed him as a "snarling cur" and insisted, "The fact is, our Executive Committee individually and as a body heartily favor the proposition to enfranchise the colored men."[96] Though Wood soon fell ill and ceased almost all activity, he had returned negative campaigning for negative campaigning, and failed to support black suffrage while he was still regarded as the leading voice of the woman suffrage movement in the state.[97]

Charles Langston allowed himself to be drawn into an open quarrel with Sam Wood, perhaps urged on by the *Leavenworth Daily Conservative*.[98] In a public letter of August 20, Langston blamed Wood for falsely reporting that black men were opposed to woman suffrage. "The colored men as a mass have made no public expression of hostility to the rights of woman by resolution, motion, printed document or speech." True, he admitted, a few had expressed this senti-ment at a meeting in Topeka the previous winter, but "an overwhelming majority" was in favor of woman suffrage. Langston complained that Wood and his com-rades had previously ignored black men and their suffrage efforts: "If they expected or desired the cooperation of colored men in this great movement, why did they not meet with us when repeatedly urged to do so, and aid us in orga-nizing such a movement as all interested thought best?"[99] Langston had every right to complain of Wood's uncooperative behavior, but he apparently did not notice how often the false reports of black-woman conflict came from woman suffrage *opponents,* who took the pose of merely reporting what they had heard. As those opponents kept repeating the "indisputable fact" that woman suffrage advocates wanted to defeat black suffrage, they were egging on Charles Langston to "prompt retaliation" against Wood and company.[100]

Hearing it said that black men opposed woman suffrage, Wood took the bait. He issued a campaign sheet that read, "The fight that the negroes, backed by McBurney, Eskridge, Hoyt, Thad Walker and others are making against woman suffrage is about sure to kill negro suffrage in the State.... We confess that if these scalawags are going to defeat female suffrage, we hope and pray that negro suffrage may be defeated at the same time. If either class must wait, let it be the negro."[101] Wood thus appeared to confirm the Eskridgeite charge that the advo-cates of woman suffrage opposed black suffrage.

The burden of defending the AERA's principled position in favor of both refer-enda fell heavily on Olympia Brown, who was speaking two or even three times a day and traveling great distances across the prairies.[102] As Brown soldiered on through the heat of the summer, she increasingly took Wood's place as the most prominent exponent of woman suffrage, and soon she too was charged with assailing black men. Sol Miller reported, "Miss Olympia Brown, in her speech at Fort Scott, is said to have very indignantly declaimed against placing the dirty, ignorant, degraded negroes ahead of white women."[103] This report originated with the *Fort Scott Press* and was publicized by the *Atchison Daily Champion*, both vociferous opponents of woman suffrage.[104] There is no independent evidence to confirm that Brown said this. She herself denied it, and at least one contemporary immediately smelled a rat: the *Lawrence State Journal* said the language imputed to Brown was not "reasonable or probable" and suggested that the *Fort Scott Press* reporter "introduced and sandwiched his own ideas for those of Miss Brown."[105] Other suspicious reports fanned the flames of blacks-versus-women. One anonymous "correspondent" reported that in Wyandotte black people said "the women have no right to vote and they hope they will be defeated." Another reported that in Miami County woman suffragists were excluding "people of African descent, particularly those of the female persuasion" from their meetings.[106] False reports could be amplified through the echo chamber of the numerous newspapers that were swinging behind the Eskridge gambit, while honest journalists who supported both black and woman suffrage found it impossible to track down the facts and publicize the truth fast enough to blunt their impact.

Sam Wood's undeniably anti-black comments in his newspaper lent an air of plausibility to the charge against Olympia Brown, and Sol Miller repeated the report about Brown's Fort Scott comments with an implicit question mark over it. But he added, "The *Chase County Banner*, which is doubtless under the editorial supervision of Sam Wood, takes substantially the same position." Miller wrote, "A condition of the question is fast approaching which we have endeavored to avert—a bitter antagonism between negro and female suffrage."[107] Miller warned presciently that if this antagonism continued, it would defeat woman suffrage and perhaps black (male) suffrage as well.

Of course, there was more than a grain of truth in all the reports of conflict between blacks and women. Wood *had* snubbed Langston, repeatedly, and Wood and Langston *had* publicly assailed each other. Twine probably *did* perceive that Lucy Stone thought him "ignorant," and he had to feel insulted when Wood sarcastically called him "Brother Twine." Twine complained that woman suffrage was being used "as a club with which to beat out our brains" and at one point simply declared neutrality on the issue.[108] Still, Twine understood that the friends of black suffrage were mostly also friends of woman suffrage, and he tried to be politic: he explained publicly that he regarded woman suffrage as "foreign to American politics," but nevertheless, "as opposition to this question might prejudice the enfranchisement of his race, he was in favor of it."[109] Understandably, when Langston and Twine tried to be supportive of woman suffrage, they could sound grudging.[110]

For her part, Olympia Brown was probably grudging, too, because she carried unpleasant memories of divinity school, where one group of students had particularly resisted her admission and tried to force her out. Her opponents then had been young Republicans who were busy demanding freedom for blacks "while opposing with all their might the education of women in the Theological school."[111] Brown sometimes did not confront racism while campaigning. In her speech at Wyandotte, she clarified that she "did not oppose negro suffrage, said she was in favor of it, but chose to devote her efforts specially to the enfranchisement of women."[112] However in Shawnee Town, a rough place where "they *hate* the Negro beyond measure," she was careful to mention only woman suffrage. "If anybody else goes there," she wrote Sam Wood, "be sure and warn them against speaking of the Negro it is the roughest place I ever saw."[113] When Brown thus tailored her arguments to fit her audience, it was a natural speaker's tactic but not helpful to the black-and-woman suffrage coalition, and in at least one instance Brown may have gone further and argued comparative cases. In a debate at Oskaloosa, Brown reportedly suggested that women were more deserving of the ballot than black men.[114] Susan B. Anthony was at one point moved to tell her, "Olympia, you have no right to say one word more for women than you do for the Negro."[115]

Nevertheless, the real friends of both causes saw that it was crucial that they stick together, and Woodson Twine and Olympia Brown tried gamely to do so. They held joint meetings at which woman suffrage proponents and black men publicly stated their mutual support. For example, in Atchison the friends of impartial suffrage met in early September at a restaurant owned by a black entrepreneur, Nick Johnston. After dinner, there were toasts, in the course of which Olympia Brown said, "Extend the ballot—enfranchise my brother (pointing to Mr. Johnston) and the race he represents—give the ballot to myself and the sex I represent, and you will strengthen the bulwarks of liberty." To which Nick Johnston responded, "I want the ballot, but not for myself alone; the ladies should have it too." He acknowledged the two measures had a rocky history, but affirmed their common interests.[116] At another such meeting, in Highland on September 24, Olympia Brown addressed the black community "and explained that she and the other friends of female suffrage were not enemies of negro suffrage—they had been among the most earnest workers to secure freedom and civil rights." She declared, "Reports to the effect that she had spoken against negro suffrage were false." The black audience, pleased with her remarks, unanimously adopted a resolution in the name of "the colored people of Kansas" announcing "We deprecate any conflict between the friends of the two propositions," and endorsing "Impartial Suffrage, without regard to sex or color."[117]

To undermine the impact of such joint appearances and mutual support, the Eskridge-ites relied on false reports and slanted coverage in cooperative newspapers, and they may even have sent ringers into some meetings to cause trouble. At a suffrage meeting in Atchison, for example, while Olympia Brown and Bessie Bisbee spoke, Reverend Twine had a seat on the stage in a show of mutual support. But after the meeting adjourned, some members of the audience stayed behind and began calling derisively for Twine while "hooting, stamping, and whistling." When Twine rose and made a few remarks, he was "interrupted by jeers and mock-applause." The anti-woman suffrage press then reported the incident as if it reflected upon the audience as a whole and showed hostility toward blacks among woman suffrage supporters.[118] The Democratic press in effect supported the Eskridge-ites by refusing to credit expressions of mutual support. A Democratic reporter who covered a Charles Langston speech complained that Langston spent an hour and fifteen minutes talking about black suffrage and only five minutes talking about woman suffrage, and concluded, "The probabilities, however, are that Langston, like all the negroes, is opposed to female suffrage, and that his five minutes talk in its behalf was but a blind."[119]

The Eskridge gambit was converted into an organized campaign against woman suffrage at a meeting held in Lawrence on September 5 to create an Anti-Female Suffrage State Committee.[120] The meeting trumpeted the principle of "manhood suffrage" but did this ambiguous phrase mean *favoring* suffrage for black men, or just *opposing* suffrage for women? The answer was revealed when "Not one word was uttered in favor of Negro suffrage from first to last."[121] The Anti-Female committee members were so conservative on a range of issues that a radical editor dubbed them the "Kansas Association of Political Fossils." The fossils hoped to take over political offices while defeating the referendum, intending to "vote down the proposition and vote all its supporters out of office."[122] Radical Republicans who supported both referenda warned that the false friends of black suffrage were in fact undermining it and questioned the need for the new organization.[123] Editor Joel Moody called the Anti-Female faction a "bastard offshoot" of the Republican Party composed of "a few of the forlorn, degraded office seekers," and he charged the new editor of the *Leavenworth Daily Conservative,* George Hoyt, with having "sold his influence in the Republican party for a miserable mess of potage."[124] But Hoyt and the Anti-Female crowd turned out to have more power than Moody and the radicals to define Republicanism in Kansas. On September 18 the Republican State chairman announced that the party would canvass the state on behalf of striking out the word "white" from the constitution, while its speakers could "express their individual convictions upon other issues if they desire." Since the announced speakers included Eskridge and other prominent anti-woman suffragists, it was obvious the Anti-Female committee had at that point gained effective control over the party apparatus.[125]

Losing support within Republican Party ranks, proponents of woman suffrage did what they could. The arrival of Anthony and Stanton in early September gave the campaign a shot in the arm. Stanton prevailed upon Governor Robinson to drive her to her speaking engagements, and by all accounts she was effective and impressive even to opponents.[126] The two AERA leaders brought tracts and generated headlines, and the Hutchinson family singers added spirit and interest to their meetings, while Olympia Brown kept up her own killing pace. Woman suffrage supporters also fought back by appealing to temperance sentiment, though this move may have served only to deepen opposition among Germans and saloonkeepers.[127] Eastern supporters tried to help by sending details of Kalloch's seamy past in Boston, which were then publicized. Anthony began to refer to the Anti-Female canvassers as "old Jack Falstaff and his followers."[128]

Stanton and Anthony made a point of affirming their support for black (male) suffrage. When Stanton and Olympia Brown spoke at Wyandotte, they supported both referenda so unambiguously that the local Democratic paper taunted, "They went the whole figger, for the woman and the big buck nigger."[129] Anthony was eager to squelch the blacks-versus-women story, and she spoke out strongly, saying "certain editors" were mistaken in supposing the advocates of female suffrage were, in any sense, opposed to black suffrage.[130] Anthony knew Charles Langston from her earlier residency in Kansas, and she had especially strong reason to broker reconciliation because the needs of black women were fresh in her mind. On the trip west, Anthony had spoken at a meeting in a large African American church in St. Louis, and there she "told the men that they must not stop with asking equal rights for themselves, but must include their wives and daughters also." To her delight, when she delivered that line, the women of the congregation "brought down the house," bursting out in applause and even stamping their feet.[131] But when Anthony got to Kansas and spoke out for both black (male) suffrage and woman suffrage, the editor of the *Leavenworth Daily Conservative* said she was "ignorant of conditions in Kansas," and suggested that she ought to read Sam Wood's latest publication.[132]

Charles Langston briefly cooperated with the Anti-Female committee by appearing on the same stage with Eskridge and Kalloch in Leavenworth on September 17.[133] He thus gained access to a larger audience, but he "afterwards vowed he would never be caught in such company again for it did the negro far more harm than good."[134] The most insightful Kansas editor, Sol Miller, explained, "A persistent effort has been made by the enemies of female suffrage to get up a fight between that and negro suffrage." "The negroes are very anxious to vote," he wrote, "and their pretended champions have poured such stuff as this into their ears, until they have begun to think that the female suffrage people are their worst enemies, and some of them have been led into public demonstrations against the woman movement."[135] He reproached Langston for appearing with

Kalloch and Eskridge, but Langston himself already regretted it and sought to mend the damage with a letter explaining that his position on woman suffrage had been misunderstood and he would "resist all the attempts that are being made to draw him into the fight on that question."[136]

In lieu of outside speakers who could have helped to unite the advocates of black suffrage and woman suffrage, editorial support in key eastern newspapers like Greeley's *Tribune* and Tilton's *Independent* might have educated Kansas voters on the merits of both measures. Years later, Anthony and Stanton recalled that those papers were scanned "wistfully" for "some inspiring editorials on the woman's movement," and argued, "Those two papers, extensively taken all over Kansas, had they been as true to woman as to the Negro, could have revolution-ized the state."[137] Stone and Blackwell worked to lobby eastern editors, and on October 1 the result, an appeal "to the voters of the United States," was pub-lished in the *New York Tribune*.[138] The appeal was widely reprinted in Kansas newspapers, and the signers were an impressive list, including the whole con-gressional delegation from Kansas as well as congressional Radicals like Ben Wade and George Julian, and familiar abolitionist names, including Garrison, Phillips, and Beecher. Yet the appeal was terse rather than eloquent. It simply declared that on the principle that governments derive their just powers from the consent of the governed, "Suffrage is the right of every adult citizen, irrespec-tive of sex or color. Women are governed, therefore they are rightly entitled to vote."[139] In connection with this appeal, Horace Greeley "endorsed" woman suffrage in Kansas in a *New York Tribune* editorial characterizing woman suffrage as an "experiment." He grudgingly conceded, "While we regard it with mistrust, we are quite willing to see it pioneered by Kansas." But he also predicted the women of Kansas would find the vote "a plague rather than a profit," and "should the experiment work as we apprehend, they will soon be glad to give it up."[140] Of course such a backhanded "endorsement" only furnished fodder for the Anti-Female crowd.[141]

In early October, the results of the elections in Ohio and Pennsylvania (where election day fell on earlier dates) created panic in the ranks of Kansas Republicans. Voters in those other states rejected black suffrage and Republican incumbents, and conservatives in the party interpreted this as voter rejection of the key tenet of radicalism.[142] Some conservative Republicans actually welcomed the defeats as a check to the power of radicalism within the party.[143] Kalloch made no bones about ditching black suffrage. "The party has tried to carry too much," he edito-rialized, and in a speech at Wyandotte he declared he was "tired of niggerism," as one report put it.[144] Editor Sol Miller explained, "Since Ohio has defeated negro suffrage, a number in Kansas who were in favor of it, have turned square around, and many who were prepared to do right, have gone back and are among the hardest opponents of the measure."[145] Miller pointed out that Kalloch and "a large number of smaller caliber, all professing the deepest interest in the question of negro suffrage," did little or nothing to aid it, but instead spent their efforts in a furious campaign against female suffrage.[146] The *Leavenworth Daily Conservative* demonstrated how to abandon black suffrage smoothly by blaming its impending defeat on the women. "Lucy Stone and her outfit," the editor wrote, "may have succeeded in so disgusting the people of Kansas that they will vote down all amendments—the odious and repulsive measure to vote women carrying down with it the enfranchisement of the colored man."[147] Some radical Republicans, including Susan B. Anthony's brother, felt enough principled concern about black (male) suffrage that they hurriedly formed a new organization to canvass for it—indicating that the work of the State Central Committee under the aegis of the Anti-Female group had been inadequate.[148] Meanwhile the Anti-Female faction took advantage of the county nominating conventions to cement their hold on the Kansas Republican Party by eliminating candidates for local office who favored woman suffrage and perhaps even black suffrage. At the county convention in Atchison, for example, supporters of woman suffrage were "kicked aside as unworthy," but there was also no mention of black suffrage in its "dishwater" platform.[149] By October 24, Sol Miller was ready to refer to woman suffrage as "a hopeless issue," and at about the same time Henry Blackwell wrote to Lucy Stone saying, "*We are beat*," and black suffrage is in "great danger."[150]

At this point, in the last two weeks of the campaign, George Francis Train burst onto the scene and seized the headlines. Train had been invited to join the Kansas woman suffrage campaign by a number of different individuals and groups because he was a well-known proponent of woman suffrage and a magnetic speaker, and he was already in nearby Omaha.[151] Train was willing to help and able to pay his own way, but along with resources he injected added controversy and complexity into the last phase of the Kansas campaign. Train's outsized personality overshadowed and distorted the history of the two referenda.

An orphan, Train had climbed in Horatio-Alger style and amassed wealth in clipper ships, the China trade, and the all-important field of railroad promotion.[152] He was using his entrepreneurial success as a platform from which to run as an independent candidate for president, and crowds flocked to hear him because Train offered what amounted to stand-up comedy with content and an edge. He was cheerful and witty, always talking rapid-fire while acting out vignettes and dead-on impersonations, spewing puns and rhymes, and composing doggerel satire on the spot. His performances could last for hours and he often took his topics from audience members with whom he traded jests and jibes; large numbers eagerly paid admission and were loath to leave at the end of the evening. After attending a two-and-a-half-hour Train speech in San

Francisco, one journalist declared, "The phrase 'as good as a play,' would fall far short of describing the performance. I was never present at any entertainment so interesting and exciting. I never saw any man hold an audience so perfectly or handle it with so little effort."[153] Train's opinions were many and varied, but he always took the stance of the crusading outsider, delivering zestful jeremiads against moral rot and evildoing in high places, and throughout this period, government corruption had Train at a white-heat of indignation. But he also liked to remind his audience that he was a player in the world of high finance, and his role in railroad promotion gave him special cachet in Kansas. With his tongue-in-cheek grandiosity and his hectic pace, Train confounded journalists who could neither transcribe his words nor reproduce the points he was making as he careened around the stage, especially since his ideas defied categorization.[154] For the woman suffrage cause, Train drew in larger and more diverse audiences, but he also stepped into and widened the rift between black and woman suffrage.

Train was a political maverick because his pet causes—temperance, green-backs, the eight-hour day, Irish independence, and women's rights—cut across party lines. Before the war he had defended slavery, arguing it was civilizing an inferior race, but once the South seceded, he became a fierce unionist, though he also critiqued the Lincoln administration for violating civil liberties and blasted abolitionists for their emancipationist goals. In 1864, Train attended the Democratic convention but became disgusted with the peace platform, refused to support McClellan, and ended up campaigning vigorously for Lincoln in Pennsylvania.[155] Upon arriving in Kansas he happily proclaimed the death of both the Democrats and the Republicans.[156] But his appeal tilted toward the Democrats because his Fenian sympathies gave him many Irish fans and because his attacks on the status quo targeted the party in power. In Kansas, Republican newspapers tried to dismiss him by painting him as a lunatic and a Democrat pure and simple, while Democratic papers cheered him on to discomfit their Republican opponents.[157] These partisan effects were heightened because the editor of one local Democratic paper was an old friend of Train's.[158] Democrats understand, Train said, "that by voting W. S. they beat the Republicans at their own game," and he urged, "Democrats, do your duty on the fifth of November and vote for woman suffrage."[159] When he thus seemed to side with the Democrats, Train offended rock-ribbed Kansas Republicans.

When he spoke of black people, Train made bigoted and derogatory comments, referring sometimes to "the nig." "Sambo must wait for Sarah," he declared, and "woman first and negro last is my programme."[160] He repeatedly argued that white women were better qualified and more deserving of the ballot than black men, and that black men opposed woman suffrage.[161] Train's impact certainly worked against the black suffrage referendum and probably comforted skeptics who opposed both measures. Thus the specious charges that Eskridge and the

Anti-Female group had made seemed confirmed by Train, and under his aegis, the last few days of the campaign took on the appearance of "a regular Kilkenny fight" in which each measure killed off the other.[162]

On October 25, Langston and other black leaders scheduled a mass meeting in Leavenworth to clear up "certain misrepresentations made by some speakers engaged in the present canvass, with reference to the position of colored men in the present momentous political struggle." It sounded as though they intended yet another statement of neutrality on woman suffrage, or even mutual support, but Train had just arrived and begun campaigning in high gear. By the time the meeting was actually held, on October 31, the announced list of speakers had changed, and Langston was joined on stage by General Blunt and George Hoyt, two notorious opponents of woman suffrage.[163] In the interim, a meeting in the Second Ward seemed to signal a change of position by black leaders.[164]

Langston's last-minute shift would cause woman suffrage proponents to recall his earlier grudging comments, and revise their views accordingly.[165] In hindsight, the idea that blacks opposed women, which had been largely a canard at the outset, gained credibility from these developments at the end of the campaign. Looking back some years later, Olympia Brown would be critical of Charles Langston for having "added his mite of bitter words to make the path a little harder for women, who had spent years in pleading the cause of the colored man."[166] Brown recalled what she took to be personal remarks, as when Langston asked one public meeting if they "wanted every old maid to vote."[167] In a less stressful situation Brown might have overlooked such comments, but Kansas left her exhausted, and privately she feared she would end the campaign "burnt out, disgraced, disappointed, and penniless."[168] In unpublished reminiscences she would go so far as to characterize black men as "among the bitterest opponents of the enfranchisement of women." But Brown understood which factor was determinative, and she blamed the Kansas defeat squarely on white Republican politicians, discussing their motives in some detail while refusing to publish her comments on African Americans.[169]

Train threw himself into attacking the local opponents of woman suffrage, about whom he was well briefed. He recited,

> When Legate and Blunt, and Kalloch and Sears
> Go back on the women, voting negroes their peers,
> Morality says to our daughters and wives,
> When Kalloch approaches, run for your lives.[170]

He called out eastern abolitionists by name, crying, "Where is Wendell Phillips today? Lost caste everywhere. Inconsistent in all things and cowardly in this."[171] For the woman suffrage leaders it must have been exhilarating to have someone who could strike back against the opponents who had been so freely abusing them, and complain openly of the allies who had deserted them. If they tried to curb Train's racist pronouncements there is little evidence to show.[172] Elizabeth Cady Stanton, who was especially quick to forgive Democrats their sins, thought Train's appeal to them was a legitimate last-minute tactic. "We worked untiringly and hopefully, not seeing through the game of the politicians until nearly the end of the canvass, when we saw that our only chance was in getting the Democratic vote. Accordingly, George Francis Train, then a most effective and popular speaker, was invited to see what could be done to win the Democracy."[173] Henry Blackwell, who returned to Kansas in late October to look after some real estate investments, may also have entered into last-minute "negotiations with the Democrats."[174]

On election day, Anthony and Stanton gamely worked the polling places in Leavenworth, but the cause was lost. Printed party "tickets" provided one last opportunity for unscrupulous Kansas politicians to manipulate the referenda results. In one area they undercut support for both referenda by printing Republican tickets in which the voter was required to fill in a blank space with the word "for" or "against" opposite each amendment—an added bit of work that surely suppressed the vote.[175] In at least one other area, Republican tickets included a printed "no" on woman suffrage.[176] The last-minute appeal to Democrats apparently had little effect except in Leavenworth County, where prominent local Democrats had some party tickets printed "yes" for woman suffrage, with the result that Democrats voted for it unawares.[177] Woman suffrage went down to defeat 19,857 to 9,070, while black suffrage was also defeated, 19,421 to 10,483.

Analysis of the referenda results shows that woman suffrage supporters and black suffrage supporters were substantially the same people—despite all the efforts to cause a fight between them.[178] There were very few voters of the type Eskridge and Kalloch purported to speak for, those who opposed woman suffrage but still supported black suffrage. As Charles Robinson observed a few weeks later, woman suffrage won votes in Kansas from "the old school, liberal thinking, antislavery men & women"—precisely the same people who voted for black suffrage.[179] But negative campaigning by the Eskridgites against women and by Democrats against blacks combined to produce a solid bloc of voters opposed to *both* measures.[180]

From the New York referendum on black suffrage in 1860, to the Connecticut referendum on the same issue in 1865, to the 1867 Kansas results, one thing was clear: without active positive campaigning, black suffrage referenda would not pass. Advocates of black (male) suffrage in Kansas might have imagined that, had woman suffrage never been mentioned, they would have had smooth sailing, but the record demonstrates otherwise. Black (male) suffrage also went down to defeat on its own in Ohio and Minnesota in 1867, because part of the nominally Republican electorate needed convincing about equal rights and because Republicans of the Eskridge stripe could find plenty of excuses other than woman suffrage to sit on their hands. What might active campaigning and effective leadership have accomplished in Kansas? Sol Miller remarked that if Jim Lane were still alive and wanted to, "He could have carried the state for Negro suffrage by a large majority."[181] Just a year later, Iowa Republicans would show how it was done: there radical leaders led a vigorous positive campaign for black suffrage, overruling conservative Republicans who warned it was "liable to bring party defeat," and persuading white voters to do the right thing.[182] As modern political scientists have found, voters lean toward voting "no" in referenda as their default position, so vigorous "vote yes" campaigns are crucial for passage.[183]

With a power vacuum at the top of the Kansas Republican Party, Eskridge and Kalloch had exploited the situation to advance themselves. Although they did not forge a lasting faction, they helped define a version of Republicanism that excluded radicalism and focused on patronage. Charles Eskridge became the next Republican lieutenant-governor, and although his tenure was marked by corruption scandals in Topeka, he remained a power among Kansas Republicans for thirty years thereafter.[184] Isaac Kalloch was a contender for the congressional nomination in 1868 and was appointed a presidential elector, but he could not live down the story of the Boston sex scandal and eventually concluded that Kansas was too small a pond for his ambitions.[185] Before he left, however, he defrauded the Baptist Home Missionary Society and profited handsomely in railroad manipulations. Upon relocating to San Francisco, Kalloch would use his oratorical talents to scapegoat the Chinese and be elected mayor of the city.[186] These two colorful miscreants, who despised woman suffrage and cared little or nothing for black suffrage, gave Anthony and Stanton an unforgettable lesson in what some elements of the Republican Party were capable of.

On the morning after the election, Elizabeth Cady Stanton and Charles Langston met on the sidewalk in Leavenworth. Langston looked so sad and downcast that, Stanton recalled, she forgave him and shook his hand. "We still stand with idiots, lunatics, minors, criminals, paupers, and rebels," she remarked on their continued disenfranchisement, saying that it was "evidently the design of providence" that the two causes should be fought and won together. Next time, she said, we must work side by side. "Yes," Langston replied, "if we had done so, we should have triumphed."[187] They had been set against each other by ambitious local politicians who cared little or nothing for either cause, ill-served by supposed local allies who failed to work together for both causes, and starved for resources that might have brought in outside opinion leaders and altered the local dynamics. Certainly some of the advocates on one side or the other betrayed sexism or racism, but until Train arrived, the resulting antagonism was limited, especially considering all the efforts made by politicians and editors to fan the flames. Although Train was obnoxious, he had arrived on the scene after the die was cast.

Kansas left the women's rights leaders haunted by a gnawing sense of what might have been. Victories in Kansas in 1867 might have suggested that woman suffrage was a source of strength to black (male) suffrage, which was going down to defeat elsewhere. Victories here might even have suggested that pairing the two was a winning position for radicals within the party. Kansas in 1867 was part of a turning point of historic proportions in national political history, as the Republican Party began to redefine itself. Radical Republicans were losing out to moderates and conservatives who saw the party primarily as a patronage machine. "All depends on carrying Kansas," the editor of the *New York Evening Post* predicted, but the radicals lost.[188] A year later, black (male) suffrage would win in Iowa, but its victory came too late to affect Republican strategy. By then moderates and conservatives had already seized on the defeats of 1867 to hammer the radicals and shift the balance of power within the party.[189] No one who understood politics as well as Stanton and Anthony did could look back on Kansas without desperate regret.

6

Revolutionary Journalism
and Political Opportunism

It was so late at night that the ferry boats across the Missouri River had stopped running, but Susan B. Anthony prevailed upon someone to row her across in a skiff. She was in a hurry to catch up with George Francis Train to ask about his casual offer to finance an equal rights newspaper. She had not taken it seriously until Train announced it on the platform, stating "name, price, editor, motto and everything complete."[1] Now that the Kansas campaign was over, he also offered to pay all the expenses of Anthony and Elizabeth Cady Stanton on their trip back east and to join them to "lecture for *our treasury's benefit* all the way down to Boston."[2] Anthony needed to be sure this was more than just Train-style grandiosity and hot air. Once reassured that he was serious, she presented the offer to Stanton, and after "prolonged consultation," they decided to accept. They both understood that Train's reputation as a racist and a copperhead made his offer a "deal with the devil," but where else could they find funding, and without funding, how could they fight on?[3]

Accepting help from Train inaugurated a new phase of Stanton and Anthony's activism because it set them off on a new journalistic project and papered over the real history of what happened in Kansas. Train was no saint, but some of the criticism Stanton and Anthony took was unfair, which only made them more determined to forge ahead. Nobody back east wanted to hear the complex story of Kansas political infighting, and Lucy Stone, who was reemerging into full-time activism, was deeply offended by Train. Stanton and Anthony suffered harsh public criticism for having killed black suffrage, much of it from the backers of Wendell Phillips—who was, they believed, largely responsible for the Kansas defeats in the first place. Once Stanton and Anthony began their Train-financed newspaper, the *Revolution*, their aims and their tactics began to shift, because as journalists they needed to produce more commentary and could focus less on campaigning, while their national circulation increasingly led them to comment on national politics, losing the state-level focus that had marked their bellwether strategy. They identified a new fighting chance to win woman suffrage in the short term in Washington, D.C., and began to cultivate new allies among labor activists and working women. But the first year of the *Revolution*, 1868, was remarkable mostly for their attempts to exploit political opportunities.

After election day in Kansas in 1867, the faction that took control of the Kansas Republican Party had some explaining to do. After all, black suffrage, which was ostensibly a party measure, went down to defeat by a wide margin and polled only a few more votes than woman suffrage. The winning faction rarely mentioned their own "absolute lukewarmness" about, and failure to campaign for, black suffrage.[4] Nor did they acknowledge that the great majority of woman suffrage voters had also supported black suffrage and vice versa. Instead they had a cover story—blaming woman suffrage for defeating black suffrage by loading it down with a "side issue." Some even floated the bogus charge that "the large majority of the female suffrage advocates *sold their votes to the Democrats to obtain votes for that dogma.*"[5] Republican editors and readers in other states picked up their lead from party organs like the *Leavenworth Daily Conservative,* which pushed an explanation of events in which woman suffrage was the enemy of black suffrage—and of course George Francis Train's ebullient racism provided a kernel of truth in what was otherwise a false account. Knowledgeable Kansans like Sol Miller might excoriate the woman suffrage advocates for importing Train and yet not blame them for the defeat of black suffrage.[6] But such distinctions were lost on easterners who got their news secondhand.

Back east, most of Stanton and Anthony's old abolitionist allies concluded that Train and the woman suffrage advocates had ruined black men's chances. After all, Wendell Phillips had long predicted that black suffrage would be harmed by simultaneous campaigning for woman suffrage. Accustomed to viewing events through the lens of personal morality rather than political maneuver, few abolitionists could wrap their minds around the complexities of a faction fight inside the Kansas Republican Party. Instead, they reproached Stanton and Anthony for having "killed negro suffrage."[7] The charge was unfair but it stuck because George Francis Train became strongly identified with the Kansas campaign in retrospect, and the two women became, in turn, strongly identified with Train. "All the friends" were sure they were wrong, but Anthony and Stanton decided, eyes open, to commit what their critics called "Trainism" because they needed money.[8] After years of effort, they faced the possibility of having to leave the field for lack of the means to continue.[9] They still felt that woman suffrage had a fighting chance. And so they weighed money for continued women's rights campaigning against loyalty to black men's rights and an end to active campaigning, and they chose the money.

Train's generosity was, at first, extraordinary. He spent $3,000 on their joint lecture tour, renting the finest halls and reserving rooms in the best hotels.[10] His commitment to the newspaper dwarfed the old Jackson and Hovey funds—later reports pegged it at $100,000—although the two women had no way of knowing that only a tiny fraction of that amount would ever materialize.[11] Susan B. Anthony was especially inclined to make allowances and even excuses for this new donor because Train had traveled with her for most of his two weeks in Kansas. He had glanced at the hectic schedule before him and tried to demur, but Anthony responded firmly that the engagements were made and the handbills sent, and if he refused, she would go alone. "Miss Anthony," he replied, "you know how to make a man ashamed," and off they went. It was "entirely unforeseen and decidedly embarrassing" to be traveling alone with a man, and soon opponents mocked them with suggestive comments, but she was unafraid.[12] They rode across the prairies in a lumber wagon, drove on through the pouring rain, got lost in the dark and stuck in the mud—and sharing these hardships forged an unlikely bond of mutual respect.[13] Afterward, George Francis Train trusted Susan B. Anthony with money and encouraged her to assert herself. Eventually she thanked him, "For every word you have spoken—for every vote you have taken—for every dollar you have given—and more than all for the increase of respect for and faith in myself with which you have inspired me."[14] None of the grandees of eastern abolition had ever given her that kind of trust and responsibility, so when Lucretia Mott challenged her on her "disloyal affiliations," Anthony made no excuses.[15]

His critics were understandably loath to admit it, but George Francis Train had his virtues. He always asked his large audiences to "vote" on woman suffrage and he always cajoled a "yes" vote, even from the Irish Americans who flocked to see him because of his Fenian sympathies.[16] He helped the women reach out, after decades of promoting their ideas inside abolitionist circles, to different groups, especially to working-class men and women.[17] He commanded press attention at a time when the women's movement was in danger of being ignored, even before he solved their press problems with the gift of the *Revolution*. He did not drink, smoke, chew, swear, or gamble: indeed, Train was such a muscular Christian that the YMCA would later hire him to deliver inspirational speeches.[18] He also had an irreverent sense of humor which he usually trained on those in high places: he never saw Ulysses S. Grant, he claimed, "that I don't feel like saying, 'General, I've only five minutes, tell me all you know!'"[19] Though changeable, eccentric, and inclined to drop projects without seeing them through to completion, Train was capable of focusing and he did so, for a while at least, on the subject of woman suffrage.[20] Train's habitually frantic pace matched their mood, and the manic energy he brought to their cause in 1867 and 1868 was simply incandescent, especially in comparison to the wan enthusiasm and faint candlepower of their old abolitionist allies.

George Francis Train. Library of Congress.

Train's undoubted racism was probably something Anthony and Stanton believed they could change. His opinions were certainly volatile, and the history of the last few years had shown how far and how fast men could change their minds about race. Bostonians knew Train mostly from his high-profile antics in 1862, when he had disrupted a speech by Charles Sumner at Fanueil Hall, raising the usual copperhead cry against emancipating the "niggers."[21] But they probably did *not* know that two years later Train had campaigned for Abraham Lincoln. Train expressed more progressive views in private and was already not as bad as he sounded, Elizabeth Cady Stanton thought: "So long as Mr. Train speaks nobly for woman, why should we repudiate his services?" she asked; "even if he does ring the changes on 'nigger, nigger, nigger,' though we traveled with him through nine states,... [we] never heard him in public or private ignore the black man's rights."[22] Perhaps they expected that their abolitionist friends would help persuade Train to change, while in turn meeting the man would reassure them that he was not an irredeemable ogre. But when Anthony tried to introduce him, Lucy Stone turned her back.[23] Their chance to persuade him suffered another blow when Train traveled to England, offended British authorities with his Fenian stand, and refused to pay what he considered an unjust fine, with the result that he spent most of 1868 in jail there.[24] With Train removed from the American scene, a debate ensued *about* his racism, rather than a debate *with* him about race. If Train was changing his mind about black people—and there is some indication in his letters that by mid-1868 he began to do so—it was too little and too late.[25]

Anthony summed up what their Boston friends were implicitly advising: "*They want to keep still*—nothing less, nothing more—*Kid Gloves and Silver Slippers* ways and means is their motto for action."[26] Unwilling to "keep still" and quit the fight at what still seemed like a remarkably propitious historic moment, or to await more genteel "ways and means," Anthony and Stanton forged ahead. Years later Stanton defended their decision tartly: if the "fastidious ladies and gentlemen" who criticized them had come out to Kansas and/or provided "the sinews of war," there would have been "no field for Mr. Train's labors."[27] Arriving back east, the two women immediately used Train's money to launch their new weekly newspaper, the *Revolution*, with Elizabeth Cady Stanton sharing the editor's chair with Parker Pillsbury, while Susan B. Anthony served as manager and "proprietor." Their first issue hit the newsstands on January 8, 1868.

Because Train provided indispensable resources, Anthony and Stanton indulged his self-important perspective on Kansas events. Train had saved them from overwhelming defeat in Kansas, they wrote, and, "We say, 'God bless you, we have triumphed, and to you belongs this great victory—for this is our Bunker's Hill battle.'"[28] In speeches on the way east, Anthony was willing to attribute "much–most" of the woman suffrage vote in Kansas to Train.[29] Stanton and Anthony continued to tell this inaccurate story in the *Revolution*, although they also printed long letters from knowledgeable Kansans who disagreed.[30] Train probably had little impact on Kansas votes either way, but saying so would have seemed ungrateful.[31] They preferred to give Train credit he did not deserve, but they had to admit he offended many friends and allies.[32] Once they had thrown in their lot with Train, the chances dwindled for an accurate postmortem assessment of events in Kansas.

Train burned their bridges with Wendell Phillips, who may have been inclined to regret his own course in Kansas. Phillips sounded unusually defensive at the next American Anti-Slavery Society meeting, in May 1868, as he protested, "It is not my fault that this hour is the Negro's."[33] Phillips betrayed himself by posing an awkward rhetorical question: "Suppose I should go to Kansas today and argue the woman question. Is it fit?" No, he answered himself rhetorically, because "there is no question alert and afoot." But he had *not* gone to Kansas when the question *was* afoot six months earlier. And he equivocated on the subject of money: "I would not keep one dollar due to it [women's rights] hidden from actual service one instant."[34] Wendell Phillips had reason to feel sore, because Train, who had known Charles Hovey from his early days in Boston, used the very first edition of the *Revolution* to accuse Phillips of "breach of trust" for sinking "so much of the $5000 fund of my old friend Hovey into the *Anti-Slavery Standard*."[35]

Train's barbs made it easier for Phillips to quiet his conscience and to write off the whole Kansas campaign as the fiasco he had long predicted, one in which woman suffrage agitation had indeed sabotaged black male suffrage. His *National Anti-Slavery Standard* would, accordingly, refuse to acknowledge the *Revolution*'s existence, and he personally tried to avoid its editors.[36] In a testy conversation the following summer, Susan B. Anthony asked Wendell Phillips to justify his inaction in 1867 in the New York Constitutional Convention and in Kansas, and he responded, "I didn't believe in your work in either place." Anthony apparently understood about New York, but she was incredulous about Kansas: "Not in the Kansas Campaign?" she gasped.[37] Unfortunately Phillips's reply and the rest of their conversation went unrecorded, but the exchange revealed the power of Kansas "lessons." Phillips, who was predisposed to accept the orthodox Republican explanation of Kansas events and irritated by Train's attacks, looked back and saw joint race and gender campaigning as inimical to black suffrage. But Anthony and Stanton looked back and saw Kansas as a missed opportunity for joint race and gender campaigning that might have led to victory for both causes.[38]

George Francis Train also offended William Lloyd Garrison, who blasted him as a "crack-brained harlequin," a "semi-lunatic," a "ranting egotist," and a "low blackguard." He upbraided Anthony and Stanton for working with him and charged that "the colored people and their advocates" had "no more abusive assailant" than this man who "delights to ring the changes upon the 'nigger,' 'nigger,' 'nigger' ad nauseum."[39] Garrison exaggerated: it was easy to find worse negrophobes in almost any issue of the *New York World,* not to mention the whole of the former Confederacy. Probably Garrison was glad to attack Train, Anthony, and Stanton because they made him look good by comparison after an embarrassing squabble with Wendell Phillips about the remainder of the Jackson bequest. Garrison had insisted that for the ex-slaves, education was more important than the vote, and he steered the money in that direction until Phillips cried foul.[40] What began as a private dispute was then publicized and Garrison's reputation suffered.[41] Garrison's holier-than-thou attitude toward Anthony and Stanton was especially irksome because he himself was a laggard on the issue of black suffrage.

And Train certainly offended Lucy Stone. She left Kansas in the spring of 1867 with high hopes, and it was natural to blame those who came later for the disappointing outcome. She had legitimate reason to be upset when she found her name affixed, without her permission, to the public letter in which Anthony and Stanton praised Train, and she was understandably disgusted when they published Train's self-promotional "Great Epigram Campaign" pamphlet under the AERA imprimatur. Probably at Stone's urging, the chairman of the AERA Executive Committee wrote to Stanton and Anthony and complained that they were compromising the AERA by associating with Train. But Stanton replied, "We are traveling as individuals, in no way compromising the AERA, leaving you free in N.Y. to inaugurate what work you see best while we raise the money to help you do it."[42] The Executive Committee of the AERA then met and resolved, "This association disclaims all responsibility for or endorsement of" the public events held by Train, Anthony, and Stanton. A copy of the resolution was sent to the press signed by "Lucy Stone, Secretary."[43]

Stanton and Anthony were offended, too. Phillips left Anthony and Stanton to pay their own Kansas expenses but shortly after election day, he sent Lucy Stone a check for $500 to cover expenses she and Henry Blackwell had incurred in Kansas, thus disbursing what was apparently the very last of the Jackson Fund.[44] It was an ironic payment because Stone and her husband had an independent income and could afford to continue to agitate causes as they chose. Stone and Blackwell's decision to accept those scarce women's rights funds, even while they enjoyed the personal resources to vacation on Martha's Vineyard and speculate in Kansas real estate, was tacky. But to take the money and then proceed to criticize Anthony and Stanton for the makeshift of their poverty—the Train alliance—was decidedly provoking. In her huffy response, Elizabeth Cady Stanton said nothing more about raising money for the AERA and instead declared, "I went to Kansas as an individual ... without being supplied by [the AERA] with either brains or money." She twitted Stone's inconsistency: Stone was demanding proper organizational procedure but she signed the press release as AERA "secretary"—a position actually held by her husband. "From Lucy Stone's known probity of character, her signature to the above card must have been unauthorized," Stanton commented sarcastically.[45]

Thus even before the first issue of the *Revolution* appeared, Stone saw herself engaged in "a serious quarrel" with Anthony and Stanton.[46] As she later explained the situation, "They brought Train, the Revolution, and the 'Epigram Campaign' of Mr. Train...to our office, without so much as saying 'by your leave' and literally turned us out."[47] Stone referred to an episode when some of the AREA Executive Board tried to prevent Anthony from moving the *Revolution*'s operations into an office at 37 Park Row in New York, which had been rented in the

AERA's name. But Anthony had been forced to raise the Park Row rent money herself and had taken out a personal loan to do so.[48] There was a moment of angry personal confrontation when Anthony told Stone that, in effect, "*I* am the American Equal Rights Association."[49]Anthony was high-handed, but she had a point because she had paid the rent personally and because the AERA was organizationally incoherent. At the annual meeting in 1867, the members had elected a figurehead president, Lucretia Mott, and no less than *seventeen* vice presidents. Elizabeth Cady Stanton was a vice president but so were Frederick Douglass, Henry Ward Beecher, and Sam Wood. Henry Blackwell was one of two recording secretaries, Susan B. Anthony one of three corresponding secretaries, and Stone, Anthony, and Stanton were all members of a fifteen-member Executive Committee.[50] In other words, Stone had no better claim than Anthony to decision-making power, and a rump meeting of the Executive Committee without Stanton and Anthony only highlighted the fact that the organizational underdevelopment of the women's movement was beginning to prove costly.

Stone complained that the *Revolution* editors hurt the cause by associating with Train, but she was not in a good position to claim superior loyalty to black rights. After all, she and Henry Blackwell had themselves contemplated working with the Democrats in Kansas, and Blackwell may in fact have followed through on the idea.[51] Given the white supremacist thrust of her husband's pamphlet, "What the South Can Do," published just a year earlier, Lucy Stone cannot have been terribly vigilant against racism. Probably she was hypersensitive about the *Revolution.* After all, she and Blackwell had been angling for some time to begin a women's rights newspaper themselves, and as recently as November 1866, they had proposed to "give their time and labor" to edit such a paper if supporters would put together $10,000 to bankroll the venture. Anthony had then supported their proposal, telling Wendell Phillips, "We *surely must have a paper* through which those who demand the *whole loaf of republicanism* may speak."[52] But thanks to Train that whole-loaf newspaper now belonged to Anthony, not Stone.

The situation was even more complicated: Lucy Stone was probably disposed to quarrel because she was enduring a terrible personal crisis. At about this same time she became aware that Henry Blackwell was involved in an affair with a younger woman.[53] Stone chose to stay in the marriage, trying to keep her husband's infidelity a secret and to redirect his interests, but her distress and denial probably colored her decision making. She came to believe that lecturing was "not consistent with any home life or any proper care of my family," whereas editing a newspaper would avoid the separations of the lecture tour and provide plenty of work for Blackwell's idle hands and restless nature.[54] To have that newspaper project snatched away, and by the same man who she thought had spoiled women's chances in Kansas, was understandably infuriating. Perhaps quarreling with Anthony and Stanton about Train, who Stone despised but never met, gave her a place to redirect her anger.[55] The way Blackwell's infidelity coincided with the "Train Cloud" could only have deepened a growing rift between Stone and her old friends.[56]

Money became the principal medium through which the emerging quarrel was carried on. Before the *Revolution* was a month old, Train had been jailed in England and his ability to subsidize the paper evaporated, so Anthony requested that the AERA pay her outstanding salary and expenses dating from the Kansas campaign. She was asking for scarce AERA resources, and Stone and Blackwell, who were at that point contributors as well as officers in the AERA, bridled. They criticized Anthony for having used AERA money to print posters advertising Train in Kansas. They were right to criticize an association with a notorious racist, but their focus on money strained the point because Train had covered his own expenses in Kansas and thus had arguably subsidized the AERA more than the reverse. They complained about Anthony privately and then publicly, at the May 1868 AERA anniversary, and afterward Anthony nursed hurt feelings.[57] "I have not *two hundred dollars more* than I had the day I entered upon the public work of Woman's Rights and AntiSlavery," she reflected, making an implicit comparison between herself and Lucy Stone, who had come into money.[58] Two months later Anthony reported that "*Lucy Stone* & Co have voted to leave me out of pocket" for "a cool sum of $1000," including $600 in salary and $400 in expenses.[59] Anthony needed the money badly, and of course she resented it. As late as January 1869, Henry Blackwell was still complaining that Anthony had never submitted proper receipts for Kansas expenses, and he went over her account with a sharp pencil until the bottom line showed the AERA owed her nothing at all.[60] The unfair charge that Anthony had misspent AERA money in Kansas would linger for years to come.[61]

Frederick Douglass also disapproved of George Francis Train but was not quite so quick to criticize. He finally did so at the May 1868 AERA meeting, saying he was appalled by Train's reported boast that he had converted Susan B. Anthony's concerns from "three fourths Negro and one fourth woman" to the reverse proportion.[62] And he disagreed with Olympia Brown about Kansas: she scorned Kansas Republicans as worthless hypocrites, while he saw their merits and preferred them to the Democrats. Who was to blame for the defeat of black suffrage in Kansas? Brown unhesitatingly blamed Republican politicians but Douglass blamed George Francis Train. Brown refused to concede his point: if Train was to blame in Kansas, she asked, what about Minnesota where the Republicans "voted the negro down" without Train?[63] Douglass remained unconvinced, but his criticisms were comparatively collegial: "Our revolutionary friends need to have somebody to tell them when they are a little out of the way…. This Train has led some of them astray." He added a personal comment, saying "I know well … the heart of the lady in our presidential chair [Stanton]," and declaring, "I will not be driven away from her by any such comet as George Francis Train."[64] Douglass did not know the facts about the Republican faction fight in Kansas and he accepted an element of the cover story by blaming Train. But he did understand how impecunious activists' need for funding might trump other concerns, and he was enough of a realist to see that black men, armed with the vote, might have to work with unsavory political coadjutors themselves.[65] He might even have recalled his own stinging disappointment in 1860, when the black suffrage referendum in New York State was defeated "by the supineness of our friends," and thereby understood Stanton and Anthony's feelings after Kansas.[66]

George Francis Train was certainly a racist and legitimately irritating, but Lucy Stone, Wendell Phillips, and William Lloyd Garrison also overreacted to him for personal reasons. Frederick Douglass complained of the women's choice of allies, although he did not play the scandalized purist. But neither Stanton nor Anthony had patience for criticism, legitimate or otherwise, as they published their *Revolution* and pressed to "be heard *now*."[67] These two women were determined to ride roughshod over obstacles, ignore critics, and take help wherever they could get it because Kansas left them with an urgent sense that woman suffrage should have been won *yesterday.*

A paper like the new *Revolution* was much needed. "We have decidedly lost [ground] in connection with the daily press," declared Boston feminist Caroline Dall in 1866.[68] Dall suggested that the women's movement ought to purchase a half column in the *New York Tribune,* but of course that took money they did not have. Susan B. Anthony actually confronted a *Tribune* editor when she could not get the paper to run a call for an AERA meeting, telling him, "A good wholesome abuse by acknowledged enemies is a thousand times more desirable that this *chilling letting alone of professed friends."*[69] Elizabeth Cady Stanton's decision to run for Congress in 1866 was probably undertaken partly in hopes of getting press coverage and thereby public discussion of her ideas, but her experiment in cost-free publicity was not much of a success.[70]

Reformers of all stripes no longer had reliable friends at the great New York dailies.[71] Henry J. Raymond's *New York Times* was hostile: Raymond backed Andrew Johnson long after most Republicans had abandoned him, and the *Times* of this period was an administration sheet known for trimming and truckling.[72] Horace Greeley's *New York Tribune* was no help either: his maddeningly erratic course since the war, which included making bail for Jefferson Davis, drove genuine radicals to tear their hair.[73] Meanwhile Manton Marble was building the *New York World* into a national powerhouse. Marble took over the *World* in 1862 and made it clever, lively, and readable, but he was also a cunning and relentless Democratic partisan who attacked radicalism on all fronts.[74] Reformers needed editorial friends because newspapers of the day exercised an unusual degree of power but had little inclination to objective reporting. On the contrary, they indulged in chronic puffery and personal "slang-whanging," none of it much inhibited by the facts.[75] One contemporary journalist remarked coolly that the power of the press consisted "not in its logic or eloquence, but in its ability to manufacture facts, or to give coloring to facts that have occurred."[76]

Though radicals found themselves increasingly bereft of friendly coverage, other efforts to establish a sympathetic paper had foundered. *The Nation*, a new weekly journal launched in July 1865, was hailed as the successor to the *Liberator*, but it was almost immediately hijacked by its editor E. L. Godkin, who took a more conservative stance than its financial backers—mostly abolitionists—had been led to expect.[77] The *Commonwealth*, subsidized heavily by abolitionist George Luther Stearns, did not long survive his death, and though the *Independent*, a weekly edited by Theodore Tilton, took progressive stances on many issues, the paper's primary commitment was to religion rather than public affairs.[78]

In this context, Wendell Phillips's *National Anti-Slavery Standard* was especially important, but it refused to cover woman suffrage. At a scant four pages, the weekly *Standard* was scarcely more than an organizational newsletter for the American Anti-Slavery Society, but it was a voice of integrity among the puffers and the screamers, and it was sent to every congressman, every major newspaper, and to a "free list" of radical individuals in the South.[79] But ever since Phillips's "Negro's hour" pronouncement, the *Standard* was closed to women's issues. When it rejected a letter from Elizabeth Cady Stanton, Anthony fumed, "All there is to be said is '*it aint as it used to was*,'" and editor Aaron Macy Powell at one point informed Anthony that notices of AERA events must be paid for at the regular advertising rates.[80] Eventually the *NASS* editors offered the AERA a certain amount of space in its columns, but its leaders felt obliged to reject the offer because everything they submitted would still be subject to "editorial revision."[81] Parker Pillsbury worried so much about the newspaper's dependence on the Hovey funds that he finally decided he could not "in conscience" continue to work as an editor of the *NASS* "unless it should advocate woman's claims equally with those of the negro."[82] It did not, and for this reason Pillsbury was free to join the *Revolution*.

It was all the more important to get press access because women's rights was no longer a novel subject, and mainstream papers could not be induced to provide coverage on the basis of curiosity, as they often had ten or fifteen years earlier. On the contrary, the women's rights movement looked like old news and was even disparaged for being "fashionable."[83] Instead, the press gave coverage to a flock of anti-woman suffragists who suddenly emerged in 1866–67. These ranged from Tayler Lewis, published in the *Independent*, to the Reverend John Todd, out with a new book condemning women's rights, to Dr. Francis Lieber, a German American jurist and political philosopher who taught at Columbia University.[84] They were joined by other commentators who reacted to the corruption of New York's Tweed ring by concluding that it was time to take the ballot away from unworthy white men, let alone extend it to anyone else.[85] The metropolitan New York press was missing the story on woman suffrage because no editor was willing to bring together the scattered state and local news items that attested to the mushrooming of women's rights enthusiasm at the grassroots. Thus when, in Michigan, the Constitutional Convention voted in *favor* of woman suffrage on July 22, 1867, but on August 12 reversed itself and defeated the measure, the New York press scarcely noticed. The *New York Times* gave Michigan two inches and told its readers the first vote was "buncombe."[86]

Anthony and Stanton had therefore been grateful when Manton Marble gave them coverage in the *New York World* as soon as they issued their first woman suffrage petitions back in December 1865.[87] "Go ahead, Susan," the *World* urged, while it described the speakers at a woman suffrage meeting as "really very good" and the turnout as a "great crowd."[88] Especially after the disastrous Democratic losses in the election of 1866, Marble focused on fault lines within the ruling Republican Party and looked to use woman suffrage as a wedge issue. He high-lighted Elizabeth Cady Stanton in particular, emphasizing her critiques of Republicans and kind words for Democrats. In connection with Stanton's run for Congress in 1866, Marble wrote, "The country will owe Mrs. Stanton thanks for her agency in exposing for once the hugger-muggering Pecksniffian dishon-esty of this party of 'great moral ideas.' "[89] Once Radical Reconstruction enfran-chised black men in the South in 1867, the *World* harped on the theme that the freedmen all opposed woman suffrage. This was reported as fact: "Now that the negroes have pronounced against the extension of the elective franchise to women, the leading Radical journals are preparing to fall in behind and to follow in the footsteps of their negro leaders."[90] Marble's *World* gave Stanton's ideas a selective reading, highlighting her invidious comments about black men and ignoring her egalitarian comments when she still came out in favor of their voting rights.[91] The *World* also downplayed episodes when the activists empha-sized black women's rights, and Marble never actually declared in favor of woman suffrage, coyly pushing the argument while backing off an endorsement.[92]

The *World's* coverage of the woman suffrage movement was surrounded by columns packed with accounts of "outrages" in the South that were grotesquely exaggerated or manufactured out of whole cloth.[93] The *World* reported that pro-miscuous sex prevailed among the freedpeople because there were no longer any slave masters to enforce marriage and morality.[94] One *World* correspondent even suggested that if black people could not be returned to slavery, "speedy extermination" was "the best thing for them."[95] George Francis Train's rhetoric could sound mild by comparison, and coverage for the women's movement came at a high price when it was accompanied by the *World's* vile bigotry. Manton Marble was especially dangerous because he was helping to craft policy for a resurgent Democratic Party. Dogged by a bad reputation among northern voters who recalled their copperhead sympathies during the war, Democrats like Marble were discovering a new appeal based on economic issues—a ballooning national debt, unprecedented federal spending, and inflation that doubled the cost of living while wages failed to keep pace.[96] Because the *New York World* packaged together legitimate economic concerns, woman suffrage, and violent bigotry, it was important for the woman suffrage advocates to launch a paper of their own where they could clarify their positions.

True to George Francis Train's entrepreneurial inspiration, Anthony and Stanton hoped to make their new paper a paying proposition, because a profitable paper could fund future activism, meet their personal financial needs, and provide work for other women.[97] They immodestly aspired to reach 100,000 subscribers in a daily that would surpass the *World* and the *Tribune* combined.[98] Such an ascent was not impossible: in 1862 Manton Marble needed $25,000 cash to keep his paper afloat, but Marble found the investor he needed and by 1865 he was living in a mansion on Fifth Avenue and sponsoring charity balls.[99] Stanton and Anthony believed they had the financial backing they needed, even though a significant capital sum was required. The *Revolution* needs "no eleemosynary aid," Susan B. Anthony declared, "and I hope it never will."[100] With Horace Greeley's *New York Tribune* having lapsed into opportunism, a profitable market niche for a progressive paper lay open.[101]

The *Revolution* aimed for wide popularity by offering a lively mixture of politics, culture, finance, and the arts, and its editorials flowed from Elizabeth Cady Stanton's pen in a voice full of "life and snap."[102] It printed many criticisms of itself and (except in some editorials by Parker Pillsbury) avoided the ponderous tone of "very respectable Miss Nancy journals" like the *Nation*.[103] It took the tone of a "sharp and spicy" inside-scoop sheet, and by one account it was humorous enough to preempt "the imagined necessity for an American *Punch*."[104] This style was lost on humorless crusaders like William Lloyd Garrison or Lucy Stone, but it certainly fell in step with the contemporary market, which favored rapid-fire satire by Fanny Fern and comic "burlesque" in New York theaters.[105] The paper also fit Elizabeth Cady Stanton's ebullient personality, and she moved into a new phase of life in its pages, independent of family cares and very much a self-possessed public intellectual. "I feel as if I have just begun to live," she wrote a friend.[106]

It was not to last. Within months or even weeks after their first issue hit the streets, it became clear that Train was stuck in England and would actually supply only $3,000. Though David Mellis, who hoped to make the paper's financial pages a window on Wall Street, provided another $7,000, the venture was never adequately capitalized. Soon Anthony and Stanton began a search for additional backing, during which they would investigate the possibility of an infusion of capital from Harriet Beecher Stowe.[107] But they never found a substitute investor, and Anthony began to borrow personally to continue to publish the paper. When the *Revolution* editors decided in their very first issue to refuse advertisements for patent medicines, they may have unwittingly sealed its fate.[108] Later in the game, as the paper shriveled for want of resources, the editors would claim that it had not been started with a view to making money, but this rationale only helped to dignify failure.[109] An increasingly urgent desire to be heard before its voice was stilled began to creep into the *Revolution*'s editorial tone.

Stanton and Anthony's *Revolution* broke the silence that had been imposed upon their movement. They commented on "the deceitfulness of the press," and took shots at Phillips's *NASS* for refusing to notice their new paper, and at Greeley's *Tribune* for ignoring women.[110] They tried to reach a large general audience and insert themselves into the national editorial conversation by imitating Garrison, who had brilliantly manipulated the system of editorial exchange.[111] They sent out 6,000 copies of the *Revolution* to newspapers all over the country, half of which replied soliciting an exchange, and with the results they initiated a lively column, "What the Press Says of Us." They understood how to get attention and used cheeky publicity stunts, like getting President Andrew Johnson to subscribe, in order to make a splash.[112] The *Revolution* confirmed Stanton and Anthony's status as nationally renowned figures.

But their move into journalism also muddied the waters strategically. Their old bellwether strategy had focused on state-level campaigning, assuming that work at the national level was mostly worthwhile as reinforcement. With no state campaign in view, a national audience in mind, and column inches to fill, they began to talk more vaguely and from an increasingly national perspective. Looking backward, they argued that suppressing women's cause to further black (male) suffrage had been counterproductive. If Wendell Phillips and his friends had been true to the women of the country in 1867, "they would have at least saved the negro," and in Kansas and Wisconsin they "might and probably would have" achieved woman suffrage to boot.[113] The *Revolution* editors were still keening over the loss in Kansas, but by making this argument they seemed to imply that what had been true at the state level in Kansas—that the two causes would have been stronger together—was still true at the national level. The point was highly debatable.

Although they had become journalists, the *Revolution* editors were not quite ready to limit themselves to commentary and general agitation. They still wanted to campaign and win, but what was the target and what was the plan? Ever since being faced with Phillips's "Negro's hour" strategy, Stanton had been quoting Daniel O'Connell's "claim the uttermost," but that produced scattershot arguments except when used in support of agreed-upon goals.[114] The *Revolution* leaders could be misread as campaigning when they were only complaining. The *Revolution*'s first issue pointed out that black men, at least in the South, had already been granted many rights women were denied: "Black men [are] already at the ballot box, exercising the right of suffrage, in constitutional conventions, framing the fundamental laws of states, in courts of justice, pleading at the bar, and sitting in the jury-box."[115] But it was one thing to express resentment at this fait accompli, quite another to say what—if anything—to do about it at this point. In search of a single practical goal that could clarify their immediate priorities, they again considered and then abandoned educated suffrage, and finally returned to their bellwether strategy.[116]

Washington, D.C., made a good bellwether for woman suffrage because it was small, highly visible, and more winnable than a state. Woman suffrage could be accomplished by a simple majority vote in Congress, and then play out as a highly visible experiment in the national capital. Nor did Stanton and Anthony have to create a Washington campaign from the bottom up: happily for these busy journalists they could endorse the efforts of a Washington, D.C., group called the Universal Franchise Association. Its titular president was Senator Samuel Pomeroy of Kansas, and its Advisory Committee was studded with prestigious names including Ben Wade, Salmon P. Chase, and John Stuart Mill, but the real leader of the group was Josephine Griffing, a veteran abolitionist and women's rights activist.[117] Griffing had been a stalwart in the Women's Loyal National League, and she worked extensively with a number of black women including Sojourner Truth in freedmen's relief efforts in postwar Washington.[118] In early 1868 Griffing's Universal Franchise Association was already engaged in a petition campaign for woman suffrage in Washington.

Best of all, in Washington black male suffrage was already a fact and there could be no objection that woman suffrage might harm black men's chances. In fact, woman suffrage in D.C. could positively serve the needs of the whole black community. Black male voters, just enfranchised in 1867, were sufficiently numerous to have aroused considerable local opposition, and not just among negrophobic Democrats. A group of conservative Republican businessmen looking to redefine local Republicanism were promoting a consolidation of the city of Washington with Georgetown and the county, so as to dilute black men's votes.[119] Because the black population of Washington was disproportionately female and the white population was imbalanced in the other direction, woman suffrage had the potential to hand local black leaders a margin with which to repel the consolidation drive.[120] It was thus in the interests of black men to enfranchise black women, and the UFA's petition protesting an "aristocracy of sex" was signed by none other than George Downing, the African American leader who had claimed priority for black male suffrage at the 1867 AERA meeting.[121] The UFA's campaign for voting rights for women in Washington offered a win-win scenario for the advocates of black suffrage and woman suffrage.

The UFA's interracial coalition was threatened briefly in June 1868 when a "White Woman Suffrage Association" meeting was held in Washington to discuss a resolution framed in deliberately divisive terms: "To deny to white women the right of suffrage is most positively and practically to assert that white women are inferior to black men."[122] The Civil War physician Dr. Mary Walker, best known for her penchant for wearing men's clothes, was said to provide leadership for the new organization, but the whole thing sounded suspiciously like a stalking horse designed to break up the UFA. If so, it failed because the white woman suffrage group fizzled out, though not before the *Revolution* had incautiously praised it saying, "Intelligent, cultivated white women are beginning to wake up to the fact of their political degradation."[123] Under Josephine Griffing's leadership, the local advocates of woman suffrage were wiser, and stuck to their campaign for universal suffrage with a series of meetings as well as their petition campaign.[124] The annual meeting of the UFA in September 1868 showed that its coalition between black men and black and white women was still in good working order.[125] Stanton and Anthony's choice of Washington as a bellwether showed they had not entirely lost the penchant for practical plans, local results, and universal human rights that marked their earlier efforts in New York and Kansas. But their editorial comments also indicated that they were willing to fling out contradictory and racist arguments.

The *Revolution* editors employed a mixed bag of arguments for woman suffrage, just as Stanton had long been accustomed to. They repeated often-used claims to equal rights for all citizens, including women, and they elaborated familiar arguments about how black women had especially urgent need of the vote and were "as precious in the scale of being as the men."[126] But Stanton also indulged the "women will outweigh" argument she had used in her 1866 congressional campaign and in her response to George Downing at the 1867 AERA meeting. In an early *Revolution* editorial she returned to this note, arguing that "the wealth, the virtue, the education of woman" would "outweigh ignorance, poverty and vice."[127] The argument was apparently based on an assumption about class differences in female voter turnout, with middle-class women more likely to vote than poor women. (Otherwise newly enfranchised women would merely have reproduced the demographic characteristics of their male relatives.) But such an assumption simply opened the door for opponents to counter with their own predictions that "Bridget" and "Dinah"—Irish and black domestic servants—or even prostitutes, would be more likely to vote than respectable women.

The *Revolution* introduced another questionable line of argument by claiming that "the woman element" was especially needed in civilization and government to counterbalance "the male element." This "rhetoric of sexual difference" may have sprung from Elizabeth Cady Stanton's new interest in the social theories of August Comte.[128] Exclusively male suffrage, Stanton argued, is "opposed to all the recent revelations of science."[129] Here, too, the argument was problematic, and not just because it contradicted the equal rights reasoning they had long favored. It also emphasized natural, inherent differences between the sexes, differences just as easily—indeed, more easily—invoked by reactionaries in support of traditional sex roles.

Among the *Revolution*'s most troubling arguments was the charge that black men opposed woman suffrage, and therefore enfranchising them first would be an added roadblock to woman suffrage. Kansas events were cited as proof positive: the first page of the first issue saw Stanton explaining the Kansas defeat in part by citing "the hostility everywhere of black men themselves, some even stumping the state against woman's suffrage."[130] This description did violence to the real history of all but the last two weeks of the campaign. The *Revolution* even named Charles Langston as an open opponent, apparently on the strength of that one last meeting in Leavenworth just before election day.[131] Of course, the *Revolution* editors knew that *some* black men *supported* woman suffrage, and there was no way to know, in an era before opinion polls, what proportion lined up on either side. The only fair question was whether black men were any *more* sexist than white men, and sometimes Stanton was careful to describe black men as no better but also no worse than white ones: "We have no reason to suppose that the black man understands the principles of equity, or will practice the Christian virtues better than his Saxon masters."[132] But in the pages of the *Revolution* "no better than" often shaded into "worse" or even "all opposed"— the same sort of biased overgeneralization that so infuriated Anthony and Stanton when their opponents asserted that "women" did not want the vote.

The argument that black men were opposed was made by two of their most prominent black allies. Robert Purvis had predicted that black men would be "like a dead weight" against woman suffrage.[133] And in May 1868 even Frederick Douglass conceded the point, saying, "The race to which I belong have not generally taken the right ground on this [woman suffrage] question."[134] Douglass remarked that it was "natural and habitual" to clamor for one's own rights while ignoring or denying those of others, but he immediately followed up this observation by endorsing woman suffrage himself. He seemed to think that the freedmen's tendency to oppose woman suffrage was real but not a fixed fact; instead, it was one more thing reformers—and black leaders like himself—would have to work on.

But for Stanton and Anthony, the idea that black men were generally opposed to woman suffrage led to a different conclusion, one that popped up in a throw-away line Stanton used in speeches while heading back east from Kansas: "She protested against the enfranchisement of the negro, or another man, until woman had been given her rights."[135] Earlier Stanton had resisted Phillips's black-men-first priorities, but when pushed in an exchange with George Downing in 1867, she had conceded that she preferred women and "the educated classes" over black men. Stanton now repeated the "not another man" line in a key editorial in the *Revolution*: "Every far-seeing woman who has a proper self-respect or an intelligent love of country will protest against the enfranchisement of another man, either black or white, until the women of the nation are crowned with all the rights of citizenship."[136] Yet the meaning of the "not another man" catch-phrase was unclear: when challenged, the *Revolution* denied it meant reversing priorities so that white women must go first, but rather meant simply holding out for simultaneous enfranchisement.[137]

The cry of "not another man" offended many old abolitionist allies, one of whom questioned Stanton's use of inconsistent arguments. J. Elizabeth Jones, a veteran of the 1859–60 New York State canvass, believed that any expansion of rights, even if incomplete, was a step in the right direction. "What means this new system of ethics of Mrs. Stanton?" Jones demanded, and in response, Stanton explained, "It is not a question of necessary precedence for one or the other.... Our demand has long been suffrage for all, white and black, male and female, of legal age and sound mind." But, she concluded, "We say today, edu-cated women first, ignorant men afterward."[138] Jones shot back that Stanton was inconsistent:

> You say "the franchise is not a question of necessary precedence for one
> class or the other." Why, then, make it a question of precedence and say,
> "educated women first, ignorant men afterward?" Again you say, "our
> demand has long been suffrage for all, white and black, male and female,
> of legal age and sound mind," but in speaking of manhood suffrage you
> also declare, "we have enough of that already. We say not another man,
> black or white, until woman is inside the citadel."[139]

Thus pressed, Stanton explained that since the abolitionists now claimed it was the "Negro's hour," the *Revolution* was entitled in turn to descend "to their low ground of expediency" and advocate "educated women first, ignorant men after-ward."[140] It was one of Stanton's most explicit acknowledgments of her "in the alternative" style of argument that put a desire to win the case above principle.

The key difference between Jones and Stanton lay in their sense of the moment, their assessment of its possibilities and its urgency. Jones clearly assumed that woman suffrage was not possible in the short run and was willing to settle down to educate and agitate the issue over the long haul, for which alternative pleading could be contradictory and confusing. But Stanton had breathed Kansas air, and she still believed there was a fighting chance to win woman suffrage at this moment. As a result she was quite ready to deploy a whole range of arguments, including the "outweigh" argument, the rhetoric of sexual difference, the "black men opposed," and the "not another man" argument, all of which involved contradictory logic when employed alongside the classic egalitarian arguments that Stanton also continued to make. It was as if she was a lawyer and woman suffrage was her client, for whose sake she would throw out any argument that might sway the jury. But what was the case to be decided? What was the specific political opportunity at hand? Washington, D.C., still presented one last opportunity to win woman suffrage, but Stanton could not resist scanning the larger, national political landscape for another fighting chance, tempted by the volatility of an election year in an era of crisis.

Reconstruction was a moment in American history when politics was clearly "where the action was," when the political arena seemed to hold the answers to all sorts of social and humanitarian questions, and the party landscape was fluid, offering unusual opportunities to outsiders like Stanton. After four years of dealing with a headstrong accidental president, 1868 found both of the major political parties ill-defined.[141] Inside the Republican Party, ex-Whigs and ex-Democrats differed on important economic issues, and although the party in the South was closely identified with black suffrage, elsewhere many Republicans were decidedly leery. Radical Republicans had tried to insist that black men's voting rights were central to the party's purpose, but the 1867 election results had delivered a body blow to those hopes, and radical leadership at the national level was increasingly ineffectual. Charles Sumner was in the midst of a marital breakup that delighted Capital Hill gossips and left him more isolated than ever, while Thaddeus Stevens was gravely ill and would die before the summer was over. Instead, conservative Republicans like William Pitt Fessenden, Lyman Trumbull, and Roscoe Conkling wielded increasing power in Congress. The only aims that united Republicans were a determination to hold onto the gains of the war and to their party's patronage control, and most hoped to accomplish those ends by nominating a popular war hero, Ulysses S. Grant, for president. The corruption and cynicism of Republicans like Isaac Kalloch would fuel rising resentment among radicals, and in a few years, many radical or reform-minded or "liberal" Republicans would find themselves willing to bolt the party en masse.

Democrats faced an identity crisis of their own: they had scored gains in the 1867 elections in part by appealing to white bigotry, but many northern Democrats were also interested in redefining the party around economic issues and limited government. Western Democrats looked to new leadership in George Pendleton, while other northerners wanted to beat the drums against taxes and government spending, now that federal taxes were being levied on ordinary individuals for the first time.[142] Southern Democrats were reentering the political arena, seeking to reclaim their own political rights and party leadership at the national level. Were southerners and the Democrats as a whole willing to recognize that "General Jackson is dead," as Anthony put it, and with him their traditional party foundations of slavery and racism?[143] Or would they persist in identifying the party with white southerners' diehard intransigence on race and Reconstruction? Here, too the definition of the party was in play.

In the pages of the *Revolution,* Stanton and Anthony analyzed this political landscape and tried to find openings for women. In their editorials, Anthony and Stanton urged the "true men in both parties" to mutiny. They should "step out from the ranks, clear the deck of its time-serving faithless crew, lay hold the helm and guide the ship of state to safety."[144] They envisioned Ben Wade or Ben Butler as president and Frederick Douglass as vice president.[145] The *Revolution* signaled its lack of respect for existing political alignments by refusing to capitalize either "republican" or "democratic," but they criticized the Republicans especially fiercely, and readers in the grip of binary thinking therefore labeled them Democrats.[146] They were not, but Stanton in particular leaned that way and tried to encourage "progressive democracy" and urge "liberal democrats" to assert themselves.[147] "If the democratic party were wise," she advised, it would reorient itself by embracing universal suffrage and women's rights.[148]

The process of sorting out party identities temporarily took a back seat to the drama of impeachment. President Andrew Johnson had done everything in his power to stymie or dismantle Radical Reconstruction, and in December 1867 he used his annual message to Congress to declare black voters "corrupt in principle" and to state openly that he had contemplated using force to seize control of the Congress in order to put a halt to what he deemed "unconstitutional" Reconstruction Acts. Many thoughtful people believed that Johnson and southern intransigents had planned, and perhaps still were planning, nothing less than a coup d'etat. But when Radicals demanded impeachment, they were outmaneuvered by conservative Republicans who feared the radicalism of Ben Wade, next in line for the presidency. Then Johnson brought matters to a head by seeking to remove Secretary of War Edwin Stanton, provocative behavior that finally left the conservatives no choice. Impeachment proceedings dragged on through the first winter and spring of the *Revolution's* existence, and though they differed on other questions, Stanton and Anthony agreed with Douglass and

Phillips on the political question of the hour: they all wanted impeachment and saw Ben Wade as the country's best hope.[149]

In May 1868 the Senate refused, by one vote, to remove Andrew Johnson from office. This scotched the last hope for a political breakthrough that might have secured black (male) suffrage and helped woman suffrage at the same time—Ben Wade's elevation to the presidency. It also broke the political logjam, and just days later the Republicans proceeded to nominate Ulysses S. Grant for president on a platform that did not even dare to endorse black suffrage, despite the fact that the party had just imposed it upon the South as a condition of Reconstruction. Wendell Phillips was devastated by this turn of events. A year earlier he had rallied the AASS to back the Republican Party, asking only "if we sell out" to get the best price, and the impeachment of Andrew Johnson had been his price.[150] Phillips now condemned both parties as "essentially indifferent to the rights and the welfare of the colored race," and even urged abolitionists to abstain from voting.[151]

"The last Republican lamp has gone out," the *Revolution* announced when impeachment failed. Unlike Phillips, Stanton and Anthony had never hoped for much from the party of Eskridge and Kalloch and they pivoted quickly toward the Democrats. Stanton declared for "universal suffrage and universal amnesty," condemned the Republicans' financial policies, and lent support to a boomlet for Salmon P. Chase as the Democratic presidential candidate.[152] Chase would have returned from the Republicans to shift his old party in a progressive direction "on a platform of universal suffrage, the rights of labor, greenbacks, and free trade."[153] Chase had pre-convention support that ranged from Gerrit Smith to the Democratic press, including the *New York Herald* and for a time even Manton Marble's *World*, and he came surprisingly close to pulling off this seemingly unlikely swap of parties.[154] Anticipating a strong run by Chase, Stanton and Anthony decided to appeal to the Democrats directly: they sought and won a chance to present their ideas to the Democratic national convention when it met at Tammany Hall.[155] This time they were angling for something bigger than woman suffrage in D.C. and hoping for a reorientation of the Democratic Party, even though it was heavily staffed with white racists.

Stanton and Anthony's 1868 "Tammany Hall Platform" included some Democratic orthodoxy on economic matters (including greenbacks, repeal of the income tax, and retrenchment in government expenditure), but its main thrust was to endorse universal suffrage.[156] Republican papers reported that the Democrats laughed at Susan B. Anthony when she appeared in person to present it, though the *Revolution* tried to insist that the laughter in the hall had been directed at the follies of Republicans.[157] Still, the Democratic convention was deeply discouraging because it rejected both Chase and universal suffrage. The tone was set by Missouri politician and former Union Army General Frank

Blair, who circulated a so-called Brodhead letter that threw red meat to unre-
pentant ex-Confederates. Blair's letter argued that a Democratic president could
simply declare the Reconstruction governments in the South "null and void"
and use the army to disperse them and restore white rule.[158] After Chase's candidacy crumbled, the Democrats nominated Horatio Seymour (against whom
Anthony had campaigned back in the 1862 gubernatorial election), an old
stager who was acceptable to all factions. They then energized the ticket by
nominating Frank Blair for vice president and constructing a platform that
echoed extreme white southern intransigence and attacked Reconstruction as
fundamentally illegitimate. Anthony could scarcely believe the Democrats
made "such a stupid nomination."[159] She even tried to persuade Chase to persist
as a third-party candidate.[160]

Confronted with the possibility of a Democratic administration determined
to destroy Reconstruction root and branch, Wendell Phillips slunk back into
Republican ranks. In a key editorial in the NASS at the end of August, he taxed
his considerable eloquence to excoriate the Republicans as "shuffling, evasive,
unprincipled, corrupt, cowardly and mean, almost beyond the power of words
to describe." But then, after having reviled Republican leaders as "mad for office,
cankered with gold, poisoned with spite, cowards from the first, ... ridiculously
incompetent," he proceeded to endorse them. Grant and Colfax were, he said,
"the salvation of the union and the best hope for the negro."[161] This about-face
was, his biographer writes, "perhaps the single most humiliating public act of his
career."[162] Anthony and Stanton agreed with Phillips's description of the
Republican Party but were disgusted with his nonsequitur endorsement.[163]

In response, Stanton and Anthony cultivated new alliances with the labor
movement, which also was disenchanted with both major parties and threatening third party action.[164] They turned to the National Labor Union and its
leader William Sylvis, running editorials of their own on capital and labor, and
printing articles by and about Sylvis. In September 1868 Anthony helped form a
Working Woman's Association in New York City, most of whose members were
typesetters.[165] At about the same time, Anthony and Stanton attended the
National Labor Congress, where they tried to make the case for woman suffrage
as essential to working women. Although Sylvis declared in favor of "universal
suffrage, regardless of sex or color," he could not carry with him the more conservative white men of the craft unions who dominated the organization.[166] The
Revolution editorialized in favor of the Labor Congress as the basis for a third
party in 1872, prophesied it would give greater recognition to women in the
future, and regretted that black representation had been lacking in its ranks.[167]
But it was clear that forging alliances with organized labor and mobilizing
working women offered no immediate leverage for woman suffrage. What else
might be done now, in 1868?

In a remarkable move, Elizabeth Cady Stanton identified an astonishing expedient: having been disappointed in her hopes for Ben Wade or Salmon P. Chase, she now endorsed Frank Blair! Stanton used the front page of the *Revolution* to urge every woman in the country to read Blair's "able" Indianapolis speech in the New York *World*, "showing most clearly and conclusively what is to be the fate of American women under the radical policy of manhood suffrage." "We have not room to copy in full," Stanton regretted, and concluded, "In the name of the educated women of this country, we protest against the enfranchisement of another man of any race or clime until the daughters of Jefferson, Hancock, and Adams are crowned with all their rights."[168] She also wrote a personal letter to Blair congratulating him on the speech, using most of the same phrasing found in her *Revolution* piece. Lest anyone fail to notice, her vice-presidential endorsement was publicized in the *New York World*.[169] With these actions, Elizabeth Cady Stanton clasped hands with the lowest and most violent racism.

Frank Blair's Indianapolis speech, delivered before a huge crowd and widely covered in Democratic newspapers, was a carefully thought out position paper that was read, not delivered extemporaneously.[170] In it, Blair shifted ground by arguing not that Reconstruction was unconstitutional but instead that it was catastrophic because enfranchising black men would unleash a "despotism of bestial passions."[171] Blair was seeking to alter the terms of the presidential contest because his Brodhead letter, together with fiery speeches by ex-Confederates, had backfired. Republicans were scoring points by charging that "Seymour was opposed to the last war, and Blair is in favor of the next one."[172] In Indianapolis, Blair offered his new argument: he attacked black male suffrage, the centerpiece of Radical Reconstruction, on the basis of the sexual behavior of black men and their threat to white womanhood. Assuming the mantle of up-to-date science, Blair quoted at length from two professors who opined that Africans always practiced "promiscuous concubinage." He predicted that suffrage in the hands of black men would result in "the loss of popular liberty, the establishment of a military despotism in the place of the Constitution, the establishment of different social institutions, and the degradation of the fairer sex," but he emphasized the last of these. Would not black men who could vote, Blair asked, "use that power to the worst extremity that their passions may suggest toward the softer sex?" Blair's speech was an early, high-profile expression of a deeply racist mythology that would be constructed around the figure of the black rapist.[173]

Stanton seized upon a point in Blair's speech when he seemed to endorse woman suffrage, which would have been an unprecedented embrace of the women's cause by a major party candidate in a presidential race. But Blair only appeared to do so by way of complaining that abolitionists who had formerly pushed woman suffrage, such as Wendell Phillips, had abandoned white women in favor of black men: "They deny it [the vote] to their own fair countrywomen,

Frank Blair, the Democratic vice-presidential candidate in 1868. Print Collection,
Miriam and Ira D. Wallach Division of Art, Prints and Photographs, New York
Public Library, Astor, Lenox, and Tilden Foundations.

however intellectual and cultivated, and give to the gross, ignorant, hateful
African caste."[174] Stanton's own comments about "outweighing" black men and
vowing "not another man" certainly projected hostile views of black male voters,
but with this endorsement she took a step well beyond any previous arguments
of "low expediency."

The election of 1868 was the first presidential contest conducted after the
freedmen of the former Confederacy were enfranchised, and the situation in the
South was volatile and violent. As Louisiana's carpetbagger governor Henry Clay
Warmoth later recalled, "there never was such bitterness" when "it was believed
by both parties that the whole question of Reconstruction was to be settled by
the result of this Presidential election."[175] All over the South, black voters were
intimidated, beaten, and killed as the Ku Klux Klan demonstrated the lengths to
which it would go to elect Democrats. The *NASS* tried to alert its readers with
headlines like "Desperadoism in Tennessee," and "Persecution and Murder of

Union Men in Kentucky and Tennessee."[176] But Marble's *World* dismissed such reports as "Radical Forgeries" and brazenly insisted the violence was all on the other side.[177] In the summer and fall of 1868, Warmoth tried and failed to stop the murder of black Republicans in Louisiana. Ultimately, hundreds died in Klan violence, and Republican voters stayed at home or hid in the woods on election day, which guaranteed a Democratic victory. Similar Klan violence in Georgia enabled the Democrats to carry that state as well.[178]

When Frank Blair campaigned against a "semi-barbarous race" whose "rule" would "subject the white women to their unbridled lust," he was invoking the black rapist as an excuse for the reign of terror being unleashed in the South, and Stanton's endorsement implicated her in these violent southern realities.[179] Marble immediately publicized Stanton's endorsement, and southern Democrats picked up the cue. The *Georgia Weekly Telegraph* doctored Stanton's remarks slightly and quoted her to its readers, declaring that Elizabeth Cady Stanton urged every patriot to "unite with us in the great approaching struggle to elect Horatio Seymour and Frank Blair, that the war for the Union, the Constitution, and the laws may be commenced in earnest."[180] Thus Stanton's comments literally gave aid and comfort to Georgia Klansmen.

Why did she do it? Stanton's endorsement coincided with—and may have been influenced by—a calculated campaign by Manton Marble in the *New York World*. As the presidential campaign heated up in the late summer of 1868, Marble's *World* was one in which a supposed wave of "negro outrages" swept the South, purportedly the work of black rioters, thieves, thugs, arsonists, and assassins.[181] But in mid-September 1868 a new type of black criminal appeared in its pages: black rapists suddenly became prominent.[182] Many of the alleged rapes happened in the North, but no matter, Marble drew the connection anyway. On the very same day he ran Blair's Indianapolis speech, Marble warned soberly of a supposed upsurge in black-on-white rape:

> Since this devilish work began of stimulating the southern negroes into envy, hatred, and jealousy of their former masters, negro outrages upon whites at the North also have been enormously more frequent than of old. This is especially true of the worst form of such outrages. Scarcely a week has passed since the spring began that the public press has not been called upon to chronicle one or more instances of hideous outrage perpetrated upon white women in lonely places by negro scoundrels.[183]

Marble was easily shrewd enough to understand that the specter of the black rapist was useful precisely because it got traction among northern progressives who were normally unsympathetic to the ex-Confederates—progressives like Elizabeth Cady Stanton.

The motto of the Blair campaign. Photographs and Prints Division, Schomburg Center for Research in Black Culture, New York Public Library, Astor, Lenox, and Tilden Foundations.

Perhaps Stanton believed the Democrats were going to win the election and if so she might as well encourage them to make good on woman suffrage. Reports coming out of Louisiana might have forecast such a victory, and she had connections with both the former governor Michael Hahn and the current governor Henry Clay Warmoth. And Frank Blair was Warmoth's former brigade, division, and corps commander during the war, and a "personal friend."[184] Stanton also had Democratic Party connections: 1868 was the year when her husband took a step back toward his old party by signing up as a journalist for Charles A. Dana, who had just taken over the *New York Sun*. Dana is said to have believed for a while that a new coalition of Radical Republicans and working-class Democrats could remake the Democratic Party.[185] Stanton's son Neil would soon head to Louisiana as a carpetbagger, perhaps because of his father's connections to the *Sun* and the Warmoth administration.[186] The threads cannot be connected, but they all suggest Stanton had an insider's perspective on Louisiana and on Democratic prospects in 1868. It may be telling that Stanton's correspondence with her husband in these years was almost entirely destroyed.

Of course, Stanton's Blair endorsement disgusted Frederick Douglass, who had been up to this point remarkably tolerant of Stanton's flights of rhetoric denigrating black men. In frosty tones, Douglass refused Josephine Griffing's request to speak on behalf of woman suffrage adding, "I never suspected you of sympathizing with Miss Anthony and Mrs. Stanton in this course."[187] To Douglass the Republican Party, however imperfect, was the best hope for black people, and in 1868 he gave Grant an early endorsement. At one point he even considered running for Congress himself, which would certainly have been as a Republican.[188] Douglass insisted that while woman suffrage might be desirable, the vote for black men was literally a matter of life and death. "The South today," he editorialized, "is a field of blood." Douglass called on every loyal man and woman in the country to rally: "Our one work now is to elect Grant and Colfax."[189] Stanton and Anthony were far too busy to campaign for the Democratic ticket: they had a paper to edit, Anthony was organizing her Working Woman's Association, and Stanton was building a new house in New Jersey.[190] But with this editorial endorsement of Frank Blair, they had taken a step that set them poles apart from longtime ally Frederick Douglass. It was political opportunism of the worst sort: ill-informed, ineffective, and unprincipled.

Stanton's Blair endorsement dropped out of sight almost immediately. Indeed, Blair's speech itself was quickly forgotten, because the campaign took a new turn shortly thereafter, when early balloting in Pennsylvania and Ohio showed the Democrats stumbling in the North. Before long Manton Marble was hinting that Blair himself was a drag on the Democratic ticket and ought to be axed.[191] Stanton understandably never mentioned the Blair endorsement in her autobiography or in the *History of Woman Suffrage*. Most likely she was ashamed of it, because her year-end editorial in the *Revolution* included an otherwise mysterious apology. In what was, for her, an unusual tone of contrition, she wrote that she was sorry "if by a heedless word or act we have added one pang to any human heart, one jarring note to the world's discordant strain of misery."[192]

The *Revolution* had been nothing if not inconsistent: the editors had actually *attacked* Frank Blair two months before they endorsed him—on the grounds that he opposed black suffrage.[193] They never could decide what to say about the southern situation. Early on, Stanton, Anthony, and Train had proposed to speak on educated suffrage in all the chief cities in the South, but that idea quickly disappeared.[194] They ran a letter from an ex-slave endorsing them, and an editorial countering the *World*'s depiction of black misrule in the South.[195] But they also claimed to be receiving "many excellent letters from southern [white] women" and seemed to think they were a promising constituency.[196] Southern black women only sometimes claimed the *Revolution*'s attention.

Instead of covering political matters, the *Revolution* of late 1868 turned increasingly to the old debates about marriage and sexual behavior which had been hot button issues before the war. A flap occurred when George Francis Train used the *Revolution* columns to ask breezily, "Have Not Women the Same Right to Have Paramours that Men Have to keep Mistresses?"[197] When critics howled, Train pointed out they obviously assumed that men *did* have a right to keep mistresses. The controversy played on for months.[198] The paper also took up the case of Hester Vaughn, a domestic servant who had been seduced and abandoned and then became a cause celebre after she was convicted on circumstantial evidence of murdering her newborn infant.[199] Elizabeth Cady Stanton began to use *Revolution* columns to respond to queries about her position on marriage and divorce.[200] This turn toward issues of marriage and sexual morality responded to deep concerns among contemporary women, concerns far more powerful than their interest in the ballot, but public discussion of marriage and morality had tended to rebound against the women's rights cause. After the Blair endorsement, however, it may have seemed like familiar and safer ground.

By late 1868, Train's financial backing had long since evaporated and it was becoming apparent that their paper was not going to yield a profit, not soon and perhaps not ever. Every passing week ran Anthony deeper into debt.[201] Stanton and Anthony's year was winding down with no results, a major mistake, and a terrible, growing suspicion that the moment of opportunity might already have come and gone, back on the plains of Kansas.

7

The Fight over the Fifteenth Amendment

It was an obvious slap in the face. With Wendell Phillips's encouragement, the Boston woman suffragists had called a convention in late November 1868, shortly after Ulysses S. Grant was elected president. It was bad enough that the organizers failed to invite Susan B. Anthony. But when they first invited Elizabeth Cady Stanton to speak and then *withdrew* the invitation claiming it had been issued "by mistake," Stanton was furious.[1] She retaliated by publicizing the maladroit episode in the *Revolution*. The Boston women had called "a little private convention of their own," she wrote, to which she had been finally invited despite fears that doing so "would be endorsing Seymour, Blair, Tammany, the *New York World*, and the *Revolution*." "We accepted the invitation," she wrote, "and began to plan the threads of our discourse, and the fitting bonnet, cloak and dress (for these innocent vanities will creep into the souls of the most strong minded)." But then, she concluded in mock-heroic tones, "Lo! Like the milkmaid in the fable, our visions of glory were all suddenly dashed to the ground; for in an evil moment the committee repented themselves, and we were duly informed that the invitation was withdrawn!"[2] By mentioning Blair, Stanton betrayed some awareness that she might be subject to legitimate criticism, but she was not about to accept it from the stay-at-home Bostonians who had not lifted a finger to help in Kansas and lacked the courage to face her in debate. Stanton was already disturbed by the news that, by all accounts, the Republicans would shortly pass a constitutional amendment securing the right to vote for black men but not for women. The Bostonians who presumed to rescue the women's movement from her tainted leadership made the political outlook even harder to face.

Feeling sure the Fifteenth Amendment was in hand, Wendell Phillips declared a "woman's hour" in late 1868. For a moment it seemed that Stanton and Anthony might yet see woman suffrage become a reality in Washington, D.C. But when the Fifteenth Amendment slowed and stalled in Congress, Phillips reversed himself again and reannounced the "Negro's hour." This time he had the help of Lucy Stone, who finally arrived at a position of open opposition, even enmity to Anthony especially. Stanton reacted to this latest disappointment by making her "fearful outrages" claim, taking on the race hatred of Blair and the *World* and making it her own, and Anthony backed her up. By January or February 1869 there was no longer any chance, fighting or otherwise, to win woman suffrage. According to the "claim the uttermost and you are sure to get something" adage, it was time for these woman suffrage leaders to concede that the "something" they would have to settle for was black (male) suffrage. But they could not bring themselves to do it until late summer or fall 1869, and in the interim, they engaged in ugly sniping and irresponsible vituperation. They no longer had a fighting chance, but they were worn out with failure and poorer for their efforts. They were also embittered by personal attacks from rival white activists, thrown into confrontational situations because of free platform traditions, chafed by a long ratification fight, and stung by the humiliating realization that women were to be the only sensible adults without the ballot. Conflict came to a head at the 1869 AERA convention, where Stanton and Anthony clashed with Frederick Douglass and Frances Harper. Douglass and Harper kept the focus on the issues and eschewed personal attacks, but the AERA was shattered. The "saddest of all divorces" had finally come.

After Grant's election, Republicans finally determined on a Fifteenth Amendment to guarantee black (male) suffrage because they saw that Grant's margin of victory was alarmingly slim—only about 300,000 in an election in which 500,000 black men cast votes.[3] Under these circumstances, even unprincipled party hacks saw the merits of an amendment that would protect black Republicans already enfranchised in the South and add additional black Republican voters in the northern and border states. The opportunity stood open because they could take advantage of their super majority in the lame duck congressional session in the winter of 1868–69 to pass the amendment. Furthermore, because ratification took place inside state legislatures, they could keep what might be an unpopular measure buffered from the voters.[4] Thus voting rights for black men, long the goal of radicals, finally appealed to moderate and conservative Republicans as a means to secure the party's hold on power.[5]

Wendell Phillips eagerly embraced these developments. By interpreting the Fifteenth Amendment as "the last and most necessary of all the abolitionists' victories," he could "adjust emotionally" to the defeat he had suffered in his previous struggle to influence the Republican Party. Feeling vindicated after all, he urged Congress to lose no time on "needless debate" or mere "phraseology."[6] And now that he felt confident of the Fifteenth Amendment, Phillips finally lifted his "Negro's hour" proscription against woman suffrage agitation. He signaled the change in two editorials in the *National Anti-Slavery Standard* in the fall of 1868, one in anticipation of the women's rights convention in Boston, and one just after it was held.[7] Boston woman suffragists were ready to act on Phillips's signal by holding their convention in November 1868, and at the same time, in apparent coordination, a number of state woman suffrage conventions were held elsewhere in the Northeast.[8] At the Boston convention Thomas Wentworth Higginson announced that this was "emphatically the woman's hour," now that "questions that took precedence" had been cleared away.[9]

A group of Bostonians led by Caroline Severance used the convention to launch a New England Woman Suffrage Association (NEWSA). They black-balled quarrelsome Caroline Dall, eased Olympia Brown to the side, and ignored or disinvited the *Revolution* editors.[10] Instead, the New England organization elevated the socially prominent Julia Ward Howe to its top leadership position despite her being a very recent convert. Her chief credentials seemed to be her elite status and her willingness to say plainly, "I am glad we shall come in after the negro."[11] The Boston convention defined the woman's hour as a time to build a formal organization; results would come later, after black men had the vote. Frederick Douglass was there to endorse woman suffrage but also to remind the convention that black suffrage was a matter of "much greater emergency . . . a matter of life and death."[12] Massachusetts senator Henry Wilson told the convention, "For more than a dozen years . . . I would have given suffrage to the women of Massachusetts," but he also boasted of having "courage enough" to vote down woman suffrage when it had been coupled with black suffrage.[13] Other prominent attendees willing to echo those priorities included William Lloyd Garrison and Frances E. W. Harper. Wendell Phillips was not present, perhaps because he was avoiding Garrison, but the proceedings clearly had his blessing.[14] In the NEWSA, Boston woman suffragists effectively created a safe-and-sane alternative to Stanton and Anthony, making a clear commitment to backing a black (male) suffrage FIfteenth Amendment and *then* seeking a woman suffrage Sixteenth Amendment. They seemed able to tap widespread grassroots interest via state-level conventions that were held around the Northeast, and they also seemed to have access to all-important funding, because it was announced that $2,000 had been pledged toward the operation of the new NEWSA.[15]

The only thing lacking in this anti-Anthony-and-Stanton organization was Lucy Stone's leadership. In fact, Stone marred the harmony of the Boston convention by unexpectedly introducing a resolution calling for the Republican Party to "drop its watchword of 'Manhood Suffrage' " and give the vote to all men and women as a right of citizenship.[16] Although she was opposed by Douglass, Garrison, and Harper, Stone summoned up her old eloquence and won the vote. Stone was no longer friendly with Stanton and Anthony, but she still shared their preference for a combined Fifteenth Amendment that would address both race and gender discrimination in voting rights. An opponent reported that Stone "got the meeting to pass a resolution placing the woman before the negro."[17] Actually Stone's resolution called for citizenship suffrage and therefore simultaneous rather than sequential enfranchisement of women and black men, but, revealingly, opponents assumed that *challenging* the black-men-first priority meant *reversing* it. The old AERA middle ground of supporting simultaneous black and woman suffrage was slipping away.

Stanton and Anthony's new Boston rivals promptly moved to challenge them in another way, by launching a newspaper called the *Woman's Advocate*. In an obvious shot at the *Revolution,* Phillips's *Standard* quickly praised the monthly *Advocate* for its dignified "moral tone" and freedom from "partisan coquetry."[18] The appearance of the first issue in January 1869 must have been an especially bitter pill for Susan B. Anthony, because old abolitionist allies who refused to support the *Revolution* had opened their purses to fund this rival organ. Handsomely printed, carrying no advertising, and promising contributors that they would be "liberally compensated," the *Woman's Advocate* flaunted its prosperity at a time when Anthony was ever more desperate for money.[19]

The *Revolution*'s editors fought back by promoting an alternative woman suffrage convention—a national convention in Washington, D.C., hosted by the Universal Franchise Association and scheduled for January 1869.[20] Stanton criticized Senator Henry Wilson for his "disingenuous" speech in Boston and challenged him to offer support where it counted, in Washington, where woman suffrage was to be voted up or down in Congress: "Mr. Wilson's private views are of no advantage to our cause so long as he publicly declares he will vote adversely. He cunningly tells the women of Massachusetts to press the question in their Legislature. Why not in the District where the negro question is settled?"[21] Although Stanton and Anthony, like Stone, would have preferred a combined race-and-gender Fifteenth Amendment, its chances in the Congress were obviously slim to none. Senator Samuel Pomeroy led off the new congressional session in early December 1868 by introducing just such an amendment—making suffrage a right of all citizens—but Pomeroy's bill was simply ignored by his fellow legislators, and George Julian proposed a like measure in the House, to similar effect.[22] Prospects looked brighter when Henry Wilson introduced a bill in the Senate to enfranchise women in the District of Columbia (while Representative George Julian presented a similar measure in the House), because Wilson was influential and his D.C. bill would not be bottled up in the Judiciary Committee. It could instead head for the District of Columbia Committee and its friendly chair, Senator James Harlan of Iowa.[23] Phillips's *Standard* promptly declared its support for Wilson's D.C. bill, and thus at the end of 1868 it appeared that despite policy differences and personal enmity, the New England moderates would join Stanton and Anthony in backing a practical woman suffrage measure with a real chance to become law in the near term.[24] The immediate fruit of the "woman's hour" was to be woman suffrage in the nation's capital.

But hope for Washington woman suffrage was quickly squelched. On January 14, 1869, Lucy Stone was scheduled to deliver a public lecture in Washington in front of Senator Henry Wilson and "many members of Congress and their wives," and it had been announced beforehand that Stone would urge the passage of the D.C. woman suffrage bill and "a separate [i.e., sixteenth] suffrage amendment for women."[25] In the event, Stone raised the cry of "the Negro's hour" and told Wilson and the other congressmen, "Woman must wait for the negro."[26] Stone was throwing the D.C. woman suffrage bill overboard, implying it would interfere with the black (male) suffrage amendment. At the same time, George Julian indicated that it was "not probable" that a vote could be obtained on D.C. woman suffrage in the House either.[27] The woman's hour was over almost before it began.

The problem was that the Fifteenth Amendment, which had appeared poised to sail through Congress when it convened in December, had stalled out in January. Republicans had become absorbed in time-consuming debates over greenbacks and specie resumption, while black suffrage advocates were ineffective because they differed among themselves over whether to push for an amendment or a law to enforce voting rights, or both.[28] Meanwhile the clock was ticking because the 40th Congress's term would soon expire.[29] Wendell Phillips, realizing he had been overconfident, asked anxiously, "Where is the Constitutional Amendment? Has Congress forgotten it, or is there an intent to baulk the people's wish? The delay is alarming."[30] In this emergency Lucy Stone abandoned the position she had argued so passionately in Boston a few weeks earlier and helped Wendell Phillips to reinstate his old dictum: it was still the "Negro's hour."

Although Stone's actions were no help, the fate of Washington woman suffrage was also determined by local developments. The black community had to fend off a new threat to disenfranchise Washington residents altogether, and D.C. woman suffrage dropped so far off the table that when the next woman suffrage convention met, it felt obliged (rather than urging Congress to extend the vote to D.C. women), to deplore a scheme to take the vote away from D.C. men.[31] When Stanton testified before the District of Columbia Committee in favor of woman suffrage, she dismissed the threat of disenfranchisement as "puerile," but it was real.[32] In 1871, a new law would consolidate the District and make most local offices appointive rather than elective, and in 1874 Congress would eliminate representative government in the District entirely.[33] Efforts to win D.C. woman suffrage would continue, but this episode in January 1869 completed the long process whereby Stone separated from Anthony and Stanton and sided with the Bostonians against them.

Never very politically minded, Lucy Stone was probably taking her political cues from Henry Blackwell, an early proponent of the Fifteenth Amendment and a supporter of Republican policies generally.[34] In the aftermath of Kansas she had quarreled personally with Anthony over Train, money, and organizational control, but long before that, caught between Blackwell on one side and Stanton and Anthony on the other, she had begun to make her choice, as the rocky passages in her marriage only confirmed Stone's unwillingness to trust women who might have been critical. At this point, Stone took up the position with which she would be historically identified, as the most determined advocate of the voting rights of black men within the ranks of white woman suffragists. Given her history—her quarrels with Frederick Douglass, her quick conclusions that black men were all opposed to woman suffrage—it was a bit surprising. Stone's hostility to Anthony was so decided that Lucretia Mott remarked on "how perverted the understanding becomes, when personal dissension exists."[35] Stanton and Anthony were hostile right back: they were furious with Stone's reversal on D.C. woman suffrage and they publicly accused her of having "ruined Wilson and several others for any action this year."[36]

By all indicators, the last real prospect for any immediate victory on woman suffrage was dead. Stanton and Anthony had to decide how to react. Even when her hopes had been high for a D.C. suffrage bill back in December, Stanton had been unwilling to stifle her objections to a black (male) suffrage Fifteenth Amendment. In December she editorialized, "The District of Columbia certainly can be given us this very year."[37] But in the same issue, she slammed the "unwashed and unlettered ditch-diggers, bootblacks, hostlers, butchers, and barbers" who would precede women if the Fifteenth Amendment passed. "Think of Patrick and Sambo and Hans and Yung Tung" making laws for educated, refined women, she cried. She structured her rhetoric around a repeated, "We object...we object...we object" to the Fifteenth Amendment.[38] Long in the habit of including invidious comments about black men among the array of arguments she offered for woman suffrage, Stanton found it easy to mute the egalitarian arguments and turn up the volume on those that demeaned black men.

Stanton strained facts and mangled logic as her *Revolution* editorials reinterpreted Kansas. She had previously insisted that the two causes of black (male) suffrage and woman suffrage would have been stronger together, but now she changed her tune and claimed that women in Kansas had helped to defeat black suffrage. Kansas women justifiably resented black men's claims of precedence, she wrote, and their "natural pride and jealousy" were "infused into the minds of men at every hearthstone" so that the white male voters rejected black suffrage at their behest.[39] This was quite a piece of sophistry, implying that women hardly needed the ballot, so perfect was their control of male voters. With this distorted

Lucy Stone. The Schlesinger Library, Radcliffe Institute, Harvard University.

Kansas history, Stanton actually worked her way around until she nearly occupied common ground with her critics and with the women's old Kansas nemesis, the *Leavenworth Daily Conservative,* saying that women *had* defeated black suffrage in Kansas. Stanton appeared to imply that women might now do the same thing and defeat the Fifteenth Amendment. "We doubt," she speculated ominously, "whether a constitutional amendment securing 'Manhood suffrage'

Henry Blackwell. Schlesinger Library, Radcliffe Institute, Harvard University.

alone could be fairly passed in a single state in this Union."[40] Stubbornly arguing for black and woman suffrage together in a combined amendment—a measure she surely knew had no practical chance—she predicted that, if separated, "both will be defeated!!"[41] As she looked back to recall her encounter with Charles Langston on the streets of Leavenworth, Stanton was now reinterpreting Kansas, not as the last moment of harmony but as the first moment of hostility between white women and black men.

Her editorials increasingly portrayed black men as sexual offenders. She and Anthony had devoted a large part of December 1868 to stepped-up efforts to prevent the execution of Hester Vaughn, the servant convicted of infanticide.[42] Anthony's Working Women's Association mobilized on Vaughn's behalf and portrayed her as an example of working women's victimization.[43] But Manton Marble's *World* tied the Hester Vaughn case to its favorite theme, the black rapist, by referring to the father of Vaughan's child, hitherto unidentified in any way, as her "brutal black ravisher."[44] Stanton picked up on that same theme when she editorialized about another case of "supposed infanticide" involving a girl of fourteen or fifteen and a black farm worker who "effected her ruin." "With judges and jurors of negroes," Stanton asked, "how will Saxon girls fare in their courts for crimes like this?" Although she did remark that black (male) jurors might be unfair for good reason—"the generations of wrong and injustice their daughters have suffered at the white man's hands"—her sympathies were reserved for the

"Saxon girl" at the center of the case.[45] Stanton also commented on a rape case originally reported in the *World* as an "Outrage by a Negro in Tennessee."[46] Stanton reprinted the *World* article but altered the story by cutting off the last line, which indicated that the black suspect had been taken from jail and lynched by the Ku Klux Klan. Instead she concluded with the previous line, which reported that marshals had difficulty "in keeping the negroes, who had assembled, from burning him." This indefensible omission suppressed mention of deadly Klan violence and instead shifted the onus for violence onto black people's shoulders. As Stanton wrote about cases of sexual violence, she was beginning to imagine that Frank Blair and the *New York World* were right, that there was a link between black men's voting rights and the sexual abuse of white women. She would eventually write of "slender threads" of logic that linked "hideous overt acts" of rape to "creeds and codes that make an aristocracy of sex," but there were no threads and the logic was faulty.[47]

At the National Woman Suffrage Convention in Washington in January 1869—the one called to counter the Boston convention held in November—Stanton and Anthony struck out in several directions at once. Stanton opened with a speech that reiterated her demand for a Sixteenth Amendment enfranchising women, which seemed to concede that the Fifteenth Amendment was a fait accompli, but many of her arguments continued her descent into unmitigated racism. She again warned against "Patrick, Sambo, Hans, and Yung Tung," and repeated her "not another man" line.[48] Stanton went so far as to contend that a man's government (i.e., one in which black men had the right to vote) was actually *worse* than a white man's government.[49] Susan B. Anthony introduced resolutions endorsing an educational qualification for suffrage, returning to a position she and Stanton had previously abandoned.[50]

After the convention, Stanton took a deep breath and sought to mend fences in a *Revolution* editorial in which she wrote, "It has been a great grief to the leading women in our cause that there should be this antagonism with men who we respect, whose wrongs we pity, and whose hopes we would fain help them to realize." She admitted that, when contrasting white women's condition with that of black men, "There seems to be a selfishness in our present position." But, she wrote, we speak "not for ourselves alone," but on behalf of "all womankind, in poverty, ignorance and hopeless dependence, for the women of this oppressed race too."[51] Over the very long haul, she was right, and the work of these pioneering activists would indeed come to benefit all women. But in early 1869, this fine sentiment rang hollow and scarcely lasted a week. In the very next issue of the *Revolution*, Stanton and Anthony hit rock bottom.

The February 4, 1869, issue carried the infamous editorial in which Stanton predicted that enfranchising black men under the Fifteenth Amendment would "culminate in fearful outrages on womanhood especially in the southern states."[52]

At the convention, Stanton had predicted "greater injustice and oppression" in the South, but now she specifically warned of "tyranny, persecutions, insults, horrors" and introduced an unmistakable euphemism for rape—"outrages on womanhood." She thus returned to the worst of Frank Blair's hate campaign and Manton Marble's disinformation and adopted their arguments against the black-man-as-rapist as her own. This prediction of "fearful outrages" was no slip of the editorial pen, because Stanton and Anthony soon repeated it in person during a trip to Chicago and Milwaukee to attend woman suffrage meetings.[53] This same *Revolution* issue also carried the charge that Lucy Stone had "ruined" Wilson for action on women and even blamed black men for the D.C. failure. "Black men have been citizens in the District of Columbia for two years," Stanton wrote, "Have they made any move for the enfranchisement of women there? Nay, nay, they are at this moment more hostile to women than any class of men in the country."[54] Finally this issue contained a scornful report of a conversation with a black minister who spoke in dialect and complacently announced that God made man "de boss over de woman." As for women voting, the minister declared, "I is 'posed to dat, it will not do at all. . . . I tell you dat de woman was de first to commit sin."[55]

At some point in January or February 1869, Stanton and Anthony should have realized that the "uttermost" was out of reach and it was time to support black men's voting rights. But they were unwilling to endorse the Fifteenth Amendment and eager to criticize it, although not quite ready to abandon their equal rights loyalties altogether and oppose black men's voting rights directly. They had long stewed about how Wendell Phillips had denied them money to which they were entitled, and they still agonized over squandered opportunities in Kansas and resented being blamed. They knew that some of the criticism of their association with George Francis Train was justified but thought much of it was unfair and over the top. They resented the way Lucy Stone was using policy differences to dignify defensiveness and spite. They must have felt defensive themselves about the Blair endorsement, and they certainly felt sore at the treatment they had received at the hands of their holier-than-thou, well-heeled Boston competitors. And on top of all this, they felt humiliated. The elevation of black men inevitably placed women in a lower, subordinate position, as only women were to be denied the vote. Surely they felt what Frederick Douglass referred to as "that bitter and stinging element of invidiousness which attaches to disfranchisement in a republic."[56] Douglass crafted the phrase to plead for black suffrage, but it was women who ended up with that bitter and stinging feeling. Julia Ward Howe actually cited this factor in explaining her sudden interest in the cause, noting that black suffrage brought with it a surprising "scarcely anticipated condition"—woman's isolation beyond the political pale—which goaded a previously indifferent woman like Howe to demand the vote.[57] For all these reasons, Stanton and Anthony were too wrought up to reflect, to reconsider—too wrought up to do anything but battle on.

The tradition of the free platform in woman suffrage meetings set them up for continuing confrontation.[58] The free platform, which dated back to abolitionist gatherings, was a matter of principle based on the assumption that if all ideas were freely aired, truth would win out, and it was believed to be worth the trouble of dealing with bores, lunatics, and cranks.[59] In 1869, however, it aggravated dissension because Stanton and Anthony found that their critics invaded woman suffrage conventions and exploited the free platform to confront them. At the Woman Suffrage Convention in Washington, for example, Edward M. Davis and Giles Stebbins both took the floor to lecture the women on their duty to defer to black suffrage. Other attendees became impatient, raised "point of order" objections, and finally voted to impose a ten-minute restriction on all speakers, but the debate was so warm the convention failed to break for lunch.[60] Stanton and Anthony repeatedly took the position that their opponents should be allowed to speak, trying to take the high road and conciliate on procedure if not on substance. But men like these, who monopolized the floor until resentments ran high, made it hard to concede that they might be right about the Fifteenth Amendment. At one point, Mary Livermore told a male windbag he ought to leave off and allow the women to speak because "men had been talking when they please, where they pleased, about what they pleased for 6,000 years."[61]

Some of the confrontational male invaders in the Washington convention in January 1869 were black men. George Downing presented resolutions that supported voting rights for black men even if women were left behind, just as he had at the 1867 AERA convention.[62] Dr. Charles Purvis, a young physician who had served in the army and was prominent in the Washington, D.C., black community, made an impassioned plea for women to waive their claims for the present, arguing that, when enfranchised, black men would be an added power in favor of woman suffrage. But Purvis also changed his tone and charged that women (i.e., white women) were "the bitterest enemies of the negro."[63] That remark set off a row: the eccentric Dr. Mary Walker, who had the previous year been named a leader of the "white woman suffrage" group in D.C., challenged Purvis. What, she asked, had women done to the negro? Purvis replied he was "astonished at her ignorance," and George Downing chimed in with the answer: "They have ordered us to be tied up and burned alive." Perhaps Downing referred to an 1866 Georgia case in which a black man accused of raping a sixteen-year-old white girl had been tied to a stake and burned to death before a crowd of 1,000 people.[64] These women present? No, not them, Charles Purvis replied, but they did not represent the women of this country. Neither, Susan B. Anthony retorted, did Purvis and Downing represent the black men of the South.[65] Anthony and Stanton managed to direct their gaze away from the appalling southern realities to which Downing referred, and they bolstered their own position with black testimony. To counter the criticisms of Charles Purvis, they invoked the opinions of his own father, Robert Purvis, who was present and sided with them. Robert Purvis declared, "He had the same feelings for his daughter as he had for his son, and he claimed she was entitled to equal rights with him." Downing demanded to know if, because he could not secure his daughter's rights, Robert Purvis would refuse them to his son? Yes, Purvis replied, he would, and Stanton praised the spectacle of "noble" Robert Purvis rebuking his own son for his narrow position.[66] But differences of opinion within the black community were reflected within the Purvis family, and Stanton had cherry-picked the opinion she preferred.

Western woman suffrage meetings saw confrontation as well. At the founding meeting of the Illinois Woman Suffrage Association in Chicago, Susan B. Anthony presented a resolution that warned of "fearful outrages on womanhood, especially in the Southern States," though she soon moved to withdraw it, probably responding to local leaders who did not appreciate her throwing "a firebrand in the convention."[67] Then William Wells Brown and another black man identified as "Mr. Babcock" shot back from their side. Brown and Babcock objected to a resolution calling for the Illinois state constitution to make no distinction "in the exercise of suffrage on account of race, color, sex, nativity, property, education, or creed." They argued that it should mention only sex discrimination, not racial bias, so that "the negro question and the woman question" would not be linked in any way.[68] By arguing that a woman suffrage meeting had no business taking a stand against race discrimination, Brown and Babcock took a verbal shot at white women who were, they thought, piggybacking on black (male) suffrage. But they had not considered the implications of their request, which in effect condoned and even demanded a whites-only focus among woman suffragists. Brown and Babcock were ignoring the interests of black women, who would be unable to vote unless both forms of discrimination were removed, and an African American woman named Naomi Bowman Talbert objected. Saying she spoke "on behalf of the colored women of Chicago and of the state of Illinois," Talbert argued for universal suffrage.[69] But even the presence of this outspoken black woman who endorsed both black and woman suffrage was not sufficient to bridge the gap between increasingly polarized positions.

Still in denial about the end of any immediate prospects for woman suffrage, Stanton and Anthony seemed to be stumbling from confrontation to confrontation. Stanton could not resist telling audiences that if woman suffrage and black suffrage were united, they could have been won in Kansas, and she mocked Theodore Tilton as a Rip Van Winkle who thought to be encouraging when he predicted women "would *certainly* vote in *twenty years*!!"[70] Anthony, too, found it impossible to concede defeat in view of growing popular interest in the women's movement—"this rushing to our lines," she called it.[71] Maybe Stanton still entertained some faint hope that Roscoe Conkling might be converted to the woman suffrage cause and pull wires to make it happen.[72] Perhaps John Stuart Mill's just-published *On the Subjection of Women* reassured Stanton that somehow, through sheer force of argument, women's cause must soon prevail.[73]

In the midst of their western trip, Stanton and Anthony's train schedule accidentally overlapped with Frederick Douglass's and they came face to face. Stanton understandably dreaded his reaction, but Anthony stepped forward to greet Douglass, and "his hearty words of welcome and gracious smile" reassured her. Stanton and Douglass had what she called "an earnest debate ... as far as we journeyed together." She described him as "gradually working up to our ideas on the question of suffrage."[74] "Up" to what? Was she still describing her position as "claiming the uttermost?" Stanton seems to have been engaged in wishful thinking. She claimed she looked forward to the annual AERA meeting in May 1869 as an opportunity to continue "a full and free discussion" with Douglass on the whole question of woman suffrage and the Fifteenth Amendment.[75] But that convention would prove to be the occasion for the biggest confrontation of all.

If the Fifteenth Amendment had been speedily drafted and ratified, Stanton and Anthony's complaints about it would have quickly become unimportant, but it was not. As it finally emerged from Congress in late February 1869, the Fifteenth Amendment simply forbade states from denying the right to vote on grounds of race. This language was the weakest of several versions proposed: it would not, for example, prevent southern states from using proxy grounds, such as literacy tests and poll taxes, to bar blacks from the polls. Although both the House and Senate had voted stronger language, the conference committee of Republican Party sachems, including the ubiquitous Roscoe Conkling, reported language that was weaker than either. Out-maneuvered late in the session, radicals had to take what they could get. Several Republican senators, including Charles Sumner, considered the Fifteenth Amendment so anemic they refused to vote for it, and two of the most radical actually voted against it, with the Democrats.[76] Readers of the *NASS*, however, would scarcely have suspected these weaknesses. Far from criticizing, Phillips and the old abolitionists of the AASS praised the Fifteenth Amendment to the skies. The *NASS* described it as "the grandest and most Christian act ever contemplated or accomplished by any nation," and pushed for its ratification.[77]

Stanton and Anthony believed Republican Party support for black suffrage at this point was totally cynical and prompted only by low motives of party advantage, and they mocked Wendell Phillips and his followers for having reduced themselves to "a mere tail of the Republican kite."[78] The *Revolution* editors criticized the Fifteenth Amendment roundly, though they did not call for active opposition to ratification. But they ran without comment letters from correspondents who did. One wrote, "Wherever a constitutional amendment for negro suffrage alone is pending, let all efforts be concentrated there, to defeat it."[79]

Phillips made ratifying the amendment the ultimate project of the American Anti-Slavery Society. As early as November 1868, before Congress had even convened, let alone drafted and passed the amendment, Henry Wilson of Massachusetts asked Abby Kelley Foster for help in the ratification campaign, and she began to solicit funds.[80] Phillips rallied the faithful to "strain every nerve" for ratification, and the American Anti-Slavery Society women raised scarce dollars for it through their annual "subscription anniversary."[81] "The Constitutional Amendment MUST be ratified," the *Standard* told its readers in March 1869, and proposed extreme measures, suggesting that Georgia could be divided in two or Texas broken into four new states, each of which could be required to ratify as the price of readmission.[82]

Although Phillips and the AASS seldom acknowledged the Fifteenth Amendment's limitations, they were quite evident to black men in the South, whose dangerous situation was regularly cited as its primary justification. The May 1869 AASS meeting heard from Henry McNeal Turner and James Simms, black legislators who had been expelled from the white-dominated Georgia legislature and who told of the assassination of many black Republicans. When asked point-blank by Frances Harper what the men of Georgia needed, Turner did not mention the Fifteenth Amendment: instead, he asked for military intervention or even "old rusty muskets" so black men could defend themselves.[83] The AASS had little to offer him except the idea that ratifying the new amendment would stop the violence. As the *Standard* put it: "While the question covered by the Fifteenth Amendment is allowed to remain an open one, desperate and murderous opposition to it will continue."[84]

For several months in 1869, Stanton and Anthony "went negative" on the Fifteenth Amendment while their critics insisted that they ought to feel obliged to positively endorse it. This debate among radical activists over ratification became overheated in part because Wendell Phillips and the American Anti-Slavery Society overestimated their own power to push the amendment through, just as they overestimated the *Revolution*'s power to stop it. The AASS engaged five speakers to campaign for ratification in doubtful states but apparently did not realize they were preaching to the choir.[85] Phillips overestimated the women's clout in the summer of 1869 when ratification efforts stalled in Rhode Island and coincidentally the Rhode Island Woman Suffrage Association condemned "the 15th Constitutional Amendment without the 16th" as "the basest compromise a republican government could make."[86] Phillips publicly lambasted them, implying their opposition was to blame for the Rhode Island defeat and characterizing the women's movement as "essentially selfish." Even "if the negro man should in his ignorance misuse his right and delay woman's recognition many a year," Phillips preached, woman suffragists had no principled right to deny him the vote.[87] But Rhode Island's defeat of the Fifteenth Amendment probably had little to do with woman suffrage and its advocates. Instead, it stemmed from Republicans' fears that the amendment might void a state law that imposed a property qualification on naturalized citizens, most of whom were Irish and would vote Democratic if they could. Some Republicans were understandably reluctant to toe the party line, and ratification was further complicated by an ongoing rivalry between Rhode Island's two senators.[88] Once again, Phillips and the old abolitionists who backed him failed to understand the dynamics of insider politics and were quick to blame the advocates of woman suffrage when things went wrong.

At one point, Phillips may have made small concessions to Stanton and Anthony's opinions. He remarked, "The ignorant prejudice of the working class is one of the great obstacles to the recognition of Woman's Rights." He thus seemed to acknowledge a tendency among the freedmen to oppose woman suffrage but shifted its source from race to class. He also argued that the Fifteenth Amendment would pose no practical threat to state-level efforts to win woman suffrage because "the addition of seventy thousand black votes in South Carolina will not retard the action of Iowa or Massachusetts," and once northern states proceeded to enact women's suffrage, the South would follow: "Once carry this reform [woman suffrage] in half a dozen northern states and the negro looks so much to us for his example that his vote will be sure to follow ours."[89] But Stanton brushed aside these suggestions and responded to Phillips's "pronunciamento" with an editorial blast of her own.

Why, Stanton demanded, was a movement among women for the outraged and oppressed of their sex "selfish," while "Wendell Phillips pleading for black men, or Frederick Douglass for his own race" was not? She was happy to argue the case of Rhode Island because its interesting history caught Phillips in a contradiction. In 1842, when a proposal to eliminate the property qualification for white male voters had been before the voters of Rhode Island, abolitionists had gone into the state and campaigned *against* it. Abolitionists had then opposed extending the franchise piecemeal, even though it would give the vote to poor white men, because it came entailed with the continued disenfranchisement of black men—"an aristocracy of race." Their position in 1842 with respect to race was the *Revolution*'s position now with respect to an aristocracy of sex. She concluded with a personal slam, saying Wendell Phillips, "with his cry, 'this is the negro's hour,'" had done more to delay justice for women than any other man in the nation.[90] As late as June 1869 Stanton had tried to mend fences by sending

Phillips a note regretting "any personal bitterness," but there was no mending them after his "pronunciamento" and her response.[91]

Phillips felt defensive enough to reply to Stanton at length while pretending not to. He did so by responding to a letter from Frances Dana Gage in both the *NASS* and the *Woman's Advocate*. Phillips told Gage straight-faced that he had never declared a "Negro's hour" in which women's rights agitation must wait and give precedence to black suffrage. True, it had been said a hundred times, he wrote, "but said on a level where self-respect forbade me to notice it." Now, because *Mrs. Gage* repeated the charge and *she* was "a woman of integrity and intelligence," he would answer.[92] Phillips claimed he had never postponed women's claims, nor advised anyone else to, "never refused pecuniary assistance or my aid on the platform." He even claimed credit for having given woman suffrage twice as much space in the *NASS* over the last three years than it ever had before. And he patted himself on the back for "our committee" having expended $2,500 "to aid the agitation in New York and in Kansas," adding, "At my suggestion we put another thousand dollars aside to be spent in Massachusetts." These self-serving remarks were insulting to Stanton and Anthony, and they were also sadly distorted. Lumping together money spent in New York and in Kansas hid the fact that the latter effort had been starved when it meant most, and the revelation that $1,000 of Hovey money had apparently been held back from Kansas and given to the fastidious ladies of Boston for their NEWSA was particularly galling. Of course Stanton had presented distorted Kansas stories of her own, but the fact made it no easier to stomach Phillips's latest sally.

Stanton and Anthony's opposition to the Fifteenth Amendment looked more and more irresponsible as the ratification process dragged on, even while it became harder and harder for them to concede that Phillips was now in the right and that it was time to support it. Lydia Maria Child criticized Stanton by name for her reported willingness to accept the support of southern white women. Disaster loomed, Child warned, if "rebel women" got the vote while it was taken away from "loyal blacks." She deplored Stanton's "obvious readiness" to set aside the rights of blacks in order to advance the woman's cause and asked, "Shall our influence go to strengthen the hand of the murderous Ku Klux Klan?"[93] Child had a strong point—in fact, it was the same point made earlier by Frederick Douglass and even by Stanton herself three years before, in March 1866, when she had warned against this danger.[94]

The upshot in May 1869 was a tempestuous and historic meeting in which disputes about the Fifteenth Amendment destroyed the American Equal Rights Organization.[95] The Boston woman suffragists came to the 1869 AERA meeting looking to replace Stanton and Anthony and convert the AERA into a clone of the NEWSA with its Fifteenth-Amendment-first policy. Stanton had different intentions. Prior to the meeting she sent letters to all the "old friends" in which she urged "ignoring the past" and "sink[ing] all petty considerations in one united effort to secure woman suffrage."[96] It is hard to see why she thought unity in support of a woman suffrage Sixteenth Amendment would be possible if the black suffrage Fifteenth Amendment still remained unratified.

Elizabeth Cady Stanton led off the meeting with a speech that repeated, "I urge the sixteenth amendment, … I urge the sixteenth amendment," but as she developed her arguments, she soon dropped a nasty crack about the "African" from the southern plantations "in whose eyes woman is simply the being of man's lust," and she again warned of "Patrick and Sambo and Hans and Yung Tung" making laws for the daughters of Adams and Jefferson. Stanton argued for the Sixteenth Amendment by warning that manhood suffrage would be "national suicide and woman's destruction." Where was the nation tending, she asked, "when clowns make laws for queens?" Perhaps she softened the worst of her rhetoric, because she apparently dropped her prediction of "fearful outrages" and predicted instead that manhood suffrage "rouses woman's prejudices against the negro" and increases "his hostility and contempt for her."[97] But what she said was bad enough. Stanton's speech showed her usual inclination toward grand theory and broad historical perspectives couched in striking, metaphorical language, but she chose to end on a personal note: "I have asked my own soul, in moments of exaltation and humiliation, if woman … was made by her Creator to be a slave?" "No. No. NO!" she concluded, to loud applause.[98] Stanton was making no apologies; she was in fact putting her personal prestige on the line in support of her critique of the Fifteenth Amendment.

Stephen Foster had been chosen to make the attack on the *Revolution* women at this AERA meeting, perhaps because he had long supported them by pushing to include woman suffrage on the AASS platform and had only recently switched sides. The attack was personal: Foster asked for Stanton's resignation as the AERA's president, and he demanded that Stanton and Anthony disavow George Francis Train. When Anthony refused, he turned to her with the charge that she had been dishonest about money, a slur based on the disputed Kansas expenditures. Anthony hotly denied it, and then Foster in effect added the charge that she was a liar, adding that "certain persons" loved themselves more than "the cause."[99]

Stanton as chair tried to rule Foster out of order, but Frederick Douglass successfully objected, citing the traditions of the open platform. Douglass did not, however, second Foster. In fact, Douglass proceeded to ignore Foster's questions about Train and Anthony's alleged dishonesty, and he did not demand Stanton's resignation. Instead, he calmly turned attention to the important issue at hand, the Fifteenth Amendment. Douglass refused to descend to personal attacks—on the contrary, he affirmed his longtime friendship with Stanton—but he was also prepared to insist that, on the issue, she and Anthony were dead wrong: the Fifteenth Amendment was not a fait accompli, and it deserved support, not criticism. Douglass made Klan violence the fulcrum of his argument and asked how anyone could now claim that woman suffrage had the same urgency as black suffrage. He quoted Julia Ward Howe's "I am willing that the negro shall get in before me," and compared cases. "When women, because they are women, are hunted down…when they are dragged from their houses and hung upon lamp posts," only then, Douglass declared, will women "have an urgency to obtain the ballot equal to our own." A voice from the floor asked, "Is that not all true about black women?" and Douglass shot back, "Yes, yes, it is true of the black woman, but not because she is a woman but because she is black."[100] It was a clincher of an argument, but Douglass took the edge off it at the end with his own personal comment: he recalled how, many years before when he was ostracized by all white society, he had been accepted as a guest in Elizabeth Cady Stanton's home.

In the past, Susan B. Anthony would have picked up on Douglass's remark about the danger to black women and pointed out that the black woman, too, needed the vote to protect herself—rather than relying, as Douglass implied, on the black man for her protection. This time, Anthony's emotions ran high and her disjointed remarks suggest how agitated she had become. To describe how it felt to be dismissed by male-decreed priorities, she told of a pivotal conversation when two men informed her that woman suffrage must be left to the next generation. She did not mention names, but many in the crowd must have guessed she referred to Phillips and Tilton. She recalled how the two men told her the AERA's real goal was to strike out the word "white" from the New York State suffrage qualification, while striking out "male" was only "an intellectual theory" rather than "a practical thing to be accomplished." She recalled "the downright insolence of those two men, when I had canvassed the entire state from one end to the other, county by county, with petitions in my hand…that they should dare to look me in the face and speak of this great earnest purpose of mine as an 'intellectual theory' but not to be practiced or for us to hope to attain."[101]

Since then, Anthony had defied those men and pursued her "great earnest purpose," but now Frederick Douglass had, in effect, told her she must wait, just as Phillips and Tilton had done three years earlier: he looked her in the face and said, black men come first, you must wait. Anthony challenged Douglass, accusing him of male pride and declaring "he would not exchange his sex" and swap his black manhood, however oppressed on account of race, for white womanhood. Douglass responded with a question: will suffrage change anything in the nature of our sexes? Anthony immediately shot back, yes, it would change one thing very much, "the pecuniary position of woman. It will place her in a position in which she can earn her own bread." In Anthony's speech, exhausting years of work, stinging disrespect, and inexpressible disappointment had come tumbling out. But these personal comments also brought her exchange with Douglass to an odd conclusion: each activist had acknowledged, in different ways, that the ballot was not so fundamental after all—not as important as the body, and primarily a tool to gain economic justice. Two logical thinkers each veered off the question at hand and moved away from that fatal, fundamental disagreement: now, at this moment, who would win the vote and who would not?

On the second day of the 1869 AERA meeting, the confrontational tone set by Stephen Foster became general, even though Foster himself fell silent. We know little of what was said because the *World* reporter refused to transcribe "hot and heavy" debates on organizational purpose, on whether capital and labor was a legitimate topic on this platform, on whether New York or New England was the birthplace of the woman's movement. But eventually Douglass recalled the meeting to the central issue by introducing his own resolutions, including one that explicitly stated, "We gratefully welcome the pending 15th Amendment." The eccentric, irrepressible C. C. Burleigh, an AASS veteran, stepped into the role of the confrontational white man who would dictate the women's agenda. When Burleigh boasted that he would teach the members of the AERA a lesson in good manners, some of the attendees flung him hisses and catcalls.[102] Frances Harper tried to play a moderating role, asking whether Douglass's resolutions were not subsumed under another that was more vaguely worded, but when Douglass pressed for his own more explicit endorsement of the Fifteenth Amendment, she backed him unequivocally. Though the *World* reporter did not transcribe Harper's long speech, he paraphrased her as "saying that when it was a question of race she let the lesser question of sex go. But the white women all go for sex, letting race occupy a minor position."[103] Harper would not have used such colloquial phrasing, but she was clearly siding with Douglass. The meeting turned into a disorderly scene in which speakers on both sides were drowned out by opponents, but the fight was not entirely or even mostly between black men and white women—indeed, the two most quarrelsome individuals, Foster and Burleigh, were both white men.

Lucy Stone tried to maintain neutrality throughout much of this stormy AERA meeting, as did her husband. Blackwell had the decency to defend Anthony's expenditures against Foster's charges, praising Anthony's willingness "for the sake of harmony and the good of the cause" to give up her claim for $1,000.[104] Blackwell also presented a set of carefully worded resolutions that offended neither side and were adopted unanimously. Stone tried to square the circle by saying that Douglass and Stanton "both are perhaps right," and concluding, "We are lost if we turn away from the middle principle and argue for one class." But she also disputed Douglass briefly by comparing women's situation to black men's inasmuch as "the Ku Kluxes here in the North in the shape of men take away the children from the mother." Her comment suggests that, like many others, Stone could not quite grasp the new realities in the South, where the problem was no longer the breakup of the black family, as under slavery, but terror and murder outright. But eventually Stone had to get off the fence, which she did by declaring unambiguously, "I thank God for the 15th Amendment."[105]

At some point in the convention, Stanton and Anthony realized that arguing with their opponents was pointless. The Boston moderates apparently lacked the votes to take over the AERA meeting, but they were able to block its immediate conversion into a woman suffrage organization. Stone said she must oppose any motion to convert the AERA into a new Woman Suffrage Association, "until the colored man gained the right to vote."[106] Stone's opposition to reorienting the AREA explains why—if additional reasons were needed—Anthony and Stanton failed to invite her and her husband to a hastily called meeting that same evening, where they proceeded to form a new National Woman Suffrage Association.[107] Stanton and Anthony's NWSA was an independent woman suffrage association that shed any pretense of concerning itself with black rights. One of its first acts was to pass a resolution stating that although the organization rejoiced in every step to put an end to the aristocracy of color, "We repudiate the Fifteenth Amendment," because it enacted an aristocracy of sex.[108] A month later, when the NEWSA met in Boston, Lucy Stone was a loyal supporter, not a maverick, and Wendell Phillips pounded home the implications of the "Negro's hour" for the women in his camp: many ladies were "too sanguine," he claimed, about the short-term prospects for woman suffrage. Better, said Phillips, those ladies should learn to be "satisfied to labor on for another generation."[109]

At length Stanton had to face the fact that, as Phillips had long insisted, black male suffrage was a present reality while woman suffrage was still only a goal for the future. The hope of really winning the ballot, which had dawned with the Jackson and Hovey bequests and blossomed when Reconstruction threw the nation's politics into turmoil, must be relinquished. Stanton claimed she had, at least, never overestimated her political clout: "All the friends are mistaken as to the policy of opposing the 15th Amendment," she wrote. "I never had a doubt but it would pass," she claimed, but saw it only as an occasion for making "our strong arguments." She would not even mention the Fifteenth Amendment, she told Paulina Wright Davis, "unless somebody asks us to rejoice."[110] Later Stanton would rationalize that criticizing the Fifteenth Amendment had not been intended to stop it, only "the best possible means to keep up the agitation."[111] By late summer 1869, Stanton began to be able to admit that their fighting chance had come and gone: she told Davis she was thinking about writing a book and hoped to spend the next five years alone with her thoughts. At about the same time, she signed up with two lyceum lecture agencies for engagements in the fall, implicitly conceding that it was time to move on. Stanton would agitate women's issues and educate women through lecturing; she would spread the word and make a living at it, too, but with no immediate goal in sight.[112]

Anthony began to concede defeat as well. Her change of attitude was evident in September 1869 at a meeting of the Working Woman's Association, where a Mrs. Norton attacked Anthony's leadership and argued that the association was "useless" and had "never done anything for working women." In response Anthony said they might have "failed to accomplish all that we would like," but Mrs. Norton's expectations were faulty because she failed to understand that agitation was an accomplishment in itself: "The grandest work that a mortal can accomplish is to get talking, and thereby stir people up to do something," Anthony told her. "You don't think much of this talking; I tell you it makes everything in the world."[113] Mrs. Norton, in her impatience and indignation, resembled Anthony herself only a few months earlier, outraged at the idea that her efforts were "*only* a means of agitation."[114] Norton wanted results, but Anthony had learned that she must labor on without them. "First comes talk, then in due time will come action and revolution," she declared. *In due time*—but not now. "After twenty years of earnest work in this cause," Anthony bravely concluded, "I am greatly encouraged."[115]

Stone and Blackwell did not make it easy for Stanton and Anthony to back down. They insisted that the *Revolution* women ought to positively endorse the Fifteenth Amendment, not just fall silent. At a meeting of the Western Woman Suffrage Association in September 1869 the organizers asked Anthony beforehand to refrain from condemning the amendment, and she agreed, remarking unrepentantly, "I am not in the habit of shooting dead ducks."[116] But then Henry Blackwell and Lucy Stone unexpectedly produced a resolution endorsing the Fifteenth Amendment. Anthony was ready to cease the attack, but that was not good enough.[117] Finally, when the results of the off-year elections in Ohio and Pennsylvania in early October 1869 clearly signaled that the requisite number of state legislatures would ratify the Fifteenth Amendment, Phillips and his allies dialed back their attacks.[118] By November, although final ratification was not quite complete, everyone understood that it was assured, and some woman suffragists began to write about differences of opinion over the Fifteenth Amendment in the past tense.[119]

The argument lived on, however, and even flared up again because Lucy Stone used Stanton and Anthony's National Woman Suffrage Association and its opposition to the Fifteenth Amendment as a prime rationale for forming her own organization, the American Woman Suffrage Association. As early as June 1869 Stone began to solicit support by warning that "with her paper circulating largely in the doubtful Western states, [Mrs. Stanton] can defeat the 15th Amendment."[120] Hearing of Stone's intentions, Stanton exclaimed, "What a ludicrous proposition to organize a national *woman's* organization on the basis

of the 15th Amendment."[121] Yet Stone's plans also fired Stanton's ire toward the
disputed measure, and one more time she carped, "All wise women should
oppose the Fifteenth Amendment."[122] Trying to put the situation in perspective
at a point when the Fifteenth Amendment's ratification was certain, Stanton
wrote an editorial in which she pointed to the real motives of those she called
the "Boston malcontents." It was, she declared, all about "leadership and personalities," and to end it, she offered to resign the NWSA presidency, saying,
"I should prefer to be known in conventions no more forever, rather than to
fight old friends."[123] But Stone and Anthony were still angry with each other,
and arguments over supporting the Fifteenth Amendment lingered by becoming
entangled in personal enmity and organizational rivalry. Although Stone's
AWSA was founded on deference to the Fifteenth Amendment, it did not thereafter cultivate alliances with the organized defenders of black rights.[124] Neither
of the two white woman suffrage organizations offered much welcome to black
woman suffragists, some of whom attended AWSA meetings, while others went
to NWSA events or to both.[125]

African American men and women only sometimes participated in the hot arguments of 1869. They had meetings of their own to attend, they faced a number of
urgent questions, and they did not always agree among themselves. In
mid-January 1869, a National Convention of Colored Men met in Washington.
It had been called by border state African Americans, who remained disenfranchised and for whom suffrage was therefore a preeminent concern.[126] The
convention also offered northern black leaders a chance to meet with their
southern counterparts and set a national black agenda.[127] The role northern
blacks should play in Reconstruction was subject to debate: some had moved
south, while others like Frederick Douglass hoped to exercise national leadership from a base in the North. Still largely disenfranchised, northern blacks
wanted voting rights, setting their hopes on a Fifteenth Amendment and watch-
ing the D.C. disenfranchisement proposal with alarm.[128] They also wanted a
national organization to stand for black rights, the Equal Rights League having
ceased to operate.[129] In the South, African Americans had different priorities:
they wanted protection for men who were already enfranchised—and could
point to the violence of the previous year to prove their case—and they felt little
need for an organization because they already had their Union Leagues and the
Republican Party.[130] Personal rivalries overlaid these regional differences.[131] No
surprise, then, that the 1869 national "Convention of Colored Men" was often
contentious.

The black convention may have given woman suffrage, and perhaps black
women themselves, a disrespectful reception—or so it seems, though inadequate press coverage and scanty proceedings make it hard to confirm reported

insults.[132] James J. Spelman, an African American journalist from New York State who had gone to Mississippi with the Freedmen's Bureau, reported that the convention endorsed woman suffrage by a large majority, but no other source mentioned any such decision.[133] The news reports and published proceedings do agree that one black woman, Harriet Johnson of Pennsylvania, was admitted as a delegate, but only after a "spirited" debate.[134] They also indicate that when John Willis Menard, a black man elected to the House of Representatives from Louisiana, spoke to the convention in favor of woman suffrage, he was interrupted by "frequent hisses and calls to sit down."[135] Menard may have offended mostly on other grounds—he also scolded the delegates because "they all wanted to be big men."[136] But as Stanton and Anthony saw it, a black man had espoused woman suffrage and been shouted down by other black men. They saw raucous confirmation of their oft-repeated allegation that "black men on the stump and in their conventions repudiate women."[137] And they chose to focus on their opponents rather than potential allies like Spelman and Menard.

Black attitudes toward woman suffrage were complex. In the South, a strain of pro–women's rights opinion ran through Radical Republicanism, and the new state constitutions almost all secured married women's separate property rights.[138] The Reconstruction government of Arkansas considered a woman suffrage proposal, and in South Carolina the black Republican William J. Whipper pleaded for woman suffrage at the South Carolina constitutional convention.[139] By one account, black women voted in certain districts of South Carolina in 1870.[140] This southern radicalism was born of political calculation as well as idealism, because if ex-Confederate men were eventually to be reenfranchised, perhaps the best hope for radical majorities lay in enfranchising women. After all, women showed extraordinary engagement in the collective life of the black community, and some black leaders, including Whipper, Spelman, and Menard, saw the implications: black women would likely be more apt to go to the polls than white women, which made woman suffrage a way to enhance black power.[141] Menard said, "They had but one voice in the South, and that was to know no distinctions of color or sex. Unless they concentrated their power they would never attain to any political power."[142] Of course, black leaders did not speak with one voice: many or most southern black men chose to eschew woman suffrage and even to interpret voting rights as male privilege.[143] And those southern black men who did favor woman suffrage were up against the fact that the organizations through which the aspirations of the black community were expressed—the Union Leagues and the Republican Party—were heavily influenced by the northern Republican Party, which set its face against woman suffrage just as it discouraged talk of land confiscation.

Splits within the postbellum black community opened along lines of class, color, and pre-emancipation status, and they probably affected opinions about woman suffrage along with much else.[144] Some of the complications of black opinion on suffrage played out within the Purvis family, where Robert Purvis backed Stanton and Anthony and opposed the Fifteenth Amendment, while his son Charles Purvis supported it. Another son, Henry Purvis, went to South Carolina after the war, where he held several positions in the Reconstruction government. Henry Purvis voted conservatively and was associated with a set of well-to-do Charleston people of mixed race, some of whom had even owned slaves before the war. They were often at odds with darker skinned ex-slaves over direction and control of the South Carolina Republican Party.[145] Robert Purvis may have been moved to insist on woman suffrage by his daughter, Hattie Purvis, who, her father said, was "palpitating in every nerve for the recognition of her rights."[146] Or perhaps Robert Purvis did not trust the illiterate black men of the South, because of what he heard from Henry in Charleston.[147] Mistrust of southern black voters was not unheard of in the northern black community. African Americans in Washington, for example, reportedly worried that the ex-slaves, once enfranchised, would vote according to the dictates of their old masters.[148] And why should they not have worried when northern Democrats kept predicting that southern blacks were about to come to their senses, realize the planters were their true friends, and vote Democratic.[149] It was not just Stanton and Anthony who underestimated the wisdom of the freedmen when newly armed with the ballot.

Stanton and Anthony seemed not to notice these complexities, and they kept repeating that the "vast majority" of black men opposed woman suffrage. A black leader like John Mercer Langston might take time in a speech to declare in favor of "women's rights," but even if Stanton and Anthony noticed the fact, they made no move to use the information to forge cooperative practical links.[150] Instead they retold stories in which black men spoke dismissively of women—"Talk of a woman's votin'; now jess look at a woman, *she ain't nuffin*," said one.[151] The *Revolution* made sure to publicize the fact that at the Labor Congress in the summer of 1869, the black delegates voted "as a unit" against Anthony's admission despite the fact that she had long advocated their cause.[152]

And what of black women? Mostly their opinions went unrecorded. When *Harper's Weekly* illustrated "The National Colored Convention in Session at Washington, D.C." it showed a number of women in the audience at that January 1869 event, but their opinions never entered the record, even when the subject was the admission of a woman delegate.[153] Harriet C. Johnson was the principal of the female department of Avery College, but her own reaction to the debate over her credentials at the convention was not reported.[154] Even when Louisa Rollin of South Carolina, called "the black Anna Dickinson," spoke in favor of universal suffrage on the floor of the South Carolina House of Representatives, her remarks received little public attention, and though Rollin and her sisters presided over an elegant salon for radical Republicans in Reconstruction Charleston, their views apparently did not enter the historical record.[155] Like black men, black women had no organizational framework that might have encouraged them to express and record their views on woman suffrage.[156] Ultimately, black women's self-assertion found an outlet at the local level, where it flowed into the black churches, within which women fought for and won the right to vote on church matters in the 1870s.[157]

Two black women who were not content to cede precedence to black men found the means to be heard. Edmonia Highgate was a northern black woman who taught in Reconstruction Mississippi for a number of years. She reported that the freedmen were "fully convinced that women like their teachers have a greater right to vote than they, because of their superior intelligence," but "most of their colored *leaders* are opposed to the Sixteenth Amendment." Highgate declared that she was "not willing that another man, black or white, should be enfranchised" until she herself got the right of suffrage—a position that caused the *Revolution* to publicize her views.[158] Naomi Bowman Talbert, who spoke up at the February 1869 Chicago woman suffrage convention, gave an unusually lengthy statement of her views in a letter to the *Chicago Tribune*. Several of her friends supported woman suffrage, Talbert reported, but the rest of the women kept silent because of the "dictatorial spirit" of their husbands. Talbert said that female suffrage was often "the theme of conversation" among black men, and she urged them to realize that they needed black women. If they wanted to overcome prejudice, Talbert declared, they "must take the broad platform of universal suffrage."[159]

Sojourner Truth avoided the AERA meetings in 1868 and 1869. In the 1867 AERA meeting, she had demanded the vote herself, unwilling to stand aside for black men. After Stanton and Anthony returned to the East in the company of George Francis Train, she refused to associate herself with their position. But she did not bother to try to correct or quarrel with them either.[160] Truth was a working activist with her hands full as she arranged job placement for freedpeople and tried to support black claims on land in the West.

Other black women apparently made the pragmatic tactical decision to support black (male) suffrage and the Fifteenth Amendment before white audiences but also to argue for woman suffrage inside the black community. For example, Maud Molson lectured with Charles Lenox Remond in the Mohawk Valley in support of "impartial suffrage" in February 1869, and at the Colored Men's Convention in Binghamton in July 1869, Molson spoke on "Manhood Suffrage" with "great power and eloquence."[161] But when she spoke at the annual meeting of the Pennsylvania Equal Rights League in August 1869, her eloquent appeal for impartial suffrage "included *female* as well as *negro* suffrage."[162]

The most prominent black woman leader on suffrage issues, Frances E. W. Harper, seems to have taken this approach, and she famously put race ahead of sex at the climactic 1869 AERA meeting. But in her novel, *Minnie's Sacrifice*, which was being serialized in the *Christian Recorder* at the same time, Harper addressed the question differently. Her novel's heroine Minnie has a husband who says, "This hour belongs to the negro," but Minnie does not agree. She responds, "I cannot recognize that the negro man is the only one who has pressing claims at this hour. Today our government needs woman's conscience as well as man's judgment." Minnie goes on to say she "would not throw a straw in the way of the colored man, even though I know that he would vote against me as soon as he gets his vote." Minnie insists, however, that "woman should have some power to defend herself from oppression."[163] Harper, like Truth, was on her own, a self-supporting widow with children to care for; and the idea that black women could rely on black men for protection was an ideal and an abstraction.

Harper's opinions seem to have been complex and changing. Even after the *Revolution*'s "fearful outrages" rhetoric and the blowup at the 1869 AERA meeting, Harper was still willing to attend an NWSA meeting with Stanton and Anthony and to speak there.[164] Years later, Harper would describe the Reconstruction years as a time when "the colored man vaulted into power, [and] the colored woman was left behind to serve."[165] These scraps of information are inconclusive, but they seem to suggest that Harper found it hard to give up immediate hope of winning votes for women. But at the moment of truth at the 1869 AERA convention, Harper firmly backed Frederick Douglass and the Fifteenth Amendment.

Given that Stanton and Anthony had descended to despicable racism in the Blair endorsement, stooped to "fearful outrages" rhetoric, and meanly opposed the Fifteenth Amendment, it was no surprise that their oldest and most prominent black ally, Frederick Douglass, criticized them so harshly in the fall of 1868 and quarreled with them so openly in the spring of 1869. But the sequel is surprising. Not long after the blowup, Frederick Douglass and Elizabeth Cady Stanton sat down together at dinner at Theodore Tilton's house, and there they "forgot the Fifteenth Amendment," and enjoyed the oysters, chicken, jellies, and ices. They savored a good cup of coffee and good conversation and afterward parted "as they have been for twenty years, good friends."[166] So the *Revolution* reported, and even assuming that its report was shaded with rosy tints, its account of the meeting remained uncontroverted. It seems that Frederick Douglass and Elizabeth Cady Stanton did indeed remain on speaking or even friendly terms, despite all that had transpired.

Maybe Douglass could understand their position. In his 1869 lyceum lecture on "William the Silent," the founder of the Dutch republic, Douglass hinted that he understood the potential value of woman suffrage to the self-defense of the black community. There Douglass described how Dutch women literally fought alongside Dutch men to defeat the Spanish, a history lesson that played off the popular argument that the ballot and the bullet were linked, and suggested that men and women together could defeat a strong and violent foe.[167] Douglass had his own reservations about the freedmen, as expressed in a speech at the American Anti-Slavery Society in May 1869 when he remarked that although slavery was abolished, "the ignorance and servility of the slave still remain."[168] He argued that this very "ignorance and servility" necessitated passage of the Fifteenth Amendment, so that black men would be armed and educated by it. Douglass gave a reflective, multifaceted speech, in which he worried about the fate of the black intelligentsia and hesitantly pondered the mystery of how to conquer race prejudice. It was a wandering speech, but it was worlds apart from the simplistic remedy Phillips and the AASS were then promoting: ratify the Fifteenth Amendment and all will be well. Douglass knew that was not true. At one point he recalled a personal visit to Pittsfield, New Hampshire, many years before, when an outspoken enemy of abolition proved to be the only man in town willing to offer him food and shelter when he was in need—implying that nominal "allies" might be disappointing human beings.

Douglass and Stanton apparently shared a friendship old enough and durable enough to withstand the storms of 1869. In the midst of those battles, Elizabeth Cady Stanton recalled how, years before, she had entertained Frederick Douglass at her house, "and to those of her household who had objected to sitting down to the table with him, she had sent their meals to their rooms."[169] And he, too, recalled old times when "this wooly head of mine" found a bed and a pillow at Stanton's house.[170] She recalled how she had been "ostracized from society for walking in the streets of New York with Frederick Douglass." But now the very same people who then "hissed her to scorn" were "loud-mouthed Republicans" insisting that she endorse the Fifteenth Amendment.[171]

We will probably never know how Frederick Douglass was able to get past the stomach-turning racism that Stanton and Anthony displayed in that interval between September 1868 and September 1869, when they saw that their chances were dying and black men's were flowering. Douglass had always paid limited attention when abolitionists threw themselves into faction fights, and he mostly stood aside when Stanton and Anthony scrapped with Phillips and Stone and their allies. Douglass knew about the Jackson and Hovey monies, he knew how true-as-steel abolitionists could turn mean and arrogant, and he surely appreciated the extraordinary rarity of the political opportunities opened up by Reconstruction. Probably he understood politics better than any of Stanton and Anthony's abolitionist critics and knew that playing the political game meant abandoning the hope of being right or righteous at every turn. He was too much the political pragmatist not to take the ballot when the Republicans offered it, and yet he must have understood the limits of Republican sincerity about as well as Stanton did. He could remember the loss of the black suffrage referendum in New York in 1860, when pusillanimous Republicans threw the black cause overboard, when he himself had angrily blamed "drunken Irishmen and ignorant Dutchmen." For determined radicals who were also confirmed politicians—and both Stanton and Douglass were—sympathizing in defeat was a well-practiced posture. And Douglass certainly understood how, in a life devoted to activism, with spouses estranged and children grown to disappoint one's hopes, one might have to take comfort not from winning, but only from the struggle itself.

Conclusion

Although Stanton and Anthony's fighting chance to win woman suffrage was gone, three developments combined to obscure that fact. In December 1869 an actual woman suffrage victory was won in the West when the territory of Wyoming gave women the vote.[1] Wyoming had required no expensive and exhausting campaigning on Stanton and Anthony's part, only a simple majority in a tiny territorial legislature and a governor who was willing to sign the bill.[2] Eastern suffrage leaders could cheer and take credit for having inspired others to act. But this promising development in the West went sour when the territory of Utah followed suit in granting woman suffrage a few weeks later, in February 1870, and Mormon women soon voted in support of polygamy.[3] Suffrage feminists had a terrible time trying to explain the Utah results, which seemed to confirm their opponents' dire predictions that woman suffrage would undermine the family.[4] Late 1869 also saw the emergence of a promising "new departure" legal strategy. Missouri attorney Francis Minor proposed an interpretation of the Fourteenth and Fifteenth Amendments in which women already had an implied constitutional right to vote.[5] Pursuing this strategy also required scant resources and little effort on Stanton and Anthony's part. All that was needed were suffragists who were willing to create a test case by voting illegally and some pro bono legal help in the courts. Before long, however, in 1875, the Supreme Court would kill "new departure" hopes in *Minor v. Happersett*.[6] Meanwhile in New York City, a charming female stockbroker with a shady past began generating publicity for woman suffrage. Victoria Woodhull may have given Stanton and Anthony one last glimmer of false hope for early enfranchisement, with her promise of funding and her ability to gain a hearing in Congress.[7] But Woodhull soon caused such a furor—by publicly espousing free love and by exposing the scandal of the century, the Beecher-Tilton affair—that the early years of the 1870s gave Stanton, Anthony, and other participants little opportunity for retrospection about events of the late 1860s.[8]

By late 1869, the moment of opportunity was gone and so was the money that helped to spark and underwrite this interval of active campaigning.

Thereafter, the women's movement lacked two of the three prerequisites for success—material resources and political opportunity—and would not regain them for decades to come. No new donor took the place of Jackson, Hovey, and Train. Susan B. Anthony conceded financial defeat and turned the *Revolution* over to others, walking away with a sizable debt.[9] Stanton and Anthony's organization, the National Woman Suffrage Association, scraped along financially and they even needed an additional small bequest from Francis Jackson's daughter to publish *The History of Woman Suffrage*.[10] Stone and Blackwell were personally well off and their *Woman's Journal* kept going, but the paper never thrived, nor did their American Woman Suffrage Association.[11] Anthony was, however, able to pay off her personal debt, and she and Stanton found they could support themselves nicely thanks to the postbellum lyceum circuit. The lyceums would welcome suffragist speakers and reward them with "profit and emolument" as they circulated far and wide in the 1870s and 1880s. But lyceum opportunities in the absence of any other types of funding decentered the women's movement, reduced it to individual entrepreneurial initiative, and obliged suffragists to craft arguments that would, literally, sell.[12]

Their moment of political opportunity had fled as well. Could Stanton and Anthony really have won woman suffrage in the 1860s? Victory is impossible to affirm. But they had good reason to believe they had a fighting chance, because they had identified a narrow entering wedge—woman suffrage in a bellwether state or district—and they had (or thought they had) arguments, talent, allies, resources, energy, and a fluid political scene. True, had women won the vote in Kansas or the District of Columbia, victory might have proved limited or even reversible. Kansas might have been bracketed just as Wyoming territory was, as western and no precedent for anywhere else, and Washington women might have lost the vote along with the men in years to come. But Stanton and Anthony cannot be dismissed as naïve for trying to fight and win. Labor historian David Montgomery has argued that woman suffragists and other "sentimental reformers" of this period tended to lose themselves in elaborate schemes involving insider influence, rather than doing the hard work of organizing rank-and-file workers or ordinary citizens.[13] Stanton and Anthony did work hard in a grassroots campaign among ordinary voters in Kansas. Beyond that, they also understood that their cause lacked widespread popular support, and a focus on insiders seemed appropriate given their options. In this period, political outcomes *were* often decided in small rooms behind closed doors, as surely indicated by the drafting of the Fourteenth and Fifteenth Amendments, or the nominations for president in 1868. If Stanton and Anthony's political acumen led them to think that an "inside job" could, for example, return Salmon P. Chase from the ranks of the Republican Party to lead the Democrats in 1868, bringing with him a policy of universal suffrage, that did not make them unrealistic, let alone "sentimental." Reconstruction-era politics were extraordinarily fluid and the rules of the game and the composition of the teams—the parties—kept changing. In short, their political knowledge was real, though their insight paid them limited dividends. Stanton and Anthony understood much about "the art of the possible," but their understanding only lured them on step by step to positions they would have found indefensible a few years before.

After 1869 the modes of suffrage activism had to change. In a speech at the 1895 National American Woman Suffrage Association convention, shortly after the two rival organizations merged, Carrie Chapman Catt declared, "The chief work of suffragists for the past forty years has been education and agitation," but now the time had come for "organization" and what she would later call a "winning plan."[14] Though Catt tactfully credited earlier activists with having changed public opinion through their education and agitation, she overlooked the way Stanton and Anthony tried, in the Reconstruction era, to do just what she recommended—to organize and win. There is often no bright line between the two styles of activism—between educating and agitating to raise consciousness, and campaigning to win legal change—and activists vary in their awareness of the difference.[15] Susan B. Anthony found it easier than Elizabeth Cady Stanton to make the transition back to education and agitation, though she had hoped, as she admitted, that the woman suffrage movement would not have to spend "forty years in the Wilderness" and might go into "political Canaan" by a shorter, more direct route.[16] Social movements depend on individuals like Anthony who are willing to "carry it on" for long periods of time, insisting, despite all appearances to the contrary, that "the dream never dies." And yet at some point activists must shift gears to formulate winnable plans and push through practical legislation, as Stanton and Anthony had sought to do after the Jackson and Hovey bequests. In 1871, Anthony scolded Stanton for her inability to shift back: "To my mind there was never such suicidal letting go the helm of a ship in a stormy sea as has been that of yours, these last two years."[17]

The money was significant to these women emotionally as well as practically. Wendell Phillips insisted that in the "Negro's hour" women should not only put aside their own suffrage goals but also devote themselves to the cause of black men. Of course Stanton and Anthony resented being told what to do, but they resented it even more when Phillips tried to force them to comply by abusing his power as Hovey trustee to deny them funding. Most women's rights activists did not like to talk openly about money, preferring euphemisms like "sinews of war," but funding was terribly important to them—far more important than it was to white male abolitionists who had greater property rights and more opportunities to earn money for themselves. Phillips's shifty move hit them in a sore spot. Perhaps Lucy Stone's newfound affluence (after Henry Blackwell's speculations paid off in 1864) did the same.

Although so much turned on Kansas, events there were falsely reported and confusion only served to compound resentments. In fact, a conservative faction of the Kansas Republican Party deliberately set out to provoke and exploit a quarrel between black suffrage and woman suffrage in 1867. By attacking woman suffrage and failing to campaign for black suffrage, and then blaming the lagging fortunes of black suffrage on women, the conservative faction succeeded in taking over party power and, incidentally, defeating both referenda. Kansas politicians who supported woman suffrage bungled, failing to cement an alliance with black leaders, and the AERA was too underfunded and understaffed to alter these local dynamics. But the bogus charges of the winning conservatives, together with George Francis Train's flamboyant presence during the last two weeks of the campaign, created confusion about what had happened and who was to blame. Stanton and Anthony felt bitter at being blamed for the Kansas defeats after having been denied resources to which they were entitled. They believed Wendell Phillips was too stubborn about his definition of the "Negro's hour" to see the opportunity Kansas offered both causes, and they believed that with outside reinforcements, Kansas Republicans might have rallied to a different standard from that raised by Eskridge and Kalloch. Perhaps they were wrong and the referenda would have been defeated all the same. But if the woman suffrage leaders had been able to participate in a full-out positive drive for both measures, as the AERA platform called for, Stanton and Anthony could have left there knowing they had given it the best possible effort, regardless of the outcome. And with other speakers on hand, George Francis Train might not have entered the picture. Counterfactual speculation is risky business, but in the absence of post-Kansas bitterness, it is hard to imagine that the rest of the story would have played out unchanged.

Wendell Phillips undoubtedly told himself he was acting for the best, cutting corners in the service of worthy goals as he strained every nerve to win rights for black men in the face of powerful opposition. Taking the long view, he accomplished much of lasting good, and maybe he needed every dollar of the Hovey Fund to do so. But his arrogance made it hard to disentangle the merits of the priorities he was promoting from the sexism he displayed in pursuing them. He was relatively inexperienced in politics, especially compared to Stanton, and his lack of savvy took a toll when it came time to decide on funding for Kansas. Accustomed to being the smartest man in the room, Phillips was unwilling to second-guess himself as he tried to operate in the unaccustomed realm of political maneuver. He was sometimes ill-informed as well as self-righteous and underhanded—a particularly galling combination.

Lucy Stone played a more equivocal role than her biographers suggest.[18] Stone was quick to decide that in Kansas black men were all opposed to woman suffrage, at a point when neither Anthony nor Stanton had arrived at that conclusion. "These men *ought not* to be allowed to vote before we do," she told Anthony, "because they will be just so much more dead weight to lift."[19] But later she would claim superior loyalty to black rights and criticize Stanton and Anthony for arguing the same point. Stone did not chart a steady course because she did not think politically and therefore found it hard to assess political situations or to understand Stanton and Anthony when they did. In the late 1860s Stone endured a crisis in her marriage, but at the same time she increasingly followed her husband's political lead, and Henry Blackwell was a partisan Republican with an impulsive streak. Lucy Stone certainly deserves credit, when it came to the moment of truth in 1869, for supporting the Fifteenth Amendment and for refraining from making racist remarks. But Stone's strong personal animosity toward Anthony (which seems out of proportion to the provocations she suffered) helped make the overall situation worse. Perhaps Stone was suffering from menopausal depression, as Stanton at one point speculated, or perhaps she was envious of the *Revolution* or defensive about her decision to stay in the marriage with Blackwell.[20] Whatever the reason, this old friend's deep hostility probably encouraged Anthony and Stanton to overreach because they were determined to show Stone they were right and because, already under attack, they felt, as the proverb has it, that they "might as well be hung for a sheep as a lamb."

Black activists were much less emotionally engaged in these quarrels. In the South, black men needed to act as political insiders in a fight for their lives, and for that, the regular Republican Party both locally and nationally was a far stronger ally than outsider, activist women. In the North, where black men were still political outsiders until the Fifteenth Amendment passed, they sometimes did need to ally with activist white women, as in New York or Kansas or Washington, D.C. But the results depended mostly upon local circumstances, and failure was not magnified by personal rivalry or resentment. Although some black men like George Downing and ultimately Frederick Douglass chose to debate and confront Stanton and Anthony at AERA meetings, they spent little time on personal rancor. Black women, too, were mostly focused elsewhere, perhaps sensing that they would be unwelcome at the mostly white women's meetings. But black women activists were typically unafraid of confronting bigotry, and an additional reason for their absence was that they had their hands full coping with another project, trying to relieve the sufferings of the refugee freedpeople. Throughout this drama, the absence of significant numbers of black women activists was like an empty chair at center stage. Black leaders were present only in small numbers and they did not speak with one voice, so as Stanton and Anthony plowed ahead they could always reassure themselves that some black people shared some of their opinions. From Sojourner Truth, who claimed the ballot when they did, to Robert Purvis, who voiced strong reservations about the capacities of the freedmen, they could often find black validation if they looked hard enough. And Frederick Douglass's personal friendship with

Elizabeth Cady Stanton probably reassured her at moments when she should have been reassessing her position.

The founding mothers of suffrage feminism were not racially enlightened. On the contrary, they engaged in plenty of racial stereotyping and racialist thinking. Even as radical outsiders, they inevitably partook of the social attitudes and scientific arguments of their day. Held up to our standards, no white individuals of the nineteenth century, with the possible exception of John Brown, would escape censure entirely. But effective political coalitions to serve the interests of black Americans did not require perfect enlightenment; they needed only white people willing to "do the right thing" under the circumstances. It is easy to overlook longtime cooperation between those who later became antagonists, knowing how the story would end in 1869 and writing backward from that debacle as if everything pointed to it. But for a period from about June 1866 to March 1867, Frederick Douglass and Wendell Phillips joined with Elizabeth Cady Stanton and Susan B. Anthony in opposing the Fourteenth Amendment, and with Hovey funds the AERA—a working coalition across race and gender lines—campaigned against the amendment and for universal suffrage. Cooperation and money were related: as long as the funding held up, practical joint work kept conflicts to manageable dimensions, but when Phillips withdrew the funding, occasions for cooperation dwindled and unenlightened attitudes could come to the fore. The record shows that activist leaders had personal biases but they could subordinate those biases to promising alliances in a given situation, as Stanton did during the AERA's New York campaign in the winter of 1866–67. Black-white teamwork in that campaign was not flawless, and both black men and white women had occasion to wonder whether their erstwhile allies had enlightened attitudes at heart. But this was a political campaign, not a marriage, so hearts were not at issue.

Stanton's style of argument has made it hard for history to get a read on her racism. Her lawyerly willingness to argue "in the alternative" dated back to the 1850s or earlier. It was not that Stanton made egalitarian arguments in her better moments; she made both kinds of arguments at the same time, one after the other. She understood that an affirmative answer to the "threshold question"—will you enfranchise women based on egalitarian arguments?— would render her additional "lower" arguments moot. Her intent was to offer two alternative rationales to arrive at the same conclusion, woman suffrage, but she appeared to abandon morally grounded egalitarian arguments when she tried to leverage invidious distinctions based on race. Stanton apparently assumed that her moral stance on black rights was not impaired by adding appeals for woman suffrage based on "low" arguments as long as she also continued to argue in the first instance for black and women's rights alike on the "high" ground of equal rights for all citizens. But making "low" arguments always risked giving aid and comfort to opponents of black rights, and arguing on both high and low levels set up a slippery slope she could easily descend. The Blair endorsement amounted to abandoning the high ground altogether, and many of Stanton's comments in 1869 were little more than white supremacist venting. Given her powerful way with words, those racist pronouncements have tended to overshadow and even to obscure the egalitarian arguments she had used for decades.

Stanton had a long-standing commitment to equal human rights for all, dating back to 1848 and earlier. She and other antebellum feminists deserve more credit for their egalitarian convictions than has been granted by a skeptic who refers to their "so-called" egalitarian arguments.[21] Despite their occasional condescending comments or hierarchical assumptions, these feminists also held on to equal rights convictions and battled to change others' minds.[22] What Stanton said and did in the late 1860s amounted to a significant change—though not an entirely unprecedented departure—from her earlier beliefs. Stanton shifted her position on race, but why did she go so far? She not only abandoned alliance and sympathy with black men but she also adopted the black-man-as-rapist charge, arguably the ultimate in racial slander. In the postbellum South, that charge would be used to justify lynching—hideous torture and ritual public murder—the real purpose of which was to intimidate the entire black population and maintain absolute control by whites even after slavery was dead. By 1869, Stanton was certainly stressed to the breaking point—exhausted, disappointed, and frus-trated—which may account for some of the shift.[23] But she also began from a standpoint of legitimate concern for the Hester Vaughns of this world. She cared about that penniless, friendless servant girl who lay in prison condemned to death "while he who betrayed her walks this green earth in freedom."[24] For Stanton, rape was connected to the concerns about marital power and sexual autonomy that underlay her prewar divorce initiative: it harked back to marriage issues she and Anthony had laid on the shelf, with some reluctance, in order to pursue the vote. Perhaps alone among nineteenth-century feminists, Stanton had a grasp of the mind-boggling dimensions of sexual abuse and violence against women, abuse and violence kept hidden until second wave feminism.[25] Ironically, Stanton's multifaceted feminism and her critique of the family and sexual mores may have predisposed her to accept the white South's cover story for its hateful violence.

Anthony followed Stanton's lead in this interval, relying on her friend's political insights and backing her up even when she made those "fearful outrage" charges. It would be 1872 before Stanton's misjudgments in the Woodhull affair finally undermined her credibility with Anthony. Years later in their *History of Woman Suffrage*, the two women agreed on an interpretation of their actions from 1865 to 1869 that emphasized the outcome—the founding of an independent women's rights movement. But what was the value of that women's movement, since it was so deeply flawed by white supremacy and marked by notorious incidents of racial bias? The answer depends upon whether one assumes that the vote and other aspects of women's liberation were inevitable components of modernity. If all the progress American women would see by the twenty-first century was coming anyway, was in effect waiting just around the bend of history, why cut Stanton and Anthony any slack for selling out to racism in the 1860s? Unfortunately, nothing in the historical record suggests that women's autonomy and full citizenship would have emerged effortlessly in the fullness of time. As the women's liberation movement of the 1970s revealed, forging any women's movement worthy of the name is a tough business in which fallible individuals make great sacrifices and also, sometimes, big mistakes.

Stanton and Anthony were goaded by the bad behavior of others, and they were sinned against as well as sinning, but their moral failure was massive. When Stanton wrote to Frank Blair in October 1868 praising his "able" speech for showing "what is to be the fate of American women under the radical policy of 'manhood suffrage,'" she was in essence praising him for predicting that black men would become rapists once they were politically empowered. That endorsement fell so far outside Stanton's usual line that her daughter, Harriot Stanton Blatch, felt she had to explain. When sorting through her mother's papers, Blatch added a handwritten note to her mother's letter to Frank Blair. In it she attributed "the attitude of Mrs. Stanton and Miss Anthony" to "a certain party of suffragists" who criticized Stanton and questioned Anthony's honesty.[26] Blatch explained her mother's actions in terms of a dispute among suffragists—an explanation that was both historically accurate and sadly inadequate to the magnitude of the letter's betrayal. Stanton and Anthony came to this sorry pass by pursuing political opportunities—opportunities they believed, quite rightly, would never recur in their lifetime. Eventually they came to the point of doing "whatever it took"—a decision they could only hope to justify if they succeeded. If it ended well, if women somehow somewhere gained the vote, they must have hoped that the indefensible steps they took to get it would be forgotten and forgiven. Stanton was "a famous storyteller" who knew, as every storyteller does, that the meaning of a story lies in its sense of an ending, and stands open until its conclusion is told. In effect, Stanton and Anthony gambled on "moral luck" and a happy ending, but they lost.[27]

In 1868 and 1869, Stanton and Anthony provided ample evidence to convict them of all the racism with which they have been charged in recent years. They had begun, a few years earlier, from a more principled position in favor of rights for all citizens, black and white, male and female, but they compromised and then sold out completely on their better, higher convictions. Wendell Phillips, for once in his otherwise grand and admirable life, acted in ways that were mean and petty, while Lucy Stone vacillated, criticized, and finally sided with Phillips, and one by one people and events fell into place so as to stymie Stanton and Anthony's hopes. Their disappointment and resentment were such that, for a while, they could scarcely bring themselves to speak responsibly or behave decently, as they sought to deny and then struggled to digest the contingent results of their unavailing struggles. Historian Eleanor Flexner remarks that it was "fortunate" that the woman suffrage leaders were not at that point "political realists," because the path that lay ahead after the defeat of their Reconstruction era hopes was so "staggering."[28] But they *were* political realists, which was why they had stooped so low to stave off this appalling prospect. Decades later, after the vote was finally won in 1920, Carrie Chapman Catt totted up what woman suffrage cost over the intervening years:

> To get the word "male" in effect out of the Constitution cost the women of the country fifty-two years of pauseless campaign....During that time they were forced to conduct 56 campaigns of referenda to male voters; 480 campaigns to get Legislatures to submit suffrage amendments to voters; 47 campaigns to get State constitutional conventions to write woman suffrage into state constitutions; 277 campaigns to get State party conventions to include woman suffrage planks; 30 campaigns to get presidential party conventions to adopt woman suffrage planks in party platforms, and 19 campaigns with 19 successive Congresses.[29]

Stanton and Anthony did not live to see it. Each died shortly after the turn of the century, in the midst of the "doldrum" years between 1896 and 1910 when not a single suffrage victory was won.

As the woman suffrage movement struggled on through the Gilded Age, its partisans no longer needed to defend equal rights for all citizens. Instead they crafted arguments fitted to women alone, essentialist arguments about how women—*white* women—had special qualities needed to elevate government and spread civilization.[30] As they tapped the scientific racism and imperial pretensions of the late nineteenth century for rationales to justify woman suffrage, white suffragists snubbed black women and tried to reassure southern bigots that woman suffrage would serve their interests.

Meanwhile, black men lost the suffrage that had seemed so secure with the ratification of the Fifteenth Amendment in 1870. Failing to make suffrage a right of citizenship had been not only unjust to women but also risky to black men, whose Republican Party champions might eventually desert them for the same reason they had embraced them—for partisan advantage. It did not take long for the Republican Party to do just that. When Reconstruction ended in the deal known as the "Compromise of 1877," national Republicans took the White House and in exchange left black men in the South to the tender mercies of the so-called Redeemers. Black men's voting rights were mauled by Reconstruction-era violence, crushed under the weight of debt peonage and the respectability of "scientific" racism, and extinguished by Jim Crow laws and Supreme Court decisions that whittled the Reconstruction amendments down to nothing. By the time W. E. B. Du Bois published his *Souls of Black Folk* in 1903, it was "like fireworks going off in a cemetery" where black hopes lay dead.[31]

After 1910, the woman suffrage movement would revive, when the Progressive era's enthusiasm for reform opened up a new window of political opportunity. By then women had better access to resources. Activists could turn to a new cohort of self-supporting, college-educated women, as well as rich women like Miriam Follen Leslie or Alva Belmont, whose million dollar donations helped to put woman's cause over the top.[32] Appropriately enough, Stanton's own daughter, Harriot Stanton Blatch, would exemplify the new political savvy among that generation of suffrage leaders. Blatch was also adept at cultivating wealthy women who could cover the expenses of an expanded mass movement.[33]

The black drive to reclaim civil and voting rights lay much further in the future, awaiting a shift in the science of race, a changing of the guard at the Supreme Court, and a Cold War in which the United States found it could not credibly preach about the values of freedom among peoples of color in faraway parts of the globe if it continued to discriminate at home. The failures of Reconstruction bequeathed unfinished business to the twentieth century, for women as well as people of color. The victories of white women in the early twentieth century, when they won the vote while black rights still lay at their "nadir," proved limited and even disappointing because they were undermined by enduring sexist attitudes that the suffrage movement and the vote itself did little to budge. It fell to civil rights activists and second wave feminists to pick up and try again to realize the essential vision of universal human rights at the core of Reconstruction radicalism.

As the movement for black rights and the movement for women's rights went their separate ways after 1869, each carried on without the challenging and enlivening presence of the other, and America thus forfeited chances, if only among a small cohort of activists, to learn how to lean across difference and negotiate a cosmopolitan world. The leading feminists of the Reconstruction era ultimately led the way to a terrible racism that warped their movement and betrayed women and men who needed their help. How sad and ironic given the way they had previously, persistently championed equal rights for all.

ABBREVIATIONS

AASS	American Anti-Slavery Society
Abolitionist Papers	Abolitionist Papers, Boston Public Library, Boston, Mass.
AERA	American Equal Rights Association
AFUC	American Freedmen's Union Commission
BAP	Black Abolitionist Papers. 17 reels. Sanford, N.C.: Microfilming Corp. of America, 1999.
BFP/LC	Blackwell Family Papers, Library of Congress, Washington, D.C.
BFP/Schlesinger	Blackwell Family Papers, Schlesinger Library, Radcliffe Institute for Advanced Study, Harvard University, Cambridge, Mass.
Brown Papers	Olympia Brown Papers, Schlesinger Library, Radcliffe Institute for Advanced Study, Harvard University
CHD	Caroline Healey Dall
Dall Papers	Caroline Healey Dall Papers, Massachusetts Historical Society, Boston, Mass.
ECS	Elizabeth Cady Stanton
FD	Frederick Douglass
HBB	Henry B. Blackwell
HBS	Henry B. Stanton
HWS	Elizabeth Cady Stanton, Susan B. Anthony, and Matilda Joslyn Gage, eds. *History of Woman Suffrage.* 6 vols. Rochester, N.Y.: Susan B. Anthony and Charles Mann Printing, 1881–1922.
LS	Lucy Stone
MCW	Martha C. Wright
NASS	*National Anti-Slavery Standard*

NAWSA Papers	National American Woman Suffrage Papers, Library of Congress
Phillips Papers	Wendell Phillips Papers, Houghton Library, Harvard University, Cambridge, Mass.
PP	Parker Pillsbury
Papers	Patricia D. Holland and Ann D. Gordon, eds. *Papers of Elizabeth Cady Stanton and Susan B. Anthony.* 45 reels. Wilmington, Del.: Scholarly Resources, 1991. Citations show reel number: frame number.
SBA	Susan B. Anthony
Selected Papers	Ann D. Gordon, ed. *The Selected Papers of Elizabeth Cady Stanton and Susan B. Anthony,* 5 vols. New Brunswick, N.J.: Rutgers University Press, 1997–2009.
Smith Papers	Gerrit Smith Papers, Special Collections Research Center, Syracuse University Library, Syracuse, New York
UFA	Universal Franchise Association
Wood Papers	Samuel Newitt Wood Papers, Kansas State Historical Society, Topeka, Kans.
WP	Wendell Phillips
WLG	William Lloyd Garrison

NOTES

Introduction

1. "Women and Black Men," *Revolution* 3 (February 4, 1869): 88.
2. Ibid.
3. ECS, "Editorial Correspondence,"*Revolution* 3 (January 28, 1869): 49.
4. William S. McFeely, *Frederick Douglass* (New York: W.W. Norton, 1991), 266.
5. "Anniversary of the American Equal Rights Association," *Revolution* 3 (May 13, 1869): 289.
6. Olympia Brown as cited by Ellen Carol DuBois, "Outgrowing the Compact of the Fathers: Equal Rights, Woman Suffrage, and the United States Constitution, 1820–1878," in DuBois, *Woman Suffrage and Women's Rights* (New York: New York University Press, 1998), 91.
7. The biographical literature began with Elizabeth Cady Stanton, *Eighty Years and More: Reminiscences, 1815–1897* (1898; reprint, Boston: Northeastern University Press, 1993); and Ida Husted Harper, *The Life and Work of Susan B. Anthony*, 3 vols. (Indianapolis: Hollenbeck Press, 1898–1908). Adult children sought to vindicate their mothers in Theodore Stanton and Harriot Stanton Blatch, eds., *Elizabeth Cady Stanton as Revealed in Her Letters, Diary, and Reminiscences*, 2 vols. (New York: Harper, 1922); and Alice Stone Blackwell, *Lucy Stone: Pioneer of Women's Rights* (Boston: Little, Brown, 1930). Subsequent biographies of Stone include Elinor Rice Hays, *Morning Star: A Biography of Lucy Stone, 1818–1893* (New York: Harcourt, Brace and World, 1961); Andrea Moore Kerr, *Lucy Stone: Speaking Out for Equality* (New Brunswick, N.J.: Rutgers University Press, 1992); Dorothea McClain Moore, "Reclaiming Lucy Stone: A Literary and Historical Appraisal," (Ph.D. diss., University of Texas at Arlington, 1996); and Joelle Million, *Woman's Voice, Woman's Place: Lucy Stone and the Birth of the Woman's Rights Movement* (Westport, Conn.: Praeger, 2003). Subsequent biographies of Anthony include Rheta Childe Dorr, *Susan B. Anthony: The Woman Who Changed the Mind of a Nation* (New York: Frederick A. Stokes, 1928); Katharine Susan Anthony, *Susan B. Anthony: Her Personal History and Her Era* (New York: Doubleday, 1954); Alma Lutz, *Susan B. Anthony: Rebel, Crusader, Humanitarian* (Boston: Beacon, 1950); Kathleen Barry, *Susan B. Anthony: A Biography of a Singular Feminist* (New York: Ballantine, 1988). Biographies of Stanton include Alma Lutz, *Created Equal: A Biography of Elizabeth Cady Stanton* (New York: John Day, 1940); Lois Banner, *Elizabeth Cady Stanton: A Radical for Woman's Rights* (Boston: Little, Brown, 1980); Elisabeth Griffith, *In Her Own Right: The Life of Elizabeth Cady Stanton* (New York: Oxford University Press, 1984); Lori Ginzberg, *Elizabeth Cady Stanton: An American Life* (New York: Hill & Wang, 2009).
8. SBA in *Philadelphia Evening Bulletin*, October 18, 1854, in *Papers* 8: 68.

9. Blackwell, *Lucy Stone*, 100; Kerr, *Lucy Stone*, 1, 50, 55–56.

10. In the following biographical sketches, I generally rely on information available in the works cited above. Otherwise, my interpretation of Henry Blackwell's personality is based on Lois Bannister Merk, "Massachusetts and the Woman Suffrage Movement" (Ph.D. diss., Harvard University, 1961), chap. 2, p. 12 and n. 17; and I rely on Kerr and Moore, who see the Stone-Blackwell marriage as troubled, rather than Million who portrays it as happy. On SBA's inability to attend the 1851 convention, see SBA to Uncle Albert and Aunt Ann Eliza Dickinson, November 9, 1851, Dickinson Papers, Susan B. Anthony House, Rochester, N.Y.; on SBA as tongue-tied see Aaron M. Powell, *Personal Reminiscences of the Anti-Slavery and other Reforms and Reformers* (1899; reprint, Westport, Conn.: Negro Universities Press, 1970), 170. On Daniel Cady's legal skills see "Death of Daniel Cady," *Albany Evening Journal*, November 1, 1859, and "A Venerable Lawyer," *Albany Evening Journal*, April 25, 1859.

11. SBA to Sarah Pellet, August 8, 1854, in *Papers* 8: 60.

12. Stanton, *Eighty Years*, 53, 55, 59.

13. ECS to Isabella Beecher Hooker, September 8, 1869, in *Selected Papers*, 2: 264; on the Stanton marriage, see also Ellen DuBois, "On Labor and Free Love: Two Unpublished Speeches of Elizabeth Cady Stanton," *Signs* 1 (1975): 264.

14. ECS to SBA, June 10, 1856, in *Selected Papers*, 1: 325.

15. "Meeting of the American Equal Rights Association in New York," May 9, 1867, in *Selected Papers*, 2: 61–62.

16. According to social movement theory, social movements need three prerequisites to have a chance at success. First, activists must develop a set of arguments that mesh with and appeal to their society's prevailing cultural discourse. Second, activists must mobilize resources, especially money but also in-kind resources and "human assets." Third, social movements may seek to educate and agitate, but sooner or later they must also institutionalize their goals in law and policy, and to do this, they must seize political opportunity when it arises. See Lee Ann Banaszak, *Why Movements Succeed or Fail: Opportunity, Culture, and the Struggle for Woman Suffrage* (Princeton, N.J.: Princeton University Press, 1996), chap. 2; Doug McAdam, *Political Process and the Development of Black Insurgency, 1830–1970*, 2nd ed. (Chicago: University of Chicago Press, 1999), vii–xlii; Doug McAdam, John D. McCarthy, and Mayer N. Zald, eds., *Comparative Perspectives on Social Movements* (Cambridge: Cambridge University Press, 1996), introduction; J. Craig Jenkins, "Resource Mobilization Theory and the Study of Social Movements," *Annual Review of Sociology* 9 (1983): 527–53.

17. *HWS*, 1: chap.19, on Kansas.

18. Ibid., 2: 267.

19. Eleanor Flexner, *Century of Struggle: The Woman's Rights Movement in the United States* (1959; reprint, New York: Atheneum, 1972), 148.

20. Second wave refers to the women's movement that began in the 1960s and flourished in the 1970s, in contrast to "first wave" which began in the 1830s and culminated with the passage of the Nineteenth Amendment in 1920. Of course the term "feminism" is anachronistic, as it was not invented and brought into general use until the 1910s, but I find it useful and not misleading as shorthand to refer to the partisans of women's rights in the nineteenth century. See Nancy Cott, *The Grounding of Modern Feminism* (New Haven: Yale University Press, 1987), 3–10. Similarly I will use the anachronistic term "activist" to describe these women.

21. Ellen DuBois, *Feminism and Suffrage: The Emergence of an Independent Women's Movement in America, 1848–1869* (Ithaca: Cornell University Press, 1978).

22. Ibid., 200.

23. Some of the earliest criticisms of Stanton and Anthony on race were advanced by Rosalyn Terborg-Penn, "Discrimination against Afro-American Women in the Woman's Movement, 1830–1920," in *The Afro-American Woman*, ed. Sharon Harley and Rosalyn

Terborg-Penn (Port Washington, N.Y.: Kennikat, 1978), 17–27; Bettina Aptheker, "Abolitionism, Women's Rights, and the Battle over the Fifteenth Amendment," in *Women's Legacy: Essays on Race, Sex, and Class in American History* (Amherst: University of Massachusetts Press, 1982); and Angela Davis, *Women, Race and Class* (New York: Random House, 1981), 70–86.

24. Important works included Nell Irvin Painter, *Sojourner Truth: A Life, A Symbol* (New York: W.W. Norton, 1996); Rosalyn Terborg-Penn, *African-American Women in the Struggle for the Vote, 1850–1920* (Bloomington: Indiana University Press, 1998); Roslyn Terborg-Penn, "African American Women and the Vote: An Overview," in *African American Women and the Vote, 1837–1965*, ed. Ann D. Gordon with Bettye Collier-Thomas (Amherst: University of Massachusetts Press, 1997), 10–23. DuBois saw the merit of the new scholarship and shifted the emphasis in her interpretation. Previously she had celebrated the emergence of an autonomous women's movement but now, with race in mind, she saw the events of 1869 as more equivocal, even tragic, "a political defeat with reactionary consequences for both the suffrage movement and the American constitutional tradition." Ellen DuBois, "The Last Suffragist: An Intellectual and Political Autobiography," in her *Woman Suffrage and Women's Rights* (New York: New York University Press, 1998), 11.

25. Emphasis is placed on the racism of the founders of the women's movement in Barbara Hilkert Andolsen, *"Daughters of Jefferson, Daughters of Bootblacks": Racism in American Feminism* (Macon, Ga.: Mercer University Press, 1986); and Nancie Caraway, *Segregated Sisterhood: Racism and the Politics of American Feminism* (Knoxville: University of Tennessee Press, 1991), chap. 5. The entire feminist project is questioned as racist in Louise Michele Newman, *White Women's Rights: The Racial Origins of Feminism in the United States* (New York: Oxford University Press, 1999).

26. One scholar who did focus on the 1860s was Michele Mitchell, "'Lower Orders,' Racial Hierarchies, and Rights Rhetoric: Evolutionary Echoes in Elizabeth Cady Stanton's Thought during the Late 1860s," in *Elizabeth Cady Stanton: Feminist as Thinker*, ed. Ellen Carol DuBois and Richard Candida Smith (New York: New York University Press, 2007), 128–15.

27. DuBois, *Feminism and Suffrage*, 71–73, describes Phillips as an "evasive" opponent but does not uncover the conflict over the Hovey bequest.

28. Primary sources unavailable to DuBois in 1978 include Patricia D. Holland and Ann D. Gordon, eds., *Papers of Elizabeth Cady Stanton and Susan B. Anthony* (Wilmington, Del.: Scholarly Resources, 1991), which more than doubled the previously known sources in a microfilm edition of forty-five reels. Invaluable edited selections became available thanks to Ann D. Gordon, ed., *The Selected Papers of Elizabeth Cady Stanton and Susan B. Anthony: Volume 1, In the School of Anti-Slavery, 1840–1866* (New Brunswick, N.J.: Rutgers University Press, 1997); followed by *Volume II, Against an Aristocracy of Sex, 1866–1873* (2000); *Volume III, National Protection for National Citizens, 1873–1880* (2003); *Volume IV, When Clowns Make Laws for Queens* (2006); and *Volume V, Their Place Inside the Body Politic* (2009). And the extant Kansas local newspapers have been collected on microfilm at the Kansas State Historical Society in Topeka. Although DuBois shifted her own research attention to later periods, she in effect invited others to persist, calling 1869 "one of those turning points in history that requires, indeed deserves, continually revised interpretation, so fundamental were the issues involved, so irresolvable the conflicts facing the participants, so painful the choices they faced." DuBois, *Woman Suffrage and Women's Rights*, 10.

29. DuBois, *Feminism and Suffrage*, 77, describes the AERA as neither a "stable organization or a viable political strategy."

30. See Ibid., 80, 87–88, 96–97, where DuBois describes Kansas as a major turning point, but pulls her punches about the women's actual chance to win and the reasons for their failure. She points to the national rather than the state Republican Party, but notes that Train's impact was exaggerated.

31. Andrea Moore Kerr charges Stanton and Anthony with racism and political naivete in order to elevate Lucy Stone as the true feminist heroine of the Reconstruction period in "White Women's Rights, Black Men's Wrongs, Free Love, Blackmail, and the Formation of the American Woman Suffrage Association," in *One Woman One Vote: Rediscovering the Woman Suffrage Movement*, ed. Marjorie Spruill Wheeler (Troutdale, Ore.: New Sage Press, 1995), 61–79.

32. McFeely, *Frederick Douglass*, 238, 264.

Chapter 1

1. *New York Daily Tribune* May 14, 1858, in *Papers* 8: 1124 describes Mozart Hall as "nearly filled"; a standing room crowd in the same hall was estimated at 1,700 in "Woman's Rights Anniversary," *Sibyl*, June 1, 1859, in *Papers* 9: 298.

2. "Practical Susan" in Antoinette Brown Blackwell to ECS, April 5, 1866, in *Papers* 11: 431; an admission charge of 25 cents to the evening sessions in *HWS*, 1: 669.

3. On women's failure to organize their movement, see DuBois, "Women's Rights and Abolition," in DuBois, *Feminism and Suffrage*, 38–39, 50–52; DuBois, *Woman Suffrage and Women's Rights*, 54–67; Sylvia D. Hoffert, *When Hens Crow: The Woman's Rights Movement in Antebellum America* (Bloomington: Indiana University Press, 1995), 17–21; Suzanne M. Marilley, *Woman Suffrage and the Origins of Liberal Feminism in the United States, 1820–1920* (Cambridge: Harvard University Press, 1996), 44–46.

4. Concerning convention financing, see Antoinette Brown Blackwell to Caroline Healey Dall, June 3, 1859, Dall Papers; Lucretia Mott to Lucy Stone, July 1, 1857, BFP/LC LS to SBA, November 2, 1855, in *Papers* 8: 299.

5. *Liberator* 28 (April 30, 1858): 70; *HWS*, 1:668.

6. The fact that the featured speaker was George William Curtis, editor of the popular *Harper's Weekly*, attested to growing mainstream appeal. Curtis would soon advise Anthony that the endorsements of prominent men like himself were carrying women's rights past the tipping point. See Harper, *Life and Work*, 1:172.

7. There is a large literature dealing with women in the nineteenth-century literary marketplace, and with the extent to which fiction challenged ideals of female submissiveness. See for example, Nina Baym, *Women's Fiction: A Guide to Novels by and about Women in America, 1820–1870* (Ithaca: Cornell University Press, 1978); Mary Kelley, *Private Woman, Public Stage: Literary Domesticity in Nineteenth-Century America* (New York: Oxford University Press, 1984); Susan M. Coultrap-McQuin, *Doing Literary Business: American Women Writers in the Nineteenth Century* (Chapel Hill: University of North Carolina Press, 1990); Laura McCall, "'Shall I Fetter Her Will?': Literary Americans Confront Feminine Submission, 1820–1860," *Journal of the Early Republic* 21 (Spring 2001): 95–113.

8. "Address by ECS to the Eighth National Woman's Rights Convention," [May 13, 1858], in *Selected Papers*, 1:369; "Women's Rights Convention," *New York Tribune*, May 15, 1858, in *Papers*: 8: 1125.

9. "Woman's Rights Convention," *New York Tribune*, May 14, 1858, in *Papers* 8: 1124.

10. See Lori D. Ginsberg, *Untidy Origins: A Story of Woman's Rights in Antebellum New York* (Chapel Hill: University of North Carolina Press, 2005); Nancy Isenberg, *Sex and Citizenship in Antebellum America* (Chapel Hill: University of North Carolina Press, 1998); DuBois, "Women's Rights and Abolition," in DuBois, *Woman Suffrage and Women's Rights*, 57.

11. Lucretia Mott to Elizabeth Neall Gay, May 7, 1858, in Beverly Wilson Palmer, ed., *Selected Letters of Lucretia Coffin Mott* (Urbana: University of Illinois Press, 2002), 271.

12. DuBois, "Woman's Rights and Abolition," in *Woman Suffrage and Women's Rights*, 62–63.

13. "ECS to the Woman's Rights Convention at Akron, Ohio," May 16, 1851, in *Papers* 7: 80.

14. Hoffert, *When Hens Crow*, 22–23; ECS to SBA, February 19, 1854, in *Papers* 7: 998.

15. "Woman's Rights Convention," *New York Tribune*, May 14, 1858, in *Papers*, 8: 1124; "Report of the Eighth National Woman's Rights Convention," *The Lily*, June 1, 1858, in *Papers* 8: 1127.

16. Lori D. Ginzberg, *Women and the Work of Benevolence: Morality, Politics, and Class in the Nineteenth-Century United States* (New Haven: Yale University Press, 1990), chap. 4.

17. See *American National Biography Online*, s.v. "Higginson, Thomas Wentworth," by Tilden G. Edelstein, accessed October 7, 2010, http://0-www.anb.org.library.colgate.edu/; Tilden G. Edelstein, *Strange Enthusiasm: A Life of Thomas Wentworth Higginson* (New Haven: Yale University Press, 1968).

18. *HWS*, 1:70–71. See also Judith Wellman, *The Road to Seneca Falls* (Urbana: University of Illinois Press, 2004), 195–204.

19. On the women's rights press strategy in the 1850s, see Hoffert, *When Hens Crow*, chap. 4. The exchange system, whereby local and regional papers freely reprinted material from the metropolitan dailies, is described in Mark Wahlgren Summers, *The Press Gang: Newspapers and Politics, 1865–1878* (Chapel Hill: University of North Carolina Press, 1994), 20. On New York newspapers reaching a national audience, see ECS to WP, January 12, 1866, in *Selected Papers*, 1: 570; Thomas Bender, *New York Intellect: A History of Intellectual Life in New York City, from 1750 to the Beginnings of Our Own Time* (New York: Knopf, 1987), 156–66.

20. On the abolitionists' agency system, modeled after both American benevolent organizations and the British antslavery campaign, see John Lytle Myers, "The Agency System of the Anti-Slavery Movement, 1832–1837, and Its Antecedents in Other Benevolent and Reform Societies" (Ph.D. diss., University of Michigan, 1960); Samuel May Jr. to LS, June 5, 1884, NAWSA Papers, microfilm frame 265–68; and Ginzberg, *Women and the Work of Benevolence*, 54–59.

21. "Woman's Rights. Circulate the Petition," enclosure in SBA to Matilda Joslyn Gage, June 28, 1854, in *Selected Papers*, 1: 274.

22. Frederick Douglass, *The Life and Times of Frederick Douglass* (1892; reprint, New York: Macmillan, Collier, 1962), 469. On women's fund-raising, see Julie Roy Jeffrey, *The Great Silent Army of Abolitionism: Ordinary Women in the Antislavery Movement* (Chapel Hill : University of North Carolina Press, 1998), esp. chap. 3; Julie Roy Jeffrey, "'Stranger, *Buy* Lest Our Mission Fail:' The Complex Culture of Women's Abolitionist Fairs," *American Nineteenth-Century History* 4 (Spring 2003): 1–24.; Lee Chambers-Schiller, "'A Good Work among the People': The Political Culture of the Boston Antislavery Fair," in *Women's Political Culture in Antebellum America*, Jean Fagan Yellin and John C. Van Horne, eds. (Ithaca: Cornell University Press, 1994), 249–74.

23. DuBois argues that the prior existence of organized abolition freed activist women from the need to organize, thus enabling them to elaborate their arguments and become accustomed to public roles. DuBois, *Feminism and Suffrage*, 32–39, 50–52; DuBois, "Women's Rights and Abolition," in DuBois, *Woman Suffrage and Women's Rights*, 57–65.

24. There is a large literature on married women's property rights. See, for example, Normal Basch, *In the Eyes of the Law: Women, Marriage, and Property in Nineteenth-Century New York* (Ithaca: Cornell University Press, 1982).

25. On female benevolent organizations as an important transitional step out of domesticity and into the public realm, see Anne M. Boylan, "Women and Politics in the Era before Seneca Falls," *Journal of the Early Republic* 10 (Fall 1990): 363–82; Anne M. Boylan, *The Origins of Women's Activism: New York and Boston, 1797–1840* (Chapel Hill: University of North Carolina Press, 2002), esp. chap. 5 and appendix 2; Nancy A. Hewitt, *Women's Activism and Social Change: Rochester, New York, 1822–1872* (Ithaca: Cornell University Press, 1984).

26. See Amy Swerdlow, "Abolition's Conservative Sisters: The Ladies' New York Anti-Slavery Societies, 1834–1840;" Nancy Hewitt, "On Their Own Terms: A Historiographical Essay," in Yellin and Van Horne, *The Abolitionist Sisterhood*, 23–44; ECS, "The Purchase of Mount Vernon," *NASS*, September 4, 1858, in *Papers* 9: 59.

27. I make this argument in *Serving Women: Household Service in Nineteenth-Century America* (Middletown, CT: Wesleyan University Press, 1983). The availability of affordable domestic service cut both ways: while it enabled some middle-class women to engage in reform work, for others it made confinement to the domestic sphere a comfortable berth.

28. Gerda Lerner, *The Grimké Sisters from South Carolina: Pioneers for Woman's Rights and Abolition* (New York: Schocken Books, 1971), 300, 315, passim. Lydia Maria Child, another early abolitionist with feminist sympathies, was obliged to curtail her contributions to both causes and spend much of her time on domestic chores and writing for pay because her husband was a chronic bankrupt. Carolyn L. Karcher, *The First Woman in the Republic: A Cultural Biography of Lydia Maria Child* (Durham: Duke University Press, 1994), 265, 290, 293, 368.

29. Palmer, *Selected Letters of Lucretia Mott,* 219, 231 n. 3.

30. Jean R. Soderlund, "Priorities and Power: The Philadelphia Female Anti-Slavery Society," in Yellin and Van Horne, *The Abolitionist Sisterhood,* 74–75, indicates that Sarah Pugh and Margaretta Forten curtailed antislavery activism to care for aging parents.

31. Kerr, *Lucy Stone,* 52–54; Million, *Woman's Voice,* 172, 174, 200.

32. "Woman's Rights Convention," *New York Daily Tribune,* May 14, 1858, in *Papers* 8: 1124.

33. *New York Herald,* May 15, 1858, in *Papers* 8: 1139; *American National Biography Online,* s.v. "Remond, Charles Lenox" by Stacey Kinlock Sewell, accessed October 7, 2010, http://0-www.anb.org.library.colgate.edu/.

34. There is a large and growing literature on the black activists of the North, summarized in Manisha Sinha, "Coming of Age: The Historiography of Black Abolitionism," in Timothy Patrick McCarthy and John Stauffer, eds., *Prophets of Protest: Reconsidering the History of American Abolitionism* (New York: New Press, 2006), 23–38. See Jane H. Pease and William H. Pease, *They Who Would Be Free: Blacks' Search for Freedom, 1830–1861* (New York: Atheneum, 1974); Benjamin Quarles, *Black Abolitionists* (New York: Oxford University Press, 1969); Leon Litwack, *North of Slavery: The Negro in the Free States* (Chicago: University of Chicago Press, 1961); James Oliver Horton and Lois E. Horton, *In Hope of Liberty: Culture, Community and Protest among Northern Free Blacks* (New York: Oxford University Press, 1997); Patrick Rael, *Black Identity and Black Protest in the Antebellum North* (Chapel Hill: University of North Carolina Press, 2002); and Shirley J. Yee, *Black Women Abolitionists: A Study in Activism, 1828–1860* (Knoxville: University of Tennessee Press, 1992).

35. Howard Holman Bell, "A Survey of the Negro Convention Movement, 1830–1861" (Ph.D. diss., Northwestern University, 1953); Jane H. Pease and William H. Pease, "Negro Conventions and the Problem of Black Leadership," *Journal of Black Studies* 2 (September 1971): 29–44; *Proceedings of the Black State Conventions, 1840–1865,* ed. Philip S. Foner and George E. Walker (Philadelphia: Temple University Press, 1979); Rael, *Black Identity and Black Protest,* chap. 1.

36. Chris Dixon, *African America and Haiti: Emigration and Black Nationalism in the Nineteenth Century* (Westport, Conn.: Greenwood Press, 200), introduction, 1–13, but cf. Sinha, "Coming of Age," 33–35, warning that emigration and integration were not always competitive and mutually exclusive goals.

37. Pease and Pease, *They Who Would be Free,* 123.

38. Rael, *Black Identity and Black Protest,* 31–35. Women's rights conventions, in contrast, were open to all comers but used admission fees to screen out rowdies bent on disrupting their meetings. Black conventions preferred credentialing to fees.

39. The importance of voluntary groups within the black community is emphasized throughout the historical literature; see Sinha, "Coming of Age," 34.

40. Martha S. Jones, *All Bound Up Together: The Woman Question in African-American Public Culture, 1830–1900* (Chapel Hill: University of North Carolina Press, 2007), 72–82; Yee, *Black Women Abolitionists,* 143–46.

41. Jones, *All Bound Up Together*, 80–81; James Oliver Horton, "Freedom's Yoke: Gender Conventions among Antebellum Blacks," *Feminist Studies* 12 (Spring 1986): 69–70.

42. There were exceptions: the New England Convention of Colored Citizens in 1859 admitted women and even elected some to leadership positions. Jones, *All Bound Up Together*, 101–105; Bell, "Survey of the Negro Convention Movement," 105; *The Frederick Douglass Papers. Series One: Speeches, Debates and Interviews, Volume 3: 1855–1863*, ed. John W. Blassingame (New Haven: Yale University Press, 1985), 97; Yee, *Black Women Abolitionists*, 145; Terborg-Penn, *African American Women in the Struggle for the Vote*, 19–21.

43. Stewart's importance is highlighted in Paula Giddings, *When and Where I Enter: The Impact of Black Women on Race and Sex in America* (New York: William Morrow, 1984), 50–53.

44. Painter, *Sojourner Truth*, chaps. 14, 18, and 26, makes a strong case for Truth as in some respects an "invented great."

45. Margaret Washington, *Sojourner Truth's America* (Urbana: University of Illinois Press, 2009), 132–33; 170–71, discusses Truth's lack of literacy as a choice but also notes its effect on her organizing abilities.

46. Janice Sumler-Lewis, "The Forten-Purvis Women of Philadelphia and the American Anti-Slavery Crusade," *Journal of Negro History* 66 (Winter 1981–82): 281–88.

47. Beth A. Salerno, *Sister Societies: Women's Antislavery Organizations in Antebellum America* (DeKalb: Northern Illinois University Press, 2005); but see also Jean R. Soderlund, "Priorities and Power: The Philadelphia Female Anti-Slavery Society," in Yellin and Van Horne, *The Abolitionist Sisterhood*, 67–88. The Philadelphia Female Antislavery Society, which included black women among its founders and leaders, endured but it remained small, local, and focused on antislavery without branching out to women's rights.

48. Ruth Bogin, "Sarah Parker Remond: Black Abolitionist from Salem," *Essex Institute Historical Collections* 110(1973): 12–150.

49. *New York Herald*, May 14, 1858, in *Papers* 8:1135.

50. Black participants in 1858 included Sarah Parker Remond, Robert Purvis, Frederick Douglass, and Charles Lenox Remond. See *Papers* 8: 1125, 1127, 1139. In 1859, no black persons were mentioned in the *Proceedings* or the press coverage (*Papers* 9: 280–301), while in 1860, Robert Purvis was listed as a vice president, but no black speakers were mentioned in the *Proceedings* or press coverage. *Papers* 9: 612–68.

51. This dilemma would resurface in second-wave black feminism, as discussed in the aptly titled *All the Women Are White, All the Blacks Are Men, But Some of Us Are Brave*, Gloria T. Hull, Patricia Bell Scott, and Barbara Smith, eds. (Old Westbury, N.Y.: Feminist Press, 1982).

52. Anne M. Boylan, "Benevolence and Antislavery Activity among African American Women in New York and Boston, 1820–1840," in Yellin and Van Horne, *The Abolitionist Sisterhood*, 119–37; Dorothy Sterling, ed., *We Are Your Sisters: Black Women in the Nineteenth Century* (New York: W.W. Norton, 1984), 117–19; Yee, *Black Women Abolitionists*, 8. Cf. Caraway, *Segregated Sisterhood*, 121, for an interpretation that emphasizes white exclusion more than black women's choices.

53. John Stauffer, *The Black Hearts of Men: Radical Abolitionists and the Transformation of Race* (Cambridge: Harvard University Press, 2001), 102–8, 127–30, 135–41, argues that Gerrit Smith's generosity was literally unique.

54. Pease and Pease, *They Who Would Be Free*, 12–13, 75–79, 84.

55. Eliza Legett to WP, April 24, 1864, in Phillips Papers, bMS Am 1953 (810).

56. Bettye Collier-Thomas, "Frances Ellen Watkins Harper: Abolitionist and Feminist Reformer, 1825–1911," in Ann Gordon and Bettye Collier-Thomas, eds., *African-American Women and the Vote, 1837–1965* (Amherst: University of Massachusetts Press, 1997), 43.

57. David Roediger, *The Wages of Whiteness: Race and the Making of the American Working Class* (London: Verso, 1991); Noel Ignatiev, *How the Irish Became White* (New York:

Routledge, 1995); Ronald P. Formisano, "The Edge of Caste: Colored Suffrage in Michigan, 1827–1861," *Michigan History* 66 (Spring 1972): 38. Concerning defeats of black suffrage referenda, see Pease and Pease, *They Who Would Be Free* 190–92. There are also notable state studies, such as Michael McManus, *Political Abolition in Wisconsin, 1840–1861* (Kent, Ohio: Kent State University Press, 1998). An overview of the scholarship is found in Robert P. Forbes, "'Truth Systematised': The Changing Debate over Slavery and Abolition, 1761–1916," in McCarthy and Stauffer, *Prophets of Protest*, 16–17.

58. David Blight, *Frederick Douglass's Civil War: Keeping Faith in Jubilee* (Baton Rouge: Louisiana State University Press, 1989).

59. Horton, "Freedom's Yoke," and Yee, *Black Abolitionist Women*, 45, 50, 55–57.

60. Charles L. Remond to Charles B. Ray, June 30, 1840, in *Liberator* (October 16, 1840): 165. On black men but not black women among recognized women's rights supporters, see Caraway, *Segregated Sisterhood*, 241 n. 49.

61. See *American National Biography Online*, s.v., Purvis, Robert, by Joseph A. Borome, accessed October 7, 2010, http://0-www.anb.org.library.colgate.edu/; Margaret Hope Bacon, *But One Race: The Life of Robert Purvis* (Albany: State University of New York Press, 2007); Nell's activities in upstate New York are mentioned in Nancy Hewitt, "'Seeking a Larger Liberty': Remapping First Wave Feminism," in *Women's Rights and Transatlantic Antislavery in the Era of Emancipation,* ed. Kathryn Kish Sklar and James Brewer Stewart (New Haven: Yale University Press, 2007), 266–78.

62. Benjamin Quarles, "Frederick Douglass and the Woman's Rights Movement," *Journal of Negro History* 25 (January 1940): 35–44; *Frederick Douglass on Women's Rights,* ed. and introduction by Philip S. Foner (Westport, Conn.: Greenwood Press, 1976).

63. Swisshelm in the *Pittsburgh Saturday Visiter [sic]*, November 2 and 23, 1850, in John F. McClymer, *This High and Holy Moment: The First National Woman's Rights Convention, Worcester, 1850* (Orlando: Harcourt Brace, 1999), 170–74. See also Sylvia D. Hoffert, *Jane Grey Swisshelm: An Unconventional Life, 1815–1884* (Chapel Hill: University of North Carolina Press, 2004), 143–48.

64. Leonard L. Richards, *"Gentlemen of Property and Standing": Anti-Abolition Mobs in Jacksonian America* (New York: Oxford University Press, 1970), 41–46, 114–16.

65. *Albany Argus,* ca. January 3–4, 1861, in *Papers* 9: 982.

66. Jones, *All Bound Up Together*, 98–100.

67. *Liberator,* December 9, 1853; January 13, 1854; and February 24, 1854; Leslie Wheeler, ed., *Loving Warriors: Selected Letters of Lucy Stone and Henry B. Blackwell, 1853–1893* (New York: Dial Press, 1981), 64; Million, *Woman's Voice*, 160–66.

68. *Frederick Douglass' Paper,* February 17 and March 17, 1854, in Foner, *Frederick Douglass on Women's Rights,* 67–73.

69. In October 1859, a hoax purported to show that Lucy Stone had invited the notoriously racist Illinois Senator Stephen Douglas to a women's rights convention in Chicago. Although Garrison and others were not taken in, Douglass found the report believable and wrote, "Lucy Stone has too frequently compromised her anti-slavery principles by a feverish desire for prominence and popularity." *Douglass' Monthly,* October 1859, in Foner, *Frederick Douglass on Women's Rights,* 74–77; *Liberator,* October 21, 1859. Hays, *Morning Star,* 133, says Stone considered Douglass "unprincipled and mean."

70. "Accounts of SBA with the American Anti-Slavery Society," in *Selected Papers,* 1: 330–34; SBA to LS, July 12, 1853, in *Papers* 7: 779, which indicates that Anthony asked Douglass's advice about movement tactics.

71. *American National Biography Online,* s.v., Smith, Gerrit, by John R. McKivigan, accessed October 7, 2010, http://0-www.anb.org.library.colgate.edu/; Octavius B. Frothingham, *Gerrit Smith: A Biography* (New York: G.P. Putnam's, 1878); Stauffer, *The Black Hearts of Men.* Stauffer contends that Smith's friendships across the color line made him unique among white abolitionists. However, Christine Stansell argues that black women remained largely unknown to Stanton, in part because she did not participate in the biracial female

antislavery societies that flourished in the 1830s. See her "Missed Connections: Abolitionist Feminism in the Nineteenth Century," in DuBois and Smith, *Elizabeth Cady Stanton: Feminist as Thinker*, 32–49.

72. *Life and Times of Frederick Douglass Written by Himself* (1893), in *Frederick Douglass: Autobiographies* (New York: Library of America, 1994), 904.

73. *HWS*, 1: 73.

74. See *Selected Papers*, 1: 287. Stanton's remark was criticized by the black activist George T. Downing. See Pease and Pease, *They Who Would Be Free*, 87.

75. SBA to Antoinette Brown Blackwell, before September 29, 1858, in *Papers* 9: 103.

76. "Home Notes. The Bequests of the Late Francis Jackson," *Commonwealth*, February 9, 1867, and "Concerning Wills," *Commonwealth*, February 16, 1867. The actual text is found on pages 1–3 of *Edmund Jackson v. Wendell Phillips & others*, Supreme Court of Massachusetts, Suffolk; 96 Mass. 539; 867 Mass. LEXIS 113; 14 Allen 539.

77. *Edmund Jackson v. Wendell Phillips*, 1–2. Jackson's sympathy for women's rights stemmed in part from the suffering of his daughter, Eliza Jackson Eddy, whose husband abused her. He directed that income from the property he left for the support of his daughter and granddaughter should revert to the women's cause upon their decease. SBA to LS, June 16, 1857, in *Papers* 8: 930; LS to SBA, July 20, 1857, BFP/LC.

78. WP to LS and SBA, November 6, 1858, in *Selected Papers*, 1: 381.

79. "Extracts from the Will of the Late Charles F. Hovey, Esq," in *HWS*, 1: 667–68; *Selected Papers*, 1:391.

80. ECS to SBA, 1 December [1858], in *Selected Papers*, 1:382. Dorr, *Susan B. Anthony*, 129 notes this crucial juncture but overstates when she writes, "With money enough in the bank…victory seemed certain."

81. *New York Tribune*, October 26, 1850, in McClymer, *This High and Holy Moment*, 149.

82. LS to HBB, n.d.,1854, in BFP/LC.

83. Wheeler, *Loving Warriors*, 93, 98; "Miss Stone's Lecture" *Brattleboro Democrat*, reprinted in the *Liberator*, September 2, 1853.

84. Hendrik Booraem, *The Formation of the Republican Party in New York* (New York: New York University Press, 1983), 53; Harper, *Life and Work*, 1: 121.

85. Harper, *Life and Work*, 1: 65, 173; SBA to William Lloyd Garrison, in *Papers* 9: 230.

86. *American National Biography Online*, s.v. "Weed, Thurlow," by Phyllis F. Field, accessed October 7, 2010, http://0-www.anb.org.library.colgate.edu/; Glyndon Van Deusen, *Thurlow Weed: Wizard of the Lobby* (Boston: Little, Brown, 1947); Hendrik Booraem, *The Formation of the Republican Party in New York* (New York: New York University Press, 1983), 89, 110; Glyndon G. VanDeusen, *William Henry Seward* (New York: Oxford University Press, 1967).

87. Arthur H. Rice, "Henry B. Stanton as a Political Abolitionist" (Ph.D. diss., Teachers College of Columbia University, 1968); Rosalie Margolin, "Henry B. Stanton: A Forgotten Abolitionist," (M.A. thesis, Columbia University, 1962); Henry B. Stanton, *Random Recollections*, 2nd ed. (New York: McGowan & Slipper, 1886).

88. Henry B. Stanton's views are evident in his "New York Finances," *The United States Magazine and Democratic Review* 18 (March 1851): 274. On Democrats like Stanton, see Jonathan H. Earle, *Jacksonian Antislavery and the Politics of Free Soil, 1824–1854* (Chapel Hill: University of North Carolina Press, 2004); Sean Wilentz, "Slavery, Antislavery, and Jacksonian Democracy," in *The Market Revolution in America: Social, Political, and Religious Expressions, 1800–1880*, ed. Melvyn Stokes and Stephen Conway (Charlottesville: University of Virginia Press, 1996), 202–23.

89. ECS to Elizabeth Smith Miller, June 4–[5], 1851, in *Papers* 7: 86.

90. A large literature on the split includes Aileen Kraditor, *Means and Ends in American Abolitionism: Garrison and His Critics on Strategy and Tactics, 1834–1850* (1967; reprint, New York: Vintage Books, 1970); and Ronald G. Walters, *The Antislavery Appeal: American Abolitionism after 1830* (Baltimore: Johns Hopkins University Press, 1976). Henry B.

Stanton argued that rational reformers, standing between "ultraists" on the one hand and "conservatives" on the other, must use political means despite the risk of compromise, in *Ultraists, Conservatives, Reformers: An Address before the Phoenix and Union Societies of Hamilton College* (Utica: Roberts & Sherman, 1850). For his role in the 1840 split, Stanton was vilified by the Garrisonians, and even today historians immersed in Garrisonian sources tend to be drawn into their venomous assessments of Stanton—for example, Henry Mayer, *All on Fire: William Lloyd Garrison and the Abolition of Slavery* (New York: St. Martin's Press, 1998), 268.

91. HBS to Gerrit Smith and Elizabeth Smith Miller, May 2, 1849, in *Papers* 6:910; Rice, "Henry B. Stanton," 311–51; Richard H. Sewell, *Ballots for Freedom: Antislavery Politics in the United States, 1837–1860* (New York: Oxford University Press, 1976), 223–30, 249–51.

92. ECS to HBS, [February 27, 1851], in *Papers* 7:56; Griffith, *In Her Own Right*, 64; Stanton, *Random Recollections*, 83.

93. He was one of the first of the Barnburners to switch over to the Republicans. Booream, *Formation of the Republican Party*, 129–33, 263. Her interest is evident in ECS to SBA, [November 4, 1856], in *Papers* 8: 785.

94. At the time of the abolitionist split in 1840, Henry B. Stanton said he agreed with the Garrisonians on women's rights, but it is not clear how he voted on the seating of women delegates at the World's Anti-Slavery Convention in London. See Rice, "Henry B. Stanton," 207; Kraditor, *Means and Ends*, 72–73, 77. "Henry sides with my friends, who oppose me in all that is dearest to my heart," Stanton wrote at one point. ECS to SBA, September 10, 1855, in *Papers* 8: 281.

95. ECS, "A Woman's View of Our Late Elections," *New York Semi-Weekly Tribune*, December 8, 1854, in *Papers* 8: 94. She discussed the Maine Law, Know-Nothing, Soft and Hard-Shell Democrats, Woolly-Head and Silver Grey Whigs, Free Soil, and Liberty Party factions.

96. According to Million, *Woman's Voice*, 257, Stone suffered a series of miscarriages.

97. ECS to SBA, April 10, [1859], in *Papers* 9: 267.

98. *Selected Papers*, 1:386 n. 1. On personal liberty laws, intended to thwart the federal Fugitive Slave Law, see Thomas D. Morris, *Free Men All: The Personal Liberty Laws of the North, 1780–1861* (Baltimore: Johns Hopkins University Press, 1974).

99. Anthony's personal responsibility is seen in Antoinette Brown Blackwell to LS, August 29, 1859, in Lasser and Merrill, *Friends and Sisters*, 157–58.

100. A list of the speakers is found in *Proceedings of the Tenth National Woman's Rights Convention Held at the Cooper Institute, New York City, May 10th and 11th, 1860* (Boston: Yerrinton and Garrison, 1860), 6, in *Papers* 9: 617. Concerning expenses and salaries, see Antoinette Brown Blackwell to LS, July 22 and August 29, 1859, in Lasser and Merrill, *Friends and Sisters*, 155.

101. ECS, "To the Women of the Empire State," c. July 12, 1859, in *Selected Papers*, 1: 389.

102. *Proceedings of the Tenth National Woman's Rights Convention*, 6, in *Papers* 9: 617.

103. Million, *Women's Voice*, 262.

104. Her father died the previous fall, and although he had disapproved of her women's rights work and threatened to cut her off, she inherited an estimated $50,000 worth of property upon his death. Henry Stanton's performance as a breadwinner—erratic at best—was no longer an issue. Never the sort of mother to hover, Stanton had long made use of domestic servants as the family budget allowed, and now her resources were ample. See Griffith, *In Her Own Right*, 97–98.

105. On the 1854 campaign, see Harper, *Life and Work*, 1: 108–11; *HWS*, 1: 577–619. Stanton's 1854 address was delivered at a public meeting and copies were distributed to state legislators. *Selected Papers*, 1:239–61.

106. SBA to LS, December 13, 1853, in *Selected Papers*, 1:233.

107. Harper, *Life and Work*, 1: 122–28.

108. *Selected Papers*, 1:406 n.2. See Norma Basch, *In the Eyes of the Law: Women, Marriage, and Property in Nineteenth-Century New York* (Ithaca: Cornell University Press, 1982), chap. 4; and Amy Dru Stanley, *From Bondage to Contract: Wage Labor, Marriage, and the Market in the Age of Slave Emancipation* (Cambridge: Cambridge University Press, 1998), chap. 5, on the significance of an earnings rather than a property law.

109. SBA, Secretary's Report, Speech of ECS in *Proceedings of the Tenth National Woman's Rights Convention*, 4–7, 34–46, in *Papers* 9: 615–16, 630–35.

110. *Proceedings of the Tenth National Woman's Rights Convention*, 34 in *Papers* 9: 630.

111. *Selected Papers*, 1:304, 406; Basch, *In the Eyes of the Law*, chap. 4.

112. Mark Wahlgren Summers, "'A Band of Brigands:'Albany Lawmakers and Republican National Politics, 1860," *Civil War History* 30 (June 1984): 101–19; David M. Ellis, et al., *A Short History of New York State* (Ithaca: Cornell University Press, 1957), 238.

113. *Proceedings of the Tenth National Woman's Rights Convention*, 11, 47 in *Papers* 9: 618, 635.

114. "The Women Movement," *New York Daily Tribune*, February 18, 1860, in *Papers* 9: 530.

115. The Assembly voted 67–19 for the bill, the Senate voted 21 in favor, with no opposition recorded, out of a total of 32 senators, and finally the Assembly voted to accept the Senate's version 92–95. See *Journal of the New York State Assembly, 1860* (Albany: Van Benthuysen, 1860), 334, 663; *Journal of the Senate of the State of New York, 1860* (Albany: Van Benthuysen, 1860), 301.

116. *Proceedings of the Tenth National Woman's Rights Convention*, 7, in *Papers* 9: 616.

117. *Journal of the New York State Assembly, 1859*, 605; "The Female Suffrage Question," *New York Times*, March 18, 1859; William D. Murphy, *Biographical Sketches of the State Officers and Members of the Legislature of the State of New York in 1859* (Albany: Van Benthuysen, 1859), 184–85.

118. *Selected Papers*, 1: 406, 408.

119. This problematic indifference provided the topic for two pamphlets Stanton wrote for use in the previous state canvass, "I Have All the Rights I Want," and "It Is So Unladylike." *Selected Papers*, 1: 391–92, 402–405.

120. *Proceedings of the Tenth National Woman's Rights Convention*, 40–43, in *Papers* 9: 632–33.

121. The pattern Stanton envisioned would, in a later era, account for women's inclusion in Title VII of the 1964 Civil Rights Act. This was accomplished by congressional insiders acting without any pressure from an organized women's movement. The National Organization for Women was established afterward, to press for enforcement, not passage, of this law outlawing employment discrimination by sex.

122. *Proceedings of the Tenth National Woman's Rights Convention*, 7, in *Papers*, 9: 616.

123. Catherine Allgor, *Parlor Politics: In Which the Ladies of Washington Help Build a City and a Government* (Charlottesville: University Press of Virginia, 2000).

124. Cf. William E. Gienapp, " 'Politics Seem to Enter into Everything': Political Culture in the North, 1840–1860," in William E. Gienapp, et al., eds., *Essays on American Antebellum Politics, 1840–1860* (College Station: Texas A & M University Press, 1982), 15–69; and the revisionist Glenn C. Altshuler and Stuart M. Blumin, *Rude Republic: Americans and Their Politics in the Nineteenth Century* (Princeton: Princeton University Press, 2000).

125. The literature on "woman's sphere" is quite extensive; influential pioneering works include Kathryn Kish Sklar, *Catharine Beecher, A Study in American Domesticity* (New Haven: Yale University Press, 1973); Nancy Cott, *The Bonds of Womanhood: "Woman's Sphere" in New England, 1870–1835* (New Haven: Yale University Press, 1977); and Barbara Welter, "The Cult of True Womanhood: 1820–1860," *American Quarterly* 18 (Summer 1966): 151–74.

126. See Mary Kelley, *Learning to Stand and Speak: Women, Education, and Public Life in America's Republic* (Chapel Hill: University of North Carolina Press, 2006); Carolyn Eastman, *A Nation of Speechifiers: Making an American Public after the Revolution* (Chicago: University of Chicago Press, 2009).

127. See Ginzberg, *Women and the Work of Benevolence,* 68–69; Mary Hershberger, "Mobilizing Women, Anticipating Abolition: The Struggle against Indian Removal in the 1830s," *Journal of American History* 86 (June 1999): 15–40; Linda Kerber, "Separate Spheres, Female Worlds, Woman's Place: The Rhetoric of Women's History," *Journal of American History* 75 (June 1988): 9–39; Elizabeth R. Varon, *"We Mean to Be Counted": White Women and Party Politics in Antebellum Virginia* (Chapel Hill: University of North Carolina Press, 1998); Jean Gould Hales, "'Co-Laborers in the Cause': Women in the Ante-bellum Nativist Movement," *Civil War History* 25 (June 1979): 119–38.

128. On politics as extending beyond parties and elections to encompass all of "public culture," and women's "protopolitical" activities, see Jean Harvey Baker, "Politics, Paradigms, and Public Culture," *Journal of American History* 84 (December 1997): 894–99; Ronald J. Zboray and Mary Saracino Zboray, "Whig Women, Politics, and Culture in the Campaign of 1840: Three Perspectives from Massachusetts," *Journal of the Early Republic* 17 (Summer 1997): 277–315.

129. Ronald P. Formisano, "The 'Party Period' Revisited," *Journal of American History* 86 (June 1999),116; Melanie Susan Gustafson, *Women and the Republican Party, 1854–1924* (Urbana: University of Illinois Press, 2001), 7–24; Rebecca Edwards, *Angels in the Machinery: Gender in American Party Politics from the Civil War to the Progressive Era* (New York: Oxford University Press, 1997), 19–35.

130. Pamela Herr, *Jessie Benton Fremont: A Biography* (New York: Franklin Watts, 1987), 262–63, and chaps. 17–18 generally; *The Letters of Jessie Benton Fremont,* ed. Pamela Herr and Mary Lee Spence (Urbana: University of Illinois Press, 1993); Jeffrey, *The Great Silent Army of Abolitionism,* 169; Michael D. Pierson, *Free Hearts and Free Homes: Gender and American Antislavery Politics* (Chapel Hill: University of North Carolina Press, 2003).

131. Janet L. Coryell, "Superseding Gender: The Role of the Woman Politico in Antebellum Partisan Politics," in *Women and the Unstable State in Nineteenth-Century America,* ed. Alison M. Parker and Stephanie Cole (Arlington: Texas A & M University Press, 2000), 84–112.

132. Jean H. Baker, *Mary Todd Lincoln: A Biography* (New York: W. W. Norton, 1987), 160–62, 180–81.

133. Jessie Benton Fremont to Sydney Howard Gay, June 21, [1862], in *Letters of Jessie Benton Fremont,* 329; ECS to Martha C. Wright, January 20, 1866, in *Papers* 11: 297.

134. ECS to SBA, [November 4, 1856] in *Papers* 8:785.

135. Charles Bright, "The State in the United States during the Nineteenth Century," in *Statemaking and Social Movements: Essays in History and Theory,* ed. Charles Bright and Susan Harding (Ann Arbor: University of Michigan Press, 1984),121–58; Richard Franklin Bensel, *Yankee Leviathan: The Origins of Central State Authority in America, 1859–1877* (Cambridge: Cambridge University Press, 1990). It is significant that in the *HWS,* vol. 1, seven of fifteen chapters are devoted to developments in a given state, e.g., chapter 10 is entitled, "Pennsylvania."

136. In 1860, for example, New York's thirty-five electoral votes were key to Lincoln's victory: without them he might have won all the rest of the North and the West and still have seen the election tossed into the House of Representatives. Sidney David Brummer, *Political History of New York during the Period of the Civil War* (New York: Columbia University Studies in History, Economics and Public Law, 39:2; reprint, New York: AMS Press, 1967), 70. See also Edwin G. Burrows and Mike Wallace, *Gotham: A History of New York City to 1898* (New York: Oxford University Press, 1999), chap. 39; Bender, *New York Intellect,* 146–67.

137. "To the Friends of Woman's Rights," *Liberator,* September 2, 1853.

138. *HWS,* 1: 99. On state-level legal reform paving the way for the 1848 Seneca Falls convention, see Judith Wellman, "The Seneca Falls Women's Rights Convention: A Study of Social Networks," *Journal of Women's History* 3 (Spring 1991): 17–22; Wellman, "Women's Rights, Republicanism,"369–84; Ginzberg, *Untidy Origins,* chap. 6.

139. These included Antoinette Brown Blackwell in the Rochester area, Lydia Mott in Albany, Ernestine Rose in New York City, and Martha C. Wright (and her friends Frances Seward and Lazette Worden) in Auburn. See Elizabeth Cazden, *Antoinette Brown Blackwell: A Biography* (Old Westbury, N.Y.: Feminist Press, 1983); Harper, *Life and Work*, 1: 199; *HWS*, 1: 745; *Selected Papers*, 1:28 n.10, 75 n.3, 433 n.2; Lydia Mott's obituary in *The Woman's Journal*, August 28, 1875; Carol Kolmerten, *The American Life of Ernestine Rose* (Syracuse, N.Y.: Syracuse University Press, 1999); Sherry Penney and James D. Livingston, *A Very Dangerous Woman: Martha Wright and Women's Rights* (Amherst: University of Massachusetts Press, 2004); Judith Wellman, "Women's Rights, Republicanism, and Revolutionary Rhetoric in Antebellum New York State," *New York History* 69 (July 1988): 375–81.

140. *HWS*, 1: 472.

141. *Proceedings of the Tenth National Woman's Rights Convention*, 34, in *Papers* 9: 630.

142. Booraem, *Formation of the Republican Party*, 3.

143. Ellis, *Short History of New York*, chap.18; DeAlva Stanwood Alexander, *Political History of New York* (New York: Henry Holt, 1909), vols. 2–3; Sewell, *Ballots for Freedom*, chap. 3; Whitney R. Cross, *The Burned Over District: The Social and Intellectual History of Enthusiastic Religion in Western New York, 1800–1850* (Ithaca: Cornell University Press, 1950).

144. Booraem, *Formation of the Republican Party*, 3. "Organization Needed in Ohio," *New York Daily Tribune*, January 26, 1860, claims that a competent speaker with $1,000 for traveling and expenses could "add 10,000 ballots to the Republican vote" in northern Ohio. Parties levied assessments on officeholders and extorted payoffs in exchange for legislation. See, for example, Ellis, *Short History of New York*, 238, concerning Weed's support for New York City transit interests in return for contributions to Seward's presidential campaign.

145. *Proceedings of the Tenth National Woman's Rights Convention*, 4, 7, in *Papers* 9: 615–16. The *HWS* 1: 743 indicates about half—$1,993.66—came out of the Jackson Fund.

146. The literature on free love includes John C. Spurlock, *Free Love: Marriage and Middle-Class Radicalism in America, 1825–1860* (New York: New York University Press, 1988); Taylor Stoehr, *Free Love in America: A Documentary History* (New York: AMS Press, 1979); Joanne E. Passet, *Sex Radicals and the Quest for Women's Equality* (Urbana: University of Illinois Press, 2003); Jean Silver-Isenstadt, *Shameless: The Visionary Life of Mary Gove Nichols* (Baltimore: Johns Hopkins University Press, 2002).

147. See, for example, the Call to the Third National Woman's Rights Convention in 1852: "Our platform will, as ever, be free to all who are capable of discussing the subject with seriousness, candor, and truth," in *Papers*, 7: 312.

148. "The Petticoats in Council," *New York Herald*, May 14, 1858, in *Papers* 8: 1135.

149. *Selected Papers*, 1:431.

150. Helen Lefkowitz Horowitz, *Rereading Sex: Battles over Sexual Knowledge and Suppression in Nineteenth-Century America* (New York: Knopf, 2002); Timothy J. Gilfoyle, *City of Eros: New York City, Prostitution, and the Commercialization of Sex, 1790–1920* (New York: W. W. Norton, 1992).

151. See Janet Farrell Brody, *Contraception and Abortion in Nineteenth-Century America* (Ithaca: Cornell University Press, 1994); Andrea Tone, *Devices and Desires: A History of Contraceptives in America* (New York: Hill & Wang, 2001); Linda Gordon, *The Moral Property of Women: A History of Birth Control Politics in America* (Urbana: University of Illinois Press, 2002).

152. Horowitz, *Rereading Sex*, 125–248; Gilfoyle, *City of Eros*.

153. See Nancy Cott, *Public Vows: A History of Marriage and the Nation* (Cambridge: Harvard University Press, 2000). Spiritualists were especially prominent. See Ann Braude, *Radical Spirits: Spiritualism and Women's Rights in Nineteenth-Century America* (Boston: Beacon Press, 1989).

154. Helen Deese, "Caroline Healey Dall: Transcendentalist Activist," in *Ordinary Women, Extraordinary Lives: Women in American History*, ed. Kriste Lindenmeyer (Wilmington,

Del.: Scholarly Resources, 2000), 59–71; Helen R. Deese, ed., *Daughter of Boston: The Extraordinary Diary of a Nineteenth-Century Woman, Caroline Healey Dall* (Boston: Beacon Press, 2005); Barbara Welter, "The Merchant's Daughter: A Tale from Life," *New England Quarterly* 42 (1969): 3–22; William Leach, *True Love and Perfect Union: The Feminist Reform of Sex and Society* (New York: Basic Books, 1980), chap.10.

155. Dall exemplified what Lewis Perry aptly terms the "invincible parochialism" of Boston reformers. Lewis Perry, *Childhood, Marriage, and Reform: Henry Clarke Wright, 1797–1870* (Chicago: University of Chicago Press, 1980), 42. Cf. "Our Boston Letter," *Chicago Tribune?* April 13, 1860, clipping in scrapbooks; and Diary, October 26, 1858, Dall Papers.

156. SBA to Antoinette Brown Blackwell, April 6, 1859, in *Papers* 9: 260.

157. The privilege only resulted in friction because time constraints bore heavily on Dall, who was known for reading long, prosy reports, and Anthony had to insist she limit herself to thirty minutes. SBA to CHD, April 5, April 9, and April 17, 1859, Dall Papers; SBA to Antoinette Brown Blackwell, April 6, 1859, in *Papers* 9: 254.

158. Diary, May 12, 1859, Dall Papers; *New York Daily Tribune* May 13, 1859.

159. *HWS*, 1: 674.

160. Diary, May 13, 1859, Dall Papers.

161. Diary, May 27, 1859, Dall Papers; *Report of the Woman's Rights Meeting at Mercantile Hall, May 27, 1859* (Boston: S.Urbino, 1859), 8.

162. Diary, May 27, 1859, in Dall Papers.

163. CHD to WP, June 6, 1859 and Saturday n.d., 1859?, in Phillips Papers, bMS Am 1953 (461); *Liberator,* June 10, 1859; list of addressees in Dall Papers, Schlesinger Library, Box 3, Folder 46, "Progress of the Women's Cause," "Reports (W.R.) Mailed, 1859."

164. Caroline Severance to CHD, [May 1859], Dall Papers. See also WP to CHD, June 6, [1859], Dall Papers.

165. WP to LS, July 11, 1859, BFP/LC.

166. CHD to Rev. F. D. Huntington, October 20, 1858, in outgoing letterbook, Dall Papers.

167. One of Dall's own friends rebuked her for "irritability, pettishness, selfishness." Diary, May 20, 1858, Dall Papers. Some money, apparently from the Jackson Fund, went to Kansas for lobbying a convention to draft a new state constitution: see Clarina I. H. Nichols to SBA, June 18, 1859, in *Papers* 9:328–31; C. I. H. Nichols to SBA, July 21, 1859, in *Papers* 9:352. Anthony also used some to hire "phonographic" shorthand reporters to transcribe woman's rights convention proceedings and then have them published, in hopes that doing so could foil misrepresentations in the press. Cf. SBA to LS, May 23, 1854, in *Papers* 7: 1042, and SBA to James M.W. Yerrinton, July 2, 1859, in *Papers,* 9: 336.

168. She had mentioned divorce briefly in her speech to the New York State legislature in March, and now she expanded on the subject. "Hearing before New York Senate and Assembly Judiciary Committee," *NASS,* March 31, 1860, in *Papers* 9:547.

169. Basch, *Framing American Divorce;* Glenda Riley, *Divorce: An American Tradition* (New York: Oxford University Press, 1991); Hendrik Hartog, *Man and Wife in America: A History* (Cambridge: Harvard University Press, 2000); Richard H. Chused, *Private Acts in Public Places: A Social History of Divorce in the Formative Era of American Family Law* (Philadelphia: University of Pennsylvania Press, 1994).

170. In Connecticut an "omnibus clause" enacted in 1849 permitted divorce almost at will. Riley, *Divorce,* 46; Basch, *Framing American Divorce,* 8, 39–40, 90–92.

171. See *New York Daily Tribune,* March 1, 5, 6, 12, 17, 28, April 7, 21, and May 1, 1860.

172. *Proceedings of the Tenth National Woman's Rights Convention,* 74, in *Papers,* 9: 650.

173. Ibid., 80, in *Papers,* 9: 653.

174. Ibid., 83–84, in *Papers,* 9: 654–55.

175. Ibid., 85–86, in *Papers,* 9: 655–56.

176. The definitive modern biography is James Brewer Stewart, *Wendell Phillips: Liberty's Hero* (Baton Rouge: Louisiana State University Press, 1986).

177. Phillips may have been sensitive because of a Boston divorce scandal. William Francis Channing, son of the prominent Boston minister William Ellery Channing and a supporter of women's rights, had deserted his wife and was threatening to make a career of pro-divorce agitation. *HWS*, 1: 255; *Boston Weekly Telegraph*, September 19–20, 1855, in *Papers* 8: 282; *New York Evening Post*, November 19, 1859; William Francis Channing to WP, November 5, 1859, Phillips Papers, bMS Am 1952 (384).

178. The bill provided three new grounds for divorce: willful desertion (after three years), habitual drunkenness (after three years), and "continuous and repeated instances of cruel and inhuman treatment…so as to greatly impair the health or endanger the life of the other party" (after one year). *Journal of the New York State Senate, 1860*, 525. Stanton went back to Albany in 1861 to testify before the Senate Judiciary Committee on behalf of divorce reform. *HWS*, 1: 745–46; *Selected Papers*, 1: 458, n. 6; Stanton, *Eighty Years*, 215.

179. *Selected Papers*, 1:431; *New York Evening Post*, May 12 and 16, 1860.

180. *New York Herald*, May 16, 1860, 6.

181. ECS to Martha C. Wright, June 2, 1860, in *Papers* 9: 714.

182. Stanton, *Eighty Years*, 225; ECS to Martha C. Wright, June 2, 1860, in *Papers* 9:713–14.

183. SBA to Amy Kirby Post, [May 1860] in *Papers* 9: 686.

184. ECS, "Mrs. Dall's Fraternity Lecture," *Liberator*, November 16, 1860, in *Selected Papers*, 1: 445–48.

185. LS to ECS, August 14, 1853, in *Selected Papers*, 1: 223–24.

186. LS to Antoinette Brown Blackwell, 1856, in Wheeler, *Loving Warriors*, 186; LS to ECS, September 17, [1856], in *Papers* 8:584.

187. Frances Dana Gage in *Selected Papers*, 1:312 n.1; *Proceedings of the Tenth National Woman's Rights Convention*, 34 in *Papers* 9: 630.

188. Basch, *Framing American Divorce*, 61, 117.

189. DuBois, *Feminism and Suffrage*, 40–47.

190. ECS to SBA, June 14, 1860, in *Papers* 9:725.

191. Martha C. Wright to SBA, June 8, 1858, in *Selected Papers*, 1: 372–74.

Chapter 2

1. "Political Anti-Slavery Convention," *NASS*, August 25, 1860; *Selected Papers*, 1: 441 n. 2; John M. Sterling to ECS, August 17, 1860, in *Papers* 9: 785; ECS to Gerrit Smith, [August after 17, 1860], in *Papers* 9: 786; Stephen S. Foster to ECS, August 21, 1860, in *Papers* 9: 790–98.

2. ECS to Gerrit Smith, August 24, [1860], in *Papers* 9: 807–8.

3. FD to ECS, August 25, 1860, in *Papers* 9: 816.

4. Quarles, *Black Abolitionists*, 182–90; Phyllis F. Field, *The Politics of Race in New York: The Struggle for Black Suffrage in the Civil War Era* (Ithaca: Cornell University Press, 1982), 98 and chaps. 2–3 generally.

5. "Our Albany Letter," *Weekly Anglo African*, February 18, 1860, in *Black Abolitionist Papers, 1830–1865* (Sanford, N.C.: Microfilming Corp of America, 1999), reel 12, frame 498; on Myers, see C. Peter Ripley et al., eds., *The Black Abolitionist Papers [BAP]*, 5 vols. (Chapel Hill: University of North Carolina Press, 1991), 3: 378–79 n.3.

6. "Our Albany Letter," *Weekly Anglo African*, March 31, 1860, in *BAP*, reel 12, frame 599.

7. "Universal Suffrage," *New York Daily Tribune*, February 11, 1860.

8. Assemblyman Ellsworth of Saratoga County as quoted in the *New York Daily Tribune*, February 11, 1860. The women's bill passed the Assembly 67–19, while black suffrage carried 70–36. See *Weekly Anglo-African*, February 18, 1860, in *BAP*, reel 12, frame 499; *New York Daily Tribune*, March 19, 1860; Field, *Politics of Race*, 101–2; *Journal of the New York Assembly, 1860*, 332; *Journal of the New York Senate, 1860*, 468.

9. On county committees printing tickets, see Booraem, *Formation of the Republican Party*, 45–46.

10. Nancy Hewitt, "'Seeking a Larger Liberty': Remapping First Wave Feminism," in Sklar and Stewart, eds., *Women's Rights and Transatlantic Slavery*, 266–78.

11. Judith Wellman, "The Landscape of the Early Woman's Rights Movement in Upstate New York: Sites and Trails," paper delivered at the Susan B. Anthony and the Struggle for Equal Rights Conference, University of Rochester, March 30–April 1, 2006; *HWS*, 1: 578.

12. "Equal Suffrage Defeated," *Douglass' Monthly* 3 (December 1860): 369.

13. James M. McPherson, *The Struggle for Equality: Abolitionists and the Negro in the Civil War and Reconstruction,* 2nd ed. (1964; reprint, Princeton, N.J.: Princeton University Press, 1995), 25–26; *Douglass' Monthly* issues for October, November, and December 1860; and James McCune Smith to Stephen A. Myers, September 21, 1860, in Ripley, *Black Abolitionist Papers*, 5: 84–85.

14. James McCune Smith to Stephen A. Myers, September 21, 1860, and James McCune Smith to Gerrit Smith, October 20, 1860, in Ripley, *Black Abolitionist Papers*, 5: 84–87.

15. In 1860, the Haitian Emigration Bureau, headed by James Redpath and armed with an annual budget of $20,000, hired lecturing agents including Henry Highland Garnet, William Wells Brown, and H. Ford Douglas. Ripley, *Black Abolitionist Papers*, 5:103–109.

16. Lincoln won 362,646 to 312,510, but equal suffrage for blacks lost, 197,889 for and 345,791 opposed. The most thorough analysis of the 1860 referendum is found in Phyllis F. Field, "Republicans and Black Suffrage in New York State: The Grass Roots Response," *Civil War History* 21 (June 1975): 140–46; and Field, *Politics of Race in New York*, chap. 4.

17. "Equal Suffrage Defeated," *Douglass' Monthly* 3 (December 1860): 369. See also "Republican Opposition to the Right of Suffrage," *Douglass' Monthly* 3 (October 1860): 339.

18. Beman Brockway, *Fifty Years in Journalism, Embracing Recollections and Personal Experiences with an Autobiography* (Watertown, N.Y.: Daily Times Printing and Publishing, 1891), 79, on how one faction would beat another "in the execution."

19. "The Suffrage Vote," *NASS*, February 2, 1861.

20. "The 'Convention' at Saint James Hall," *Buffalo Commercial Advertiser* reprinted in the *NASS*, January 19, 1861, in *Papers* 9: 982.

21. "Equal Suffrage Defeated," *Douglass' Monthly* 3 (December 1860): 369.

22. William C. Bishop and William H. Attree, *Report of the Debates and Proceedings of the Convention for the Revision of the Constitution of the State of New York, 1846* (Albany: Albany Atlas, 1846), 1027, 1033; Judith Wellman, "Women's Rights, Republicanism, and Revolutionary Rhetoric in Antebellum New York State," *New York History* 69 (July 1988): 365–67, 381. The same argument was used in the Massachusetts constitutional convention of 1821. See Alexander Keyssar, *The Right to Vote: The Contested History of Democracy in the United States* (New York: Basic Books, 2000), 44.

23. Field, *Politics of Race in New York*, 91.

24. "Address by ECS to the Legislature of New York," in *Selected Papers*, 1: 240–63.

25. Ibid., 241.

26. Ibid., 243.

27. "Address to the Legislature, etc." *Frederick Douglass' Paper*, March 3, 1854.

28. Thus, in 1844, Connecticut resolved its inconsistency on the principle of "no taxation without representation" by repealing the tax on black men rather than by extending them voting rights. Lex Renda, "'A White Man's State in New England': Race, Party, and Suffrage in Civil War Connecticut," in *An Uncommon Time: The Civil War and the Northern Home Front,* ed. Paul A. Cimbala and Randall M. Miller (New York: Fordham University Press, 2002), 248.

29. *Proceedings of the Tenth National Woman's Rights Convention*, 35, in *Papers* 9: 630. Stanton repeated her Albany address delivered in March before the National Woman's Rights Convention in May.

30. *Proceedings*, 36, in *Papers* 9: 631.

31. *Proceedings*, 38, in *Papers* 9: 632.please make sure all are same size 12 point

32. *Proceedings*, 36, in *Papers* 9: 631.
33. *Proceedings*, 37 in *Papers* 9: 631.
34. *Proceedings*, 40, in *Papers* 9: 633.
35. *Proceedings*, 38, in *Papers* 9: 632.
36. *Proceedings*, 40, in *Papers* 9: 633.
37. *Proceedings*, 38, in *Papers* 9: 631.
38. *Proceedings*, 40 in *Papers*, 9: 633.
39. Ann D. Gordon notes Stanton's ability to sustain "contradictory strains of thought" in her "Stanton and the Right to Vote: On Account of Race or Sex," in DuBois and Smith, *Elizabeth Cady Stanton: Feminist as Thinker*, 124, 117.
40. *Black's Law Dictionary*, 8th ed. (St. Paul: Thomson West, 1999), 1191, s.v., "alternative pleading."
41. Stanton, *Eighty Years*, 13–14; William A. Stanton, *A Record, Genealogical, Biographical, Statistical of Thomas Stanton of Connecticut and His Descendants, 1635–1891* (Albany: Joel Munsell's Sons, 1891), 460–61.
42. SBA to ECS, August 25, 1860, in *Selected Papers*, 1: 439–41.
43. Waldo Martin, *The Mind of Frederick Douglass* (Chapel Hill: University of North Carolina Press, 1984), chap. 3; McFeely, *Frederick Douglass*, 172–73.
44. Blight, *Frederick Douglass' Civil War*, 30.
45. "Mrs. Stanton and the Wide-Awakes," *NASS*, October 13, 1869, in *Papers* 9: 831.
46. ECS to Gerrit Smith, [June? 1860], in *Papers* 9: 729–30.
47. "The Political Abolition Convention at Worcester, Mass.," and "Political Anti-Slavery Convention," *Douglass' Monthly* (November 1860): 354–55, 361.
48. LS to HBB, September 20, 1860, BFP/LC; "The Political Anti-Slavery Convention at Worcester," *Liberator*, September 28, 1860.
49. ECS to SBA, April 24, 1860, in *Papers* 9: 562.
50. "Appeal to the Women of New York," November 1860, in *Papers* 9: 941–44; ECS, "The Slave's Appeal" in *Papers* 9: 937–39. The women intended to take advantage of Republican federal authority to send abolitionist materials through the mails for the first time since the 1830s. Lydia Mott to ECS, November 28, 1860, in *Papers* 9: 932–34.
51. SBA to ECS, November 23, 1860, in *Papers* 9: 929.
52. Harper, *Life and Work*, 1: 208–14; and Stanton, *Eighty Years*, 210–13 both connect the mob tour to the political situation but not specifically to Weed's initiative. For Weed's proposals and reaction to them, see Brummer, *Political History of New York State*, 99–101; *Albany Evening Journal*, 24, November 27, 1860; "Personal Liberty Laws," *NASS*, December 1, 1860, and "Doughfaced Republicanism," *NASS*, December 15, 1860. I infer that SBA was reacting to Weed from the timing of her decision to schedule the tour; see MCW to Ellen Wright Garrison, December 4, 1860, Garrison Family Papers, Sophia Smith Collection, Smith College, Amherst, MA; SBA to Gerrit Smith, December 2, 1860, in *Papers* 9: 951. Press coverage of the "No Compromise with Slaveholders" tour is found in *Papers* 9: 982, 1057–59, 1064, passim.
53. Harper, *Life and Work*, 1: 207–13; Stanton, *Eighty Years*, 210–13.
54. SBA to Unknown, [January 18, 1861], in *Papers* 9:1074.
55. Harper, *Life and Work*, 1: 216.
56. "Abolition Convention at Auburn," *NASS*, February 16, 1861.
57. McPherson, *Struggle for Equality*, 49–51. McPherson's work is the best overall guide to the activities of abolitionists during the war. On the wartime ⌐avities of abolitionist women, see Wendy Hamand Venet, *Neither Ballots nor Bullets: Women Abolitionists and the Civil War* (Charlottesville: University Press of Virginia, 1991).
58. Wendell Phillips, *Speeches, Letters, and Letters* (Boston: Lee & Shepard, 1872), 396–414.
59. Harper, *Life and Work*, 1: 214, on "one of the matchless speeches of all history."
60. SBA to WP, April 29, 1861, in *Selected Papers*, 1: 464–65.
61. Frederick Douglass, May 1861, as quoted in McPherson, *Struggle for Equality*, 62.

62. Wendell Phillips, as quoted in McPherson, *Struggle for Equality,* 27.
63. See Jeannie Attie, *Patriotic Toil: Northern Women and the American Civil War* (Ithaca: Cornell University Press, 1998); Nina Silber, *Daughters of the Union: Northern Women Fight the Civil War* (Cambridge: Harvard University Press, 2005); Judith Ann Geisberg, *Civil War Sisterhood: The U.S. Sanitary Commission and Women's Politics in Transition* (Boston: Northeastern University Press, 2000); and Ginzburg, *Women and the Work of Benevolence.*
64. *HWS,* 1: 747–52; SBA to Lydia Mott, after April 10, 1862, in *Selected Papers,* 1: 475–76.
65. Rice, "Henry B. Stanton as a Political Abolitionist," 378, 384, 398–99. Lincoln gave top Customs House positions to radicals like Henry B. Stanton and his boss Hiram Barney, but conservative Republicans like Thurlow Weed looked on covetously because the Customs House was a rich patronage prize: its 800–1200 patronage employees were expected to pay an assessment of 2 percent of their salaries for political purposes. Brummer, *Political History of New York State during the Period of the Civil War,* 137 n.1; Mark E. Neely, Jr., *The Union Divided: Party Conflict in the Civil War North* (Cambridge: Harvard University Press, 2002), 23–27.
66. Louis M. Starr, *Bohemian Brigade: Civil War Newsmen in Action* (New York: Knopf, 1954), 67–68: "He [Wilkeson] introduced the era of the inside operator, the man who sought not merely to report news, but to find out about everything he was not permitted to report, to make arrangements for getting confidential information, and to keep his editor posted on what was going on and what was likely to happen next."
67. Harper, *Life and Work,* 1: 217.
68. McPherson, *Struggle for Equality,* 72–73. Lucretia Mott's son-in-law was Edward M. Davis.
69. Sarah Pugh, as quoted in McPherson, *Struggle for Equality,* 89–90.
70. McPherson, *Struggle for Equality,* 86. DuBois, *Feminism and Suffrage,* 54–55, notes how women's abolitionist allies were emerging as influential actors on the national scene.
71. As cited in McFeely, *Frederick Douglass,* 212–14.
72. Stephen S. Foster to WP, November 8, 1861, Phillips Papers, bMS Am 1953 (559).
73. McPherson, *Struggle for Equality,* 80, 93–94, 110.
74. Guy James Gibson, "Lincoln's League: The Union League Movement during the Civil War" (Ph.D. diss., University of Illinois, 1957); Clement Silvestro, "None but Patriots: The Union Leagues in Civil War and Reconstruction" (Ph.D. diss., University of Wisconsin, 1959).
75. Harper, *Life and Work,* 1: 226, mentions Theodore Tilton, Wendell Phillips, and Henry B. Stanton. Stanton, *Eighty Years,* 236, says they consulted with Horace Greeley, William Lloyd Garrison, Governor John Andrews of Massachusetts, and Robert Dale Owen. Anthony's brother D. R., who helped to found the Kansas Union League, probably put in a word as well. See Gibson, "Lincoln's League," 111, 335.
76. Gibson, "Lincoln's League," chaps. 10–12, and 299, 240–45 re. HBS and Gerrit Smith; Brummer, *Political History of New York State,* chap. 10. Later, a third national group, the Union League of America, set up in New York State more on the lines of a fraternal order, and an exclusive New York City men's club called the Union League Club, also complicated the picture. Henry W. Bellows, *Historical Sketch of the Union League Club of New York* (New York: G. P. Putnam's for private distribution, 1879).
77. *Proceedings of the Meeting of the Loyal Women of the Republic, held in New York, May 14, 1863* (New York: Phair, 1863), 32, 15; SBA to Anna Dickinson, April 3, 1863, in *Papers* 10: 402. The most important scholarly study of the Women's Loyal National League is found in Venet, *Neither Ballots nor Bullets,* 101–22. The title of the organization varies, even within the *HWS;* I use the version preferred by Gordon in *Selected Papers.*
78. J. Matthew Gallman, *America's Joan of Arc: The Life of Anna Elizabeth Dickinson* (New York: Oxford University Press, 2006), 40, 59; Venet, *Neither Ballots nor Bullets,* chap. 3.
79. *Proceedings of the Meeting of the Loyal Women,* 10, 32.

80. Ibid., 15.
81. Ibid., 20–21, 23.
82. Kerr, "White Women's Rights," 64, suggests Hoyt feared that "adding women's rights to antislavery would encumber the push for freedom and civil rights for slaves," and thus presaged postwar struggles, but Hoyt also wanted to exclude antislavery issues from the convention and focus only on "the maintenance of the authority of the government." *Proceedings of the Meeting of the Loyal Women,* 19, 21; *Selected Papers,* 1: 492.
83. "Proceedings of Congress," *NASS,* April 19, 1862, indicates that well before the WLNL was founded, Charles Sumner presented a petition for the abolition of slavery signed by 15,000 women. Anthony requested Senator Sumner to gather up "scattering petitions" and return them to her so they might be counted toward the organization's grand total. SBA to Charles Sumner, March 1, 1864, *Papers* 10: 729. See Jeffrey, *Great Silent Army of Abolition;* and Susan Zaeske, *Signatures of Citizenship: Petitioning, Antislavery, and Women's Political Identity* (Chapel Hill: University of North Carolina Press, 2003) on earlier abolitionist women's petitioning.
84. "Meeting of the Women's Loyal National League," May 29, 1863, in *Selected Papers,* 1: 497–99; Harper, *Life and Work,* 1: 230.
85. Michael Vorenberg, *Final Freedom: The Civil War, the Abolition of Slavery, and the Thirteenth Amendment* (New York: Cambridge University Press, 2001). The Thirteenth Amendment passed the Senate in April 1864, partly in response to the women's mammoth petition, but it was not passed by the House until January 1865, when the votes of a few holdouts switched in response to "negotiations." Vorenberg shows that the women's petitions had an impact but were not the only factor at work.
86. Stanton, *Eighty Years,* 236–41; Harper, *Life and Work,* 1: 225–40; *HWS,* 2: 81–86.
87. Owen was an associate of Fanny Wright and the author of an important early publication on fertility control who also served as an Indiana legislator and a U.S. diplomat in Naples. He had debated Horace Greeley on divorce and published a book on spiritualism, but he also had business ability, and during the war Owen served on a special committee to audit war department contracts, in which capacity he saved the federal government some $17 million dollars. *American National Biography Online,* s.v. "Owen, Robert Dale," by Mary Ferrell Bednarowski, accessed October 8, 2010, http://www.anb.org/articles/; Richard William Leopold, *Robert Dale Owen: A Biography* (Cambridge: Harvard University Press, 1940), 347–49, 360–66; Garrett Epps, *Democracy Reborn: The Fourteenth Amendment and the Fight for Equal Rights in Post–Civil War America* (New York: Henry Holt, 2006), 185–96, and passim.
88. On the disappearance of British funding and the suspension of the ladies' antislavery fair in Boston, see WLG to Oliver Johnson, July 3, 1861, in Abolitionist Papers, Ms.A.1.1, vol. 6, p. 10. On soldiers' aid, see Attie, *Patriotic Toil,* chap. 7. By 1864, according to one contemporary estimate, $24 million dollars had been raised for soldiers' aid throughout the North, and over $1 million for freedmen's aid. Linus P. Brockett, as cited in Gallman, *Mastering Wartime,* 132. The AASS still appealed for donations every January in an "anniversary subscription"—in lieu of a fair—run by women. See the *NASS,* January 4, 1862, January 10, 1863, January 9, 1864. A wartime price index pegged at 100 in 1860 shot up to 176 by 1864: Gallman, *Mastering Wartime,* 225.
89. WLG to Oliver Johnson, December 14, 1862, Abolitionist Papers, Ms. A. 1.1, vol. 6, p. 56; WLG to Oliver Johnson, September 24, 1862, Abolitionist Papers, Ms. A. 111, vol. 6, p. 44. McPherson, *Struggle for Equality,* 82; Parker Pillsbury to WP, August 27, 1864, in Phillips Papers, bMs Am 1953 (1001); Aaron M. Powell to WP, September 19, 1864, Phillips Papers, bMs Am 1953 (1010). AASS finances are noted in the *Liberator,* May 16, 1862, May 22, 1863, and May 20, 1864; *NASS,* May 20, 1865, but the sources of income are not indicated.
90. Robert Dale Owen to WP, June 1, 1863, in Phillips Papers, bMS Am 1953 (946); SBA to Samuel May. Jr., July 1, 1863, in *Papers* 10: 527.

91. Parker Pillsbury to Friend Whipple, New York, March 1, 1864, Phillips Papers, Ms.Am. 1307 (2); SBA to Gerrit Smith July 1, 1863, *Papers* 10: 529. According to Harper, Hovey's contributions to the WLNL totaled $155 plus SBA's salary. Harper, *Life and Work,* 1: 234. Wendell Phillips's memo of the Jackson account seems to show that Susan B. Anthony received $1,131 from the Jackson Fund in 1864, which, if the date were accurate, must have gone to the work of the WLNL. However, because Phillips's memo is repetitive and out of chronological order, and because the entries listed for SBA under "1864" closely track the dates and amounts listed for her under "1866," it seems likely that the "1864" date is simply an error. See "The acct of Francis Jackson and Wendell Phillips with the Francis Jackson Fund," NAWSA Papers, reel 11 frame 353.

92. Harper, *Life and Work,* 1: 235; SBA to Gerrit Smith July 1, 1863, *Papers* 10:529; SBA to Senator Edwin D. Morgan, 1863 [after June 24], in *Selected Papers* 1: 499–500.

93. SBA and S. E. Draper to "Madam," June 20, 1863, in *Papers* 10: 513–15.

94. Harper, *Life and Work,* 1: 232.

95. Ibid., 235.

96. Steven E. Woodworth, *Beneath a Northern Sky: A Short History of the Gettysburg Campaign,* 2nd ed. (New York: Rowman & Littlefield, 2008), 86–87; Harry W. Pfanz, *Gettysburg— The First Day* (Chapel Hill: University of North Carolina Press, 2001), 232, 234–35. Today historical markers at the Gettysburg National Park and online sources such as http://www.brotherswar.com/Gettysburg-1l.htm familiarize park visitors and Civil War buffs with Bayard Wilkeson's story. His father Sam Wilkeson, who was covering the battle for the *Tribune,* "wrote one of the great dispatches of the war" while sitting beside his son's freshly dug grave. Starr, *Bohemian Brigades,* 212.

97. Harper, *Life and Work,* 1: 230–31.

98. ECS to Ann Fitzhugh Smith, July 1863, in *Papers* 10: 543.

99. McPherson, *Struggle for Equality,* 204–205.

100. Ibid., 240.

101. Carol Faulkner, *Women's Radical Reconstruction: The Freedmen's Aid Movement* (Philadelphia: University of Pennsylvania Press, 2004) provides an excellent entrée into the large general literature on freedmen's aid. See also Paula Giddings, *When and Where I Enter: The Impact of Black Women on Race and Sex in America* (New York: Holmes & Meier, 1984), chaps. 4–6; Sterling, *We Are Your Sisters,* 245–305; Jeffrey, *Great Silent Army,* 217– 23 on the freedmen's aid activities of black women.

102. See DuBois, *Feminism and Suffrage,* 68–71, although emphasizing a later period.

103. ECS to Elizabeth Smith Miller, September 1, 1863, in *Papers* 10: 551.

104. *New York World,* July 25, 1863, June 13, 1863, July 10, 1863, in *Papers* 10: 547, 509, 540.

105. "The Ladies' Loyal League," *New York Herald,* May 15, 1864, and "Ladies Loyal League," *New York World,* May 16, 1864, in *Papers,* 10: 808–9.

106. Sidney Kaplan, "The Miscegenation Issue in the Election of 1864," *Journal of Negro History* 34 (July 1949): 274–343.

107. *Proceedings of the National Convention of Colored Men, held in the City of Syracuse, NY, October 4–7, 1864* (Boston: J. Rock and G. Ruffin, 1864), 36–42, 55–61, grievances on 41. The *Proceedings* are reprinted in Howard Holman Bell, ed., *Minutes of the Proceedings of the National Negro Conventions, 1830–1864* (New York: Arno Press, 1969). On the Equal Rights Leagues, see also McPherson, *Struggle for Equality,* 234–35.

108. *Proceedings of the National Convention of Colored Men,* 15 and 25. Their speeches are mentioned but there is no transcript and only the most general description. Edmonia Highgate is identified in Sterling, *We Are Your Sisters,* 294–305.

109. ECS to SBA, December 29, 1864, in *Papers* 10: 918.

110. McPherson, *Struggle for Equality,* 110; Harper, *Life and Work,* 1: 219; SBA to Lydia Mott, cited in Harper, *Life and Work,* 1: 222.

111. Brummer, *Political History of New York,* chap. 8; Alexander, *Political History of the State of New York,* vol. 3, chap. 3.

112. Brockway, *Fifty Years in Journalism*, 83 on Wadsworth's background.
113. A speech, marked in Anthony's handwriting, "SBA—during the Gen. Wadsworth campaign—1862" in *Papers*, 10:339, is probably the speech mentioned in Harper, *Life and Work*, 1: 222, as delivered at Mecklenburg in Schuyler County in the fall of 1862 on "Emancipation the Duty of the Government." Anthony spoke in five different locations in Schuyler County—Burdett, Peach Orchard, Searsburg, Mecklenburg, and Havana—in the last week before the election; see the *Havana* (N.Y.) *Journal*, October 25 and November 1, 1862. Havana, New York, was later renamed Montour Falls.
114. Brummer, *Political History of New York*, 250–51, 290; Van Deusen, *Thurlow Weed*, 301–2. The sabotage could not be proven, but charges began to fly as soon as the election was over. Stanton, *Random Recollections*, 216.
115. SBA to Samuel May, Jr., September 21, 1863, in *Selected Papers*, 1: 500–501.
116. SBA to ECS, October 10, 1863, in *Selected Papers*, 1: 502–3. Nell Irvin Painter, "Difference, Slavery, and Meaning: Sojourner Truth in Feminist Abolition," in Yellin & Van Horne, *Abolitionist Sisterhood*, 157, cites Anthony's failure to stipulate that there would be a black woman on each team as an example of black women's "invisibility." Indeed it was, but given Anthony's willingness to recognize black women at other points, it may also have reflected her awareness of who was available for the lecture tour she proposed.
117. *Selected Papers*, 1: 503 n. 1 and 2; SBA to ECS, October 10, 1863, in *Papers* 10: 565–66; and remarks of Stephen Foster in the AASS annual meeting in May 1865, as reported in the *NASS*, May 20, 1865.
118. "Special Notices," *NASS*, December 26, 1863, lists two veteran speakers, Aaron Macy Powell and Stephen Foster; a novice, Garrison's twenty-three year old son, Wendell Phillips Garrison; and a team comprised of the Reverend A.T. Foss and William A. Jackson, the latter billed as "Jeff Davis's Coachman." The AASS speakers thus included several white men, one black man, and no women.
119. James Miller McKim took the lead, resigning as the general agent of the Pennsylvania Anti-Slavery Society in order to switch over to work for freedmen's education and urging others to follow suit. McPherson, *Struggle for Equality*, 161–62; McKim in *NASS*, May 3, 1862; Maria Weston Chapman to Anne Greene Chapman, June 21, 1862, as cited in Venet, *Neither Ballots Nor Bullets*, 106.
120. See coverage of the Massachusetts Anti-Slavery Society meeting in *NASS*, February 7, 1863.
121. McPherson, *Struggle for Equality*, 161, 225, 287–95.
122. Anthony sided unequivocally with Phillips at the Third Decade Anniversary Celebration of the American Anti-Slavery Society in December 1863: see *NASS*, December 26, 1863. WLG to Helen E. Garrison, May 14, 1863, in *The Papers of William Lloyd Garrison*, Walter M. Merrill, ed., (Cambridge: Belknap Press of Harvard University Press, 1979), 5:154.
123. Rice, "Henry B. Stanton as a Political Abolitionist," 422–62; Griffith, *In Her Own Right*, 114–15; ECS to Horace Greeley, January 18, 1864, *Papers* 10: 702–3. Rice, 446, concludes that Neil Stanton was "untrustworthy, mendacious and sly." The struggle over the Customs House is discussed in Neely, *Union Divided*, 28–30. See also the results of the congressional investigation: 38th Congress, First Session, United States House of Representatives, Reports of Committees, Report N. 111, "New York Custom-House."
124. John Niven, *Salmon P. Chase* (New York: Oxford University Press, 1995), 351–52; Frederick J. Blue, *Salmon P. Chase: A Life in Politics* (Kent, Ohio: Kent State University Press, 1987), 233–35.
125. 38th Congress, Report No. 111, "New York Custom-House," 3.
126. An example of large scale misconduct might have involved Thurlow Weed himself, who profited handsomely from shady and only marginally legal trade in Confederate cotton through the lines in the South, and was sued for libel by another Republican politician, George Opdyke, whom he had accused of profiteering on shoddy goods. The suit, a classic case of pot versus kettle, ended in a hung jury. *The Great Libel Case: Opdyke vs. Weed. A Full*

Report of the Speeches of Counsel, Testimony, etc. (New York: American News, 1865). Smearing Henry B. Stanton was a way of striking at Hiram Barney, who was too radical for the Weed conservatives and a disappointment to patronage hounds of all stripes, according to Neely, *Union Divided,* 22–26.

127. Samuel Wilkeson to Sidney Howard Gay, [July 1, 1864], Sidney Howard Gay Papers, Columbia University; ECS to Gerrit Smith, July 3, 1864, in *Selected Papers,* 1: 528–30; HBS to Gerrit Smith, July 27, 1864, Smith Papers. Hulburd was probably doing Weed's bidding, but he may have been running a removals racket of his own which the Weed faction exploited. Customs House operations were so lax they could almost always justify an inquiry, so Hulburd, as chairman of the House Committee on Public Expenditures, was in a position to sell removals to eager office seekers who would profit if a position came open—or to sell vindication to the incumbent if paid a counterbribe. Cf. Henry A. Smythe to Ben F. Butler, March 20, 1867, Benjamin F. Butler Papers, LC.

128. ECS to Gerrit Smith, July 3, [1864], in *Selected Papers,* 1: 528–30. The most thorough exploration of the Customs House scandal, by Arthur Harry Rice, concludes that HBS was the victim of "scoundrels" and "the committee report was grossly unfair." Rice, "Henry B. Stanton," 422–61, 462.

129. Stanton, "The Future of the Republic," *Papers* 10: 599–656, quote on 634. The WLNL leaders also signaled political ambitions by inviting Jessie Benton Fremont and Ben Butler to address their meetings. See Jessie Benton Fremont to ECS, May 4, 1863, in *Papers* 10: 431; Benjamin F. Butler to ECS, SBA, et al., [1863 before November 28], *Papers* 10: 576.

130. Stone spoke at the Women's Loyal National League meeting in May 1863 and at AASS in December 1863. (Million, *Woman's Voice,* 268) But see Cazden, *Antoinette Brown Blackwell,* 129: "The Civil War had surprisingly little direct impact on the Blackwell family." In LS to SBA, July 12, 1864, in Wheeler, ed., *Loving Warriors,* 195, Stone remarks it is too bad Garrison has lived long enough to make a fool of himself.

131. McPherson, *Struggle for Equality,* 260–61.

132. ECS to Jessie Benton Fremont, [April? 1864], in *Papers* 10: 774–75; SBA to Charles Sumner, March 6, 1864, in *Selected Papers,* 1: 513; "Important Convention," *Principia,* May 26, 1864, in *Papers* 10: 806–7.

133. "Important Convention," *Principia,* May 26, 1864, in *Papers* 10: 806–7 includes Stanton's letter dated May 14, 1864.

134. ECS to GS, June 2, 1864, in *Papers* 10: 827.

135. Deese, *Daughter of Boston,* 304–9.

136. "Letter from Mrs. C. H. Dall," *Liberator,* May 6, 1864, and *NASS,* May 7, 1864. Dall's diary for May 1, 1864, reveals that she sought and received Garrison's advice about this letter. Dall Papers.

137. Stanton's reply in ECS to Caroline Dall, dated May 7, 1864, in *Papers* 10: 795, which ran in the *Liberator,* June 3, 1864, and *NASS,* June 11, 1864.

138. CHD to Elizabeth Neall Gay, June 23, 1864, Sidney Howard Gay Papers, Columbia University; Sarah Pugh to CHD, May 13, 1864, and William Darrah Kelley to CHD, June 12, 1864, Dall Papers, confirm Lincoln's having read and appreciated Dall's letter.

139. She describes her Washington visit in ECS to Gerrit Smith, May 6, [1864], and ECS to WP, May 6, [1864], *Papers* 10: 785 and 789. Stanton wrote these letters on WLNL letterhead printed "1863," but she was using old letterhead, and the date has been corrected on the basis of internal evidence to 1864 by Ann Gordon, editor of the *Selected Papers.*

140. *American National Biography Online,* s.v. "Dickinson, Anna Elizabeth," by Kathleen C. Berkeley, accessed October 8, 2010, http://www.anb.org/articles/; Gallman, *America's Joan of Arc,* 39.

141. *NASS,* May 28, 1864; Harper, *Life and Work,* 1: 237. Knowing that both the *Liberator* and *NASS* were slanting and/or suppressing their coverage, Anthony at one point told Stanton, "you will have to read *under* the ink." SBA to ECS, May 30, 1864, in *Selected Papers,* 1: 523.

142. Phillips even directed the treasurer of the AASS to stop paying for the *Standard* because it had become a "Lincoln sheet," thus precipitating a battle among AASS leaders. WLG to Samuel May, Jr., June 17, 1864, Abolitionist Papers, MsA 1.1, vol. 6, p. 84; Oliver Johnson to WP, June 22, 1864, Phillips Papers, bMS Am 1953 (759); Parker Pillsbury to WP, July 6, 1864, Phillips Papers, bMs Am 1953(1001). SBA to ECS, June 12, 1864, in *Selected Papers*, 1: 526–27.

143. *New York Herald*, May 15, 1864, in *Papers* 10: 808.

144. *New York Tribune*, May 28, 1864, in *Papers* 10: 810; *HWS*, 2: 83.85, 87.

145. *New York Tribune*, May 28, 1864, in *Papers* 10: 810.

146. SBA to ECS, June 12, 1864, in *Papers* 10: 837.

147. McFeely, *Frederick Douglass*, 234.

148. ECS to WP, June 6 and July 3, [1864], and WP to ECS, July 20, 1864, in *Papers* 10: 847–52, 869–73. Scholars agree that Lincoln was the consummate politician, master of a party system in which personal profit motivated officeholders from top to bottom, so Stanton's attitude was not entirely unreasonable. Summers, *The Plundering Generation*; Harry J. Carman and Reinhard H. Luthin, *Lincoln and the Patronage* (New York: Columbia University Press, 1943), 288–89, 299.

149. Rice, "Henry B. Stanton," 469–70. Stanton returned to the practice of law and wrote for the *New York Tribune* and the *New York Sun*, although never with notable success.

150. Brummer, *Political History of New York State*, 394–95, 439; Van Deusen, *Thurlow Weed*, 285–94; David Donald, *Lincoln*, 495, 528–29, 532–33. Lincoln ultimately dismissed Barney in September 1864, which gave Weed total control of the Customs House. Opposed to Lincoln's emancipation policy, Weed had flirted with the Democrats and demanded compensation for party loyalty. Since Lincoln won New York by fewer than 7,000 votes, it could be argued that he had little choice.

151. SBA to ECS, June 1 and June 12, 1864; ECS to WP, November 6, 1864, *Papers* 10: 908–10.

152. It is sometimes suggested, as a way to explain the ugliness of 1869, that Stanton was never really very interested in abolition (e.g., Washington, *Truth's America*, 336; or Terborg-Penn, *African American Women*, 22–23), but the wartime record does not support this, nor do earlier sources, which show that she was a regular reader of the *Liberator* and the *National Anti-Slavery Standard*, referred to Charles Lenox Remond as among her "good Boston friends," attended Massachusetts Anti-Slavery Society meetings etc. *Selected Papers*, 1: 8–11, 25, 29, 31, 41.

Chapter 3

1. Donald, *Lincoln*, 584–85, 588.

2. "Thirty-Second Anniversary of the American Anti-Slavery Society," *NASS*, May 13, 1865.

3. DuBois, *Feminism and Suffrage*, 60, notes that Phillips's "unprovoked" announcement shows how "obvious and compelling" the connection between black suffrage and woman suffrage seemed.

4. "Thirty-Second Anniversary of the American Anti-Slavery Society," *NASS*, May 20, 1865.

5. Charles Sumner to WP, Phillips Papers, May 1, 1865, bMs Am 1953 (1188); Samuel May, Jr., to Richard Davis Webb, January 29, 1867, Abolitionist Papers, Ms.B. 1.6, vol. 10, p. 46a.

6. WP to ECS, [May 10, 1865], in *Papers* 11: 185.

7. Elizur Wright as quoted in Kraditor, *Means and Ends*, 57.

8. "The Political Anti-Slavery Convention at Worcester," *Liberator*, September 28, 1860.

9. WP to ECS, May 10, 1865, in *Papers* 11: 185.

10. ECS to WP, May 25, 1865, in *Selected Papers*, 1: 549 n. 2.

11. One resolution presented to the Eleventh National Woman's Rights Convention in May 1866 read, "Resolved That Liberty and Equality are the inherent rights of man in civilization,

and no constitution or code should be accepted as law that does not secure them to every citizen." *Proceedings of the Eleventh National Woman's Rights Convention* (New York: Robert J. Johnston, 1866), 5, in *Papers* 11: 477.

12. DuBois, *Feminism and Suffrage*, 54, notes this important transition.

13. ECS, "Universal Suffrage," *NASS*, July 29, 1865.

14. Harper, *Life and Work*, 1: 243; *Selected Papers*, 1: 538–43. Anthony spoke explicitly of the need to fight for "absolute justice and equality for the black man." SBA to Unknown, approx April 1865, in Harper, *Life and Work*, 1: 245.

15. SBA, "Reconstruction," Oration for Independence Day, July 4, 1865, in *Papers*, 11:197–98.

16. Contextual information on Reconstruction is drawn from Eric Foner, *Reconstruction: America's Unfinished Revolution, 1863–1877* (New York: Harper and Row, 1988); or an overview in David H. Donald, Jean Harvey Baker, and Michael F. Holt, *The Civil War and Reconstruction* (New York: W. W. Norton, 2001).

17. Diary of SBA, July 18, 1865, referring to a letter from ECS with an enclosure from WP, in *Selected Papers*, 1: 550.

18. ECS to SBA, August 11, 1865, in *Papers* 11: 208.

19. *Leavenworth Daily Bulletin*, August 5, 1865, reprinted in *NASS*, August 19, 1865: "Miss Susan B. Anthony started for her home in Rochester this morning."

20. "Miss Anthony in Chicago" *NASS*, September 16, 1865. It seems that Stanton and Anthony may have differed briefly over whether to defer to black (male) suffrage, because in September 1865 Stanton told Anthony, "I am not willing to be bullied when I honestly differ from you in opinion, as I do in the matter you mention." ECS to SBA, September 10, 1865, in *Papers* 11: 214. The record indicates that Anthony was otherwise in consistent agreement with Stanton during the late 1860s (though they differed significantly at other times in their long lives together), and where the record is silent, I have assumed Anthony backed Stanton.

21. "Suffrage in Connecticut," *Commonwealth*, October 7, 1865; "The Vote in Connecticut," *Liberator*, October 13, 1865; Lex Renda, "'A White Man's State in New England': Race, Party, and Suffrage in Civil War Connecticut," in *An Uncommon Time: The Civil War and the Northern Home Front*, ed. Paul A. Cimbala and Randall M. Miller (New York: Fordham University Press, 2002), 243–79.

22. "Speech of the President to the First Regiment D.C. Colored Troops, Oct 10," *Liberator*, October 20, 1865.

23. A useful overview of Reconstruction events as seen from the abolitionists' point of view is found in McPherson, *Struggle for Equality*. See p. 331.

24. "The South Victorious," *NASS*, October 29, 1865; Stewart, *Wendell Phillips*, 268–69.

25. SBA spoke with Amy Post, Martha C. Wright, James and Lucretia Mott, Clemence Lozier, Lydia Mott, Mattie Griffith, Mary Grew, Anna Dickinson, Parker Pillsbury, Aaron Macy Powell, Henry Blackwell, Lucy Stone, Theodore Tilton, Abby Kelley Foster, Stephen S. Foster, Mary Love Davis, Antoinette Brown Blackwell, Dr. Cheever, Dr. Harriet Hunt, Dr. Marie Zakrzewska, Ernestine Rose, Caroline Dall, Caroline Severance, Phebe Jones, as well as Elizabeth Cady Stanton, Stanton's sister Catherine Wilkeson, and her cousin Nellie Eaton. Diary of SBA, October–early December 1865, in *Papers* 11: 39–100, passim.

26. Diary of SBA, November 28, 1865, in *Papers* 11: 84.

27. Kerr, *Lucy Stone*, 113–18; Moore, "Reclaiming Lucy Stone," 262–98; Million, *Woman's Voice*, 267–71.

28. LS to HBB August 9, 1864, BFP/LC; LS to Mrs. Blackwell, October 23, 1864, BFP/LC, where Stone refers to Harry's "freedom from business...with several thousands in his pocket." Blackwell described his 1864 windfall as "a modest competence," but less than ten years later he would estimate that he was worth $50,000 and Lucy worth another $50,000. HBB autobiography, holo., and HBB to George Blackwell, April 23, 1872, BFP/Schlesinger.

29. LS to HBB, December 4, 1864, BFP/LC.

30. In 1866 Thomas Wentworth Higginson referred to Lucy Stone's "entire absorption in her own household," and in 1867, when her own daughter became of school age, Stone would adopt a rambunctious five year old. Thomas Wentworth Higginson to ECS, May 2, 1866, in *Selected Papers*, 1: 578; Kerr, *Lucy Stone*, 127.

31. These included the meeting of the New England Anti-Slavery Society in June, a celebration of West Indian Emancipation in August, the meeting of the Pennsylvania Progressive Friends in August, and a Friends of Progress convention in September. See *Liberator*, June 16, August 11, August 18, September 8, 1865.

32. *Liberator*, April 14, 1865; Benjamin Gratz Brown, *Universal Suffrage: An Address Delivered at Turner Hall, St. Louis, Missouri, September 22, 1865* (St. Louis: The Democrat, 1865).

33. Harriet Beecher Stowe, "The Woman Question: Or, What Will You Do with Her?" *Atlantic Monthly* 15 (December 1865): 672–83.

34. "Letter from Mrs. Gage," *NASS*, November 25, 1865. Gage's significant role is noted in DuBois, *Feminism and Suffrage*, 68.

35. One of the best explanations of the operation of this clause and the implications of its having been voided by the Thirteenth Amendment is found in Epps, *Democracy Reborn*, 56–59.

36. "Letter from Robert Dale Owen. Negro Suffrage and Representative Population," *Liberator*, July 7, 1865.

37. ECS, "Political Rights of Woman," *Liberator*, December 29, 1865; ECS to Gerrit Smith, January 1, 1866, in *Papers* 11: 254; ECS to Editor, "Joint Resolutions before Congress Affecting Women," *NASS*, January 6, 1866, in *Papers* 11: 259.

38. Joseph B. James, *The Framing of the Fourteenth Amendment* (Urbana: University of Illinois Press, 1956), 21–23.

39. Diary of SBA, December 4 and 11, 1865, in *Papers* 11: 90, 97. Harper, *Life and Work*, 1: 251, says the Hovey Committee appropriated $500, but the only dedicated "W.R. fund" was the Jackson fund.

40. Diary of SBA, December 25, 1865, in *Selected Papers*, 1: 562.

41. "A Petition for Universal Suffrage," *Liberator*, December 29, 1865. Directed to the Senate and the House of Representatives, it asked for "an amendment of the Constitution that shall prohibit the several states from disfranchising any of their citizens on the ground of sex." This petition declared the vote was the right of "every citizen," and seemed to assume black (male) suffrage was already happening, leaving women "the only class who stand outside the pale of political recognition."

42. "Extracts from the Will of the Late Charles F. Hovey, Esq." in *HWS*, 1: 667–68; *Selected Papers*, 1: 391, n. 4.

43. SBA probably referred to this strained interpretation of the Hovey will in a diary entry of November 6, 1865: "Tried to write to Phillips of the Hovey Committee's vote but couldn't succeed." Diary of SBA, November 6, 1865, in *Papers* 11: 64.

44. WLG to Henry C. Wright, February 9, 1866, Abolitionist Papers, Ms.A.1.1, vol. 7, p. 5a; "National Testimonial to William Lloyd Garrison," April 25, 1866, Abolitionist Papers, Ms.B.1.6, vol. 10, p. 41; *Boston Daily Advertiser*, October 8, 1867, Supplement, "The Testimonial to Mr. Garrison," Abolitionist Papers, Ms.A.1.1, vol. 7, p. 50.

45. "General Sherman," *Weekly Anglo-African*, April 29, 1865.

46. J. Miller McKim to R. E. Secard, June 8, 1866, American Freedmen's Union Commission Letterbooks, Department of Rare Books and Manuscripts, Cornell University, indicates the sums involved: "We have raised during the last year money to the amount of $422,928, and supplies worth $367,709."

47. Lucretia Coffin Mott to Martha C. Wright and Anna Temple Brown, April 9–10, 1865, in Palmer, *Selected Letters of Lucretia Mott*, 357–58. The tensions within freedmen's aid organizations between the women who did much of the work and the men who were salaried officers are discussed in Faulkner, *Women's Radical Reconstruction*, chap. 3.

48. See, for example, J. Miller McKim to Mrs. E. J. Jones, November 24, 1865, AFUC Letterbooks, Department of Rare Books and Manuscripts, Cornell University.

49. See American Freedmen's Aid Commission Board of Managers Minutes, November 9, 1865; J. Miller McKim to Mr. Child, December 9, 1865, AFUC Letterbooks, Cornell University.

50. "Miss Anthony in Chicago," *NASS*, September 16, 1865, in *Papers* 11: 213.

51. SBA to Unknown, [1865 August after 20], in *Papers*, 11: 210.

52. This experiment can be followed in the letters of George Smalley and Parker Pillsbury to Wendell Phillips in the Phillips Papers.

53. George Smalley to WP, January 7, 1866, Phillips Papers, bMS Am 1953 (1120) and (1001); Diary of SBA, October 19 and 26 and November 8, 1865, in *Papers* 11: 47, 53, 66; Parker Pillsbury to Charles K. Whipple, December 28, 1865, Abolitionist Papers, Ms. Am.123.72.

54. WP to SBA, April 1865, in Harper, *Life and Work*, 1: 245.

55. ECS to WP, April 7, [1866], in *Papers* 11: 435–39. DuBois, *Feminism and Suffrage*, 73, notes that by preventing coverage Phillips blocked their access to a "political resource."

56. WP to ECS, [1866 April after 7], in *Papers* 11: 441–42.

57. WP to ECS, January 14, 1866, in *Papers* 11: 284. At the same time he informed her he would not "do much or go out of my way or spend money or time on it [women's suffrage]."

58. ECS, "Political Rights of Woman," *Liberator*, December 29, 1865.

59. ECS, "This Is the Negro's Hour," *NASS*, December 30, 1865, in *Selected Papers*, 1: 564–66.

60. Her use of the term "Sambo" is all the more striking because she had earlier written sympathetically about the way it objectified and made nameless "our colored brethren." ECS to Rebecca R. Myster, May 12, 1847?, in *Papers* 6: 662. On the other hand, she used it colloquially in ECS to SBA, April 2, 1852, in *Papers* 7: 189.

61. ECS, "This Is the Negro's Hour," *NASS*, December 30, 1865, in *Selected Papers*, 1: 564–66.

62. "Woman's Rights," *NASS*, December 30, 1865.

63. The third letter was prepared for the meeting of the AASS in Boston on January 24, 1866, in the form of an open letter to Phillips as president of the organization. ECS to WP, January 24, 1866, in *NASS*, February 3, 1866, in *Papers* 11: 305.

64. The dilemma was reminiscent of the antebellum "condition" debate about free blacks in the North, in which "black intellectuals endlessly debated the problems of locating responsibility for the 'degraded condition' of most people of color," and it became harder to blame slavery as the period of legal northern slavery receded into the past. Joanne Pope Melish, "The 'Condition' Debate and Racial Discourse in the Antebellum North," *Journal of the Early Republic* 19 (Winter 1999): 651–72, quoted passage on 662.

65. Sidney Howard Gay, *New York Tribune*, February 5, 1863, as cited in McPherson, *Struggle for Equality*, 150.

66. *Congressional Globe*, 39th Congress, 1st Session, p. 215, Rep. Thomas T. Davis, R of New York.

67. McPherson, *Struggle for Equality*, 327–28; ECS to Martha C. Wright, December 20, 1865, in *Papers* 11: 235; ECS to WP, January 12, 1866, in *Papers* 11: 278. Ann Gordon notes that Stanton endorsed educated suffrage at sporadic intervals later in her career. Gordon, "Stanton and the Right to Vote," 118.

68. Isenberg, *Sex and Citizenship*, 30–33.

69. See arguments that influenced ECS in Elisha P. Hurlbut, *Essays on Human Rights and Their Political Guaranties* (New York: Greeley and McElrath, 1845); Isenberg, *Sex and Citizenship*, 25, on Hurlbut.

70. "An Appeal to the Congress of the United States for the Enfranchisement of Women," *NASS*, June 9, 1866; WP in "Thirty-Third Annual Meeting of the American Anti-Slavery Society," *NASS*, May 19, 1866.

71. Gordon, "Stanton and the Right to Vote," 118.

72. ECS to WP, January 15, 1866, in *Papers* 11:287. O'Connell was well known to abolitionists: W. Caleb McDaniel, "Repealing Unions: American Abolitionists, Irish Repeal, and the Origins of Garrisonian Disunionism," *Journal of the Early Republic* 28 (Summer 2008): 243–69.

73. "Woman's Rights," *NASS*, December 30, 1865.

74. WP to ECS, between January 9 and 12, 1866, *Papers* 11: 274.

75. ECS to WP, January 12, 1866, in *Selected Papers* 1: 571.

76. Ginzberg, *Elizabeth Cady Stanton*, 73.

77. Cf. Lori D. Ginzberg, "'The Hearts of Your Readers Will Shudder': Fanny Wright, Infidelity, and American Freethought," *American Quarterly* 46 (June 1994): 195–226, 218 on freethinkers who considered calling themselves "infidels" in order to deprive the term of odium, and comparisons to "recent struggles to retrieve 'queer' from the depths of opprobrium."

78. Lucretia Coffin Mott to MCW and Martha Mott Lord, November 2, 1865, in Palmer, *Selected Letters of Lucretia Mott*, 365; Pennsylvania Anti-Slavery Society Minute Book, December 27, 1865, as cited in *Selected Papers*, 1: 568 n.1; Diary of SBA, December 27, 1865, in *Papers* 11: 101.

79. "Special Meeting of the American Anti-Slavery Society," *NASS*, February 3, 1866.

80. See DuBois, *Feminism and Suffrage*, 57, 75, on the relationship of the AASS to the Republican Party.

81. Harper, *Life and Work*, 1: 256.

82. WP to ECS, between January 9 and 12, 1866, in *Papers* 11: 274.

83. ECS to Wendell Phillips, February 10, [1866], in *Papers* 11: 343–44.

84. WP to ECS, between January 9 and 12, 1866, *Papers* 11: 275.

85. Three sources tell us of this meeting, though none describes it directly and contemporaneously. WP to ECS, between January 9 and 12, 1866, *Papers* 11: 274 looks forward to the meeting; ECS to Anne Greene Phillips, [February 15, 1866], *Papers* 11: 360–63, reflects back on it, and "Remarks by SBA to the American Equal Rights Association," May 12, 1869, in *Selected Papers*, 2: 239 probably refers to it.

86. ECS to Anne Greene Phillips, [February 15, 1866], in *Papers* 11: 363.

87. Ibid.

88. SBA, ECS to WP, January 28, 1866, in *Papers* 11: 315. When Caroline Dall tried to get up a different petition which only protested against inserting the word "male" but did not ask positively for women's suffrage, Anthony protested. ECS, SBA to CHD, January 31, [1866], in *Papers* 11: 337.

89. At first Mott thought that reviving the women's rights movement would be "in vain, while the all-absorbing negro question is up." Lucretia Coffin Mott to Martha C. Wright and Martha Mott Lord, November 2, 1865, in Palmer, *Selected Letters of Lucretia Mott*, 365. She explains the three reasons she changed her mind in Lucretia Coffin Mott to WP, April 17, 1866, in Palmer, *Selected Letters of Lucretia Mott*, 371.

90. SBA to CHD, December 26, 1865, in *Papers* 11: 240; *Congressional Globe*, 39th Congress, 1st Session, January 24, 1866, 390; Norma L. Peterson, *Freedom and Franchise: The Political Career of B. Gratz Brown* (Columbia: University of Missouri Press, 1965), 159–64.

91. *American National Biography Online*, s.v. "Wade, Benjamin Franklin," by Hans L. Trefousse, accessed October 9, 2010, http://0-www.anb.org.library.colgate.edu/articles; Hans Trefousse, *Benjamin Franklin Wade: Radical Republican from Ohio* (New York: Twayne, 1963).

92. *Congressional Globe*, 39th Congress, 1st Session, February 21, 1866, 951–52.

93. Stanton, *Eighty Years*, 242; Harper, *Life and Work*, 1: 256; David Herbert Donald, *Charles Sumner* (New York: DaCapo Press, 1996); and on Sumner's inability to draft legislation, George Frisbee Hoar, *Autobiography of Seventy Years* (New York: C. Scribner's, 1903), 214.

94. *American National Biography Online*, s.v. "Stevens, Thaddeus," by Josh Zeitz, accessed October 9, 2010, http://0-www.anb.org.library.colgate.edu/articlesOctober 9, 2010; Trefousse, *Thaddeus Stevens: Nineteenth Century Egalitarian* (Chapel Hill: University of North Carolina Press, 1997).

95. SBA to James Brooks, January 20, 1866, in *Selected Papers*, 1: 572.

96. Epps, *Democracy Reborn*, 62–63, 216.

97. SBA to CHD, January 30, 1866, in *Papers* 11: 331–32; ECS to Martha C. Wright, January 6, 1866, in *Papers* 11: 263.

98. SBA to James Brooks, January 20, 1866, in *Selected Papers*, 1: 572; ECS to Charles Sumner, February 15, [1866], in *Papers* 11: 358–59.

99. *Congressional Globe*, 39th Congress, 1st session, 379–80; Epps, *Democracy Reborn*, 110–11.

100. James, *Framing of the Fourteenth Amendment*, 59–61; Epps, *Democracy Reborn*, 107. Stevens explained his opposition to inserting the word "male" in the Constitution: see James, *Framing of the Fourteenth Amendment*, 66; *Congressional Globe*, 39th Congress, 1st Session, 537.

101. SBA to Ottilia Assing, March 1, 1866, in *Papers* 11: 380.

102. Epps, *Democracy Reborn*, 113–15; James, *Framing of the Fourteenth Amendment*, 67–68.

103. She was probably reacting to a proposal by Senator Doolittle, whose formula was endorsed by *Harper's Weekly* and the *Nation*, and was said to be supported by the western states and the president. James, *Framing of the Fourteenth Amendment*, 91.

104. ECS, "Legal Voters," *NASS*, March 17, 1866, in *Papers* 11: 393. She may have been clarifying her position, which was unclear in another article in the same issue: ECS, "Constitutional Amendments," *NASS*, March 17, 1866, in *Papers* 11: 392.

105. James, *Framing of the Fourteenth Amendment*, 92–95.

106. Epps, *Democracy Reborn*, 198–204.

107. Leopold, *Robert Dale Owen*, 367–72; and Robert Dale Owen, "Political Results from the Varioloid," *Atlantic Monthly* 35 (June 1875): 660–70. Epps, *Democracy Reborn*, 203, gives a more complicated account.

108. Epps, *Democracy Reborn*, 198–203; Owen, "Political Results from the Varioloid," 660–70.

109. Differing accounts, all of which indicate limited debate over section one, are found in Epps, *Democracy Reborn*, 225–39; Eric L. McKitrick, *Andrew Johnson and Reconstruction* (Chicago: University of Chicago Press, 1960), chap. 11; James, *Framing of the Fourteenth Amendment*, 124–31, 142–50; Benedict, *Compromise of Principle*, 169–86. Section one seemed only to reiterate provisions of the Civil Rights bill that Congress had just passed.

110. Tilton and Stevens as quoted in Benedict, *Compromise of Principle*, 186–87, Phillips as quoted in McPherson, *Struggle for Equality*, 354–55.

111. Douglass as quoted in McPherson, *Struggle for Equality*, 355.

112. "An Equal Rights League in Toledo," *Weekly Anglo-African*, April 23, 1865; *Trenton Gazette*, July 15, 1865, in Marian Thompson Wright, "Negro Suffrage in New Jersey," *Journal of Negro History* 33 (1948): 207–8. At a "Convention of Colored Citizens" in Boston, no women were mentioned among the participants and the stated aim was to deal with "matters concerning the colored man and his status." "Convention of Colored Citizens in Boston," *Liberator*, December 9, 1865.

113. "Speech by John Mercer Langston," Indianapolis, October 25, 1865, in Ripley, *Black Abolitionist Papers*, 5: 374, 383.

114. *Proceedings of the First Annual Meeting of the National Equal Rights League Held in Cleveland, Ohio, October 19, 20, and 21, 1865* (Philadelphia: E. C. Markley, 1865), 35.

115. Elsa Barkley Brown, "Negotiating and Transforming the Public Sphere: African American Political Life in the Transition from Slavery to Freedom," *Public Culture* 7 (1994): 107–46; Elsa Barkley Brown, "To Catch the Vision of Freedom: Reconstructing Southern Black

Women's Political History, 1865–1880," in Ann D. Gordon and Bettye Collier-Thomas, eds., *African-American Women and the Vote, 1837–1965* (Amherst: University of Massachusetts Press, 1997), 66–99.

116. "The First Colored Men's Convention of Virginia," *Weekly Anglo-African*, August 19, 1865; "Constitution of the Colored Men's Equal Rights League of Richmond," May 9, 1865, in Ripley, *Black Abolitionist Papers*, 5: 324–29.

117. Barkley Brown, "Negotiating and Transforming," 112 n.8; Sterling, *We Are Your Sisters*, 344–55; Lisa Cardyn, "Sexual Terror in the Reconstruction South," in Catherine Clinton and Nina Silber, eds., *Battle Scars: Gender and Sexuality in the American Civil War* (New York: Oxford University Press, 2006), 140–67; Tera W. Hunter, *To 'Joy My Freedom: Southern Black Women's Lives and Labors after the Civil War* (Cambridge: Harvard University Press, 1997), 32–33.

118. "Our Platform," *New Orleans Tribune,* reprinted in *Liberator,* March 31, 1865.

119. Lucretia Coffin Mott to Martha C. Wright, October 2, 1865, in Palmer, *Selected Letters of Lucretia Mott,* 364.

120. Catherine Clinton, *Harriet Tubman: The Road to Freedom* (New York: Little, Brown, 2004), 191–92, 211–12; Sterling, *We Are Your Sisters,* 411.

121. SBA to Sojourner Truth, January 13, 1866, in *Papers* 11: 280.

122. Washington, *Sojourner Truth's America,* 316–29; Painter, *Sojourner Truth,* 209–19; Sumler-Lewis, "The Forten-Purvis Women," 281–88; Faulker, *Women's Radical Reconstruction,* 67–82; Sterling, *We Are Your Sisters,* 250–56.

123. Collier-Thomas, "Frances Ellen Watkins Harper,"48–49; Carla L. Peterson, "Literary Transnationalism and Diasporic History: Frances Watkins Harper's 'Fancy Sketches,' 1859–1860," in Sklar and Stewart, *Women's Rights and Transatlantic Antislavery,* 189–208; Peterson, *Doers of the Word,* 120–33; Margaret Hope Bacon, "'One Great Bundle of Humanity': Frances Ellen Watkins Harper (1825–1911)," *Pennsylvania Magazine of History and Biography* 113 (January 1989): 21–43.

124. Collier-Thomas, "Frances Ellen Watkins Harper," 46; "Mrs. Frances E. W. Harper on Reconstruction," *Liberator,* March 3, 1865. Her lectures and her conduct in the debate over disbanding the AASS in May 1865 seem at odds. In that debate Charles Lenox Remond, George T. Downing, Frederick Douglass, and Robert Purvis all opposed William Lloyd Garrison because they wanted to keep the organization going to fight for black (male) suffrage, but Frances Harper did not, perhaps out of respect for father's friendship with Garrison (Bacon, "One Great Bundle of Humanity," 23). Her speech was unrecorded, but I infer her position from the fact that Garrison considered her remarks "excellent," which he would not have done had she opposed him. WLG to Helen Benson Garrison, May 10, 1865, Abolitionist Papers, Ms A.1.1, vol. 6, p. 103.

125. "What the Black Man Wants," *Commonwealth,* February 25, 1865.

126. Ibid.

127. McPherson, *Struggle for Equality,* 343, 346–47.

128. Douglass did say "This is the hour" when referring to black men's voting rights in his January 1865 speech, but that was months *before* Phillips announced his policy. Blassingame and McKivigan, *Papers of Frederick Douglass,* Series One, 4:62. I am unable to find the phrase "the Negro's hour" in Douglass's speeches or writings from this period.

129. "The Waterloo Yearly Meeting," *NASS,* June 16, 1866. DuBois, *Feminism and Suffrage,* 177 appears to misstate Douglass's position when she says that he, like Phillips, believed "woman suffrage agitation itself a betrayal of the ex-slave." But she may be referring in this passage to a state of affairs that had developed by 1869, when Douglass backed the Fifteenth Amendment and moved over to affirm Phillips's priorities.

130. FD to ECS, February 16, 1866, in *Papers* 11: 367.

131. ECS to WP, February 10, [1866], in *Papers* 11: 343–44.

132. Harper, *Life and Work,* 1: 256–59.

133. *NASS*, May 19, 1866, only listed participants and summarized debate, as in, "The sixth, and one or two other [resolutions] elicited considerable discussion, and were amended." Cf. *New York World*, May 9 and 10, 1866, in *Papers* 11:466–72; *New York Tribune*, May 10, 1866, in *Papers* 11: 473–74.

134. *Proceedings of the Eleventh National Woman's Rights Convention, Held at the Church of the Puritans, New York, May 10, 1866* (New York: Robert J. Johnston, 1866), 52 in *Papers* 11: 501.

135. Ibid., 5, 54, in *Papers* 11: 477, 502.

136. Ibid., 3–4, in *Papers* 11: 476–77.

137. Ibid., 7, 8,12, in *Papers* 11: 478–79, 481.

138. Ibid., 9, in *Papers* 11: 479.

139. Ibid., 20, in *Papers* 11: 486.

140. "Mr. Phillips throws a Pail of Cold Water on the Audience," *New York World*, May 11, 1866, in *Papers* 11: 520.

141. *Proceedings of the Eleventh National Woman's Rights Convention*, 37–42, in *Papers* 11: 493–96; Olympia Brown, "An Autobiography, Edited and Compiled by Gwendolyn B. Willis," *Annual Journal of the Universalist Historical Society* 4 (1963): 48.

142. Two months earlier, Harper had positioned herself between Garrison and Phillips, on "the moderate ground." "Philadelphia Correspondence," *NASS*, March 10, 1866. She relied on Garrison to endorse her as a lyceum lecturer: "To Lyceum Managers," *NASS*, January 19, 1866.

143. Peterson, *Doers of the Word*, 228–30.

144. *Proceedings of the Eleventh National Woman's Rights Convention*, 46, in *Papers* 11: 498.

145. Ibid., 47, in *Papers* 11: 498.

146. *Proceedings of the Eleventh National Woman's Rights Convention*, 48. This page is omitted from the microfilm and must be consulted in the original pamphlet.

147. This argument is highlighted by Nell Painter, who sees in Harper's remarks a strong critique of white feminists: *Sojourner Truth*, 224–25.

148. "Our Boston Correspondent," *NASS*, June 9, 1866.

149. *Proceedings of the Eleventh National Woman's Rights Convention*, 55, in *Papers* 11: 502.

150. Harper, *Life and Work*, 1: 261.

151. *Proceedings of the Eleventh National Woman's Rights Convention*, 56, in *Papers* 11: 503.

152. On this AERA meeting, attended by Anthony but not Stanton or Stone, see "Our Boston Correspondence," *NASS*, June 9, 1866; "Equal Rights Meeting in Boston," *NASS*, June 16, 1866. Phillips's opposition to the Fourteenth Amendment is seen in "The Congressional Fraud," *NASS*, June 23, 1866; and "Political Huckstering," *NASS*, July 7, 1866.

153. "Our Boston Correspondence," *NASS*, June 9, 1866; "Equal Rights Meeting in Boston," *NASS*, June 16, 1866; "Personal," *NASS*, June 23, 1866.

154. Historians have often suggested that it did. For example, Flexner, *Century of Struggle*, 145 indicates that Phillips favored passage of the Fourteenth Amendment "at all costs" while Stanton and Anthony opposed it; Painter, *Sojourner Truth*, 226, says Truth supported the Fourteenth Amendment while Stanton and Anthony opposed it; Newman, *White Women's Rights*, 4, says Douglass favored the Fourteenth Amendment while Stanton and Anthony opposed it. DuBois, *Feminism and Suffrage*, 58, 65, avoids such inaccuracies but offers an ambiguous account. She writes that abolitionists like Phillips were deeply dissatisfied with the Fourteenth Amendment "but ultimately could not oppose it," but she also indicates that the amendment was "so unsatisfactory from the perspective of black suffrage" that Stanton and Anthony's AERA "found it difficult to make its feminist criticisms heard above those of abolitionists and Radicals."

155. *HWS*, 2: 322. They discussed the two amendments together in chapter 21 of the second volume of the *HWS*, in an account that was generally confusing, (and in the quoted passage, positively misleading). Discussing the two amendments together saved them from having to be specific about their record of opposition to the subsequent Fifteenth Amendment, the details of which were indefensible.

Chapter 4

1. "Wendell Phillips and Congress," *NASS*, September 29, 1866; ECS, "Should Radical Abolitionists Go to Congress?" *NASS*, October 6, 1866.
2. "Elizabeth Cady Stanton for Congress," October 10, 1866, in *Selected Papers*, 1: 593–94.
3. "The Negro Compromised," *NASS*, September 22, 1866; "The Amendment and Its New Advocate," *NASS*, September 29, 1866.
4. "State Constitutional Convention," *NASS*, October 6, 1866.
5. *Proceedings of the Eleventh National Woman's Rights Convention*, 49.
6. SBA to WP, November 6, 1866, in *Papers* 11: 627–31. In the enclosure, Henry B. Blackwell, recording secretary, conveys a resolution from the AERA executive committee.
7. *HWS*, 2: 923–26; ECS to Ellen Dwight Eaton, April 5, [1866], in *Papers* 11: 426.
8. Coverage of the Tweddle Hall convention in the major New York dailies was garbled, as noted in *Selected Papers*, 1:599. But the 3,000 attendance figure comes from what appears to be a sober eyewitness: "Our New York Letter, December 3, 1866" unidentified clipping in scrapbook #5, "Progress of the Woman's Cause," Dall Papers.
9. "Equal Rights," *New York Tribune*, November 21, 1866, in *Papers* 11: 648.
10. Ibid., 648–49.
11. "New York State Equal Rights Convention," in *Selected Papers*, 1: 600. Cf. Philip S. Foner, *Frederick Douglass on Women's Rights* (Westport: Greenwood Press, 1976), 28–29, who sees a "clash" between Douglass and Stanton and Anthony that anticipated 1869.
12. On Blackwell's "pugnacity" as "greater than his discretion," see Merk, "Massachusetts and the Woman Suffrage Movement," chap. 2, p. 12 and n. 17.
13. "New York State Equal Rights Convention," in *Selected Papers*, 1: 600–601.
14. Congressional Globe, 39th Congress, 2nd Session, 46–47, 55–66, 76–84, December 10–12, 1866.
15. Ibid., 59.
16. Ibid., 47.
17. Ibid., 55–56.
18. Ibid., 62–63.
19. Ibid., 76–78.
20. Ibid., 60.
21. Ibid., 63–64.
22. Ibid., 84. Six senators were absent.
23. Mary Clemmer Ames, "A Woman's Letters from Washington," *Independent*, December 27, 1867; Congressional Globe, 39th Congress, 2nd Session, 311, January 18, 1867.
24. Salmon P. Chase ("Father") to Nettie, December 12, 1866, in *"Spur Up Your Pegasus": Family Letters of Salmon, Kate, and Nettie Chase, 1844–1873*, ed. Jane P. McClure, Peg A. Lamphier, and Erika M. Kreger (Kent, Ohio: Kent State University Press, 2009), 343.
25. SBA to Anna Dickinson, December 2, 1866, in *Papers* 11: 671; SBA to Gerrit Smith, [December 8, 1866] in *Papers* 11: 729–30; *Penn Yan Democrat*, December 28, 1866, in *Papers* 11: 800; *Rochester Democrat and American*, December 13, 1866, in *Papers* 11: 791; "Shall Women Vote?" *New York World*, December 7, 1866, in *Papers* 11: 685. Little is known about the local chapters. In the Utica Equal Rights Club, all the participants but one were women. *Utica Morning Herald and Daily Gazette*, December 11, 1866. In Philadelphia, PA, the local AERA chapter attracted "several intelligent colored young men and women." Lucretia Coffin Mott to Martha C. Wright, September 3, 1867, and January 21, 1868, in Palmer, *Selected Letters of Lucretia Mott*, 394, 399.
26. *NASS*, January 26, February 2, February 23, March 2, March 9, March 16, March 23, March 30, re. meetings in Canandaigua, Little Falls, Herkimer, Cohoes, Troy, Hudson, Rondout, Kingston Newburg, Schenectady, Amsterdam, Fultonville, Canajoharie, Gloversville, Johnstown, Fort Plain, Ilion, St. Johnsville, Oswego, Fulton, Baldwinsville, Syracuse, Marcellus, Perry, Warsaw, Gainesville, Pike, Nunda, Clyde, Lyons, Port Byron.

27. SBA to Amy Kirby Post, February 17, 1867, in *Papers* 11: 1050–51.

28. In Rochester, the AERA convention charged 25 cents admission for the evening meeting, but offered free tickets to "women who earn their own bread." SBA to Amy Kirby Post, December 2, 1866, in *Papers* 11: 678.

29. "Remarks by SBA to the Pennsylvania Anti-Slavery Society," *NASS*, December 1, 1866, in *Selected Papers*, 1: 605.

30. ECS, "Lecture for AERA Meeting and Tour of New York State," [December 6, 1866, & after], in *Papers*, 11: 694–728; ECS, *Address in Favor of Universal Suffrage for the Election of Delegates to the Constitutional Convention* (Albany: Weed, Parsons, 1867), in *Papers* 11: 894–906.

31. A manuscript copy of ECS, "'Reconstruction' Lecture for Tour of New York State," [December 10 and later, 1866], in *Papers* 11: 741–88 does contain invidious remarks about black men, but a note in the hand of Harriot Stanton Blatch (at 11: 758) describes it as "first used" when the Fourteenth Amendment was about to be ratified, suggesting it was subsequently reused and therefore possibly altered. Phillips's *NASS*, which was presumably keen to detect and reject any comments deleterious to black men's chances, praised Stanton's speech as "a very earnest and effective plea for the enfranchisement of women and such colored men as are proscribed by the property qualification." *NASS*, February 23, 1867.

32. Henry B. Blackwell, *What the South Can Do: How the Southern States Can Make Themselves Masters of the Situation. To the Legislatures of the Southern States, January 15, 1867* (New York: Robert J. Johnston, 1867).Library of Congress American Memory Web site, http://memory.loc.gov/cgi-bin/query.

33. Ibid.

34. "Henry W. Blackwell. New York. Southern States," *Dallas Herald*, February 23, 1867.

35. The silence may be meaningless because so many papers were destroyed, but SBA and ECS made a point of including this embarrassing document in the *HWS*, 2: 929. The proposal closely paralleled one Henry Blackwell would make in 1890, in what became known as his "southern strategy" for women's suffrage. Kerr, *Lucy Stone*, 229–30; Aileen Kraditor, *The Ideas of the Woman Suffrage Movement, 1890–1920* (New York: W. W. Norton, 1981), 168–69.

36. They published an important piece of historical research in the *Newark Daily Advertiser* describing how women had had the right to vote in New Jersey until 1807, and Stone went on to address New Jersey legislators asking that they amend the state constitution to strike the words "white" and "male" from the franchise clause. She argued that the Republicans could bolster their thin majority in the state with the votes of grateful blacks and women, but they were too timid to try it. "Women and the Ballot in New Jersey," *NASS*, January 5, 1867; *Woman Suffrage in New Jersey, An Address Delivered by Lucy Stone at a Hearing before the New Jersey Legislature, March 6, 1867* (Boston: C. H. Simonds, 1867), in BFP/ Schlesinger; "The Notorious Thirteen," *NASS*, April 20, 1867; Marion Wright, "Negro Suffrage in New Jersey," *Journal of Negro History* 33 (1948): 211–18.

37. Olympia Brown, "An Autobiography," 34–35, in Brown Papers.

38. LS to Abby Kelley Foster, January 24, 1867, in Wheeler, *Loving Warriors*, 215–16; "Equal Rights," *NASS*, February 2, 1867.

39. The presence of Mott, Stanton, and Anthony is noted in "Correspondence. Letter from Philadelphia," *Commonwealth*, January 26, 1867.

40. *American National Biography Online*, s.v. "Purvis, Robert," by Joseph A Borome, accessed October 9, 2010, http://0-www.anb.org.library.colgate.edu/articles/; Margaret Hope Bacon, *But One Race: The Life of Robert Purvis* (Albany: State University of New York Press, 2007).

41. The last meeting of the AERA canvass seems to have been April 12: "Personal," *NASS*, April 6, 1867.

42. SBA to Gerrit Smith, March 5, 1867, in *Papers* 12: 85–89

43. Peabody, the partner of J. P. Morgan's father, later increased his gift to $2 million. In practice, "to avoid antagonizing white southern sentiment," the trust devoted more of its resources to white schools than to black schools. Robert H. Bremner, *The Public Good: Philanthropy and Welfare in the Civil War Era* (New York: Knopf, 1980), 186–88.

44. SBA to Gerrit Smith, March 5, 1867, in *Papers* 12: 85–89.

45. SBA to Anna Dickinson, March 24, 1867, in *Selected Papers*, 2: 45.

46. Benedict, *Compromise of Principle*, 216–40; Foner, *Reconstruction*, 271–80.

47. James, *Framing of the 14th Amendment*, 193. Gordon, "Stanton and the Right to Vote," 115 notes that section two of the Fourteenth Amendment had no effect on black suffrage, but it did have a negative impact on women by reinforcing their disenfranchisement. This passage was cited, among others, by the Supreme Court in turning down Virginia Minor's contention that she had the right to vote as an implied right of citizenship, in *Minor v. Happersett* (1875).

48. "The Situation," *NASS*, March 16, 1867; Wendell Phillips, "The West—Congress—Impeachment," *NASS*, March 23, 1867.

49. These were the anniversary of the AASS on May 7 and 8 in New York City; the anniversary of the AERA on May 9 and 10 in New York City; and the 37th Annual New England Anti-Slavery Convention on May 29 in Boston.

50. *Proceedings of the First Anniversary of the American Equal Rights Association, held at the Church of the Puritans, New York, May 9 and 10, 1867* (New York: Robert J. Johnston, 1867), 57, in *Papers* 12: 182.

51. "Thirty-Fourth Annual Meeting of the American Anti-Slavery Society," *NASS*, May 18, 1867.

52. "Thirty-Fourth Annual Meeting of the American Anti-Slavery Society," *NASS*, May 25, 1867; Stewart, *Wendell Phillips*, 283–85. '

53. "Business Meeting," *NASS*, May 25, 1867.

54. "Speech of Col. T.W. Higginson," *NASS*, May 18, 1867.

55. "Business Meeting," *NASS*, May 25, 1867. The original reads "hypercritical," which I take to be a misspelling.

56. ECS to Sojourner Truth, March 24, 1867, in *Selected Papers*, 2: 47. Painter, *Sojourner Truth*, 225, implies that Truth was being used by Anthony and Stanton as a foil against Harper's criticisms of them in the AERA meeting of the previous year. But Margaret Washington, *Sojourner Truth's America*, 336–40, portrays Truth as self-directed woman who dominated the 1867 platform.

57. *Proceedings of the First Anniversary of the AERA*, 20–21, in *Papers* 12: 164.

58. "Twenty-Ninth Annual Meeting of the Pennsylvania Anti-Slavery society," *NASS*, December 8, 1866.

59. "Twenty-Ninth Annual Meeting of the Pennsylvania Anti-Slavery Society," *NASS*, December 8, 1866; "Our Boston Correspondent," *NASS*, February 16, 1867; *Proceedings of the First Anniversary of the AERA*, 26, in *Papers* 12:167.

60. *Proceedings of the First Anniversary of the AERA*, 20, in *Papers* 12: 164.

61. *Proceedings of the First Anniversary of the AERA*, 53. in *Papers* 12: 180.

62. As Amy Stanley has explained, the freedwomen were just then discovering that they were not really free to control their own bodies or to possess the proceeds of their own labor. The prerogatives of their husbands infringed upon freedwomen's newly won and highly prized right of self-ownership, and sorting through the contradictions involved in the post-emancipation project of defining "freedom" for wives who were still legally subject to their husbands was going to trouble black women, legislators, jurists, and feminists for some time to come. Amy Dru Stanley, *From Bondage to Contract: Wage Labor, Marriage, and the Market in the Age of Slave Emancipation* (Cambridge: Cambridge University Press, 1998), chaps. 1 and 5.

63. *American National Biography Online*, s.v. "Downing, George Thomas" by Leslie H. Fishel, accessed October 9, 2010, http://0-www.anb.org.library.colgate.edu/articles/; John H.

Hewitt, "Mr. Downing and His Oyster House: The Life and Good Works of an African-American Entrepreneur," *New York History* 74 (1993): 229–52. He took the lead in pushing for black male suffrage in Washington, DC: "Suffrage in the District," *NASS*, December 15, 1866.

64. *Selected Papers*, 2: 71 n.11.

65. *Proceedings of the First Anniversary of the AERA*, 53, in *Papers* 12: 180.

66. *Proceedings of the First Anniversary of the AERA*, 54–55, in *Papers* 12: 181.

67. "Annual Meeting of the Equal Rights Association," *NASS*, June 1, 1867. There are two different versions of Truth's remarks: cf. *Proceedings of the First Anniversary of the AERA*, 63, in *Papers* 12: 185. Although the *NASS* account cut many of the speeches at the AERA meeting including the whole exchange between Downing and Stanton, it presented a much longer version of Truth's second speech in what certainly sounds like Truth's voice. It is not clear why the published *Proceedings*, which were described as a "phonographic report," should have omitted this material. The *HWS*, 2: 182–226 contains the same version found in the published *Proceedings*.

68. "Annual Meeting of the Equal Rights Association," *NASS*, June 1, 1867.

69. *Proceedings of the First Anniversary of the AERA*, 67, in *Papers* 12: 187.

70. Painter, *Sojourner Truth*, 228–29, characterizes the exchange between Downing and Stanton as "furious" and "a firestorm," a reading that seems quite reasonable except when viewed in the light of these final comments by Truth.

71. The proceedings of the AERA meeting were published immediately in pamphlet form, which contributed to the dynamics of an ongoing debate. See "American Equal Rights Association," *NASS*, June 1, 1867, announcing the pamphlet at 25 cents a copy.

72. "Proceedings of the New England Anti-Slavery Convention," *NASS*, June 8, 1867.

73. "Proceedings of the New England Anti-Slavery Convention," *NASS*, June 15, 1867.

74. Ibid.

75. Ibid.

76. Stanton declared Greeley "will ignore us and the Negro too if he thinks party necessity demands it." ECS to Gerrit Smith, [1866 after November 11], in *Papers* 11: 635.

77. Brockway, *Fifty Years in Journalism*, 299.

78. Richard Hofstadter, *The American Political Tradition and the Men Who Made It* (New York: Knopf, 1948), chap. 7; *American National Biography Online*, s.v. "Conkling, Roscoe," by Allan Peskin, accessed October 9, 2010; http://0-www.anb.org.library.colgate.edu/articles/; David M. Jordan, *Roscoe Conkling of New York: Voice in the Senate* (Ithaca: Cornell University Press, 1971).

79. James, *Framing of the Fourteenth Amendment*, 56–57, 112.

80. ECS to Gerrit Smith, [1866 after November 11], in *Papers* 11: 635.

81. *HWS*, 2: 274.

82. Folger practiced law in Geneva, New York. He had been a Barnburner Democrat before he moved over to the Republicans because of the party's antislavery stance, and as a member of the New York State Senate from 1862 to 1869, he chaired the Judiciary Committee. *American National Biography Online*, s.v. "Folger, Charles James," by Justus D. Doenecke, accessed October 9, 2010, http://0-www.anb.org.library.colgate.edu/articles/.

83. "The State Constitutional Convention," *NASS*, February 16, 1867; untitled, *NASS*, April 6, 1867; "The State Constitutional Convention," *NASS*, February 23, 1867.

84. This was the "32-at-large" plan. James C. Mohr, *The Radical Republicans and Reform in New York during Reconstruction* (Ithaca: Cornell University Press, 1973), 211–12.

85. *HWS*, 2: 282; Lucretia Coffin Mott to SBA, February 10, 1867, in *Selected Papers*, 2: 13–14; "Correspondence. Our New York letter," *Commonwealth*, March 2, 1867.

86. *HWS*, 2: 270.

87. Ibid., 286.

88. "The State Constitutional Convention," *NASS*, July 6, 1867.

89. *HWS*, 2: 286–87.

90. *HWS*, 2: 287; *Selected Papers*, 2: 77 n. 3. Barbara Goldsmith, *Other Powers: The Age of Suffrage, Spiritualism, and the Scandalous Victoria Woodhull* (New York: Knopf, 1998), 56–62, provides a grim portrait of the Greeley marriage, but other biographers have not confirmed this.

91. ECS, "Female Suffrage Committee," in *Selected Papers*, 2: 72–73. Michele Mitchell points out that Stanton's reference in this article to "bootblacks, barbers and ignorant foreigners" making laws for white men was meant to tap into racism among the delegates to the Constitutional Convention. Mitchell, "'Lower Orders,' Racial Hierarchies, and Rights Rhetoric," 128–51. Stanton's address to the legislature in January had referred to an "incoming tide of poverty, ignorance, and vice," but she did not then connect it to black men, whose voting rights she defended. Cf. *HWS*, 2: 276 and 280.

92. George W. Cole murdered L. Harris Hiscock on June 4, 1867. *Selected Papers*, 2: 287–88 n. 4; "Terrible Tragedy in Albany," *Boston Post*, June 6, 1867; Mohr, *Radical Republicans and Reform*, 221–22.

93. "The Constitutional Convention," *New York Times*, July 30, 1867, complains of "no visible energy" and not a single accomplishment after nearly two months in session.

94. *Selected Papers*, 2: 85 n.1. Curtis's speech is found in *HWS*, 2: 288–303.

95. "The Constitutional Convention," *New York Times*, July 30, 1867.

96. ECS to Gerrit Smith, July 6, 1867, Smith Papers.

97. Untitled, *NASS*, February 16 and March 2, 1867; SBA to Amy Kirby Post, February 17, 1867, in *Papers* 11: 1051–52. The Kansas constitution declared "every white male person" an elector. Mark A. Plummer, *Frontier Governor: Samuel J. Crawford of Kansas* (Lawrence: University Press of Kansas, 1971), 4.

98. Daniel Webster Wilder, *The Annals of Kansas* (Topeka: Kansas Publishing House, 1886), 447. About 30,000 votes would be cast in the 1867 referenda statewide. *Selected Papers*, 2: 643–44, Appendix B.

99. DuBois, *Feminism and Suffrage*, 84–85 emphasizes the importance of these Kansas women.

100. Wilder, *Annals of Kansas*, 490. Republicans constituted 70 percent of the Kansas electorate in the 1860s according to LaWanda Cox and John H. Cox, "Negro Suffrage and Republican Politics: The Problem of Motivation in Reconstruction Historiography," *Journal of Southern History* 33 (August 1967): 318.

101. Elsewhere radical speakers had demonstrated their power to change attitudes: during the winter of 1866–1867 the small settlement of Mount Pleasant, Iowa, was visited by five prominent speakers—Anna Dickinson, C. C. Burleigh, Theodore Tilton, Frederick Douglass, and Wendell Phillips—who "made such an impression in the small Iowa town that the people abandoned their policy of school segregation." McPherson, *Struggle for Equality*, 367. Mount Pleasant's conversion was publicized in the *NASS*, March 30, 1867.

102. SBA to Anna Dickinson, February 18, 1867, in *Papers* 11: 1056.

103. Untitled, *NASS*, March 16, 1867, quoting an SBA letter dated March 12. In *Feminism and Suffrage*, 79, DuBois refers to "meager resources" in Kansas.

104. In SBA to Samuel N. Wood, April 21, 1867, in *Selected Papers*, 2: 53–56, Anthony mentions speakers she hopes to line up for Kansas, including Anna Dickinson and Frederick Douglass, and then breaks off saying, "But you see *the money, the money.*"

105. *Proceedings of the First Anniversary of the AERA*, 5–6, in *Papers* 12: 156–57, also excerpted in *Selected Papers*, 2: 61–62.

106. LS to SBA, May 1, 1867, in *Papers* 12: 147.The terms of the will are in the *HWS*, 1: 667–68.

107. WP to Ann Greene Phillips, April 16, 1867, Phillips Papers, bMs Am 1952(1377); "Lectures in the West," *NASS*, April 6, 1867; untitled, *NASS*, April 27, 1867.

108. News of a lawsuit involving the Jackson Fund had come before the public for the first time in February; see coverage in the *Commonwealth*, February 9 and 16, 1867. See also "The

Diversion of Francis Jackson's Bequest," *Commonwealth*, August 17, 1867; "The Jackson Bequest," *Commonwealth*, September 7, 1867.

109. "Concerning Wills," *Commonwealth*, February 16, 1867.

110. See Nina J. Crimm, "Democratization, Global Grant-Making, and the Internal Revenue Code Lobbying Restrictions," *Tulane Law Review* 79 (February 2005): 612–15. Crimm explains that after the Revolution a minority of states, including Massachusetts, retained the Elizabethan Statute of Charitable Uses, but a larger number either repealed the English statute or took some middle ground. *Jackson v. Phillips* became a much-cited precedent defining a narrow interpretation of charitable trusts so as to rule invalid bequests that aimed to change the laws. But states like Illinois and Pennsylvania rejected the notion that trusts whose objectives involved reforming the laws were noncharitable. Cf. McPherson, *Struggle for Equality*, 400–401; Bremner, *The Public Good*, 180–81.

111. *Edmund Jackson v. Wendell Phillips and others*, Supreme Court of Massachusetts, Suffolk, 99 Mass.539; 1867 Mass. LEXIS 113; 14 Allen 539, available online through http://web.lexis-nexis.com.

112. WP to Francis Jackson, October 9, 1858, Abolitionist Papers, Ms.A.1.2, vol. 28, p. 147.

113. SBA to Anna Dickinson, [August 1867], in *Papers* 12: 369–70.

114. Attorney Samuel Sewall did present a short argument on the women's behalf. *Edmund Jackson v. Wendell Phillips.*

115. SBA to Anna Dickinson, [August 1867], in *Papers* 12: 369–70.

116. *HWS*, 1: 257–58.

117. See WP to LS, November 18, 1867, and HBB to LS, October 29, 1867, BFP/LC.

118. SBA to Samuel N. Wood, August 9, 1867, in *Papers* 12: 347; SBA to Martha C. Wright, [August 26, 1867], in *Papers* 12: 368.

119. WLG to Henry I. Bowditch, March 28, 1868, Abolitionist Papers, Ms.A.1.1, vol.7, p. 76a.

Chapter 5

1. SBA to Anne Green Phillips, 1867 ca. April, Phillips Papers, bMs Am 1952 (1390).

2. SBA to S. N. Wood, June 12, 1867, in *Papers* 12: 238; Gallman, *America's Joan of Arc*, 82–86.

3. ECS to Gerrit Smith, August 6, 1867, in *Papers* 12: 337.

4. SBA to Martha C. Wright. [August 26, 1867], in *Papers* 12: 368.

5. The early history of Kansas is part of the vast literature dealing with the causes of the Civil War. See James Rawley, *Race and Politics: Bleeding Kansas and the Coming of the Civil War* (Philadelphia: J. B. Lippincott, 1969); Craig Miner, *Kansas: The History of the Sunflower State, 1854–2000* (Lawrence: University Press of Kansas, 2002).

6. Miner, *Kansas*, chaps 2–3; Albert Castel, "Jim Lane of Kansas," *Civil War Times Illustrated* 12 (April 1973): 22–29; Leverett W. Spring, "The Career of a Kansas Politician," *American Historical Review* 4 (October 1898): 80–104.

7. Albert Castel, "Civil War Kansas and the Negro," *Journal of Negro History* 51 (April 1966): 125–38; Hildegarde Rose Herklotz, "Jayhawkers in Missouri, 1858–1863," *Missouri Valley Historical Review* 18 (October 1923): 64–101.

8. Neither Senator Samuel Pomeroy, who was reelected, nor the new senator, Edmund Ross, had leadership skills, and the incumbent governor, Samuel Crawford, seems to have been an ineffective placeholder. Mark A. Plummer, *Frontier Governor: Samuel J. Crawford of Kansas* (Lawrence: University Press of Kansas, 1972).

9. "Rough and ready" is from Olympia Brown, "An Autobiography," 51. Historian Eugene H. Berwanger charged that Wood was cynically using woman suffrage to defeat black suffrage. Berwanger, *The West and Reconstruction* (Urbana: University of Illinois Press, 1981), 165–67; Berwanger, "Hardin and Langston: Western Black Spokesmen of the Reconstruction Era," *Journal of Negro History* 64 (Spring 1979):101–15. But Sister Mary Berard McKenna, "Samuel N. Wood: Chronic Agitator" (Ph.D. diss., St. Louis University, 1968) finds ample evidence of his sincerity on women's rights.

10. Cf. Sandra Arlene Madsen, "The 1867 Campaign for Woman Suffrage in Kansas: A Study in Rhetorical Situation" (Ph.D. diss., University of Kansas, 1975), 26, who refers to Wood's maneuvers in the state Senate as "political blackmail;" and the more neutral description in the reminiscence of Helen Ekin Starrett in *HWS*, 2: 250–51.

11. Henry Blackwell found that Wood had "warmer friends and bitterer enemies than almost any man in the State." HBB to ECS, April 5, 1867, in *HWS*, 2: 233; Wood's salary in "Latest Election News," *Emporia News*, November 8, 1867.

12. Sol Miller, editor of the *White Cloud Kansas Chief* and a perceptive commentator on the Kansas political scene, supported both black and woman suffrage. He worried, "We fear the female suffrage question in Kansas will be more unpopular than if taken upon its simple merits, from the fact that Sam Wood is taking such an active part on its behalf." *White Cloud Kansas Chief*, April 8, 1867.

13. Kerr, *Lucy Stone*, 267 n.16; Samuel A. Johnson, *The Battle Cry of Freedom: The New England Emigrant Aid Company in the Kansas Crusade* (Lawrence: University of Kansas Press, 1954).

14. Cf. Johnson, *The Battle Cry of Freedom*, 54; Don W. Wilson, *Governor Charles Robinson of Kansas* (Lawrence: University Press of Kansas, 1975); Thomas Wentworth Higginson, *Cheerful Yesterdays* (Boston: Houghton, Mifflin, 1898), 207–8.

15. Plummer, *Frontier Governor*, 42.

16. Gov. C. Robinson to S. N. Wood, November 9, 1866, Wood Papers; Plummer, *Frontier Governor*, 37–38; McKenna, "Samuel N. Wood," 112.

17. LS to ECS, April 10, 1867 in *Selected Papers*, 2: 49.

18. Wilder, *Annals of Kansas*, 436–37; Michael Lewis Goldberg, *An Army of Women: Gender and Politics in Gilded Age Kansas* (Baltimore: Johns Hopkins University Press, 1997), 14. Goldberg argues that Radical Republicans supported black (male) suffrage on principle, while conservative Republicans saw it as a way to pad their party's majority, assuming that black men would vote Republican reliably and yet have little claim to patronage or preferment.

19. LS to ECS, April 10, 1867, in *Selected Papers*, 2: 48–52; HBB to ECS, April 5, 1867, in *HWS*, 2: 233; Madsen, "The 1867 Campaign," 31–32.

20. "The Suffrage Convention," *Leavenworth Daily Conservative*, April 5, 1867; Plummer, *Frontier Governor*, 61; "Local and Miscellaneous," *Leavenworth Daily Conservative*, October 8, 1867.

21. *American National Biography Online*, s.v. "Langston, Charles Henry," by Thaddeus Russell, accessed October 7, 2010, http://0-www.anb.org.library.colgate.edu/; Berwanger, "Hardin and Langston," 105–13; Richard B. Sheridan, "Charles Henry Langston and the African American Struggle in Kansas," *Kansas History* 22 (Winter 1999/2000): 268–83; Frederick J. Blue, *No Taint of Compromise: Crusaders in Antislavery Politics* (Baton Rouge: Louisiana State University Press, 2005), 65–89.

22. *Selected Papers*, 1:539; Jones, *All Bound Up Together*, 80.

23. C. H. Langston to S. N. Wood, February 10, 1867, Wood Papers. Langston upbraided Wood as someone from whom he was entitled to expect support: "The radical party through their state convention, by their governor, as well as through official nominees has declared in favor of Negro suffrage. Why do you as one of that party hesitate?"

24. Charles H. Langston to S. N. Wood, April 7, 1867, Wood Papers.

25. Ibid.

26. "We desire speakers to advocate the broad doctrine of Impartial Suffrage, but welcome those who advocate either," Wood wrote. "Those [speakers] who desire colored suffrage alone, are invited to take the field; also those who favor only female suffrage. Each help the other." S. N. Wood to SBA, April 5, 1867, in *Proceedings of the First Anniversary of the AERA*, 74–75, in *Papers* 12: 191.

27. Charles Robinson to S. N. Wood, April 6, 1867, Charles and Sara T. D. Robinson Collection, Kansas State Historical Society, Topeka, KS.

28. LS to ECS, April 10, 1867, in *Selected Papers*, 1:49; HBB to ECS and SBA, April 21, 1867, in *HWS*, 2: 237.

29. LS to SBA, May 9, 1867, BFP/LC.

30. "The Issue," *Lawrence Daily Tribune*, May 17, 1867.

31. "Impartial Suffrage Association," *Leavenworth Daily Tribune*, May 30, 1867.

32. "Suffrage," *Leavenworth Daily Conservative*, June 30, 1867.

33. "Universal Suffrage," *Leavenworth Daily Conservative*, January 6, 1867. For Wood as an old enemy, see "The State Legislature," *Leavenworth Daily Conservative*, January 26, 1864.

34. "The Suffrage Convention," *Leavenworth Daily Conservative*, April 5, 1867; "Political," *Leavenworth Daily Conservative*, May 17, 1867.

35. Spring, "Career of a Kansas Politician." Lane's followers included some very conservative Republicans as well as decided radicals. In the 1850s, Lane had been a pro-slavery Democrat. On Lane's shifting position while in the Senate, see Benedict, *Compromise of Principle*, 344, 347.

36. "Negro Suffrage," *Leavenworth Daily Conservative*, May 21, 1867.

37. Martin's list of reasons that women should not vote appeared in the *Atchison Daily Champion*, April 23, 1867. See also Roberts, "How It Operates," *Oskaloosa Independent*, May 11, 1867.

38. Untitled, *Lawrence Daily Tribune*, May 22, 1867; "Lucy Stone—Again," *Emporia News*, June 18, 1867.

39. In the *HWS*, 2: 929–31 Stanton and Anthony indicate that Blackwell distributed his pamphlet "largely" in Kansas, but I find no contemporary evidence to confirm this.

40. LS to SBA, May 9, 1867, in *Selected Papers*, 2: 57.

41. Ibid.

42. Foner, *Reconstruction*, 271–307; Hahn, *A Nation under Our Feet*, 177–215.

43. The *NASS* could not resist reprinting an editorial in which Thurlow Weed claimed he had "ever been in favor "of black suffrage. "Negro Suffrage," *NASS*, April 13, 1867.

44. "Washington Correspondence," *NASS*, 6 April and April 27, 1867. The Union Republican Congressional Committee employed 118 speakers in the South in the summer of 1867, and subsidized others through the state organizations. See "Names of Speakers and Organizers Employed or Aided by the Union Republican Congressional Committee," September 12, 1867, in Robert C. Schenck Papers, Miami University Archives, Miami, Ohio.

45. McPherson, *Struggle for Equality*, 377–38; Foner, *Reconstruction*, 281–86.

46. Michael Fitzgerald, *The Union League Movement in the Deep South: Politics and Agricultural Change during Reconstruction* (Baton Rouge: Louisiana State University Press, 1989), 123.

47. From the Sea Islands of South Carolina in a letter of June 1, 1867, Laura Towne wrote, "Several speakers have been here who have advised the people to get the women into their proper place—never to tell them anything of their concerns, etc., etc." Towne thought black men welcomed the message, adding, "The notion of being bigger than woman generally is just now inflating the conceit of the males to an amazing degree. When women get the vote, too, no people will be more indignant than these, I suppose." *Letters and Diaries of Laura Towne, Written from the Sea Islands of South Carolina, 1862–1884* (1912; reprint, New York: Negro Universities Press, [1969]), 183–84.

48. Anna Dickinson to WP, May 15, 1867, Phillips Papers, bMs Am 1953 (489); Henry Wilson to S. N. Wood, May 28, 1867, Woman Suffrage History Collection, Kansas State Historical Society; John Mercer Langston, *From the Virginia Plantation to the National Capitol* (Hartford, Conn.: American Publishing, 1894), 260–61.

49. Douglass's neglect of Kansas, along with that of other prominent abolitionist speakers like Phillips, Beecher, Higginson, and Garrison, is mentioned in *HWS* 2: 265. For his whereabouts in 1867, see McFeely, *Frederick Douglass*, 256–61; John W. Blassingame, ed., *The Frederick Douglass Papers: Series One, Speeches, Debates, and Interviews* (New Haven: Yale

University Press, 1992), 4:xxii–xxiii, for a partial speaking itinerary, showing that he was most active in November and December, after election day.

50. Stone wanted Harper to come to Kansas. See LS to SBA, May 1, 1867, *HWS*, 2: 237. Although Harper was successful as a paid lyceum lecturer in the North, it seems doubtful that she could have financed her southern speaking tour on the same basis because her audiences were so impoverished. See Farah Jasmine Griffin, "Frances Ellen Watkins Harper in the Reconstruction South," *Sage: A Scholarly Journal on Black Women*, Student Supplement 1988, 45–47; and Harper's letters in Still, *Underground Railroad*, 767–70. Harper's name does not appear on the list of 188 speakers paid by the Union Congressional Republican Committee (Schenck Papers, cited earlier), but the committee subsidized additional speakers through state-level organizations, and the way Harper confined her speaking tour to Georgia and South Carolina suggests that she had state-based funding. Her whereabouts are mentioned in the *Commonwealth*, July 6, 1867; and *NASS*, July 27, 1867, August 10, 1867, and August 31, 1867.

51. HBB to ECS and SBA, April 21, 1867, in *HWS*, 2: 236, emphasis added.

52. LS to ECS, April 10, 1867, in *HWS*, 2: 234.

53. ECS to HBS, October 9, 1867, in *Selected Papers*, 2: 96.

54. ECS, "To Our Radical Friends," *Revolution* 1 (May 14, 1868): 296.

55. Henry C. Wright reports one month's lecturing in Henry C. Wright to WP, August 29, 1867, Phillips Papers, bMS Am 1935 (1349); and two months lecturing in Henry C. Wright to William Lloyd Garrison, November 23, 1867, Ms.A.1.2, v.35, p. 153, Abolitionist Papers. I infer a likely subsidy from the Hovey Fund because Wright had benefited from it before, and because he was apparently reporting on his activities to Phillips and Garrison who were Hovey trustees.

56. *Notable American Women*, s.v. "Brown, Olympia"; *American National Biography Online*, s.v. "Brown, Olympia," by Sheryl A. Kujawa, accessed October 7, 2010, http://0-www.anb. org.library.colgate.edu/; Charlotte Cote, *Olympia Brown: The Battle for Equality* (Racine, Wis.: Mother Courage Press, 1988).

57. LS to Olympia Brown, September 30, 1867, BFP/LC. It appears that Brown's salary and expenses for three months' work amounted to $495.

58. Bisbee's problems are mentioned in HBB to S. N. Wood, July 25, 1867, and Bessie Bisbee to S. N. Wood, August 25 and August 28, 1867, September 22, 1867, Woman Suffrage History Collection, Kansas State Historical Society, Topeka.

59. "Female Suffrage," *Emporia News*, June 7, 1867.

60. "Hon. C.V. Eskridge of Emporia, on Female Suffrage," (Ottawa, Kans.) *Western Home Journal*, June 13, 1867.

61. "Suffrage," (Ottawa, Kans.) *Western Home Journal*, April 25, 1867.

62. Ibid.

63. Untitled, *White Cloud Kansas Chief*, June 13, 1867.

64. Untitled, *White Cloud Kansas Chief*, January 24, 1867.

65. "Our Opinion," (Lawrence) *Kansas Daily Tribune*, April 9, 1867.

66. "Political," *Leavenworth Daily Conservative*, May 17, 1867.

67. Eskridge is described in *Autobiography of William Allen White* (New York: Macmillan, 1946), 263–64; M. M. Marbury, *The Golden Voice: A Biography of Isaac Kalloch* (New York: Farrar, Straus, 1947).

68. "Female Suffrage. Rogers versus Eskridge," *Emporia News*, June 14, 1867.

69. Untitled, *White Cloud Kansas Chief*, July 4, 1867.

70. Letter from Sam Wood, April 22, 1867, *Emporia News*, May 3, 1867.

71. C.H. Langston to S. N. Wood, Leavenworth, June 20, 1867, Woman Suffrage History Collection, Kansas State Historical Society.

72. Madsen, "The 1867 Campaign," 57; Wilson, *Governor Charles Robinson of Kansas*, 100.

73. "The Pernicious Proposition. Another Letter from Eskridge," *Emporia News*, July 12, 1867.

74. "The Suffrage Convention," *Leavenworth Daily Conservative*, April 5, 1867; Margaret Wood's response in the *Leavenworth Daily Tribune*, May 12, 1867.

75. "Female Suffrage," *Emporia News*, August 2, 1867.

76. "Our Suffrage Imbroglio," *Emporia News*, August 9, 1867.

77. "McMillan versus Wood," *Emporia News*, October 25, 1867.

78. Rev. MacBurney quoted in the *Oskaloosa Independent*, October 19, 1867, as cited in Madsen, "The 1867 Campaign," 123.

79. "How the Papers Stand," *Emporia News*, October 4, 1867. *Venus's Miscellany* is described in Horowitz, *Rereading Sex*, 239–42.

80. Untitled, *Oskaloosa Independent*, July 20, 1867.The leg show was *The Black Crook*. See "Opera House," *Leavenworth Daily Conservative*, July 20, 1867. It opened in New York in September 1866 and ran for an unprecedented fifteen months, generating huge profits; it is often cited as the first Broadway musical and/or the original "girlie" show. I describe its impact in *Women and the American Theatre: Actresses and Audiences, 1790–1870* (New Haven: Yale University Press, 1994), chap. 7.

81. Untitled, *Leavenworth Daily Conservative*, November 5, 1867.

82. "Another Shot," *White Cloud Kansas Chief*, August 15, 1867.

83. Sarah (Sallie) Brown to Auntie, September 8, 1867, John Stillman Brown Family Papers, Kansas State Historical Society, Topeka. See also "A Card," *Lawrence Daily Tribune*, September 8, 1867; "Another Reverend Liar and Slanderer," *Wyandotte Commercial Gazette*, September 17, 1867. The "free lover" charge was leveled against Julia Archibald Holmes, who was then living in Washington, DC, and was the corresponding secretary of the Equal Rights Assn. of Washington. "Letter from Mrs. Julia Archibald Holmes," *Lawrence Daily Tribune*, September 21, 1867.

84. LS to Olympia Brown, September 30, 1867, in BFP/LC; SBA to Anna E. Dickinson, September 23, 1867, in *Selected Papers*, 2: 92.

85. See, for example, "Equality," "Amalgamation," and "Didn't Suit Them," *Leavenworth Daily Commercial*, June 28, July 2 and 6, 1867.

86. "The World Moves," *Wyandotte Democrat*, July 19, 1867.

87. "Emancipation Celebration," *Wyandotte Democrat*, August 2, 1867.

88. "Womanhood and Negrohood," *Wyandotte Democrat*, June 21, 1867; "Negroes Opposed to Female Suffrage," and "Strategy of the Radicals," *Leavenworth Daily Commercial*, August 23 and 25, 1867.

89. Congressional Globe, 39th Congress, 1st Session, part 1, p. 357; Quintard Taylor, *In Search of the Racial Frontier: African Americans in the American West, 1528–1990* (New York: W.W. Norton, 1998), 97. Cf. Leslie A. Schwalm, " 'Overrun with Free Negroes': Emancipation and Wartime Migration in the Upper Midwest," *Civil War History*,1 (June 2004): 145–74, re. Wisconsin, Minnesota, and Iowa.

90. "A Canvass Needed," and "State Affairs," *Leavenworth Daily Conservative*, July 24 and 26, 1867. In mid-August, the Republican State Central Committee finally scheduled a series of mass meetings. "Republican Mass Meetings!" *Leavenworth Daily Conservative*, August 16, 1867.

91. SBA to S. N. Wood, August 9, 1867, in *Papers* 12: 344–49.

92. Kansas had more newspapers than its population could support and patronage was a necessity to many editors. William Frank Zornow, *Kansas: A History of the Jayhawk State* (Norman: University of Oklahoma Press, 1957), 119.

93. "Let Him Vote," *Leavenworth Daily Conservative*, August 16, 1867.

94. "The Fall Elections," *Leavenworth Daily Conservative*, August 10, 1867.

95. "Salutatory" and "Mr. Politics," *Chase County Banner*, August 3, 1867. Only one edition of his *Banner* is extant, so Wood's editorial stance is otherwise undocumented.

96. "A Fair Sample," *Leavenworth Daily Conservative*, August 17, 1867, quoting "Sam Wood's Topeka organ."

97. Henry Blackwell described events: "He [Wood] became discouraged, went home early in August, and has not done anything since. He was taken sick and nearly died, was in bed

three weeks, his wife and children were then sick. He was out of money. The mail to Cottonwood Falls was *robbed* and he never got any letters till a few days ago *for six weeks*. The campaign was left to run itself and of course it ran into the ground." HBB to LS, October 25, 1867, BFP/LC.

98. "Suffrage," *Leavenworth Daily Conservative*, June 30, 1867.

99. "A Letter from C. H. Langston," *Leavenworth Daily Conservative*, August 20, 1867.

100. "Consistency," *Leavenworth Daily Conservative*, August 21, 1867; and "Our Letter from Rover," *Leavenworth Daily Conservative*, August 24, 1867.

101. "What Is Intended," *Leavenworth Daily Conservative*, September 5, 1867.

102. "Reminiscences about Kansas, 1867," Brown Papers, folder 46.

103. "The Suffrage Question," *White Cloud Kansas Chief*, August 22, 1867.

104. No issues of the *Fort Scott Free Press* survive, and the other Fort Scott paper, the *Weekly Monitor*, did not cover Brown's speech. "Impartial Suffrage," *Lawrence State Journal*, August 15, 1867, quotes the *Atchison Champion* on this incident in order to reply to it. The *Champion* reported Brown to have said, "The negro is an ignorant, stupid being, unfit to exercise the right of suffrage."

105. "Impartial Suffrage," *Lawrence State Journal*, August 15, 1867. The editor writes that the *Fort Scott Press* "looks upon the negro very much as does Deacon Pogram of Nasby noto- riety." "Petroleum Nasby" sketches, created by humorist David Ross Locke, poked fun at ignorant, self-complacent racists. John M. Harrison, *The Man Who Made Nasby, David Ross Locke* (Chapel Hill: University of North Carolina Press, 1969). Olympia Brown saved a clipping of this *Lawrence State Journal* article, which expresses confidence that she would not have spoken in such a racist way, and it is found among her papers at the Schlesinger Library.

106. "Correspondence," *Leavenworth Daily Bulletin*, September 6, 1867, a letter purportedly from one who attended a women's suffrage meeting in Wyandotte at which SBA, ECS, and Olympia Brown spoke; "Our Letter from Rover," *Leavenworth Daily Conservative*, August 17, 1867, re. Miami County meetings. The presence of the Hutchinson Family singers, veteran abolitionists, at the Miami County meetings makes it unlikely that black people were actually excluded. In both cases the newspapers reported on events elsewhere, in other towns or counties; falsifying local matters would have been too easily detected by their readers.

107. "The Suffrage Question," *White Cloud Kansas Chief*, August 22, 1867.

108. "'Brother Twine,'" *Atchison Daily Champion*, September 11, 1867.

109. "The Celebration at Monrovia," *Atchison Free Press*, August 2, 1867. Here Twine admitted he had "no love for" women's suffrage as an independent proposition, "and only yielded to it a qualified support as a matter of policy."

110. "'Brother Twine,'" *Atchison Daily Champion*, September 11, 1867; "Suffrage Meeting," *Atchison Free Press*, September 27, 1867.

111. Brown, "An Autobiography," 28.

112. "Impartial Suffrage," *Wyandotte Commercial Gazette*, August 31, 1867.

113. Olympia Brown to S. N. Wood, n.d., 1867, Woman Suffrage History Collection, Kansas State Historical Society, Topeka.

114. This is implied by a newspaper account of her debate with Judge Sears. He spoke first on behalf of black suffrage, and Brown followed and reportedly "took up each point advanced by her opponent, not denying its truth, but showing by unanswerable logic that if it were good for certain reasons for the negro to vote, it was ten times better for the same reasons for the women to vote." *Kansas State Journal* in HWS, 2: 241.

115. Brown, "An Autobiography," 59.

116. "A Social Suffrage Gathering," *Atchison Free Press*, September 4, 1867.

117. "The Right Sentiment," *White Cloud Kansas Chief*, September 26, 1867. According to this account, after the first vote, "Langston expressed the belief that many had not voted their true sentiments, but had been led away with enthusiasm, and proposed another vote.

Before voting he addressed them requesting every one to vote his true sentiment, regardless of everything else. Again the vote was unanimous in favor of the resolution." Langston's motives are unclear: was he tilting against woman suffrage, or trying to ensure that the vote's results could not be questioned?

118. "Impartial Suffrage Meeting at Atchison," *Leavenworth Daily Bulletin,* September 3, 1867.

119. "Langston at Atchison," *Leavenworth Daily Commercial,* June 18, 1867.

120. "Manhood Suffrage!" *Leavenworth Daily Conservative,* September 7, 1867.

121. "Lo the Poor Negro," *Mound City Border Sentinel,* September 27, 1867. The editor, Joel Moody, warned, "If this meeting was a fair sample.... [the black man] has abundant reasons to pray to be delivered from such friends."

122. "Another Reverend Liar and Slanderer," *Wyandotte Commercial Gazette,* September 14, 1867.

123. "The Anti-Suffrage Conclave," *Atchison Free Press,* September 11, 1867; "Why This Fluttering?" *White Cloud Kansas Chief,* September 12, 1867; untitled, *Wyandotte Commercial Gazette,* September 7, 1867.

124. "The Bastard," *Mound City Border Sentinel,* September 13, 1867.

125. "To the Republicans of Kansas," *Leavenworth Daily Conservative,* September 19, 1867.

126. Madsen, "The 1867 Campaign," 80–84.

127. "State Temperance Meeting," *Leavenworth Evening Bulletin,* September 27, 1867; Madsen, "The 1867 Campaign," 11–14, 77; Goldberg, *An Army of Women,* 13–14.

128. LS to HBB, October 13, 1867, BFP/LC. SBA's Falstaff remark in "Train's Second Great Speech," *Lawrence State Journal,* in George Francis Train, *The Great Epigram Campaign of Kansas* (Leavenworth: Prescott & Hume, 1867), 19.

129. "Impartial Suffrage Meeting," *Wyandotte Democrat,* September 6, 1867. Cf. ECS, Speech for Tour for Impartial Suffrage [September 1867], in *Papers,* 12: 484–541; and ECS, Speech on Impartial Suffrage, September 4?, 1867 and later, in *Papers* 12: 375–438, which contain no invidious remarks about black men.

130. "What Is Intended," *Leavenworth Daily Conservative,* September 5, 1867.

131. "The Campaign in Kansas," *NASS,* September 14, 1867, 2–3. Anthony had also known and worked with Sattira A. Douglas when she was in Kansas in 1865, but since then Douglas had resettled in Chicago after her husband's death. *Selected Papers,* 1: 539 n.1.

132. "What Is Intended," *Leavenworth Daily Conservative,* September 5, 1867.

133. "Manhood Suffrage," *Leavenworth Daily Conservative,* September 18, 1867.

134. Untitled, *Wyandotte Commercial Gazette,* September 21, 1867.

135. "The Right Sentiment," *White Cloud Kansas Chief,* September 26, 1867.

136. "The Right Sentiment" and "His Position," *White Cloud Kansas Chief,* September 26, 1867. Before Miller went to press with his editorial remarks, he received the letter from Langston, which he printed in the adjoining column.

137. *HWS,* 2: 264–65. See also *HWS,* 2: 230, 235; LS to SBA, May 1, 1867, in *HWS,* 2: 237.

138. Lucy Stone told Olympia Brown she meant "to keep something constantly in the papers here to help the work with you." LS to Olympia Brown, September 30, 1867, BFP/LC.

139. *HWS,* 2: 247–48.

140. *HWS,* 2: 248–49.

141. The editor of the *Atchison Daily Champion* denounced the appeal as "flimsy" and pounced on Greeley's inconsistencies, saying a fledgling state should hardly be encouraged to experiment by taking such a "nauseating dose." "Take it Yourself," in *HWS,* 2: 249–50.

142. Foner, *Reconstruction,* 313–15.

143. Mohr, *Radical Republicans and Reform in New York,* 254–60; Wang, *Trial of Democracy,* 40–41.

144. "Lessons of the Elections," *Ottawa Western Home Journal,* October 17, 1867; "Kalloch's Meeting," *Wyandotte Commercial Gazette,* October 19, 1867; "Whither Tending?" *Atchison Free Press,* October 15, 1867.

145. "Stand Firm," *White Cloud Kansas Chief,* October 24, 1867; see also "Negro Suffrage," *Atchison Free Press,* October 14, 1867.

146. Untitled, *White Cloud Kansas Chief,* October 24, 1867. Cf. untitled, *Wyandotte Commercial Gazette,* October 26, 1867.

147. "Tilton," *Leavenworth Daily Conservative,* October 11, 1867.

148. "Republicans Attention!" *Leavenworth Daily Conservative,* October 15, 1867.

149. "The Ticket, the Convention," *Atchison Free Press,* October 25, 1967; "Proscription," *Atchison Free Press,* October 29, 1867.

150. Untitled, *White Cloud Kansas Chief,* October 24, 1867; HBB to LS, October 25, 1867, BFP/LC.

151. *Selected Papers,* 2: 95 n. 1, on the various invitations to Train, and SBA to Anna Dickinson, September 23, 1867, in ibid., 2: 93, indicating Anthony's surprise to learn Train was coming. Train had been in Kansas as recently as June. Wilder, *Annals of Kansas,* 456–57.

152. George Francis Train, *My Life in Many States and Foreign Lands* (London: William Heinemann, 1902).

153. "Train in the *Atlantic Monthly,*" *Revolution* 3 (November 25, 1869): 324, quoting A.D. Richardson.

154. In one Kansas speech Train described himself as "that wonderful, eccentric, independent, extraordinary, generous and patriotic reformer of America, who is sweeping off all politicians before him like a hurricane, your modest, diffident, unassuming friend, George Francis Train, the future President of America." "Geo Francis at Ottawa, Kalloch's Headquarters," *Mound City Border Sentinel,* November 1, 1867.

155. George Francis Train, *Young America on Slavery* (Liverpool: Griffin, McGhie, 1859); George Francis Train, *The Facts; or, At Whose Door Does the Sin Lie?* (New York: R. M. DeWitt, 1860); *George Francis Train in Cleaning Out the Copperheads Follows Up George B. McClellan with a Sharp Stick* (New York: American News, 1864). In Pennsylvania in 1864 he argued for protective tariffs, and laced his message with anti-British and anti-Semitic comments. Neely, *The Union Divided,* 154–55.

156. "George Francis Train's First Great Speech," reprinted from the *Leavenworth Commercial,* in Train, *The Great Epigram Campaign,* 7, 10. Train collected press reports from papers of all stripes and had them reprinted in this pamphlet.

157. In the *Great Epigram Campaign,* compare coverage in the two Leavenworth dailies, the Democratic *Commercial* versus the Republican *Conservative.*

158. "George Francis Train Stirring Up the People," *Leavenworth Daily Commercial,* October 24, 1967, shows Train's friendly relation with this Democratic editor.

159. Train, *Great Epigram Campaign,* 28, 37

160. Ibid., 32, 37, 38.

161. George Francis Train to editor of the *Kansas State Journal,* 24 and October 25, 1867, in Train, *Great Epigram Campaign,* 31, 32.

162. *HWS,* 2: 254.

163. The October 25 meeting is reported and the October 31 rally and mass meeting is announced in "The Position of the Colored Man," *Leavenworth Daily Conservative,* October 27, 1867, and *Leavenworth Evening Bulletin,* October 28, 1867. By the day of the mass meeting, the speaker list had been changed: see "Grand Rally," *Leavenworth Daily Conservative,* October 31, 1867. The only coverage of the October 31 meeting after it occurred appeared in a hostile Democratic paper, which reported a large number of blacks and a few whites had assembled, but did not describe the content of the speeches. "Meeting of the Rads," *Leavenworth Daily Commercial,* November 1, 1867.

164. According to the hostile Democratic *Leavenworth Daily Commercial,* October 29, 1867, the ward meeting declared "dat wimen had'nt a right for to vote."

165. Three months later the *Revolution* of February 5, 1868, described Langston as opposed to women's suffrage. No denial or rebuttal appeared in either the *Revolution* or the *National*

Anti-Slavery Standard, so Langston was apparently willing to live with this characterization or felt it was not worthwhile to try to correct matters.

166. Olympia Brown to SBA, March 16, 1882, in *HWS*, 2: 261.

167. Brown, "An Autobiography," 56–57.

168. LS to Olympia Brown, September 30, 1867, BFP/LC. Brown had confided in Stone, and Stone in responding quotes Brown's letter back to her.

169. "Reminiscences about Kansas, 1867," Brown Papers, box 1, folder 46.

170. "G.F.T." reprinted from the *Topeka Leader*, in Train, *Great Epigram Campaign*, 49; "Geo. Francis Train," *Mound City Border Sentinel*, November 1, 1867.

171. "George Francis Train at Ottawa," reprinted in Train, *Great Epigram Campaign*, 40.

172. Kerr, *Lucy Stone*, 129, suggests that Stone wrote to Anthony and begged her to dissociate from Train, but the sources refer to communications after election day.

173. Stanton, *Eighty Years*, 247.

174. Elizabeth Blackwell to HBB, October 22, [1867], BFP/LC. In HBB to LS, October 29, 1867, BFP/LC, Blackwell tells Stone he will "go down to Leavenworth on Wednesday and if not detained there by negotiations with the Democrats, shall start straight homeward same day."

175. "Look Well to Your Tickets," *Oskaloosa Independent*, November 2, 1867.

176. One Republican ticket printed "no" on woman suffrage and one Democratic ticket printed "yes" on woman suffrage are found in the BFP/LC.

177. "The mass of the [Democratic] voters did not know how they voted," Charles Robinson explained, "but took it for granted that they were all right as they were the regular democratic tickets." Charles Robinson to ECS, November 20, 1867, in *Selected Papers*, 2: 102–3.

178. The votes for black suffrage and woman suffrage were highly correlated, with a Pearson coefficient of .831. Excluding the anomalous returns from Leavenworth County (where Democratic leaders had some tickets printed with a yes for woman suffrage), the correlation rises to a very high .923. Official vote totals in *Selected Papers*, 2: Appendix B; statistical computations by Gavin Byrnes, research assistant. Cf. similar results reported in Madsen, "The 1867 Campaign," 102, n.2.

179. Charles Robinson to ECS, November 20, 1867, in *Selected Papers*, 2: 102.

180. Excluding Leavenworth, voting against black suffrage and against woman suffrage were remarkably correlated, with a Pearson coefficient of .976.

181. "A Leader Wanted," *White Cloud Kansas Chief*, November 21, 1867.

182. On the instructive case of Iowa, see Robert R. Dykstra, *Bright Radical Star: Black Freedom and White Supremacy on the Hawkeye Frontier* (1993; paperback edition Ames: Iowa State University Press, 1997), quoted passage 204. Iowa demonstrated that vigorous leadership and strong "vote yes" campaigning could carry black suffrage in a state where Republicans outnumbered Democrats heavily.

183. Shaun Bowler and Todd Donovan, *Demanding Choices: Opinion, Voting, and Direct Democracy* (Ann Arbor: University of Michigan Press, 1998), 35, re. "negativity bias."

184. Wilder, *The Annals of Kansas*, 491, 539, 547. Eskridge became wealthy in land speculation, was influential in the Santa Fe railroad, and continued to abuse his rivals in the pages of his own newspaper, the *Emporia Republican*. See Christopher Childers, "Emporia's Incongruent Reformer: Charles Vernon Eskridge, the *Emporia Republican*, and the Kansas Republican Party, 1860–1900," *Kansas History* 28 (Spring 2005): 2–15. (Childers contended that Eskridge was a "reformer" because in the late 1890s he supported a bimetallic currency, but this argument is not especially persuasive.)

185. Wilder, *Annals of Kansas*, 481, 488; "Kansas," *New York World*, August 31, 1868.

186. James D. Hart, review of *The Golden Voice: A Biography of Isaac Kalloch* by M. M. Marbury in the *New England Quarterly* 21 (June 1948): 273, describes Kalloch as dogged by "accusations of adultery, lawsuits, perjury, blackmail, and shootings."

187. "Stand by Your Guns, Mr. Julian," *Revolution*, January 9, 1869, in *Selected Papers*, 2: 203.

188. Editor Nordhoff as quoted in HBB to S. N. Wood, July 25, 1867, Woman Suffrage History Collection, Kansas Historical Society. Of course there were other forces moving the Republican Party in a conservative direction, especially events in the South.

189. Foner, *Reconstruction,* 313–16; Gillette, *The Right to Vote,* 26, 33; Michael Les Benedict, "The Rout of Radicalism: Republicans and the Election of 1867," *Civil War History* 18 (December 1972): 334–44.

Chapter 6

1. Harper, *Life and Work,* 1: 290–91, 299–300.
2. SBA to Olympia Brown, November 7, 1867, in *Papers* 12: 595.
3. Stanton, *Eighty Years,* 256. Stanton used this phrase repeatedly to characterize working with Train: ECS to Edwin A. Studwell, November 30, 1867, in *Selected Papers,* 2: 117; ECS to Olympia Brown, March 23, 1868, in *Papers* 12:856.
4. "The Political Situation," *Emporia News,* November 15, 1867.
5. "A Review of the Canvass," *Atchison Daily Champion,* November 9, 1867; "Defeat of the Suffrage Question," *Lawrence Daily Tribune,* November 10, 1867; "The Election," *Leavenworth Daily Conservative,* November 7, 1867.
6. "A Touch of Demagogism," *White Cloud Kansas Chief,* November 14, 1867.
7. HWS, 2: 265. In January 1868, Anthony reported that Senator Thayer of Nebraska "said we had killed the negro question in Kansas." "Woman Suffrage at Rahway, N.J.," *Revolution* 1 (January 8, 1868): 3. Horace Greeley even extended the blame to Lucy Stone: "I have always felt that Miss Anthony, Lucy Stone and Mrs. Stanton defeated negro suffrage in Kansas." "Horace Greeley," *Revolution* 3 (September 9, 1869): 52–153.
8. Diary of SBA, January 1, 1868, in *Papers* 12: 786; Lillie Chace to Anna Dickinson, May 29, 1868, Anna Dickinson Papers, Library of Congress.
9. Anthony had always needed a salary to live on, and although Stanton had her inheritance, she also had many children to educate and a husband whose earning power was limited.
10. Harper, *Life and Work,* 1: 293.
11. Dorr, *Susan B. Anthony,* 199, indicates that Train told Anthony he could easily spare $100,000; "Letter from Washington," *Revolution* 3 (February 18, 1869):100, implies that Train actually gave them $5,000; Harper, *Life and Work,* 1: 354, says Train provided about $3,000.
12. Harper, *Life and Work,* 1: 288. See Train, *Great Epigram Campaign,* 58–60, for suggestive comments that appeared in Kalloch's *Western Home Journal* and the *Kansas Radical.*
13. Harper, *Life and Work,* 1: 287–90.
14. SBA to George Francis Train, January 1, 1870, in *Selected Papers,* 2: 288.
15. "Editorial Correspondence," *Revolution* 2 (September 24, 1868): 178.
16. SBA to George Francis Train, January 1, 1870, in *Selected Papers,* 2: 288–89. Anthony wrote, "I saw you take those immense audiences of Irishmen all opposed to woman's voting—and time after time make every man of them vote *aye* before you left."
17. SBA described Train as a "good card" in "Equal Rights," *New York World,* May 15, 1868, in *Papers* 12: 897.
18. Harper, *Life and Work,* 1: 292–93; Stanton, *Eighty Years,* 256; "George Francis Train," *Revolution* 4 (October 21, 1869): 252.
19. *Nebraska City News,* October 28, 1871, in *The People's Candidate for President, 1872, the Man of Destiny etc.* (New York: n.p., 1872), 32.
20. Willis Thornton, *The Nine Lives of Citizen Train* (New York: Greenberg, 1948), 147, emphasizes Train's changeability.
21. "Lecture by George Francis Train," *Boston Journal,* September 26, 1862; "Grand Ratification Meeting," *Boston Journal,* October 7, 1862; "Lecture of George Francis Train," *Boston Journal,* October 29, 1862. Caroline Severance wrote that Anthony and Stanton's

tour with Train was "strange, insane.... They cannot know of his antecedents in Boston." *Selected Papers*, 2: 120 n.3.

22. "William Lloyd Garrison," *Revolution* 1 (January 29, 1868): 50. ECS told Charles Robinson that Train had revealed more progressive views in private, but Robinson protested, "We have to deal with the man as he stands before the public... and not with him in his private tete a tete with you and Miss A." Charles Robinson to ECS, December 5, 1867, in *Papers* 12: 635.

23. "Letter from George Francis Train," *Revolution* 3 (May 8, 1869): 279.

24. "George Francis Train in the Jaws of the British Lion," *Revolution* 1 (January 22, 1868): 43.

25. By May 1868 he was admitting that on the slavery question, "I was wrong," and vowing "I will never again spell negro with two g's." "Letter from Mr. Train," *Revolution* 1 (June 18, 1868): 379.

26. SBA to Olympia Brown, July 20, 1868, in *Selected Papers*, 2: 154–55.

27. Stanton, *Eighty Years*, 256.

28. This letter dated November 9, 1867, and "signed" by SBA and ECS, plus Lucy Stone, Olympia Brown, and others, announced the speaking tour engagements and praised Train immoderately."Suffrage Speeches," *Atchison Free Press*, November 11, 1867. See also Charles Robinson to ECS, November 20, 1867, in *Selected Papers*, 2: 102–3

29. "The Suffrage Question," *Chicago Tribune*, November 23, 1867, in *Papers* 12: 591; speech by SBA in St. Louis, November 1867, in *Selected Papers*, 2: 108–9.

30. ECS, "Kansas," *Revolution* 1 (January 8, 1868): 1, announced that Train "galvanized the Democrats...thus securing 9,000 votes for woman suffrage." "To Our Radical Friends," *Revolution* 1(May 14, 1868): 296; "Hon. Charles Robinson, Ex-Governor of Kansas," *Revolution* 1 (February 15, 1868): 68; Mrs. H. A. Monroe to Mrs. Stanton, *Revolution* 3 (January 14, 1869): 19; F. Barry, "Who Cast the Vote?" *Revolution* 1 (February 15, 1868): 68.

31. Olympia Brown, perhaps the best judge of the matter, thought Train had caused woman suffrage "to lose a few hundreds of votes" in the last weeks before the election. Autobiographical fragment, directed to Mrs. Weston, April 21, 1871, Brown Papers.

32. Gerrit Smith refers to Train as a "heavy load to carry," in *Revolution* 1 (March 12, 1868): 153; Frances Dana Gage called Train "a drag in spite of his money, his energy, and his honesty" in *Revolution* 3 (April 1, 1869): 194.

33. "The Anti-Slavery Society," *New York World*, May 14, 1868, in *Papers* 12: 893–95; see also Phillips's tone in WP to LS, November 18, 1867, BFP/LC.

34. "The Anti-Slavery Society," *New York World*, May 14, 1868, in *Papers* 12: 894–95.

35. "George Francis Train Challenges Wendell Phillips," *Revolution* 1 (January 8, 1868): 5. In February 1868 Train was on a lecture tour of New England in which he made dozens of speeches, so this charge may have been repeated widely. See also untitled, *Sunday Mercury* (New York), December 15, 1867, in *Papers* 12: 646; "George Francis Train's Crusade through New England," *Revolution* 3 (February 25, 1869): 119, where Train writes, "Our old friend Hovey gave fifty thousand dollars to women, negroes and Free Trade. W. P. kindly took forty-five thousand for negroes, and left women to be saved in Kansas by a 'Copperhead.'"

36. "Protest," *Revolution* 1 (January 22, 1868): 41; "What the People Say to Us," *Revolution* 1 (May 14, 1868): 294.

37. Anthony went to Boston in July 1868, evidently hoping that the Hovey Fund might yet be persuaded to cover some of her expenses in Kansas, but the negative response left her so shaken she left town "so *soul sick* of the *icy faces* of Boston that I felt I could not stop another minute." SBA to Olympia Brown, July 20, 1868, in *Selected Papers*, 2: 154–55.

38. "Republican Pusillanimity," *Revolution* 1 (February 5, 1868): 73.

39. WLG to SBA, January 4, [1868] in *Selected Papers*, 2: 124–25.

40. Garrison, a fund trustee, wanted the rest of the fund to go to black education, channeled through the American Freedmen's Union Commission, while Phillips wanted it to promote

black suffrage, channeled through subsidies to the *National Anti-Slavery Standard*. Pro-Garrison and pro-Phillips factions among the trustees struck a deal to divide the money, but when Congress passed the Reconstruction Act (which imposed black suffrage on the South), Garrison felt released from the deal and unbeknown to the others, he prevailed on the court-appointed "master in chancery" to rule that *all* the money should go to education. *NASS*, July 20 and August 10 and 24, 1867; "The Diversion of Francis Jackson's Bequest," *Commonwealth*, August 17, 1867; "The Jackson Bequest," *Commonwealth*, September 7, 1867; "Mr. Garrison," *Revolution* 1 (March 19, 1868): 169; WLG to Samuel May, Jr., March 10, 1867, Abolitionist Papers, Ms.A.1.1, vol. 7, p. 31a.

41. Garrison looked bad and would have looked worse had it been revealed that the educational organization to which he wanted the funds tendered was paying him a handsome salary. "Correspondence. From New York," *Commonwealth*, September 7, 1867.

42. ECS to Edwin A. Studwell, November 30, 1867, in *Papers* 12: 613–14.

43. *New York Herald*, December 15, 1867, in *Selected Papers,* 2: 120 n. 3.

44. WP to LS, November 18, 1867, BFP/LC. See also HBB to LS, October 29, 1867, BFP/LC, estimating the reimbursement needed. In LS to HBB, October 11, 1867 (Wheeler, *Loving Warriors*, 219–20), Stone told Blackwell, who was then in Kansas, "If SBA pushes to know about funds, tell her we paid a good deal from our private money—and that Phillips is willing we should draw from the Jackson fund, so much as we will give our personal guarantee for." In fact, the reimbursement flowed from the fund to Stone and Blackwell and not vice versa.

45. ECS to the editor of the *New York World*, in *Selected Papers*, 2: 119–20.

46. LS to Olympia Brown, January 6, 1868, Brown Papers.

47. LS to WLG, March 6, 1868, Abolitionist Papers, Ms.A.1.2, v. 36, p. 188.

48. Harper, *Life and Work*, 1: 298.

49. LS to WLG, March 6, 1868, Abolitionist Papers, Ms.A.1.2, v. 36, p. 188.

50. *Proceedings of the First Anniversary of the AERA*, 62–63, in *Papers* 12: 185.

51. HBB to LS, October 29, 1867, BFP/LC. One biographer argues that Henry Blackwell (together with Charles Robinson and Sam Wood) actually invited Train to Kansas in the first place, although Blackwell eventually blamed Anthony for issuing the invitation and thus harming the cause. See Barry, *Susan B. Anthony*, 180–82.

52. SBA to WP, November 4, 1866, in *Papers* 11: 621.

53. Andrea Moore Kerr, who uncovered the evidence of Henry Blackwell's infatuation with a "Mrs. P," concludes that she was probably Abby Hutchinson Patton, a much younger woman who was a member of the singing Hutchinson family and the wife of Henry's business associate Ludlow Patton. Kerr, *Lucy Stone*, 136–37, 270–71 n.26.

54. LS to Antoinette Brown Blackwell, October 31, 1869, BFP/LC.

55. George Francis Train bore some resemblance to Henry Blackwell: each was entrepreneurial, erratic, full of himself, and devoted to women's rights. Attacking the *Revolution* became all the more effective as therapy for Stone's marital difficulties when it began to air out unorthodox ideas about marriage and divorce laws, and by 1870 Stone would make this her chief explanation of her split with Anthony and Stanton. LS to HBB, November 25, 1870, BFP/LC referring to an editorial, "Woman Suffrage and Marriage," in *Harper's Weekly*, November 26, 1870.

56. SBA to Thomas Wentworth Higginson, May 20, 1868, in *Selected Papers*, 2: 141.

57. "Meeting of the American Equal Rights Association in New York," *New York World*, May 15, 1868, in *Selected Papers*, 2: 137–38.

58. SBA to Thomas Wentworth Higginson, May 20, 1868, in *Selected Papers*, 2: 141–42.

59. SBA to Anna E. Dickinson, July 10, 1868, in *Selected Papers*, 2: 152–53.

60. HBB to Edwin A. Studwell, January 16, 1869, BFP/Schlesinger.

61. The issue resurfaced at the 1869 AERA meeting. See "Women of the Period," *New York World*, May 13, 1869, in *Papers* 13: 503. By that time, SBA had given up her claim to the $1,000, agreeing to consider it a donation to the cause, and Blackwell was therefore willing

to defend her. In 1870 Anthony believed that Stone was still keeping the story alive, telling people she was a "thief." See SBA to Anna E. Dickinson, March 22, 1870, in *Selected Papers*, 2: 313.

62. "Equal Rights," *New York World*, May 15, 1868, in *Papers* 12: 898.

63. Ibid. Brown stuck to this view in the *HWS* where she blamed the Kansas defeat on Republican leaders who "selfishly and meanly" sold out principles for "a miserable mess of pottage in the shape of office and emoluments." *HWS*, 2: 260–61. In unpublished reminiscences she similarly concluded, "Every vote gained was gained in spite of political wire working and party influence." Olympia Brown, "Reminiscences about Kansas, 1867," folder 46, Brown Papers.

64. "Equal Rights," *New York World*, May 15, 1868, in *Papers* 12: 898. Douglass may have been more confrontational in the AERA business meeting, where according to the *World* reporter, SBA referred to Train spelling negro with two G's, Douglass objected, and then "a general talk ensued." "Meeting of the American Equal Rights Association in New York," May 14, 1868, in *Selected Papers*, 2: 138.

65. Much of Douglass's antebellum conflict with the Garrisonians was sparked by funding jealousies, and much of what he appreciated about Gerrit Smith was the way Smith's financial generosity did not come with strings attached. As for racist allies, Douglass had recently had the experience of seeing his own white political allies fall embarrassingly short, at a National Union Convention in August 1866. Martin, *Mind of Frederick Douglass*, 80–81; Blight, *Frederick Douglass' Civil War*, 192–93; McFeely, *Frederick Douglass*, 150–51, 250–51.

66. "Equal Suffrage Defeated," *Douglass' Monthly* 3 (December 1860): 369.

67. SBA to Olympia Brown, January 1, 1868, in *Papers* 12: 788.

68. Caroline Dall, "Report Made to the Eleventh National Woman's Rights Convention," in *Proceedings of the Eleventh National Woman's Rights Convention*, 65, in *Papers* 11: 507.

69. SBA to John Russell Young, November 16, 1866, in *Papers* 11: 645–47.

70. She did win notice in the New York papers, but largely in the form of brief and sometimes humorous paragraphs rather than opportunities for extended communication. "Mrs. Stanton for Congress," *NASS*, October 20, 1866.

71. Summers, *Press Gang*, chaps. 12 and 13, notes northern journalism's indifference or hostility to radicalism and Reconstruction. Also useful on the press of the period: William E. Huntziker, *The Popular Press, 1833–1865* (Westport, Conn.: Greenwood Press, 1999); Gerald Baldasty, *The Commercialization of News in the Nineteenth Century* (Madison: University of Wisconsin Press, 1992); Menahem Blondheim, "'Public Sentiment Is Everything:' The Union's Public Communications Strategy and the Bogus Proclamation of 1864," *Journal of American History* 89 (December 2002): 869–99.

72. Summers, *Press Gang*, 40.

73. Robert C. Williams, *Horace Greeley: Champion of American Freedom* (New York: New York University Press, 2006), 271–74.

74. George T. McJimsey, *Genteel Partisan: Manton Marble, 1834–1917* (Ames: Iowa State University Press, 1971).

75. On the power of the press in this period, see Summers, *Press Gang*, 69; Parker Pillsbury, "Deceitfulness of the Press," *Revolution* 1 (April 9, 1868): 211. "Slang-whanging" in Meyer, *All on Fire*, 40.

76. John W. Forney, *Anecdotes of Public Men* (New York: Harper Bros., 1874), 1:383, as cited in Gienapp, "Politics Seem to Enter into Everything," in *Essays on American Antebellum Politics, 1840–1860*, 41.

77. "Home Notes," *Commonwealth*, May 13, 1865; *NASS*, June 3, 1865; "The Nation," *Commonwealth*, February 17, 1866; Frank Preston Stearns, *The Life and Public Services of George Luther Stearns* (Philadelphia: J. B. Lippincott, 1907), 332–38; McPherson, *Struggle for Equality*, 323–25.

78. *American National Biography,* s.v. "Stearns, George Luther," by Louis S. Gerteis, accessed October 9, 2010, http://0-www.anb.org.library.colgate.edu/articles; "The Death of George L. Stearns," *NASS,* April 27, 1867.

79. See "Remarks of Miss [Mary] Grew," *NASS,* December 8, 1866.

80. SBA to Edwin A. Studwell, August 20, 186[6], in *Selected Papers,* 1: 590–91; SBA to Unknown, [ca.November 4, 1866], in *Papers* 11: 626.

81. Lucretia Mott to Martha C. Wright, June 10, 1866, in Palmer, *Selected Letters of Lucretia Mott,* 374; Harper, *Life and Work,* 1: 262–63.

82. SBA to Unknown, [ca. November 4, 1866], in *Papers* 11: 626.

83. Francis Lieber, *Reflections on the Changes which May Seem Necessary in the Present Constitution of the State of New York* (New York: Union League Club, 1867), 34.

84. Tayler Lewis, "Household Suffrage," *Independent,* December 6 and 20, 1866; Rev. John A. Todd, *Woman's Rights* (Boston: Lee & Shepard, 1867); "Correspondence. New York," *Commonwealth,* June 15, 1867. Lieber wrote to Professor Emory Washburn at Harvard Law School that woman suffrage must be discussed "free from namby-pamby Better-half-ism, looking plainly at God's ordinance and his Word." He boasted, "Some of my friends pretend to be in favor of woman suffrage, but all their wives are for me." Lieber to Washburn, July 14, 1867, Francis Lieber Papers, Huntington Library, San Marino, CA.

85. Keyssar, *The Right to Vote,* 181–83; David M. Quigley, *Second Founding: New York City, Reconstruction, and the Making of American Democracy* (New York: Hill & Wang, 2004); Sven Beckert, "Democracy in the Age of Capital: Contesting Suffrage Rights in Gilded Age New York," in *The Democratic Experiment: New Directions in American Political History,* ed. Meg Jacobs, William J. Novak, and Julian E. Zelizer (Princeton: Princeton University Press, 2003), 146–74.

86. See *Selected Papers,* 2: 69 n. 2, 80 n. 2, 86–87 n.1; "The Michigan Constitutional Convention–Woman Suffrage," *New York Times,* July 29, 1867.

87. "Universal Suffrage in Earnest," *New York World,* December 25, 1865; coverage of woman suffrage petitions in *New York World,* February 3, 7, 15, and 22, 1866.

88. Untitled, *New York World,* April 2, 1866; untitled, *New York World,* May 11, 1866.

89. "Mrs. Stanton and the Radicals," *New York World,* October 12, 1866.

90. "The Negroes and Woman Suffrage," *New York World,* June 15, 1867.

91. "Woman as a Voter," *New York World,* December 6, 1866.

92. An exceptional case is "Shall Women Vote?" *New York World,* December 8, 1866, re. a speech by Olympia Brown emphasizing the suffrage rights of the black woman. Marble denies his support in untitled, *New York World,* May 11, 1866; "Spinster Suffrage in the Senate," *New York World,* December 14, 1866.

93. For example, *World* headlines screamed "Reign of Terror" when reporting that a white man knocked down a black man and was therefore arrested. A "Shocking Occurrence in Georgia" involved one drunken white man shooting another, while black people who fled in all directions were somehow to blame. "Riotous Conduct of the Black Loyal Leaguers. A Reign of Terror Inaugurated," *New York World,* January 3, 1868. The *World* had the brass to insist on the accuracy of its reports, indignantly denying Republican reports to the contrary. "Reconstruction Portrayed," *New York World,* January 1, 1868.

94. Untitled, *New York World,* October 5, 1867.

95. "Washington," *New York World,* April 16, 1867.

96. Benedict, *Compromise of Principle,* 262–64, 275–76; McJimsey, *Genteel Partisan,* 99–102; "The Party in Power and Its Cost to the Country," *New York World,* February 21, 1867.

97. "The Working Woman's Association," *Revolution* 2 (November 5, 1868): 280.

98. "One Hundred Thousand Subscribers," *Revolution* 1 (April 30, 1868): 264; ECS to Ellen Dwight Eaton, December 17 [1867], in *Papers* 12: 655–58.

99. McJimsey, *Genteel Partisan,* 27–32. Whitelaw Reid also came from a family of modest means, but persuaded investors to back his bid for editorial control of the *Tribune* and

became wealthy in just a few years' time. Bingham Duncan, *Whitelaw Reid: Journalist, Politician, Diplomat* (Athens: University of Georgia Press, 1975), 20, 47, 57.

100. "Wendell Phillips a Friend Indeed," *Revolution* 1 (January 29, 1868): 52; Harper, *Life and Work,* 1: 298, quoting Stanton: "Our paper has a monied basis of $50,000, and men who understand business to push it"; and "Is the Revolution a Fact?" *Revolution* 1 (January 29, 1868): 58.

101. Wendell Phillips was assured that a newspaper with progressive politics had commercial potential in George Smalley to WP, January 7, 1866, Phillips Papers, bMS Am 1953.

102. *Boston Advertiser,* quoted in "What the Press Says of Us," *Revolution* 1 (February 5, 1868): 66.

103. Letter of Charles E. Moss, *Revolution* 2 (December 24, 1868): 390.

104. *New York World,* quoted in "What the Press Says of the Revolution," *Revolution* 1 (January 22, 1868): 34; *The Round Table,* quoted in "What the Press Says of Us," *Revolution* 1 (January 29, 1868): 51.

105. Stone as humorless in Blackwell, *Lucy Stone,* 259; popular taste in Dudden, *Women in the American Theatre,* chap. 7

106. ECS to Ellen Dwight Eaton, December 17 [1867], in *Papers* 12: 658; Stanton, *Eighty Years,* 257.

107. Harper, *Life and Work,* 1: 354–56

108. Stanton, *Eighty Years,* 257–58. On advertising rather than circulation as the source of profit for newspapers, see Richard Grant White, "The Manners and Morals of Journalism," *Galaxy* 8 (1869): 846.

109. "The Third Volume," *Revolution* 2 (July 1, 1869): 401.

110. "Woman Suffrage at Rahway, N.J.," *Revolution* 1 (January 8, 1868): 3; "George Francis Train before the Constitutional Convention at Albany," *Revolution* 1 (January 8, 1868): 6; "To Our Radical Friends," *Revolution* 1 (May 14, 1868): 296; "The Chicago Platform under the Ink," *Revolution* 1 (May 28, 1868): 328.

111. David Paul Nord, "William Lloyd Garrison," in Perry J. Ashley, ed., *American Newspaper Journalists,* in *Dictionary of Literary Biography,* vol. 43 (Detroit: Bruccoli Clark, 1985), 238; "The Chicago Tribune," *Revolution* 2 (July 30, 1868): 56.

112. Harper, *Life and Work,* 1: 295, says it "caused a sensation."

113. "Republican Pusilanimity," *Revolution* 1 (February 5, 1868): 73; "What the People Say to Us," *Revolution* 1 (May 28, 1868): 324.

114. "What the People Say to Us," *Revolution* 1 (May 28, 1868): 324; "What the People Say to Us," *Revolution* 1 (June 18, 1868): 373.

115. "Are We a Slaveholding Nation?" *Revolution* 1 (January 8, 1868): 9.

116. "To the Southern Press," *Revolution* 1 (January 15, 1868): 26; "Educated Suffrage," *Revolution* 1 (April 16, 1868): 232. Cf. Parker Pillsbury, "The Ballot," *Revolution* 1 (March 26, 1868): 184; "What the Press Says of Us," *Revolution* 1 (May 28, 1868): 322, which explains that Pillsbury remains a supporter of educated suffrage, while Stanton now opposes it.

117. *A Report on the Condition of the Cause of Woman Suffrage Made to the Universal Franchise Association, by James H. Holmes, General Agent, Together with the First Annual Report of the Corresponding Secretary* (Washington, D.C.: Universal Franchise Association, 1868). Other leaders included ex-Kansan Julia Archibald Holmes and her husband James, and Professor J. K. H. Willcox. See J. K. H. Willcox, *Suffrage a Right, Not a Privilege* (Washington, D.C.: Universal Franchise Association, 1867); HWS, 3: 809–11.

118. *Notable American Women,* s.v. "Griffing, Josephine;" HWS, 2: 26–39; Keith E. Melder, "Angel of Mercy in Washington: Josephine Griffing and the Freedmen, 1864–1872," *Records of the Columbia Historical Society of Washington, D.C.* (1963–65), 243–72.

119. Katherine Masur, "Reconstructing the Nation's Capital: The Politics of Race and Citizenship in the District of Columbia, 1862–1878" (Ph.D. diss., University of Michigan, 2001), 292–321; Alan Lessoff, *The Nation and Its City: Politics, "Corruption," and Progress in Washington, D.C., 1861–1902* (Baltimore: Johns Hopkins University Press, 1994), 52–56.

120. Professor Willcox pointed out the implications of the 1867 city census in "Rebeldom Regaining Washington," *Revolution* 3 (March 18, 1869): 171, indicating woman suffrage might yield a net gain to the Radicals of 6,000 votes.

121. "Franchise the Guarantee of Freedom," *NASS*, August 22, 1868. The backers of woman suffrage in Washington thus included black activists, the *Revolution*, and Wendell Phillips's *NASS*. See *Revolution* editions of February 19, April 9, 14, and 16, and May 21, 1868; and *NASS* editions of May 23, June 20, and August 1, 1868.

122. "White Woman's Suffrage Association," *Revolution* 1 (June 4, 1868): 337.

123. "Woman Suffrage," *Revolution* 1 (June 11, 1868): 362.

124. "Affairs in the District of Columbia," *NASS*, August 22, 1868.

125. "Annual Meeting of the Universal Franchise Association," *NASS*, October 10, 1868.

126. ECS, "Sharp Points," *Revolution* 1 (April 9, 1868): 212–13.

127. "William Lloyd Garrison," *Revolution* 1 (January 29, 1868): 50.

128. "Sharp Points," *Revolution* 1 (April 9, 1868): 212; Leach, *True Love and Perfect Union*, 143–52; Melanie Gustafson, *Women and the Republican Party, 1854–1924* (Urbana: University of Illinois Press, 2001), 39.

129. "Manhood Suffrage," *Revolution* 2 (December 24, 1868): 392.

130. ECS, "Kansas," *Revolution* 1 (January 8, 1868): 1.

131. "A Black Man on the Ballot for Women," *Revolution* 1 (February 5, 1868): 74.

132. ECS, "Sharp Points," *Revolution* 1 (April 9, 1868): 212.

133. LS to Abby Kelley Foster, January 24, 1867, in Wheeler, *Loving Warriors*, 215–16.

134. "The Anniversaries," *New York Tribune*, May 15, 1868, in *Papers* 12: 900.

135. "George Francis Train and Woman's Rights," *Buffalo Commercial Advertiser*, December 2, 1867, in *Papers* 12: 615.

136. ECS, "William Lloyd Garrison," *Revolution* 1 (January 29, 1868): 50.

137. When an Ohio paper characterized the *Revolution* as "setting forth the right of intelligent women to the ballot before ignorant negroes," the *Revolution* editors corrected them, insisting on simultaneity: "No, not exactly. We are willing to go into the kingdom with negroes; but we say, no more men at the ballot box until we too are admitted." "What the Press Says of Us," *Revolution* 2 (July 23, 1868): 36.

138. "Sharp Points," *Revolution* 1 (April 9, 1868): 212, contained a letter from J. Elizabeth Jones dated February 27, 1868.

139. "What the People Say to Us," *Revolution* 1 (June 18, 1868): 372–73, contained Jones's second letter, dated June 1, 1868, and Stanton's answer to it.

140. Ibid, 373.

141. The political history summarized below is based largely on Foner, *Reconstruction*; Benedict, *Compromise of Principle*; and Montgomery, *Beyond Equality*.

142. "Correspondence. From New York," *Commonwealth*, February 8, 1868; Heather Cox Richardson, *West from Appomattox* (New Haven: Yale University Press, 2007), 2–3, 24–25, 121.

143. "Remarks by SBA to the Union League of America (Colored)," June 22, 1868, in *Selected Papers*, 145.

144. ECS, "New Men," *Revolution* 1 (April 2, 1868): 200.

145. "A New Party," *Revolution* 1 (January 8, 1868): 10.

146. See, for example, ECS, "Going Over to the Copperheads," and PP, "The Revolution Too Democratic" in *Revolution* 1 (June 11, 1868): 361.

147. "Progressive Democracy," *Revolution* 1 (April 9, 1868): 218; ECS, "Editorial Correspondence," *Revolution* 2 (August 13, 1868): 81.

148. ECS, "To Our Radical Friends," *Revolution* 1 (May 14, 1868): 296.

149. "Women Suffrage at Rahway, New Jersey," *Revolution* 1 (January 8, 1868): 3; ECS, "Editorial Correspondence, Washington, D.C." *Revolution* 1 (February 12, 1868): 81; ECS, "Washington Gossip," *Revolution* 1 (March 5, 1868): 138.

150. Stewart, *Wendell Phillips*, 283–85. The text of the speech is found in the *NASS*, May 25, 1867.

151. "Thirty-Eighth Annual Meeting of the New England Anti-Slavery Convention," *NASS*, June 13, 1868.
152. ECS, "The Last Republican Lamp has Gone Out," *Revolution* 1 (May 21, 1868): 312.
153. ECS, "State Rights," *Revolution*, June 25, 1868, in *Selected Papers*, 2: 147–50.
154. John Niven, *Salmon P. Chase: A Biography* (New York: Oxford University Press, 1995), 428–32; *Selected Papers*, 2: 149–50, n. 1 and n. 3; "The Democratic Candidate," *New York Herald*, July 3, 1868; "Prospects of the Democratic Ticket," *New York Sun*, July 18, 1868.
155. According to Harper, ECS and SBA also approached the Republican convention but got no response. *Life and Work*, 1: 305.
156. ECS, "Will Tammany Hall Accept the Situation?" *Revolution* 1 (June 4, 1868): 347; "Tammany Hall Platform," *Revolution* 1 (July 2, 1868): 408.
157. "Andrew Johnson and Miss Anthony," *Revolution* 2 (July 9, 1968): 1.
158. Foner, *Reconstruction*, 339–40; Niven, *Salmon P. Chase*, 428–32, on the forces at work in the emergence of the Seymour-Blair ticket.
159. SBA to Anna Dickinson, July 10, 1868, in *Selected Papers*, 2: 152.
160. Salmon P. Chase to SBA, July 14, 1868, in *Papers* 12: 976.
161. "The Situation," *NASS*, August 29, 1868.
162. Stewart, *Wendell Phillips*, 290.
163. "Grant and Negro Suffrage," *Revolution* 2 (September 10, 1868): 152.
164. DuBois describes Stanton and Anthony's appeal to the Democrats but drops the thread after the Democratic National Convention, instead dealing at length with their turn toward labor alliances in *Feminism and Suffrage*, 110–61.
165. "Workingwoman's Association," *Revolution* 2 (September 24, 1868): 181–82. The group met regularly and debated ways to advance the interests of workingwomen, including producers' coops and a women's typographical union. See *Revolution* 2 (October 8 and 15, 1868): 214–15, 231.
166. "National Labor Congress," *Revolution* 2 (October 1, 1868): 197, 204–5.
167. ECS, "National Labor Congress," *Revolution* 2 (October 1, 1968): 200.
168. ECS, "Frank Blair on Woman's Suffrage," *Revolution* 2 (October 1, 1868): 200. Stanton referred her readers to the *New York World* of September 26, 1868, which carried the speech in full. The *Revolution* again recommended Blair's speech in "Frank Blair on Woman's Suffrage,"*Revolution* 2 (October 15, 1868): 235.
169. ECS to Francis Preston Blair, Jr., October 1, 1868, in *Papers* 13: 70; *New York World*, October 3, 1868.
170. "The Indiana Canvass," *New York World*, September 26, 1868, giving the speech in its entirety in four columns on page one. For its dispersion, see, for example, "Gen. Blair's Speech," *New Orleans Times*, September 29, 1868, reprinting a special dispatch to the Cincinnati *Commercial*.
171. "The Indiana Canvass," *New York World*, September 26, 1868.
172. Foner, *Reconstruction*, 341. Republican reaction in "The 'Carpetbag Governments'—Shall They Be Overthrown?" *Hartford Daily Courant*, September 16, 1868.
173. Historians agree that the trope of the black rapist became more common after the Civil War, although the attribution of uncontrolled sexuality to black men dated to the eighteenth century or earlier. Winthrop Jordan, *White over Black*, 473; Martha Hodes, "Wartime Dialogues on Illicit Sex: White Women and Black Men," in *Divided Houses: Gender and the Civil War*, ed. Catherine Clinton and Nina Silber (New York: Oxford University Press, 1992), 240–41; Martha Hodes, "The Sexualization of Reconstruction Politics: White Women and Black Men in the South after the Civil War," *Journal of the History of Sexuality* 3 (January 1993): 402–17; Diane Miller Sommerville, "The Rape Myth in the Old South Reconsidered," *Journal of Southern History* 61 (August 1995): 481–518; Diane Miller Sommerville, *Rape and Race in the Nineteenth Century South* (Chapel Hill: University of North Carolina Press, 2004). Crystal N. Feimster, *Southern Horrors:*

Women and the Politics of Rape and Lynching (Cambridge: Harvard University Press, 2009), 47–55 associates the rise of the rape myth with "redemption politics" and Democratic Party resistance to Reconstruction. . None of these sources mentions the Blair speech. Frederick Douglass and Ida B. Wells condemned the rape charge as an invention to justify violence against black people in "Why Is the Negro Lynched?" (1894) in Phillip S. Foner, *The Life and Writings of Frederick Douglass* (New York: International Publishers, 1955), 4: 501–2; "The Reason Why the Colored American Is Not in the World's Columbian Exposition," in *Selected Works of Ida B. Wells-Barnett,* ed. Trudier Harris (New York: Oxford University Press, 1991), 56, 74.

174. "The Indiana Canvass," *New York World,* September 26, 1868. Blair was eventually forced to disabuse woman suffragists of their illusions; see Frank Blair to Mrs. Francis Minor, president of the Woman Suffrage Association of Missouri, October 13, 1869, in Blair Family Papers, LC.

175. Henry Clay Warmoth, *War, Politics and Reconstruction: Stormy Days in Louisiana* (New York: Macmillan, 1930), 65.

176. See *NASS,* September 5, 1868.

177. "Radical Forgeries," *New York World,* October 2, 1868.

178. Ted Tunnell, *Crucible of Reconstruction: War, Radicalism and Race in Louisiana, 1862–1877* (Baton Rouge: Louisiana State University Press, 1984), 154–57; George C. Rable, *But There Was No Peace: The Role of Violence in the Politics of Reconstruction* (Athens: University of Georgia Press, 1984), 67–79; Allen W. Trelease, *White Terror: The Ku Klux Klan Conspiracy and Southern Reconstruction* (Baton Rouge: Louisiana State University Press, 1971), 49–185; Michael W. Fitzgerald, "Reconstruction Politics and the Politics of Reconstruction," in *Reconstructions: New Perspective on the Postbellum United States,* ed. Thomas J. Brown (New York: Oxford University Press, 2006), 97, ref. to the Democrats' "quasi-insurrectionary campaign."

179. Blair as cited in Foner, *Reconstruction,* 340.

180. "General Blair on Woman Suffrage," *New York World,* October 3, 1868; "Mrs. Elizabeth Cady Stanton," *Macon (Ga.) Weekly Telegraph,* published as *Georgia Weekly Telegraph,* September 25, 1868, accessed October 9, 2010, America's Historical Newspapers. Cf. "Woman's Suffrage," *Flakes* (Galveston, Tex.) *Bulletin,* October 13, 1868, America's Historical Newspapers.

181. Rable, *There Was No Peace,* 71. On a single particularly busy day, August 7, 1868, one page of the *World* carried articles with the following headlines: "The Texas Negro Insurrection," "Negro Riot in Mobile—Street Cars Seized by Black Radicals," "Negro Riot in Macon—Murderous Assault on a White Cripple—White Radicals Instigate the Riot," "Tragedy in Mississippi—A Man Shot Down in the Midst of His Family—The Assassination Instigated by the Loyal League."

182. *New York World,* September 10, 15, 16, 17, 1868.

183. Untitled editorial, *New York World,* September 25, 1868.

184. Warmoth, who was the same age as her son Neil, publicly endorsed Stanton's congressional bid in 1866. "Local Politics: Radical Mass and Ratification Meeting," *New York Times,* October 23, 1866. Michael Hahn called on her when he visited New York City in 1869: "What the People Say," *Revolution* 3 (June 24, 1869): 390. Warmoth, *War, Politics and Reconstruction,* 65, 29–30.

185. Rice, "Henry B. Stanton as a Political Abolitionist," 470; Janet E. Steele, *The Sun Shines for All: Journalism and Ideology in the Life of Charles A. Dana* (Syracuse, N.Y.: Syracuse University Press, 1993), 84–89.

186. *Selected Papers,* 2: xxvi.

187. FD to Josephine Griffing, September 27, 1868, in Foner, *Life and Writings of Frederick Douglass,* 4: 212–13.

188. Douglass as "warmly" in favor of Grant, in *NASS,* February 29, 1868; Douglass announces his ambition to go to Congress in *NASS,* April 25, 1868.

189. "The Work before Us," *Independent*, August 27, 1868, in Foner, *Life and Writings of Frederick Douglass*, 4: 210.

190. Stanton was in New Jersey so much that Anthony had to apologize for her absences. SBA to Anna Dickinson, October 15, 1868, in *Papers* 13: 93.

191. "Seymour and Blair," *New York World*, October 19 and 20, 1868; "Blair in New York—Seymour Nowhere," *Hartford Daily Courant*, October 29, 1868, accessed October 9, 2010, America's Historical Newspapers.

192. ECS, "The Old Year Is Gone," *Revolution* 2 (December 31, 1868): 409.

193. "Southern Suffrage," *Revolution* 2 (July 23, 1868): 42.

194. "To the Southern Press," *Revolution* 1 (January 15, 1868): 26.

195. "An Autobiography," *Revolution* 1 (January 22, 1868): 37, from Jeremiah Peck, who identified himself as a former slave from Crawford County, Georgia, welcoming their new paper; Parker Pillsbury, "Who Owns the South?" *Revolution* 1 (February 12, 1868): 88.

196. "What the People Say to Us," *Revolution* 1 (May 28, 1868): 324.

197. "Letter from George Francis Train," *Revolution* 2 (August 13, 1868): 87.

198. Untitled, *Revolution* 2 (September 3, 1868): 139; "Letter from George Francis Train," *Revolution* 2 (November 5, 1868): 279.

199. "Infanticide," *Revolution*, August 6, 1868, in *Selected Papers*, 2: 158–59; "Hester Vaughn," *Revolution* 2 (September 17, 1868): 169; "Hester Vaughan" *Revolution*, November 19, 1868, in *Selected Papers*, 2: 191–93.

200. ECS, "Marriage and Divorce," *Revolution* 2 (October 22, 1868): 249–50.

201. Eventually, after nearly two and a half years, Anthony would give up the paper after having run up a debt of some $10,000. Harper, *Life and Work*, 1: 363–64.

Chapter 7

1. ECS to Thomas Wentworth Higginson, November 3, 1868, and ECS to Stephen S. Foster, November 4, 1868, in *Papers* 13: 110–12.

2. ECS, "The Boston Woman's Suffrage Convention," *Revolution* 2 (November 12, 1868): 296–97.

3. "Ahead," *NASS*, November 21, 1868; Wang, *Trial of Democracy*, 41–42.

4. Henry Blackwell analyzed the need and the opportunity for such an amendment, largely in terms of advantages to the Republican Party, in HBB to Ainsworth Spofford, January 1, 1868, BFP/LC.

5. William Gillette, *The Right to Vote: Politics and the Passage of the Fifteenth Amendment* (Johns Hopkins University Studies in Historical and Political Science, series 83, no. 1, 1965), argues that Republicans were motivated by the desire to save their party rather than by idealistic commitment to black rights, but LaWanda and John H. Cox credit the party with having taken a principled stand despite political risk. See their "Negro Suffrage and Republican Politics: The Problem of Motivation in Reconstruction Historiography," *Journal of Southern History* 33 (August 1967): 303–30. Benedict, *Compromise of Principle*, chap. 17; and Wang, *The Trial of Democracy*, 41–48, see a combination of different motives in different wings of the party.

6. Stewart, *Wendell Phillips*, 290; "The Result—The Future," *NASS*, November 7, 1868; "Petition," *NASS*, November 21, 1868; "Suffrage Amendments," *NASS*, December 12, 1868.

7. "Woman Suffrage," *NASS*, October 10, 1868; "Woman's Rights," *NASS*, November 28, 1868.

8. The Boston convention is discussed in *Selected Papers*, 2: 184–88. On the state conventions, see "Woman's Rights in New Jersey," *Revolution* 2 (November 26, 1868): 329; "Our Boston Correspondence," *NASS*, December 12, 1868; "Woman's Suffrage Association of New Jersey," *Revolution* 2 (December 10, 1868): 359; "Rhode Island Woman's Suffrage Convention," *Revolution* 2 (December 17, 1868): 369.

9. "The Woman Question. Convention in Horticultural Hall," *Boston Post*, November 19, 1868.

10. Six months earlier, Caroline Severance and other Boston women had founded a new social organization, the New England Women's Club, open by invitation only, and no one invited Caroline Dall. When club members subsequently formed the nucleus of the new suffrage organization, Dall was effectively blackballed. "New England Women's Club," *NASS*, June 13, 1868; "New England Women's Club," *NASS*, July 25, 1868; Kate Field, "The New England Women's Club," *Woman's Advocate* 1 (January 1869): 25–33.

11. "Address by Mrs. Julia Ward Howe," *NASS*, November 28, 1868; Mary Grant, *Private Woman, Public Person: An Account of the Life of Julia Ward Howe from 1819 to 1868* (Brooklyn: Carlson, 1994), 167–69, 194–98.

12. "Woman Suffrage Convention," *Boston Post*, November 20, 1868.

13. "The Woman Question. Convention in Horticultural Hall," *Boston Post*, November 19, 1868; "Hon. Henry Wilson in the Boston Convention," *Revolution* 2 (December 3, 1868): 338.

14. The *Boston Post* reported that the invitation to Stanton was withdrawn because Wendell Phillips declared that he would not attend if she did. But then, reflecting the feud between Phillips and Garrison over the disposition of the Jackson Fund, Garrison said he would not attend if Phillips were there. In the upshot, Garrison did attend, Stanton was "dis-invited," and Phillips was conspicuously absent.

15. "Our Boston Correspondence," *NASS*, November 28, 1868.

16. "Woman Suffrage," *New York Tribune*, November 21, 1868; "Mrs. Lucy Stone and Woman Suffrage," *Commonwealth*, November 28, 1868.

17. WP to Henry C. Wright, December 7, 1868, Ms.A.1.2, v. 36, p. 62B, Abolitionist Papers. Internal evidence shows this letter was written by Phillips's wife, Anne Greene Phillips.

18. "Literary," *NASS*, January 9, 1869; "The Woman's Advocate," *NASS*, December 26, 1868. The *Advocate*'s lineup of contributors and its link to the *NASS* (Joint subscriptions were offered) marked it as an organ of the Bostonians. Stanton would later refer to the *NASS* and the *Woman's Advocate* as Wendell Phillips's "two papers." ECS, "A Pronunciamento," *Revolution* 4 (July 15, 1869): 24. The editor, William P. Tomlinson, was virtually unknown in women's rights circles but had a history as a correspondent for the *NASS* and the *New York Tribune*. See a brief biography in the *NASS*, February 15, 1868.

19. "The *Woman's Advocate*," *NASS*, December 26, 1868.

20. "Women's National Convention," *Revolution* 2 (October 15, 1868): 235; "National Woman's Suffrage Convention," *Revolution* 2 (October 22, 1868): 250. The timing of these notices suggests a tit-for-tat response to Phillips's recognition of the Boston convention and the NEWSA in the *NASS*.

21. "Hon. Henry Wilson," *Revolution* 2 (December 3, 1868): 337.

22. "Now's the Hour," *Revolution* 2 (December 10, 1868): 360; "The Right Word at Last," *Revolution* 2 (December 17, 1868): 369.

23. "Roscoe Conkling," *Revolution* 3 (January 14, 1869): 26; SBA to James Harlan, January 26, 1869, in *Papers* 13: 296–98; ECS, "Editorial Correspondence," *Revolution* 3 (February 4, 1869): 65. The less-friendly chair of the Judiciary Committee was Lyman Trumbull, described by Benedict, *Compromise of Principle*, 28, as a "consistent conservative."

24. "Woman's Rights," *NASS*, December 19, 1868; Aaron Macy Powell, "Woman a Voter," *Woman's Advocate* 1 (January 1869): 36–39.

25. Untitled, *NASS*, January 9, 1869.

26. "Stones Holding Their Peace," and "Lucy Stone and the Negro's Hour," *Revolution* 3 (February 4, 1869): 73, 89.

27. "Editorial Correspondence, Washington, Jan 18," *NASS*, January 23, 1869.

28. Robert Sharkey, *Money, Class and Party: An Economic Study of Civil War and Reconstruction* (Baltimore: Johns Hopkins University Press, 1959), 122–32; Montgomery, *Beyond Equality*, 340–48. Most radicals wanted a black suffrage amendment, but Charles Sumner

still insisted that an ordinary law would suffice. See Donald, *Charles Sumner*, 352–54, 430–31; "Universal Suffrage," *Commonwealth*, January 16, 1869; "Editorial Correspondence," *NASS*, January 23, 1869.

29. "Washington. Jan 4," *New York Tribune*, January 5, 1869, reports the session will be only fifty working days.

30. "The Congressional Amendment," *NASS*, January 16, 1869; "Congress," *NASS*, February 20, 1869.

31. Lessoff, *The Nation and Its City*, 53–55; Masur, "Reconstructing the Nation's Capitol," 312–16; "Woman's Rights Convention," [Washington] *Daily Morning Chronicle*, January 21, 1869, in *Papers* 13: 281.

32. "Mrs. Stanton Before the District Committee," *Revolution* 3 (February 4, 1869): 88.

33. Lessoff, *The Nation and Its City*, 54; Masur, "Reconstructing the Nation's Capitol," 316, 338.

34. HBB to Ainsworth Spofford, January 1, 1868, BFP/LC; "Remarks by SBA to the Radical Club of Philadelphia, June 5, 1872," in *Selected Papers*, 2: 502.

35. Lucretia Mott to Philadelphia Family, February 1, 1869, in Palmer, *Selected Letters of Lucretia Mott*, 412.

36. "Stones Holding Their Peace," *Revolution* 3 (February 4, 1869): 73.

37. "Congress Wide Awake," *Revolution* 2 (December 24, 1868): 385.

38. "Manhood Suffrage," *Revolution*, December 24, 1868, in *Selected Papers*, 2: 194–98.

39. ECS, "Stand by Your Guns, Mr. Julian," *Revolution*, January 14, 1869, in *Selected Papers*, 2: 202. In this context, Stanton exaggerated the time she spent in Kansas, neglected the many and persistent efforts that were made on both sides to hold the coalition of blacks and women together, and described a degree of hostility for which there is little evidence in the contemporary record, except as it was being encouraged and misreported by biased presses.

40. ECS, "Gerrit Smith on Petitions," *Revolution* 3 (January 14, 1869): 24–25.

41. Ibid., 25.

42. Because the evidence against Vaughan was circumstantial, they saw her as victimized twice over, by her seducer and by the court. Their efforts included a petition campaign to persuade the governor of Pennsylvania to pardon her, a large public meeting at the Cooper Union, and a personal trip to deliver the petition to and visit the prisoner. "Hester Vaughan," *Revolution*, November 19, 1868, in *Selected Papers*, 2: 191–93; ECS, "Editorial Correspondence," "Hester Vaughan," and "The Hester Vaughan Meeting at Cooper Institute," *Revolution* 2 (December 10, 1868): 353–54, 360–61.

43. DuBois, *Feminism and Suffrage*, 145–47.

44. "Hester Vaughan," *New York World*, January 23, 1869. The *New York Times* of December 4, 1868, reported that Vaughan had been raped but had refused to reveal her rapist's identity.

45. ECS, "Gerrit Smith on Petitions," *Revolution* 3 (January 14, 1869): 24–25. See also Michelle Mitchell, "'Lower Orders,' Racial Hierarchies," 137–40.

46. "Woman's Protectors," *Revolution* 3 (January 21, 1869): 40; "Outrage by a Negro in Tennessee," *New York World*, January 13, 1869.

47. ECS, "The Fifteenth Amendment," *Revolution* 3 (June 3, 1869): 344.

48. "Woman's Rights Convention," *Washington Daily Morning Chronicle*, January 20, 1869, and "Woman's Rights Convention," *Washington D.C. Evening Star*, January 20, 1869, in *Papers* 13: 280, 282.

49. "The Washington Convention," *Revolution* 3 (January 28, 1869): 56–57.

50. "Woman's Rights Convention," *Washington D.C. Evening Star*, January 20, 1869, in *Papers* 13: 282.

51. ECS, "Editorial Correspondence," *Revolution*, January 28, 1869, in *Selected Papers*, 2: 205.

52. "Women and Black Men," *Revolution* 3 (February 4, 1869): 88.

53. "Suffrage," *Chicago Times*, February 13, 1869, in *Papers*, 13: 349; "The Rights of Woman," *Evening Wisconsin*, February 25, 1869, in *Papers*, 13: 406; "The Milwaukee Convention," *Revolution* 3 (March 11, 1869): 149.

54. "Women and Black Men," *Revolution* 3 (February 4, 1869): 88.

55. "Sound Argument," *Revolution* 3 (February 4, 1869): 74.

56. Douglass, "An Appeal to Congress for Impartial Suffrage," *Atlantic Monthly* 19 (January 1867): 115.

57. Julia Ward Howe, "Women as Voters," *Galaxy* 7 (March 1869): 366.

58. Martha C. Wright announced the free platform principle at the 1860 convention: "We have always, from the first, invited all to come forward and speak." *Proceedings of the Tenth National Woman's Rights Convention*, 4, in *Papers* 9: 615.

59. Stanton, *Eighty Years*, 130. One slightly deranged woman, Abby Folsom, was a fixture at Boston reform meetings where she punctuated discussions of every topic with the same all-purpose cry: "It's the capitalists!" Thomas Wentworth Higginson, *Contemporaries* (Boston: Houghton Mifflin, 1899), 330; "Obituary. Abby Folsom," *NASS*, August 31, 1867.

60. "Local Department. Woman Suffrage Convention," (Washington, D.C.) *National Republican*, January 21, 1869, in *Papers* 13: 283.

61. "Brooklyn Equal Rights Association Founding Meeting," *Brooklyn Daily Union*, May 14, 1869.

62. "Local Department. Woman Suffrage Convention," (Washington, D.C.) *National Republican*, January 21, 1869, in *Papers* 13: 283. Downing reportedly said "nature intended man should dominate the female," though he later insisted he was not giving his opinion but only characterizing the opinions of others. "Correction," *Revolution* 3 (March 18, 1869): 169. *Selected Papers*, 2:209 n. 4 lists six black leaders who attended this woman suffrage convention: John Willis Menard, George T. Downing, John J. Moore, Robert Purvis, Charles Purvis, and William H. Lewis.

63. "Local Department. Woman Suffrage Convention," (Washington, D.C.) *National Republican*, January 21, 1869, in *Papers* 13: 283–84; "Working-Women's Association," *New York World*, January 30, 1869, in *Papers* 13: 308.

64. This case is mentioned in Hodes, "Sexualization of Reconstruction Politics," 410, citing testimony before Congress in 1872 about KKK activities.

65. "Local Department. Woman Suffrage Convention," (Washington, D.C.) *National Republican*, January 21, 1869, in *Papers* 13: 283.

66. Ibid.; ECS, "Editorial Correspondence," *Revolution*, January 28, 1869, in *Selected Papers*, 2: 205.

67. "Meeting of the Illinois Woman Suffrage Association in Chicago," in *Selected Papers*, 2: 215; "Suffrage," *Chicago Times*, February 13, 1869, in *Papers* 13: 349.

68. "Editorial Correspondence," *Revolution* 3 (February 18, 1869): 97; "Meeting of the Illinois Woman Suffrage Association in Chicago," *Chicago Tribune*, February 13, 1869, in *Selected Papers*, 2: 213, 219. In response to Babcock's challenge, Mary Livermore explained that the object of the resolution was "to include black women in the franchise." When Babcock backed off his opposition, William Wells Brown stepped into his place.

69. "Meeting of the Illinois Woman Suffrage Association in Chicago," in *Selected Papers*, 2: 214 and 220 n. 4. Naomi Talbert is discussed in Terborg-Penn, *African-American Women*, 49–50.

70. *Chicago Republican*, February 12, 1869, in *Papers* 13: 329; ECS, "Editorial Correspondence," *Revolution*, March 25, 1869, in *Selected Papers*, 2: 222–23.

71. SBA to Lucretia Coffin Mott, after March 20, 1869, in *Selected Papers*, 2: 231.

72. "Editorial Correspondence," *Revolution* 3 (January 28, 1869): 50; "Roscoe Conkling," *Revolution* 3 (January 14, 1869): 26.

73. ECS to John Stuart Mill, May 11, 1869, in *Papers* 13: 499.

74. ECS, "Editorial Correspondence," *Revolution* 3 (March 25, 1869): 177–78.

75. Ibid.

76. Benedict, *Compromise of Principle*, 331–35; Gillette, *Right to Vote*, 75–76; McPherson, *Struggle for Equality*, 356. Sumner was among the absentees who refused to vote for the Fifteenth Amendment.

77. "The Constitutional Amendment," *NASS*, March 20, 1869.

78. "The American Equal Rights Association," *Revolution* 3 (May 27, 1869): 328.

79. F. Ellen Burr, "A Rift in the Clouds," *Revolution* 3 (March 4, 1869): 131; cf. "Speech of Phoebe Couzens," *Revolution* 4 (July 8, 1869): 12.

80. Abby Kelley Foster to Gerrit Smith, January 13, 1869, Smith Papers.

81. "The Amendment," and "The Thirty-Fifth Annual National Anti-Slavery Subscription Anniversary," *NASS*, January 2, 1869.

82. "Obstacles," *NASS*, March 27, 1869.

83. "Business Meeting of the American Anti-Slavery Society," *NASS*, June 5, 1869. Turner said that 289 Republicans had been killed in Georgia, "and the first white man is yet to be arrested and put in jail for it."

84. "The Annual Meeting," *NASS*, May 8, 1869.

85. *NASS*, March 27 and June 5, 1869, named James M. Simms of Georgia, William Macy Powell, C. C. Burleigh, William Wells Brown, and Sally Holley as speakers in support of the Fifteenth Amendment. But their appeals to principle could move only radical legislators, who were already supporting the measure. Indifferent or conservative Republican legislators were persuaded to back ratification in order to get a chance at federal patronage, once the Grant administration signaled its wishes. Gillette, *Right to Vote*, 159–65; "The Fifteenth Amendment," *Commonwealth*, April 24, 1869.

86. ECS, "Editorial Correspondence," and "Meeting of the Rhode Island Woman Suffrage Association," *Revolution* 3 (July 1, 1869): 402, 410.

87. WP, "The Fifteenth Amendment," *NASS*, July 3, 1869. The same article also appeared in the July 1869 issue of the *Woman's Advocate*.

88. Gillette, *Right to Vote*, 150–53; "The Amendment in Rhode Island," *Trenton* (N.J.) *State Gazette*, June 19, 1869; "The Fifteenth Amendment," *New York Times*, May 30, 1869; "Rhode Island and Its Naturalized Citizens," *New York Times*, June 11, 1869.

89. WP, "The Fifteenth Amendment," *NASS*, July 3, 1869.

90. ECS, "A Pronunciamento," *Revolution* 4 (July 15, 1869): 24.

91. ECS to WP, June 20, 1869, in *Papers* 13: 581.

92. WP, "Woman's Rights," *NASS*, August 21, 1869. The same article was carried in the *Woman's Advocate* for September 1869.

93. Lydia Maria Child, "Women and the Freedmen," *NASS*, August 28, 1869.

94. ECS, "Legal Voters," *NASS*, March 17, 1866, in *Papers* 11: 393.

95. Unfortunately, the only extended coverage appeared in the *New York World*, whose hostile reporter emphasized personal conflict and failed to reproduce substantive argument, while the *Tribune* and the *Times* neglected the proceedings and ran summary descriptions. See *New York World*, May 13 and 14, 1869, in *Papers* 13: 500–10; *New York Tribune*, May 13 and 14, 1869, in *Papers* 13: 511–15; *New York Times*, May 13 and 14, 1869, in *Papers* 13: 516–20. Mary Livermore went so far as to complain that the New York papers either ignored the meeting or reported them "to have said what they did not say." *New York World*, May 14, 1869, *Papers* 13: 507.

96. ECS to Unknown, [1869 Apr?], in *Papers* 13: 488.

97. Before the meeting she had inserted a version of her speech in the *Revolution*, and it included her "fearful outrages" prediction, but in the event as reported she changed the language. Cf. "Anniversary of the American Equal Rights Association. Address of Elizabeth Cady Stanton," *Revolution* 3 (May 13, 1869): 292; and "Women of the Period," *New York World*, May 13, 1869, in *Papers* 13: 502.

98. "Women of the Period," *New York World*, May 13, 1869, in *Papers* 13: 501–3.

99. Foster's attack on SBA is found in "Women of the Period," *New York World*, May 13, 1869, in *Papers* 13: 503. See "Battling for the Ballot," *New York World*, May 14, 1869, in *Papers* 13: 507; "May Anniversaries. American Equal Rights Association," *New York Tribune*, May 14, 1869, in *Papers* 13: 514.

100. *New York World*, May 13, 1869, in *Papers* 13: 504.

101. "Remarks by SBA etc.," in *Selected Papers*, 2: 239.

102. "Battling for the Ballot," *New York World*, May 14, 1869, in *Papers* 13: 509.

103. Ibid., 510.

104. "Women of the Period," *New York World*, May 13, 1869, in *Papers* 13: 503–4; SBA to Edwin Studwell and Margaret Winchester, January 9, 1869, in *Papers* 13: 268.

105. "Women of the Period," *New York World*, May 13, 1869, in *Papers* 13: 504–5.

106. "Battling for the Ballot," *New York World*, May 14, 1869, in *Papers* 13: 510.

107. *Selected Papers*, 2: 242 n.1; DuBois, *Feminism and Suffrage,* 189–99, provides a thorough account of the origins of the two organizations.

108. SBA to the editor, *New York Times*, June 4, 1869, in *Selected Papers*, 2: 248.

109. "Notes and Comments," and "New England Woman Suffrage Convention," *NASS,* June 19, 1869.

110. ECS to Paulina Wright Davis, August 12?, 1869, in *Selected Papers*, 2: 256–57.

111. *HWS*, 2: 324.

112. *Selected Papers*, 2: 282, n. 3, re. a tour that took her into Ohio, Michigan, Wisconsin, Minnesota, Iowa, Illinois, Missouri, Kentucky, and Indiana, as well as Washington, D.C., and two weeks in New England.

113. "Working Woman's Association," *New York World*, September 3, 1869, in *Papers* 13: 756.

114. "The Wars of the Women," *New York Tribune*, September 3, 1869, in *Papers* 13: 757.

115. "Petticoats in Politics," *Cincinnati Enquirer*, September 16, 1869, in *Papers* 13: 809.

116. ECS, "Miss Anthony in the West," *Revolution*, September 23, 1869, in *Selected Papers*, 2: 269.

117. "Remarks by SBA to the Western Woman Suffrage Association," *Chicago Agitator,* and "Miss Anthony in the West," *Revolution*, September 23, 1869, in *Selected Papers*, 2: 265–71; Kate Doggett, "Fifteenth Amendment," *Revolution* 4 (September 30, 1869): 202–3.

118. "The Elections," *NASS*, October 23, 1869.

119. Martha C. Wright to SBA, November 4, 1869, *Selected Papers*, 2: 280.

120. LS to Elizabeth Buffum Chase, July 11, 1869, NAWSA Papers.

121. ECS to Paulina Wright Davis, August 12?, 1869, in *Papers* 13: 650.

122. "The Fifteenth Amendment," *Revolution* 4 (October 21, 1869): 248–49.

123. "The Cleveland Convention," *Revolution,* October 28, 1869, in *Selected Papers*, 2: 276–79.

124. Blackwell's editorial in the first issue of the *Woman's Journal* declared that woman suffrage must be dealt with on its own merits, and explicitly mentioned that race was an inappropriate topic for discussion in its pages. Henry Blackwell, "Political Organization," *Woman's Journal,* January 8, 1870.

125. Terborg-Penn, *African American Women*, 34, 42.

126. The border states were formerly slave-holding states that had not seceded and so were not subject to Reconstruction measures. "Call for a National Convention," *NASS*, January 2, 1869; Wang, *Trial of Democracy*, 41–42.

127. See "Proceedings of the National Convention of Colored Men of America, Held in Washington, DC, January 13, 14, 15, and 16, 1869," in *Proceedings of the Black National and State Conventions, 1865–1900,* ed. Philip S. Foner and George E. Walker (Philadelphia: Temple University Press, 1986), 344–405.

128. "The Colored People of the North: Our Work and How to Do It," *NASS*, February 6, 1869; "The Negro Race," *NASS,* June 19, 1869; "Editorial Correspondence," *NASS,* January 30, 1869.

129. "Editorial Correspondence," *NASS*, January 30, 1869, indicates "the National Equal Rights League has ceased to be an active institution."

130. In the North, the Republican Party and the Union Leagues were white-dominated and could not serve the same purposes. There was some effort in the North to create separate black Union Leagues, about which little is known. SBA spoke to a gathering of the "Union League of America (Colored)" in June 1868. See *Selected Papers*, 2: 143–50.

131. Tensions between Frederick Douglass and John Mercer Langston are noted in McFeely, *Frederick Douglass*, 260. Divisions within the black majority in South Carolina are discussed in Thomas Holt, *Black over White: Negro Political Leadership in South Carolina during Reconstruction* (Urbana: University of Illinois Press, 1977), 86, 125, and chap. 3 generally.

132. From the abbreviated version of the proceedings that was published, it is clear no phonographic record was made, and reporters from the mainstream press did not provide much detailed coverage either. Foner and Walker, *Proceedings*, 344–405.

133. "What the People Say to Us. Good for the Colored Men," *Revolution* 3 (January 28, 1869): 51. Spellman was a supporter of woman suffrage himself: see "Colored Convention in Utica," *Revolution* 2 (October 22, 1868): 241.On Spelman, see William J. Simmons, *Men of Mark: Eminent, Progressive, and Rising* (1887; reprint, New York: Arno Press, 1968), 928–31; Eric Foner, *Freedom's Lawmakers: A Directory of Black Officeholders during Reconstruction*, rev. ed. (New York: Oxford University Press, 1993), 201–2.

134. Foner and Walker, *Proceedings*, 353–54. "National Colored Convention," *NASS*, January 30, 1869, refers to "considerable discussion" and "some confusion" about her credentials.

135. Foner and Walker, *Proceedings*, 367; Menard's biography in Foner, *Freedom's Lawmakers*, 148. Menard was the first African American elected to Congress, but he was never seated owing to a dispute about the election results.

136. Menard reportedly said, "He regretted to find them so disorderly and that they were saying nothing about woman suffrage. He regretted that he had not been here to vote for the admission of Miss Johnson of Pennsylvania. He thought the greatest lever in their way was in themselves. All wanted to be big men." Foner and Walker, *Proceedings*, 367.

137. ECS to Thomas Wentworth Higginson, January 13, 1868, in *Selected Papers*, 2: 127.

138. Foner, *Reconstruction*, 320; Suzanne Lebsock, "Radical Reconstruction and the Property Rights of Southern Women," *Journal of Southern History* 43 (May 1977): 201–7.

139. SBA to Olympia Brown, February 25, 1868, in *Papers* 12: 848; Roslyn Terborg-Penn, "Nineteenth Century Black Women and Woman Suffrage," *Potomac Review* 7 (1977): 16.

140. Benjamin Quarles, "Frederick Douglass and the Woman's Rights Movement," *Journal of Negro History* 25 (January 1940): 35, unfootnoted.

141. Elsa Barkley-Brown, "Negotiating and Transforming the Public Sphere," *Public Culture* 7 (1994): 107–46. Earlier scholarship also contained scattered mention of the freedwomen's political activism, for example, Holt, *Black over White*, 34–35.

142. Foner and Walker, *Proceedings*, 367.

143. Hahn, *A Nation under Our Feet*, 212–14, infers a consensus on this issue from the fact that woman suffrage was nowhere enacted in the Reconstruction South. But Roslyn Terborg-Penn notes that although black men were widely described as opposed to woman suffrage, her research turned up very few of the "anti-woman's rights speeches or newspaper articles black men had been accused of writing." Terborg-Penn, "African American Women and the Vote: An Overview," in Gordon and Collier-Thomas, *African American Women and the Vote*, 12.

144. Holt, *Black over White*, showed that the political results of these divisions among blacks were fatal to Republican control despite South Carolina's black majority. Class differences are also discussed in David C. Rankin, "The Origins of Black Leadership in Reconstruction in New Orleans during Reconstruction," *Journal of Southern History* 40 (August 1974): 359–82; William C. Harris, "James Lynch: Black Leader in Southern Reconstruction," *Historian*, 34 (1971): 40–61.

145. Bacon, *But One Race,* is an excellent source on the whole family. Henry W. Purvis's biography is in Foner, *Freedom's Lawmakers,* 174. Purvis's voting record and associations are found in Holt, *Black over White,* 150, 162. Robert Purvis eventually came to believe that his son Henry sold out to the "redeemers," and relations between them became severely strained. Bacon, *But One Race,* 180–82, 203–4.

146. Martha C. Wright to David Wright, January 27, 1869, Garrison Family Papers.

147. At the AASS business meeting in 1869, Purvis said he had heard of bribes being offered to black legislators to persuade them to betray radical Republican positions, and he challenged Henry Turner's assertion that the freedmen never succumbed to such temptations. "Business Meeting of the American Anti-Slavery Society," *NASS,* June 5, 1869.

148. "Our Washington Correspondence," *NASS,* December 29, 1866; "Editorial Correspondence," *NASS,* January 23, 1869.

149. See, for example, "Democrats and the Negro Vote in the South," *New York Herald,* September 15, 1868; "The Revolution in the Southern Democracy," *New York Sun,* August 15, 1868. Black Democrats were publicized in northern papers. See "A New Southern Leader," *New York Sun,* August 17, 1868, on "Mr. Sandy Cameron, a colored Democrat of years and weight" in Alabama.

150. "Atlanta University," *Revolution* 3 (July 1, 1869): 407.

151. "What the People Say. L.W. to the Revolution," *Revolution* 3 (June 10, 1869): 364, emphasis original.

152. "Miss Anthony and the Labor Congress," *Revolution* 4 (September 2, 1869): 137.

153. "The National Colored Convention in Session at Washington, D.C.," *Harper's Weekly* 13 (February 6, 1869): 85; "What the People Say to Us," *Revolution* 3 (January 28, 1869): 51.

154. By the time Johnson was approved and "invited to take a seat inside the railing," she had left the hall. "Brief Notes," *Commonwealth,* January 23, 1869.

155. Roslyn Terborg-Penn, "Nineteenth Century Black Women and Woman Suffrage," *Potomac Review* 7 (1977): 16. "Personal," *NASS,* July 31, 1869, reports Rollin was appointed chief clerk in the Adjutant General's office; and "Woman's Rights in South Carolina," *Revolution* 3 (April 29, 1869): 268, reports "a colored woman spoke very ably" before the legislature but did not name her. On the "celebrated Rollin sisters," see Sterling, *We Are Your Sisters,* 365–69; Lerone Bennett, Jr., *Black Power U.S. A.: The Human Side of Reconstruction* (Baltimore: Penguin Books, 1969), 347–53, although Bennett relies on an interview in the *New York Herald,* a hostile source that apparently emphasized the appearance and social pretensions of the five Rollin sisters. *HWS,* 3: 828–29 notes Rollin's role in a Woman's Rights Convention held in Charleston in 1870.

156. Cf. Terborg-Penn, *African-American Women,* 28–35, emphasizing the silencing of black women afterward, when white woman suffragists wrote the history of the movement.

157. Jones, *All Bound Up Together,* chap. 5.

158. "Edmonia G. Highgate," and "Woman's Suffrage Meeting," *Revolution* 4 (October 2, 1869): 218, 219.

159. "Male vs. Female Suffrage. Letter from a Colored Lady," *Chicago Tribune,* March 8, 1869. Naomi Bowman Talbert Anderson's biography appears in Monroe A. Majors, *Noted Negro Women: Their Triumphs and Activities* (1893; reprint, Freeport, N.Y.: Books for Libraries Press, 1971), 82–87.

160. Washington, *Truth's America,* 347–52.

161. Untitled, *Revolution* 3 (February 25, 1869): 122; "Personal," *NASS,* July 10, 1869. Biographical information on Mary D. (Maud) Molson Hughes is found at www.buffalo.edu/uncrownedqueens/Q/bios/H/hughes_mary.

162. "Equal Rights League," *NASS,* September 25, 1869.

163. The novel appeared in the *Christian Recorder,* the organ of the African Methodist Episcopal Church. See Frances Smith Foster, ed., *Minnie's Sacrifice, Sowing and Reaping, Trial and Triumph: Three Rediscovered Novels by Frances E. W. Harper* (Boston: Beacon Press, 1994),

78–79. See also Griffin, "Frances Ellen Watkins Harper," 45–47; and Harper's letters reprinted in William Still, *The Underground Railroad* (Philadelphia: Porter and Coates, 1872), 767–74.

164. "National Woman Suffrage Association," *Revolution* 3 (June 10, 1869): 358.

165. Collier-Thomas, "Frances Ellen Watkins Harper," 54–55.

166. "What the Press Says," *Revolution* 3 (June 24, 1869): 390.

167. The *Revolution* of January 14, 1869, announces Douglass's lecture at the Cooper Institute on January 18 on this topic. His lecture on "Woman Suffrage," evidently the speech he delivered at the Boston convention in November 1868, includes a discussion of women's heroism in the defense of Leyden. See "William the Silent" folders in Frederick Douglass Papers, Library of Congress Web site.

168. "Thirty-Sixth Anniversary of the American Anti-Slavery Society," *NASS*, May 29, 1869.

169. "Woman's Rights Convention," *Washington, D.C. Evening Star*, January 20, 1869, in *Papers* 13: 282.

170. "Women of the Period," *New York World*, May 13, 1869, in *Papers* 13: 504.

171. "The Women," *Chicago Tribune*, February 13, 1869.

Conclusion

1. *Selected Papers*, 2: 303.

2. T. A. Larson, "Woman Suffrage in Wyoming," *Pacific Northwest Quarterly* 56 (April 1965): 57–66; Beverly Beeton, *Women Vote in the West: The Woman Suffrage Movement, 1869–1896* (New York: Garland, 1986).

3. *Selected Papers*, 2: 303.

4. Sarah Barringer Gordon, "'The Liberty of Self-Degradation': Polygamy, Woman Suffrage, and Consent in Nineteenth-Century America," *Journal of American History* 83 (December 1996): 815–47.

5. Francis Minor to the *Revolution*, October 14, 1869, in *Selected Papers*, 2: 273–74.

6. DuBois, "Outgrowing the Compact of the Fathers," and "Taking the Law into Our Own Hands."

7. Recent work on Woodhull includes Amanda Frisken, *Victoria Woodhull's Sexual Revolution: Political Theater and the Popular Press in Nineteenth-Century America* (Philadelphia: University of Pennsylvania Press, 2004); Joanne Passet, *Sex Radicals and the Quest for Women's Equality* (Urbana: University of Illinois Press, 2003). Barbara Goldsmith, *Other Powers: The Age of Suffrage, Spiritualism, and the Scandalous Victoria Woodhull* (New York: Knopf, 1998) is detailed but not always fully sourced.

8. Debby Applegate, *The Most Famous Man in the World: The Biography of Henry Ward Beecher* (New York: Doubleday, 2006); Richard Wightman Fox, *Trials of Intimacy: Love and Loss in the Beecher-Tilton Scandal* (Chicago: University of Chicago Press, 1999); Altina Waller, *Reverend Beecher and Mrs. Tilton: Sex and Class in Victorian America* (Amherst: University of Massachusetts Press, 1982).

9. Diary of SBA, May 1870, in *Selected Papers*, 2: 357.

10. *Selected Papers*, 4: 8, 12, 51–52, 99, 129–32 passim.

11. The AWSA muddled along on dues from a tiny membership and a yearly "festival fund" that generated $500 to $1,000; it was not even incorporated so as to be able to receive donations until 1892. See Merk, "Massachusetts and the Woman Suffrage Movement," chap. 2, 21–22, n.56. However, Kerr, "White Women's Rights," argues that it was much more prosperous in its first two years.

12. Lisa Tetrault, "The Incorporation of American Feminism: Suffragists and the Postbellum Lyceum," *Journal of American History* 96 (March 2010): 1027–56. Quote is from SBA in 1871.

13. David Montgomery, *Beyond Equality: Labor and the Radical Republicans, 1862–1872* (New York: Random House Vintage Books, 1967), chap. 10.

14. *HWS*, 4: 248–49.

15. Thus in 1910 Harriet Stanton Blatch was impatient with old-school New York State suffragists who simply assumed that educational efforts "would gradually create more and more support for suffrage" until it passed. Blatch saw them as naïve and sought to inject political realism into the campaign to influence state legislators. DuBois, *Harriet Stanton Blatch*, 123

16. SBA to Lepha Johnson Canfield, January 2, 1871, in *Selected Papers*, 2: 399.

17. SBA to ECS, January 2, 1871, in *Selected Papers*, 2: 401. That winter it was two years since the D.C. woman suffrage measure was dumped and the Fifteenth Amendment put through.

18. Andrea Moore Kerr, "White Women's Rights, Black Men's Wrongs, Free Love, Blackmail, and the Formation of the American Woman Suffrage Association," in *One Woman One Vote: Rediscovering the Woman Suffrage Movement*, ed. Marjorie Spruill Wheeler (Troutdale, Ore.: New Sage Press, 1995), 61–79. Kerr's account suffers for want of primary sources and a tendency to rely on the sometimes self-serving account of events found in the Blackwell family papers.

19. LS to SBA, May 9, 1867, in *Selected Papers*, 2: 57.

20. ECS to Paulina Wright Davis, August 12, 1869, in *Selected Papers*, 2: 257.

21. Newman, *White Women's Rights*, 18, characterizes abolitionist-suffragists as believing that the white race was "higher"; and "it was just that blacks and other racial inferiors could be 'elevated' and 'uplifted'—if freed and treated properly, educated, Christianized, and granted citizenship." This critique apparently assumes that *genuine* egalitarian arguments require a belief that individuals are literally the same in condition or capacity, so as to be entitled to equal rights, but egalitarian rights theory of the sort Stanton and Anthony subscribed to posits that individuals are entitled to equal rights subject only to minimal requirements like adulthood and mental competence. Keyssar, *Right to Vote*, 12–13, 42–44, 175–76. See also Nancy Hewitt, "Seeking a Larger Liberty" on antebellum international and interracial efforts in support of universal human rights.

22. See, for example, Anthony's response in 1868 in the *Revolution* to a correspondent who supported the "noble" cause of woman suffrage but condemned "negro equality" or "universal suffrage," citing the "barbarism" he had seen among Mexicans, Haitians, "Chinamen," and Minnesota Sioux. In reply, she stuck to her support of universal suffrage and urged him to keep reading the paper until he had imbibed its "higher ideas of human nature, its sacredness and dignity. We welcome even the poor Chinese to our shores, remembering that he is better here than in his own land. And if we establish justice on this Continent, we need have no fears that ignorance can outwit us. Your rights are only made secure as the rights of the humblest of God's children are faithfully observed and protected." "What the People Say to Us," *Revolution* 2 (December 17, 1868): 374.

23. The foundational study of prejudice was Gordon W. Allport's *The Nature of Prejudice* (New York: Addison-Wesley, 1954). Allport presented various theories of prejudice, including the frustration or scapegoat theory. See John F. Dovidio, Peter Glick, and Laurie A. Rudman, eds., *On the Nature of Prejudice: Fifty Years after Allport* (Malden: Blackwell, 2005), 25–28.

24. ECS, "Gerrit Smith on Petitions," *Revolution* 3 (January 14, 1869): 24.

25. According to one contemporary source, one in six women will be sexually assaulted in their lifetime. See http://www.rainn.org/statistics. According to another study, one in four women will be physically or sexually assaulted by a male partner. See http://new.abanet.org/domesticviolence/Pages/Statistics.aspx#prevalence.

26. ECS to Frank Blair, October 1, 1868, in *Papers* 13: 70. Blatch's handwriting is not identified here, but it is at another point, in *Papers* 11: 758.

27. On Stanton as storyteller, see Kathi Kern, *Mrs. Stanton's Bible* (Ithaca, N.Y.: Cornell University Press, 2001), 21. On "moral luck," see Stephen Greenblatt, *Will in the World: How Shakespeare Became Shakespeare* (New York: W.W. Norton, 2004), 162; Bernard

Williams, *Moral Luck: Philosophical Papers, 1973–80* (Cambridge: Cambridge University Press, 1981).

28. Flexner, *Century of Struggle*, 173. Flexner dated the death of hope at the defeat of the new departure in *Minor vs. Happersett*, in 1875, rather than 1869.

29. Carrie Chapman Catt and Nettie Rogers Shuler, *Woman Suffrage and Politics* (New York: Charles Scribner's Sons, 1926), 107.

30. See Newman, *White Women's Rights*; Allison L. Sneider, *Suffragists in an Imperial Age: U.S. Expansion and the Woman Question, 1870–1929* (New York: Oxford University Press, 2008).

31. David Levering Lewis, *W.E. B. DuBois: Biography of a Race, 1868–1919* (New York: Henry Holt, 1993), 277.

32. Sharon Hartman Strom, "Leadership and Tactics in the American Woman Suffrage Movement: A New Perspective from Massachusetts," *Journal of American History* 62 (1975–76): 296–315. Lynne Vincent Cheney, "Mrs. Frank Leslie's Illustrated Newspaper," *American Heritage* 26 (October 1975): 91; Sylvia Hoffert, "Money and Power: Alva Vanderbilt Belmont and the National Women's Party," Organization of American Historians Annual Meeting, April 20, 2006, Washington, D.C.; Ellen Carol DuBois, *Harriot Stanton Blatch and the Winning of Woman Suffrage* (New Haven: Yale University Press, 1997),106–13.

33. DuBois, *Harriot Stanton Blatch*, 106–8, 110–12, 123–26, 129–31, 165.

SELECTED BIBLIOGRAPHY

Manuscript and Archival Sources

Massachusetts Historical Society, Boston, Mass.
  Caroline Dall Papers
Library of Congress, Washington, D.C.
  Blackwell Family Papers
  National American Woman Suffrage Papers
Houghton Library, Harvard University, Cambridge, Mass.
  Wendell Phillips Papers
Boston Public Library, Boston, Mass.
  Abolitionist Papers
Kansas State Historical Society, Topeka, Kans.
  Samuel Newitt Wood Papers
  Woman Suffrage History Collection
Special Collections Research Center, Syracuse University Library, Syracuse, N.Y.
  Gerrit Smith Papers
Schlesinger Library, Radcliffe Institute for Advanced Study, Harvard University, Cambridge, Mass.
  Olympia Brown Papers
  Blackwell Family Papers

Published Sources Primary

Black Abolitionist Papers [BAP], 1830–1865. 17 reels. Sanford, N.C.: Microfilming Corp. of America, 1999.

Blackwell, Henry B. *What the South Can Do: How the Southern States Can Make Themselves Masters of the Situation. To the Legislatures of the Southern States, January 15, 1867.* New York: Robert J. Johnston, 1867. Library of Congress American Memory Web site, http://memory.loc.gov/cgi-bin/query.

Blassingame, John W., ed. *The Frederick Douglass Papers. Series One: Speeches, Debates and Interviews.* 5 vols. New Haven: Yale University Press, 1985.

Brockway, Beman. *Fifty Years in Journalism, Embracing Recollections and Personal Experiences with an Autobiography.* Watertown, N.Y.: Daily Times Printing and Publishing, 1891.

Douglass, Frederick. *The Life and Times of Frederick Douglass.* 1892. Reprint, New York: Macmillan, Collier, 1962.

Foner, Philip S., ed. *Frederick Douglass on Women's Rights.* Westport, Conn.: Greenwood Press, 1976.

Foner, Philip S., and George E. Walker, eds. *Proceedings of the Black State Conventions, 1840–1865.* Philadelphia: Temple University Press, 1979.

Foster, Frances Smith, ed. *Minnie's Sacrifice, Sowing and Reaping, Trial and Triumph: Three Rediscovered Novels by Frances E. W. Harper*. Boston: Beacon Press, 1994.

Gordon, Ann D., ed. *The Selected Papers of Elizabeth Cady Stanton and Susan B. Anthony: Volume 1, In the School of Anti-Slavery, 1840–1866*. New Brunswick, N.J.: Rutgers University Press, 1997.

———. *Volume II, Against an Aristocracy of Sex, 1866–1873*. 2000.

———. *Volume III, National Protection for National Citizens, 1873–1880*. 2003.

———. *Volume IV, When Clowns Make Laws for Queens*. 2006.

———. *Volume V, Their Place inside the Body Politic*. 2009.

Harper, Ida Husted. *Life and Work of Susan B. Anthony*. 3 vols. Indianapolis: Hollenbeck Press, 1898–1908.

Holland, Patricia D., and Ann D. Gordon, eds., *Papers of Elizabeth Cady Stanton and Susan B. Anthony*. 45 reels. Wilmington, Del.: Scholarly Resources, 1991.

Hurlbut, Elisha P. *Essays on Human Rights and Their Political Guaranties*. New York: Greeley and McElrath, 1845.

Journal of the New York State Assembly, 1860. Albany: Van Benthuysen, 1860.

Journal of the Senate of the State of New York, 1860. Albany: Van Benthuysen, 1860.

Lasser, Carol, and Marlene Deahl Merrill, eds. *Friends and Sisters: Letters between Lucy Stone and Antoinette Brown Blackwell, 1846–1893*. Urbana: University of Illinois Press, 1987.

Majors, Monroe A. *Noted Negro Women: Their Triumphs and Activities*. 1893. Reprint, Freeport, N.Y.: Books for Libraries Press, 1971.

Palmer, Beverly Wilson, ed. *Selected Letters of Lucretia Coffin Mott*. Urbana: University of Illinois Press, 2002.

Proceedings of the Eleventh National Woman's Right Convention, Held at the Church of the Puritans, New York, May 10, 1866. New York: Robert J. Johnston, 1866.

Proceedings of the First Annual Meeting of the National Equal Rights League Held in Cleveland, Ohio, October 19, 20, and 21, 1865. Philadelphia: E. C. Markley, 1865.

Proceedings of the Meeting of the Loyal Women of the Republic, Held in New York, May 14, 1863. New York: Phair, 1863.

Report of the Woman's Rights Meeting at Mercantile Hall, May 27, 1859. Boston: S. Urbino, 1859.

Ripley, C. Peter, ed., Jeffrey S. Rossback, assoc. ed. *The Black Abolitionist Papers*. 5 vols. Chapel Hill: University of North Carolina Press, 1991.

Stanton, Elizabeth Cady. *Eighty Years and More: Reminiscences, 1815–1897*. 1898. Reprint, Boston: Northeastern University Press, 1993.

Stanton, Elizabeth Cady, Susan B. Anthony, and Matilda Joslyn Gage, eds. *History of Woman Suffrage*. 6 vols. Rochester, N.Y.: Susan B. Anthony and Charles Mann Printing, 1881–1922.

Stanton, Henry B. *Random Recollections*, 2nd ed. New York: McGowan & Slipper, 1886.

Stanton, William A. *A Record, Genealogical, Biographical, Statistical of Thomas Stanton of Connecticut and His Descendants, 1635–1891*. Albany, N.Y.: Joel Munsell's Sons, 1891.

Still, William. *The Underground Railroad*. Philadelphia: Porter & Coates, 1872.

Train, George Francis. *The Great Epigram Campaign of Kansas*. Leavenworth, Kans.: Prescott & Hume, 1867.

Warmoth, Henry Clay. *War, Politics and Reconstruction: Stormy Days in Louisiana*. New York: Macmillan, 1930.

Wheeler, Leslie H., ed. *Loving Warriors: Selected Letters of Lucy Stone and Henry B. Blackwell, 1853 to 1893*. New York: Dial Press, 1981.

Published Sources Secondary

Altshuler, Glenn C., and Stuart M. Blumin. *Rude Republic: Americans and Their Politics in the Nineteenth Century*. Princeton: Princeton University Press, 2000.

Andolsen, Barbara Hilkert. *"Daughters of Jefferson, Daughters of Bootblacks": Racism in American Feminism*. Macon, Ga.: Mercer University Press, 1986.

Anthony, Katharine Susan. *Susan B. Anthony: Her Personal History and Her Era*. New York: Doubleday, 1954.

Aptheker, Bettina. "Abolitionism, Women's Rights, and the Battle over the Fifteenth Amendment." In *Women's Legacy: Essays on Race, Sex, and Class in American History*, 9–52. Amherst: University of Massachusetts Press, 1982.

Attie, Jeannie. *Patriotic Toil: Northern Women and the American Civil War*. Ithaca: Cornell University Press, 1998.

Bacon, Margaret Hope. "'One Great Bundle of Humanity': Frances Ellen Watkins Harper (1825–1911)." *Pennsylvania Magazine of History and Biography*, 113 (January 1989): 21–43.

———. *But One Race: The Life of Robert Purvis*. Albany: State University of New York Press, 2007.

Baker, Jean Harvey. "Politics, Paradigms, and Public Culture." *Journal of American History* 84 (December 1997): 894–99

Banaszak, Lee Ann. *Why Movements Succeed or Fail: Opportunity, Culture, and the Struggle for Woman Suffrage*. Princeton, N.J.: Princeton University Press, 1996.

Banner, Lois. *Elizabeth Cady Stanton: A Radical for Woman's Rights*. Boston: Little, Brown, 1980.

Barry, Kathleen. *Susan B. Anthony: A Biography of a Singular Feminist*. New York: Ballantine, 1988.

Beckert, Sven. "Democracy in the Age of Capital: Contesting Suffrage Rights in Gilded Age New York." In *The Democratic Experiment: New Directions in American Political History*, ed. Meg Jacobs, William J. Novak, and Julian E. Zelizer, 146–74. Princeton: Princeton University Press, 2003.

Bell, Howard Holman. "A Survey of the Negro Convention Movement, 1830–1861." Ph.D. diss., Northwestern University, 1953.

Benedict, Michael Les. *A Compromise of Principle: Congressional Republicans and Reconstruction, 1863–1869*. New York: W.W. Norton, 1974.

———. "The Rout of Radicalism: Republicans and the Election of 1867." *Civil War History* 18 (December 1972): 334–44.

Berwanger, Eugene H. *The West and Reconstruction*. Urbana: University of Illinois Press, 1981.

———. "Hardin and Langston: Western Black Spokesmen of the Reconstruction Era." *Journal of Negro History* 64 (Spring 1979): 101–15.

Blackwell, Alice Stone. *Lucy Stone: Pioneer of Women's Rights*. Boston: Little, Brown, 1930.

Blight, David. *Frederick Douglass's Civil War: Keeping Faith in Jubilee*. Baton Rouge: Louisiana State University Press, 1989.

Blue, Frederick J. *Salmon P. Chase: A Life in Politics*. Kent, Ohio: Kent State University Press, 1987.

———. *No Taint of Compromise: Crusaders in Antislavery Politics*. Baton Rouge: Louisiana State University Press, 2005.

Bogin, Ruth. "Sarah Parker Remond: Black Abolitionist from Salem." *Essex Institute Historical Collections* 110 (1973): 12–150.

Booraem, Hendrik. *The Formation of the Republican Party in New York*. New York: New York University Press, 1983.

Boylan, Anne M. "Women and Politics in the Era before Seneca Falls." *Journal of the Early Republic* 10 (Fall 1990): 363–82.

———. *The Origins of Women's Activism: New York and Boston, 1797–1840*. Chapel Hill: University of North Carolina Press, 2002.

Brown, Elsa Barkley. "Negotiating and Transforming the Public Sphere: African American Political Life in the Transition from Slavery to Freedom." *Public Culture* 7 (1994): 107–46.

———. "To Catch the Vision of Freedom: Reconstructing Southern Black Women's Political History, 1865–1880." In *African-American Women and the Vote, 1837–1965*, ed. Ann D. Gordon and Bettye Collier-Thomas, 66–99. Amherst: University of Massachusetts Press, 1997.

Brummer, Sidney David. *Political History of New York during the Period of the Civil War*. New York: Columbia University Studies in History, Economics and Public Law, 39: 2. Reprint, New York: AMS Press, 1967.

Burrows, Edwin G., and Mike Wallace. *Gotham: A History of New York City to 1898.* New York: Oxford University Press, 1999.

Castel, Albert. "Jim Lane of Kansas." *Civil War Times Illustrated* 12 (Apr 1973): 22–29.

———. "Civil War Kansas and the Negro." *Journal of Negro History* 51 (April 1966): 125–38.

Caraway, Nancie. *Segregated Sisterhood: Racism and the Politics of American Feminism.* Knoxville: University of Tennessee Press, 1991.

Carman, Harry J., and Reinhard H. Luthin, *Lincoln and the Patronage.* New York: Columbia University Press, 1943.

Cazden, Elizabeth. *Antoinette Brown Blackwell: A Biography.* Old Westbury, N.Y.: Feminist Press, 1983.

Cimbala, Paul A., and Randall M. Miller, eds. *An Uncommon Time: The Civil War and the Northern Home Front.* New York: Fordham University Press, 2002.

Childers, Christopher. "Emporia's Incongruent Reformer: Charles Vernon Eskridge, the *Emporia Republican,* and the Kansas Republican Party, 1860–1900." *Kansas History* 28 (Spring 2005): 2–15.

Clinton, Catherine, and Nina Silber, eds. *Battle Scars: Gender and Sexuality in the American Civil War.* New York: Oxford University Press, 2006.

Collier-Thomas, Bettye. "Frances Ellen Watkins Harper: Abolitionist and Feminist Reformer, 1825–1911." In *African-American Women and the Vote, 1837–1965,* ed. Ann Gordon and Bettye Collier-Thomas, 41–65. Amherst: University of Massachusetts Press, 1997.

Cott, Nancy. *Public Vows: A History of Marriage and the Nation.* Cambridge: Harvard University Press, 2000.

Cox, LaWanda, and John H. Cox. "Negro Suffrage and Republican Politics: The Problem of Motivation in Reconstruction Historiography." *Journal of Southern History* 33 (August 1967): 303–30.

Davis, Angela. *Women, Race and Class.* New York: Random House, 1981.

Deese, Helen R. "Caroline Healey Dall: Transcendentalist Activist." In *Ordinary Women, Extraordinary Lives: Women in American History,* ed. Kriste Lindenmeyer, 59–71. Wilmington, Del.: Scholarly Resources, 2000.

Deese, Helen R., ed. *Daughter of Boston: The Extraordinary Diary of a Nineteenth-Century Woman, Caroline Healey Dall.* Boston: Beacon Press, 2005.

Donald, David Herbert. *Charles Sumner.* New York: DaCapo Press, 1996.

Donald, David H., Jean Harvey Baker, and Michael F. Holt. *The Civil War and Reconstruction.* New York: W. W. Norton, 2001.

Dorr, Rheta Childe. *Susan B. Anthony: The Woman Who Changed the Mind of a Nation.* New York: Frederick A. Stokes, 1928.

DuBois, Ellen Carol. *Feminism and Suffrage: The Emergence of an Independent Women's Movement in America, 1848–1869.* Ithaca: Cornell University Press, 1978.

———. *Harriot Stanton Blatch and the Winning of Woman Suffrage.* New Haven: Yale University Press, 1997.

———. *Woman Suffrage and Women's Rights.* New York: New York University Press, 1998.

———. "On Labor and Free Love: Two Unpublished Speeches of Elizabeth Cady Stanton." *Signs* 1 (1975): 257–68.

DuBois, Ellen Carol and Richard Candida Smith, eds. *Elizabeth Cady Stanton: Feminist as Thinker.* New York: New York University Press, 2007.

Dykstra, Robert R. *Bright Radical Star: Black Freedom and White Supremacy on the Hawkeye Frontier.* 1993. Paperback edition, Ames: Iowa State University Press, 1997.

Earle, Jonathan H. *Jacksonian Antislavery and the Politics of Free Soil, 1824–1854.* Chapel Hill: University of North Carolina Press, 2004.

Edwards, Rebecca. *Angels in the Machinery: Gender in American Party Politics from the Civil War to the Progressive Era.* New York: Oxford University Press, 1997.

Ellis, David M., James A. Frost, Harold C. Syrett, and Harry J. Carman. *A Short History of New York State.* Ithaca, N.Y.: Cornell University Press, 1957.

Epps, Garrett. *Democracy Reborn: The Fourteenth Amendment and the Fight for Equal Rights in Post-Civil War America.* New York: Henry Holt, 2006.

Faulkner, Carol. *Women's Radical Reconstruction: The Freedmen's Aid Movement.* Philadelphia: University of Pennsylvania Press, 2004.

Feimster, Crystal N. *Southern Horrors: Women and the Politics of Rape and Lynching.* Cambridge: Harvard University Press, 2009.

Field, Phyllis F. *The Politics of Race in New York: The Struggle for Black Suffrage in the Civil War Era.* Ithaca: Cornell University Press, 1982.

―――. "Republicans and Black Suffrage in New York State: The Grass Roots Response." *Civil War History* 21 (June 1975): 140–46.

Fitzgerald, Michael. *The Union League Movement in the Deep South: Politics and Agricultural Change during Reconstruction.* Baton Rouge: Louisiana State University Press, 1989.

Flexner, Eleanor. *Century of Struggle: The Woman's Rights Movement in the United States.* 1959. Reprint, New York: Atheneum, 1972.

Foner, Eric. *Freedom's Lawmakers: A Directory of Black Officeholders during Reconstruction.* Revised. New York: Oxford University Press, 1993.

―――. *Reconstruction: America's Unfinished Revolution, 1863–1877.* New York: Harper and Row, 1988.

Formisano, Ronald P. "The 'Party Period' Revisited." *Journal of American History* 86 (June 1999): 93–120.

Frisken, Amanda. *Victoria Woodhull's Sexual Revolution: Political Theater and the Popular Press in Nineteenth-Century America.* Philadelphia: University of Pennsylvania Press, 2004.

Gallman, J. Matthew. *America's Joan of Arc: The Life of Anna Elizabeth Dickinson.* New York: Oxford University Press, 2006.

Geisberg, Judith Ann. *Civil War Sisterhood: The U.S. Sanitary Commission and Women's Politics in Transition.* Boston: Northeastern University Press, 2000.

Gienapp, William E. "'Politics Seem to Enter into Everything': Political Culture in the North, 1840–1860." In *Essays on American Antebellum Politics, 1840–1860,* ed. William E. Gienapp et al., 15–69. College Station: Texas A & M University Press, 1982.

Gillette, William. *The Right to Vote: Politics and the Passage of the Fifteenth Amendment.* Baltimore: Johns Hopkins University Press, 1965.

Ginzberg, Lori D. *Elizabeth Cady Stanton: An American Life.* New York: Hill & Wang, 2009.

―――. *Women and the Work of Benevolence: Morality, Politics, and Class in the Nineteenth-Century United States.* New Haven: Yale University Press, 1990.

―――. *Untidy Origins: A Story of Woman's Rights in Antebellum New York.* Chapel Hill: University of North Carolina Press, 2005.

Goldsmith, Barbara. *Other Powers: The Age of Suffrage, Spiritualism, and the Scandalous Victoria Woodhull.* New York: Knopf, 1998.

Gordon, Ann D., and Bettye Collier-Thomas, eds. *African American Women and the Vote, 1837–1965.* Amherst: University of Massachusetts Press, 1997.

Gordon, Sarah Barringer. "'The Liberty of Self-Degradation': Polygamy, Woman Suffrage, and Consent in Nineteenth-Century America." *Journal of American History* 83 (December 1996): 815–47.

Griffin, Farah Jasmine. "Frances Ellen Watkins Harper in the Reconstruction South." *Sage: A Scholarly Journal on Black Women* 5, Student Supplement (1988): 45–47.

Griffith, Elisabeth. *In Her Own Right: The Life of Elizabeth Cady Stanton.* New York: Oxford University Press, 1984.

Gustafson, Melanie Susan. *Women and the Republican Party, 1854–1924.* Urbana: University of Illinois Press, 2001.

Hahn, Steven. *A Nation under Our Feet: Black Political Struggles in the Rural South: From Slavery to the Great Migration.* Cambridge: Harvard University Press, 2003.

Hartog, Hendrik. *Man and Wife in America: A History.* Cambridge: Harvard University Press, 2000.

Hays, Elinor Rice. *Morning Star: A Biography of Lucy Stone, 1818–1893.* New York: Harcourt, Brace and World, 1961.

Hewitt, John H. "Mr. Downing and His Oyster House: The Life and Good Works of an African-American Entrepreneur." *New York History* 74 (1993): 229–52.

Hewitt, Nancy. "'Seeking a Larger Liberty': Remapping First Wave Feminism." In *Women's Rights and Transatlantic Antislavery in the Era of Emancipation,* ed. Katharine Kish Sklar and James Brewer Stewart, 266–78. New Haven: Yale University Press, 2007.

———. *Women's Activism and Social Change: Rochester, New York, 1822–1872.* Ithaca: Cornell University Press, 1984.

Hodes, Martha. "Wartime Dialogues on Illicit Sex: White Women and Black Men." In *Divided Houses: Gender and the Civil War,* ed. Catherine Clinton and Nina Silber, 230–42. New York: Oxford University Press, 1992.

———. "The Sexualization of Reconstruction Politics: White Women and Black Men in the South after the Civil War." *Journal of the History of Sexuality* 3 (January 1993): 402–17.

Hoffert, Sylvia D. *When Hens Crow: The Woman's Rights Movement in Antebellum America.* Bloomington: Indiana University Press, 1995.

Hoffert, Sylvia. "Money and Power: Alva Vanderbilt Belmont and the National Women's Party." Paper delivered at the Organization of American Historians Annual Meeting, April 20, 2006, Washington, D.C.

Holt, Thomas. *Black over White: Negro Political Leadership in South Carolina during Reconstruction.* Urbana: University of Illinois Press, 1977.

Horowitz, Helen Lefkowitz. *Rereading Sex: Battles over Sexual Knowledge and Suppression in Nineteenth-Century America.* New York: Knopf, 2002.

Horton, James Oliver, and Lois E. Horton. *In Hope of Liberty: Culture, Community and Protest among Northern Free Blacks.* New York: Oxford University Press, 1997.

Hunter, Tera W. *To "Joy My Freedom: Southern Black Women's Lives and Labors after the Civil War.* Cambridge: Harvard University Press, 1997.

Isenberg, Nancy. *Sex and Citizenship in Antebellum America.* Chapel Hill: University of North Carolina Press, 1998.

James, Joseph B. *The Framing of the Fourteenth Amendment.* Urbana: University of Illinois Press, 1956.

Jeffrey, Julie Roy. *The Great Silent Army of Abolitionism: Ordinary Women in the Antislavery Movement.* Chapel Hill: University of North Carolina Press, 1998.

———. "'Stranger, *Buy* Lest Our Mission Fail:' The Complex Culture of Women's Abolitionist Fairs." *American Nineteenth-Century History* 4 (Spring 2003): 1–24.

Jones, Martha S. *All Bound Up Together: The Woman Question in African-American Public Culture, 1830–1900.* Chapel Hill: University of North Carolina Press, 2007.

Karcher, Carolyn L. *The First Woman in the Republic: A Cultural Biography of Lydia Maria Child.* Durham: Duke University Press, 1994.

Kaplan, Sidney. "The Miscegenation Issue in the Election of 1864." *Journal of Negro History* 34 (July 1949): 274–343.

Kern, Kathi. *Mrs. Stanton's Bible.* Ithaca: Cornell University Press, 2001.

Kerr, Andrea Moore. *Lucy Stone: Speaking Out for Equality.* New Brunswick, N.J.: Rutgers University Press, 1992.

———. "White Women's Rights, Black Men's Wrongs, Free Love, Blackmail, and the Formation of the American Woman Suffrage Association." In *One Woman One Vote: Rediscovering the Woman Suffrage Movement,* ed. Marjorie Spruill Wheeler, 61–79. Troutdale, Ore.: New Sage Press, 1995.

Kelley, Mary. *Learning to Stand and Speak: Women, Education, and Public Life in America's Republic.* Chapel Hill: University of North Carolina Press, 2006.

Keyssar, Alexander. *The Right to Vote: The Contested History of Democracy in the United States.* New York: Basic Books, 2000.

Kraditor, Aileen. *The Ideas of the Woman Suffrage Movement, 1890–1920.* New York: W. W. Norton, 1981.

Leach, William. *True Love and Perfect Union: The Feminist Reform of Sex and Society.* New York: Basic Books, 1980.

Lessoff, Alan. *The Nation and Its City: Politics, "Corruption," and Progress in Washington, D.C., 1861–1902*. Baltimore: Johns Hopkins University Press, 1994.

Litwack, Leon. *North of Slavery: The Negro in the Free States*. Chicago: University of Chicago Press, 1961.

Lutz, Alma. *Created Equal: A Biography of Elizabeth Cady Stanton*. New York: John Day, 1940.

Lutz, Alma. *Susan B. Anthony: Rebel, Crusader, Humanitarian*. Boston: Beacon, 1950.

Madsen, Sandra Arlene. "The 1867 Campaign for Woman Suffrage in Kansas: A Study in Rhetorical Situation." Ph.D. diss., University of Kansas, 1975.

Masur, Katherine. "Reconstructing the Nation's Capital: The Politics of Race and Citizenship in the District of Columbia, 1862–1878." Ph.D. diss., University of Michigan, 2001.

Marbury, M. M. *The Golden Voice: A Biography of Isaac Kalloch*. New York: Farrar, Straus, 1947.

Margolin, Rosalie. "Henry B. Stanton: A Forgotten Abolitionist." M.A. thesis, Columbia University, 1962.

Marilley, Suzanne M. *Woman Suffrage and the Origins of Liberal Feminism in the United States, 1820–1920*. Cambridge: Harvard University Press, 1996.

Martin, Waldo. *The Mind of Frederick Douglass*. Chapel Hill: University of North Carolina Press, 1984.

McCarthy, Timothy Patrick, and John Stauffer, eds. *Prophets of Protest: Reconsidering the History of American Abolitionism*. New York: New Press, 2006.

McFeely, William S. *Frederick Douglass*. New York: W.W. Norton, 1991.

McJimsey, George T. *Genteel Partisan: Manton Marble, 1834–1917*. Ames: Iowa State University Press, 1971.

McKenna, Sister Mary Berard. "Samuel N. Wood: Chronic Agitator." Ph.D. diss., St. Louis University, 1968.

McMillen, Sally G. *Seneca Falls and the Origins of the Women's Rights Movement*. New York: Oxford University Press, 2008.

McPherson, James M. *The Struggle for Equality: Abolitionists and the Negro in the Civil War and Reconstruction*. 1964. 2nd ed. Princeton, N.J.: Princeton University Press, 1995.

Merk, Lois Bannister. "Massachusetts and the Woman Suffrage Movement." Ph.D. diss., Harvard University, 1961.

Million, Joelle. *Woman's Voice, Woman's Place: Lucy Stone and the Birth of the Woman's Rights Movement*. Westport, Conn.: Praeger, 2003.

Mohr, James C. *The Radical Republicans and Reform in New York during Reconstruction*. Ithaca: Cornell University Press, 1973.

Montgomery, David. *Beyond Equality: Labor and the Radical Republicans, 1862–1872*. New York: Random House Vintage Books, 1967.

Moore, Dorothea McClain. "Reclaiming Lucy Stone: A Literary and Historical Appraisal." Ph.D. diss., University of Texas at Arlington, 1996.

Neely, Mark E., Jr. *The Union Divided: Party Conflict in the Civil War North*. Cambridge: Harvard University Press, 2002.

Newman, Louise Michele. *White Women's Rights: The Racial Origins of Feminism in the United States*. New York: Oxford University Press, 1999.

Niven, John. *Salmon P. Chase*. New York: Oxford University Press, 1995.

Painter, Nell Irvin. *Sojourner Truth: A Life, A Symbol*. New York: W.W. Norton, 1996.

Parker, Alison M., and Stephanie Cole, eds. *Women and the Unstable State in Nineteenth-Century America*. Arlington: Texas A & M University Press, 2000.

Passet, Joanne E. *Sex Radicals and the Quest for Women's Equality*. Urbana: University of Illinois Press, 2003.

Pease, Jane H., and William H. Pease. *They Who Would Be Free: Blacks' Search for Freedom, 1830–1861*. New York: Atheneum, 1974.

———. "Negro Conventions and the Problem of Black Leadership." *Journal of Black Studies* 2 (September 1971): 29–44.

Penney, Sherry, and James D. Livingston. *A Very Dangerous Woman: Martha Wright and Women's Rights*. Amherst: University of Massachusetts Press, 2004.

Peterson, Carla L. "Literary Transnationalism and Diasporic History: Frances Watkins Harper's 'Fancy Sketches,' 1859–1860." In *Women's Rights and Transatlantic Antislavery in the Era of Emancipation*, ed. Katharine Kish Sklar and James Brewer Stewart, 189–208. New Haven: Yale University Press, 2007.

Pierson, Michael D. *Free Hearts and Free Homes: Gender and American Antislavery Politics*. Chapel Hill: University of North Carolina Press, 2003.

Quarles, Benjamin. *Black Abolitionists*. New York: Oxford University Press, 1969.

Quarles, Benjamin. "Frederick Douglass and the Woman's Rights Movement." *Journal of Negro History* 25 (January 1940): 35–44

Quigley, David M. *Second Founding: New York City, Reconstruction, and the Making of American Democracy*. New York: Hill & Wang, 2004.

Rable, George C. *But There Was No Peace: The Role of Violence in the Politics of Reconstruction*. Athens: University of Georgia Press, 1984.

Rael, Patrick. *Black Identity and Black Protest in the Antebellum North*. Chapel Hill: University of North Carolina Press, 2002.

Rice, Arthur H. "Henry B. Stanton as a Political Abolitionist." Ph.D. diss. Teachers College of Columbia University, 1968.

Riley, Glenda. *Divorce: An American Tradition*. New York: Oxford University Press, 1991.

Salerno, Beth A. *Sister Societies: Women's Antislavery Organizations in Antebellum America*. DeKalb: Northern Illinois University Press, 2005.

Sewell, Richard H. *Ballots for Freedom: Antislavery Politics in the U.S., 1837–1860*. New York: Oxford University Press, 1976.

Sheridan, Richard B. "Charles Henry Langston and the African American Struggle in Kansas." *Kansas History* 22 (Winter 1999/2000): 268–83.

Silber, Nina. *Daughters of the Union: Northern Women Fight the Civil War*. Cambridge: Harvard University Press, 2005.

Sinha, Manisha. "Coming of Age: The Historiography of Black Abolitionism." In *Prophets of Protest: Reconsidering the History of American Abolitionism*, ed. Timothy Patrick McCarthy and John Stauffer, 23–38. New York: New Press, 2006.

Sklar, Katharine Kish, and James Brewer Stewart, eds. *Women's Rights and Transatlantic Antislavery in the Era of Emancipation*. New Haven: Yale University Press, 2007.

Sommerville, Diane Miller. "The Rape Myth in the Old South Reconsidered." *Journal of Southern History* 61 (August 1995): 481–518.

———. *Rape and Race in the Nineteenth Century South*. Chapel Hill: University of North Carolina Press, 2004.

Spring, Leverett W. "The Career of a Kansas Politician." *American Historical Review* 4 (October 1898): 80–104

Spurlock, John C. *Free Love: Marriage and Middle-Class Radicalism in America, 1825–1860*. New York: New York University Press, 1988.

Stauffer, John. *The Black Hearts of Men: Radical Abolitionists and the Transformation of Race*. Cambridge: Harvard University Press, 2001.

Stanley, Amy Dru. *From Bondage to Contract: Wage Labor, Marriage, and the Market in the Age of Slave Emancipation*. Cambridge: Cambridge University Press, 1998.

Sterling, Dorothy, ed. *We Are Your Sisters: Black Women in the Nineteenth Century*. New York: W.W. Norton, 1984.

Stern, Madeleine B. *The Pantarch: A Biography of Stephen Pearl Andrews*. Austin: University of Texas Press, 1968.

Stewart, James Brewer. *Wendell Phillips: Liberty's Hero*. Baton Rouge: Louisiana State University Press, 1986.

Stoehr, Taylor. *Free Love in America: A Documentary History*. New York: AMS Press, 1979.

Strom, Sharon Hartman. "Leadership and Tactics in the American Woman Suffrage Movement: A New Perspective from Massachusetts." *Journal of American History* 62 (1975–76): 296–315.

Sumler-Lewis, Janice. "The Forten-Purvis Women of Philadelphia and the American Anti-Slavery Crusade." *Journal of Negro History* 66 (Winter 1981–82): 281–88.

Summers, Mark Wahlgren. *The Era of Good Stealings*. New York: Oxford University Press, 1993.

———. *Party Games: Getting, Keeping and Using Power in Gilded Age Politics*. Chapel Hill: University of North Carolina Press, 2001.

———. *The Press Gang: Newspapers and Politics, 1865–1878*. Chapel Hill: University of North Carolina Press, 1994.

Terborg-Penn, Rosalyn. "Discrimination against Afro-American Women in the Woman's Movement, 1830–1920." In *The Afro-American Woman*, ed. Sharon Harley and Rosalyn Terborg-Penn, 17–27. Port Washington, N.Y.: Kennikat, 1978.

Terborg-Penn, Rosalyn. *African-American Women in the Struggle for the Vote, 1850–1920*. Bloomington: Indiana University Press, 1998.

Tetrault, Lisa. "The Incorporation of American Feminism: Suffragists and the Postbellum Lyceum." *Journal of American History* 96 (March 2010): 1027–56.

Trelease, Allen W. *White Terror: The Ku Klux Klan Conspiracy and Southern Reconstruction*. Baton Rouge: Louisiana State University Press, 1971.

Tunnell, Ted. *Crucible of Reconstruction: War, Radicalism and Race in Louisiana, 1862–1877*. Baton Rouge: Louisiana State University Press, 1984.

Van Deusen, Glyndon. *Thurlow Weed: Wizard of the Lobby*. Boston: Little, Brown, 1947.

Varon, Elizabeth R. *"We Mean to Be Counted": White Women and Party Politics in Antebellum Virginia*. Chapel Hill: University of North Carolina Press, 1998.

Venet, Wendy Hamand. *Neither Ballots nor Bullets: Women Abolitionists and the Civil War*. Charlottesville: University Press of Virginia, 1991.

Vorenberg, Michael. *Final Freedom: The Civil War, the Abolition of Slavery, and the Thirteenth Amendment*. New York: Cambridge University Press, 2001.

Wang, Xi. *The Trial of Democracy: Black Suffrage and Northern Republicans, 1860–1910*. Athens: University of Georgia Press, 1997.

Washington, Margaret. *Sojourner Truth's America*. Urbana: University of Illinois Press, 2009.

Wellman, Judith. *The Road to Seneca Falls: Elizabeth Cady Stanton and the First Woman's Rights Convention*. Urbana: University of Illinois Press, 2004.

———. "The Seneca Falls Women's Rights Convention: A Study of Social Networks." *Journal of Women's History* 3 (Spring 1991): 17–22.

———. "Women's Rights, Republicanism, and Revolutionary Rhetoric in Antebellum New York State." *New York History* 69 (July 1988): 375–81.

Wilder, Daniel Webster. *The Annals of Kansas*. Topeka: Kansas Publishing House, 1886.

Wilentz, Sean. "Slavery, Antislavery, and Jacksonian Democracy." In *The Market Revolution in America: Social, Political, and Religious Expressions, 1800–1880*, ed. Melvyn Stokes and Stephen Conway, 202–23. Charlottesville: University of Virginia Press, 1996.

Yee, Shirley J. *Black Women Abolitionists: A Study in Activism, 1828–1860*. Knoxville: University of Tennessee Press, 1992.

Yellin, Jean Fagan, and John C. Van Horne, eds. *The Abolitionist Sisterhood: Women's Political Culture in Antebellum America*. Ithaca: Cornell University Press, 1994.

Zaeske, Susan. *Signatures of Citizenship: Petitioning, Antislavery, and Women's Political Identity*. Chapel Hill: University of North Carolina Press, 2003.

Zboray, Ronald J., and Mary Saracino Zboray, "Whig Women, Politics, and Culture in the Campaign of 1840: Three Perspectives from Massachusetts." *Journal of the Early Republic* 17 (Summer 1997): 277–315.

INDEX

Page numbers in bold indicate illustrations.